This DIMACS volume presents papers related to the Fifth DIMACS Challenge on Dictionaries and Priority Queues (1995–1996) and the Sixth DIMACS Challenge on Near Neighbor Searches (1998–1999).

2000 *Mathematics Subject Classification.* Primary 68-06, 68P05, 68P10, 68U05, 68W01.

Library of Congress Cataloging-in-Publication Data

Data structures, near neighbor searches, and methodology: fifth and sixth DIMACS implementation challenges: papers related to the DIMACS challenge on dictionaries and priority queues (1995–1996) and the DIMACS challenge on near neighbor searches (1998–1999)/Michael H. Goldwasser, David S. Johnson, Catherine C. McGeoch, editors.

p. cm.—(DIMACS series in discrete mathematics and theoretical computer science; v. 59)

Proceedings of workshops held October 1996 and January 1999.

Includes bibliographical references.

ISBN 0-8218-2892-4 (alk. paper)

1. Data structures (Computer science)–Congresses. I. Goldwasser, Michael H., 1969– II. Johnson, David S., 1945– III. McGeoch, Catherine C., 1959– IV. Series.

QA76.9.D35 D385 2002
005.7′3—dc21 2002038557

∞ The paper used in this book is acid-free and falls within the guidelines
established to ensure permanence and durability.
Visit the AMS home page at http://www.ams.org/

10 9 8 7 6 5 4 3 2 1 07 06 05 04 03 02

DIMACS

Series in Discrete Mathematics
and Theoretical Computer Science

Volume 59

Data Structures, Near Neighbor Searches, and Methodology: Fifth and Sixth DIMACS Implementation Challenges

Papers Related to the DIMACS Challenge on Dictionaries and Priority Queues (1995–1996) and the DIMACS Challenge on Near Neighbor Searches (1998–1999)

Michael H. Goldwasser
David S. Johnson
Catherine C. McGeoch
Editors

NSF Science and Technology Center
in Discrete Mathematics and Theoretical Computer Science
A consortium of Rutgers University, Princeton University,
AT&T Labs–Research, Bell Labs (Lucent Technologies),
Telcordia Technologies, and NEC Research Institute

American Mathematical Society

Contents

Foreword

The DIMACS Algorithm Implementation Challenges, initiated in 1991, have introduced a generation of theoretical computer scientists and mathematicians to the computer as an experimental tool for research in computer science and mathematics and to the entire field of experimental research on algorithms. This book contains papers developed in connection with the Fifth and Sixth DIMACS Challenges. These Challenges dealt, respectively, with Dictionaries and Priority Queues and with Near Neighbor Searching.

We are very grateful to the editors of this volume, Michael Goldwasser, David Johnson, and Catherine McGeoch, for tying together so much material. Thanks also go to the organizers of the Fifth Challenge, Catherine McGeoch (coordinator), David Johnson, Richard Ladner, Kurt Melhorn, Ian Munro, Robert Sedgewick, and Robert Tarjan; and to the organizers of the Sixth Challenge, Michael Goldwasser (coordinator), Jon Bentley, Ken Clarkson, David Johnson, Catherine McGeoch, and Robert Sedgewick.

DIMACS gratefully acknowledges the generous support that makes these programs possible. The National Science Foundation, through its Science and Technology Centers program, the New Jersey Commission on Science and Technology, and DIMACS's partners at Rutgers, Princeton, AT&T Labs-Research, Bell Labs, NEC Research Institute, and Telcordia Technologies generously supported these Challenges.

Fred S. Roberts
Director

Robert Tarjan
Co-Director for Princeton

Preface

The DIMACS Implementation Challenges were initiated in 1991 to promote top-quality experimental research on algorithms and data structures. Each Challenge focuses on a particular algorithmic problem area. Participants from around the world undertake year-long coordinated research projects to implement and evaluate promising algorithmic ideas. Each participating group is expected to carry out a common set of "core tests" for direct comparisons of performance, and also to undertake further experimental research to examine topics such as the effect of implementation variations, or performance on realistic input sets. A workshop held at the end of each Challenge allows participants to present their results and share their new insights about algorithmic performance. Participants are encouraged to submit their codes, instances, and instance generators to an online repository maintained at DIMACS. Those materials can be found at `www.dimacs.rutgers.edu/Challenges`.

This volume contains reviewed, revised, and expanded versions of papers that were presented at the Fifth and Sixth DIMACS Challenge workshops, held in October 1996 and in January 1999. The volume is divided into three sections. The first contains papers from participants in the Fifth Challenge, which addressed two data structure problems. The second section contains papers from participants in the Sixth Challenge, which focused on problems of near neighbor searches. The third section contains papers from participants in a special "Methodology Day" that was held as part of the Fifth Challenge workshop.

Fifth Challenge: Dictionaries and Priority Queues.

The Fifth DIMACS Challenge (1995-96) addressed two problems in data structure implementation: dictionaries and priority queues. The Challenge workshop was held in late October 1996 and included tutorials on implementation techniques, presentations by nine Challenge research teams, and panel discussions. Preliminary papers, circulated at the workshop, were reviewed by workshop participants, and three were revised and expanded for inclusion in this volume.

In the first paper, Battiti examines a data structure for persistent sets (dictionaries), with applications to Tabu Search and other heuristic search methods that employ a dictionary data structure to avoid visiting previously-visited states. A persistent data structure maintains a history of states by storing only the incremental changes between them. Since step functions in heuristic search typically impose the property that each state differs only slightly from the next state visited, a persistent dictionary leads to improvements in both time and space over standard approaches. Battiti shows that a strategy combining hashing and persistent red-black trees can be both theoretically and practically efficient.

Next, Silverstein presents a computational evaluation of a perfect hashing method to support dictionary operations. Although perfect hashing schemes can provide theoretical guarantees of constant-time lookups, they have not been considered efficient in practice because of large constant factors in time and space usage, especially when keys are long. Silverstein describes an efficient implementation that is comparable in performance to other standard hashing methods (which do not have similar theoretical guarantees).

Finally, Goldberg and Silverstein present an experimental evaluation of HOT (Heap On Top) Queues, which combine multi-level bucketing and heaps to support monotonic priority queues. Monotonicity means that at any time, a key inserted into the priority queue cannot have value smaller than the key most recently extracted. This assumption holds, for example, in event simulations and in Dijkstra's algorithm. The authors compare HOT Queues to standard alternatives for a variety of applications that use monotone priority queues.

In addition to tutorials and research talks, the Fifth Challenge workshop included several panel discussions. Panelists noted that this year's topic, Data Structures, attracted a smaller number of participants than had previous Challenges. This might be explained by a perception that priority queues and dictionaries are too well-understood to permit any fresh insights from implementation studies (although Challenge participants proved that a false perception!)

It was also noted that computational comparisons of fast data structures like these are more difficult to design and carry out than other types of algorithmic comparisons. Testing times were very much dominated by time to download and/or generate large test instances, as well as to read the inputs, which made accurate timing statistics for data structure operations relatively difficult to obtain.

Sixth Challenge: Near Neighbor Searching

The Sixth DIMACS Challenge (1998), organized in conjunction with the DIMACS Special Year on Massive Data Sets, focused on problems involving near neighbor searches. Finding near neighbors according to various distance measures arises in many domains, including but not limited to finding similar web documents, images, DNA sequences, lines of text, or audio and video clips, and more generally in application areas from statistics, data mining, information retrieval, pattern recognition and data compression.

In contrast to the Fifth Challenge, in which there was a (possibly flawed) perception that dictionaries and priority queues are well understood, there is not as rich a history of theoretical work for near neighbor searches. The most widely used general approaches are based on hierarchical decompositions of the original data points. This idea was introduced in the mid 1970s by Friedman and Bentley, as the kd-tree data structure. While these methods are theoretically and practically efficient in low-dimensional Euclidean spaces, their performance can degrade rapidly as dimensionality increases. Furthermore, there are many subtle variants based on the precise partitioning rule used for decomposition.

A Challenge Workshop was held on 15 January 1999, as an afternoon session co-located with the First Workshop on Algorithm Engineering and Experiments (ALENEX 1999). Research presentations were made by seven Challenge teams and participants were subsequently invited to submit full papers for consideration in this volume. Five such papers appear here, having been refereed and revised. The first two papers consider algorithms which always find the true nearest neighbor for a query; the other three papers consider various relaxations. All five final papers involve experiments with data from Euclidean spaces, though some presentations from the workshop discussed searches in general metric spaces.

In the first paper, Zatloukal, Johnson and Ladner evaluate nearest-neighbor search algorithms as they naturally arise within vector quantization, a common algorithm for lossy data compression. Their experiments involve the compression of 2D images drawn from an available database. In vector quantization, a codebook of representative blocks (small subimages) of a set of images is precomputed. Then images are compressed by representing each block of an image with the codebook entry which is "nearest" in appearance. The underlying nearest neighbor queries dominate the overall compression time. In this setting, Zatloukal *et al.* compare six implementations for the neighbor queries, finding the best success with a hybrid method which combines kd-trees with principal component partitioning.

Next, Katayama and Satoh consider nearest-neighbor algorithms with the goal of minimizing the number of disk accesses, as opposed to the number of internal computations. Their work is motivated by similarity retrieval within multimedia database systems. They perform experiments involving a search of 40,000 images captured from available video archives. They compare the performance of several data structures drawn from the database community as well as several variants of kd-trees. Their results show that several of the disk-based structures do indeed reduce the number of disk accesses relative to kd-trees, though with a clear increase in the number of internal computations.

Of those papers which relax the requirement of always finding the precise nearest neighbor, Maneewongvatana and Mount consider search algorithms which guarantee that the distance between the query point and the returned point is at most $(1+\epsilon)$ times the distance of the query from its true nearest neighbor. Their experiments involve synthetically generated data in 20 dimensions, drawn from a number of clustered probability distributions. The focus of their work is to evaluate alternatives for the splitting rule used by kd-trees. They evaluate the standard splitting rule as well as two new rules. One of these two new rules is designed for a setting in which training data is provided *a priori*, drawn from the same distribution as the eventual query points.

In the next paper, Perez-Cortes and Vidal also consider an algorithm which does not necessarily return the nearest neighbor. Their algorithm is based upon functions, known as space-filling curves, which map regions of a high-dimensional space to the real line. In the context of near neighbor searches, there is no absolute guarantee that the nearest neighbor in the original space will remain the nearest neighbor when mapped to the real line, however the hope is that if several, independently random mappings are computed, it is likely that a decent neighbor can be located. Their experiments, using both real and synthetic data in a variety of dimensions, characterize tradeoffs between computation time, space usage, dimensionality and the quality of the solution.

Finally, Yianilos considers a family of algorithms with the following behavior. A data structure is created using a probabilistic algorithm; after this a deterministic procedure is used for each search. The process finds the true nearest neighbor only some fixed percentage of the time, where the targeted success rate is a parameter to the algorithm. The theoretical results in this paper are limited by several assumptions on the uniformity of the data set and the queries. However, with these restrictions Yianilos proves that the expected number of distance computations is both sub-linear and independent of dimension. This approach is then tested experimentally on synthetic data using Euclidean spaces of dimension up to 1000.

Methodology for the Experimental Analysis of Algorithms

The third day of the Fifth Challenge workshop was a "Methodology Day" devoted to presentations and panel discussions on the topic of Methods and Standards in Experimental Analysis of Algorithms. Ten participants presented brief position statements, which were followed by a panel discussion on the issues raised. Subsequently, four participants prepared more formal papers about methodology for the experimental analysis of algorithms, which were reviewed and revised and appear in the final section of this volume.

Richard Anderson provides a discussion of how theory and experiment can reinforce each other and illustrates his ideas with a discussion of work on network flows. He also stresses the value of designing worthwhile experiments and highlights three situations in which uninformative experiments could have been avoided with a little more forethought.

Bernard Moret considers the potential for "experimental algorithmics" to become a formal discipline. He begins by listing the growing number of outlets for papers in experimental analysis and discussing why experimental analysis is needed, providing taxonomies of questions that should be addressed experimentally and of modes of empirical assessment. He then discusses various issues having to do with experimental setup, measurement, and analysis, and illustrates these in the context of the Minimum Spanning Tree problem.

David Johnson provides an informal "theoretician's guide" to the experimental analysis of algorithms, based on his extensive experience in writing and refereeing experimental papers. His goal is to provide useful advice on how to do worthwhile (and publishable) experimental work. The presentation is organized around ten basic principles and includes extensive lists of "pitfalls" (temptations that can lead experimenters into large wastes of time and effort) and "pet peeves" (literally "favorite annoyances" – common experimental and paper-writing practices that he argues have serious defects).

This section concludes with an extensive and lightly-annotated bibliography of papers on algorithm experimentation, prepared by Catherine McGeoch.

Acknowledgments

DIMACS Implementation Challenges are large undertakings that require the efforts of many people. In addition to the participants themselves, the Challenge Steering Committees make a major contribution, helping to formulate the Challenges, set the timelines, and evaluate the contributions. The Fifth Challenge Steering Committee consisted of Catherine McGeoch (coordinator), David Johnson, Richard Ladner, Kurt Mehlhorn, Ian Munro, Robert Sedgewick, and Robert Tarjan. The Sixth Challenge Steering Committee consisted of Michael Goldwasser (coordinator), Jon Bentley, Ken Clarkson, David Johnson, Catherine McGeoch, and Robert Sedgewick.

The staff at DIMACS were wonderful in making the Challenges go smoothly, and we are especially grateful to DIMACS Director Fred Roberts for encouraging us in continuing this series. We are also grateful to the organizers of The 1999 ALENEX Workshop for providing a home for the presentation of the Sixth Challenge papers, and to AMS, for their patience as we attempted to put the many parts of this volume together.

August 2002

MICHAEL H. GOLDWASSER
DAVID S. JOHNSON
CATHERINE C. MCGEOCH

DIMACS Series in Discrete Mathematics
and Theoretical Computer Science
Volume **59**, 2002

Partially persistent dynamic sets for history-sensitive heuristics

R. Battiti

Abstract. Effective heuristic algorithms for combinatorial problems are based on integrating local neighborhood search with *history-sensitive* schemes, where the information collected during the previous search phase is used to direct the future effort. In particular, some algorithms (like *Strict Tabu Search* and *Reactive Tabu Search*) need to detect whether a configuration has already been encountered during the previous phase of the search, either to prohibit repetitions or to determine a prohibition parameter in an adaptive way. This paper analyzes the use of *persistent dynamic sets* for storing and retrieving states and discusses the advantages of this option with respect to popular but less efficient realizations. If the search space is given by L-bit binary strings, the method complexity is $O(L)$ average-case time per search iteration when hashing is used, while the total space for a sequence of t iterations is $O(t)$.

A concrete realization of the abstract data type through a C++ class is presented. The obtained memory occupation and timing results are analyzed for selected "dictionary" benchmark tasks and for the use of the structure to support history-sensitive heuristic algorithms, in particular for the Maximum Clique problem in graphs.

Presented at the Fifth DIMACS Challenge, Rutgers, NJ, 1996. Revised: Oct 10, 1998

1. Introduction

Starting from the late eighties there has been a growing interest in *history-sensitive* heuristics that ameliorate the *Local Search* method. In particular, *Tabu Search* (*TS*) uses *prohibition-based* diversification techniques with the purpose of guiding *Local Search* beyond local optimality [**9**]. The main modifications of *Local Search* are obtained through the *temporary prohibition* (henceforth the term tabu or taboo) of selected moves available at the current point.

While ideas similar to those proposed in *TS* can be found already in the sixties, see for example the *denial* strategy of [**18**] for the Traveling Salesman problem, the current technological context, with the availability of large amounts of memory on standard computers, makes these schemes applicable for the solution of large-scale problems of applicative interest. The renaissance and full blossoming of "intelligent

1991 *Mathematics Subject Classification.* ...
Key words and phrases. heuristic algorithms, combinatorial problems, persistent data structures, tabu search, reactive search.

prohibition-based heuristics" is greatly due to the role of F. Glover [**9, 10**], but see also [**12**] for an independent seminal paper. *TS*-based algorithms have been applied to a growing number of problems in the last years, as it is witnessed by the rapidly growing number of publications. Some popular variants of *TS* algorithms will be described later.

The search space considered is given by L-bit binary strings. The main focus of this paper is on realizing mechanisms for storing *states* during the search and for checking whether a specific state has already been encountered in the past. The availability of the previous states is needed to prevent repetitions in *Strict Tabu Search* and to define in an adaptive way the suitable value of the *prohibition tenure* in *Reactive Tabu Search*, a parameter that determines the prohibited *moves*. In contrast, all previous states are not needed in *Fixed Tabu Search*, where a simple FIFO queue of space $O(L)$ is sufficient to determine the prohibited moves.

The current usage of data structures to support the history-management operations required by *Strict-TS* and *Reactive-TS* algorithms presents two sub-optimal possibilities: for a single search iteration, one method needs $O(1)$ space with a time complexity of $O(\max\{t, L\})$ [**10**], t being the current iteration; the other method needs $O(L)$ space with $O(L)$ time [**5**]. Because a large number of iterations can be executed for relevant large-size tasks (millions are not unusual) the increasing time per iteration required by the first renders the iterations progressively slower, while the memory required by the second can be excessive. In this paper we demonstrate how both goals of average time $O(L)$ per iteration, *and* $O(t)$ space for the entire sequence of t steps can be obtained by integrating *hashing* with *persistent red-black* trees.

To the best of our knowledge this is the first study to address the use of *persistent* data structure to support history-sensitive heuristics. In general, we are not aware of sound experimental studies in the area. This fact explains why comparisons with alternative approaches are lacking in the paper. Of course, this work should be extended in the future to analyze alternative implementations.

In the following sections, first the framework of history-sensitive heuristics is briefly reviewed (Sec. 2), with emphasis on *Tabu Search* principles (Sec. 2.1) and available implementations (Sec. 2.2). Then the novel use of persistent dynamic sets to support history-management in heuristics is presented (Sec. 3).

A statistical analysis of the results obtained by a realization in C++ of the proposed data structures is presented in Sec. 4. In particular the use of the structure to support the *Reactive Local Search* heuristic [**3**] is investigated.

2. Local search and history-sensitive heuristics

Let us now briefly define the main concepts and the notation related to *Local Search* and *Tabu Search*. Let $\mathcal{X}$ be the discrete search space: $\mathcal{X} = \{0,1\}^L$, and let $f : \mathcal{X} \longrightarrow R$ be the function to be minimized. In addition, let $X^{(t)} \in \mathcal{X}$ be the current configuration along the *search trajectory* at iteration t, and $N(X^{(t)})$ the neighborhood of point $X^{(t)}$, obtained by applying a set of basic moves μ_i $(1 \leq i \leq L)$, where μ_i complements the i-th bit x_i of the string: $\mu_i\ (x_1, x_2, ..., x_i, ..., x_L) = (x_1, x_2, ..., 1 - x_i, ..., x_L)$.

$$N(X^{(t)}) = \{X \in \mathcal{X} \ \text{ such that } \ X = \mu_i\ (X^{(t)}), i = 1, ...L\}$$

Local Search starts from a random initial configuration $X^{(0)} \in \mathcal{X}$ and generates a search trajectory where the next point is given by a neighbor of the current solution with a better f value. In detail, we consider a "greedy" form of *Local Search*, where the *best* neighbor is selected, as follows:

$$Y = \text{Best-Neighbor} \; (\, N(X^{(t)}) \,) \tag{1}$$

$$X^{(t+1)} = \begin{cases} Y & \textbf{if} \quad f(Y) < f(X^{(t)}) \\ X^{(t)} & \textbf{if} \quad f(Y) \geq f(X^{(t)}) \quad \textbf{local minimum: search stops} \end{cases} \tag{2}$$

where Best-Neighbor selects $Y \in N(X^{(t)})$ with the lowest f value and ties are broken randomly. Y in turn becomes the new current configuration if f decreases. Clearly, *Local Search* stops as soon as the first local minimum point is encountered, when no improving moves are available.

History–sensitive heuristics act to continue the search beyond the first local minimum without "forgetting" the part of the search already executed. *Vice versa*, the *memory-less* nature is the key property characterizing Markov chains like *Simulated Annealing* or methods based on repeating runs of *Local Search* after starting from fresh random initial points. In *TS* the history–sensitivity is obtained by generating *prohibitions*: some neighbors are *prohibited*, only a subset $N_A(X^{(t)}) \subset N(X^{(t)})$ of them is *allowed*. A move shares the same prohibition status as that of the neighbor that would be obtained by applying it. The general way of generating the search trajectory that we consider is given by:

$$N_A(X^{(t)}) = \text{Allow}(N(X^{(t)}), X^{(0)}, ..., X^{(t)}) \tag{3}$$

$$X^{(t+1)} = \text{Best-Neighbor} \; (\, N_A(X^{(t)}) \,) \tag{4}$$

The set-valued function Allow selects a subset of $N(X^{(t)})$ in a manner that depends on the entire previous history of the search $X^{(0)}, ..., X^{(t)}$. Let us note that worsening moves can be produced (see eqn. 4), as they must be in order to exit local minima.

2.1. Tabu Search: discrete dynamical systems. There are several vantage points from which to view prohibition-based algorithms like *TS*. By analogy with the concept of *abstract data type* it is useful to separate the abstract concepts and operations of *TS* with respect to the realization with specific data structures. The terminology used in this paper reflects this distinction. Now, an essential abstract concept in *TS* is given by the *discrete dynamical system* of eqn. 3–4 obtained by modifying *Local Search*.

Possibly the simplest form of *TS* is what is called **strict-TS**: a neighbor is prohibited if and only if it has already been visited [**9**]. The term "strict" is chosen to underline the rigid enforcement of its simple prohibition rule:

$$N_A(X^{(t)}) = \{X \in N(X^{(t)}) \quad \text{such that} \quad X \neq \{X^{(0)}, ..., X^{(t)}\}\}$$

Let us note that *strict-TS* is parameter-free. Two additional algorithms can be obtain by introducing a *prohibition tenure*[1] T that determines how long a move will remain prohibited after its execution. The **fixed-TS** algorithm is obtained by fixing T throughout the search [**9**]. A neighbor is allowed if and only if it is obtained from the current point by applying a move that has not been used during

[1]The term *prohibition tenure* is preferred with respect to the more traditional *list size* because *list size* refers to a specific implementation.

the last T iterations. In detail, if $\textsc{LastUsed}(\mu)$ is the last usage time of move μ ($\textsc{LastUsed}(\mu) = -\infty$ at the beginning):

$$N_A(X^{(t)}) = \{X = \mu\ (X^{(t)}) \text{ such that } \textsc{LastUsed}(\mu) < (t - T)\} \quad (5)$$

If T changes with the iteration counter t depending on the search status, the general dynamical system that generates the search trajectory comprises an additional evolution equation for $T^{(t)}$:

$$\begin{aligned} T^{(t)} &= \text{T-}\textsc{React}(T^{(t-1)}, X^{(0)}, ..., X^{(t)}) & (6)\\ N_A(X^{(t)}) &= \{X = \mu\ (X^{(t)}) \text{ such that } \textsc{LastUsed}(\mu) < (t - T^{(t)})\} & (7)\\ X^{(t+1)} &= \textsc{Best-Neighbor}\ (N_A(X^{(t)})) & (8) \end{aligned}$$

In particular, rules to determine the prohibition tenure by reacting to the repetition of previously-visited configurations have been proposed in the **Reactive-TS** algorithm, *RTS* for short. While the reader is referred to [**5**] for the details, the design principles of *RTS* are that $T^{(t)}$ (in the range $1 \le T^{(t)} \le L - 2$) increases when repetitions happen, and decreases when repetitions disappear for a sufficiently long search period. *RTS* has been applied to various problems with competitive performance with respect to alternative heuristics like *Fixed-TS*, *Simulated Annealing*, *Neural Networks*, and *Genetic Algorithms*. In particular, state-of-the-art heuristic results have been obtained for the Maximum Clique problem [**3**], Maximum Satisfiability [**4**], and Graph and Hypergraph Partitioning [**1, 2**].

The history-management operations required by *Reactive-TS* are X-$\textsc{Insert}(X, t)$ to insert a given configuration $X^{(t)}$ into memory, and X-$\textsc{Search}(X)$ to search for a given X. X-$\textsc{Search}(X)$ returns a reference to satellite data associated to the key X if X is present, NULL otherwise. Satellite data in *RTS* are the iteration t of the last visit and the total number of visits.

2.2. Implementations: REM, hashing and digital tree. Let us now consider some existing implementations in order to motivate the new technique. In particular let us focus onto the general requirements for storing and retrieving the past history and for establishing prohibitions. To this end, the binary string X can be represented by the set containing the positions of the bits equal to one (each index is in the range $[1, L]$). Without fear of confusion the same notation will be used for the configuration and for the corresponding set of indices. The computational complexities are worst-case unless stated explicitly.

Strict-TS has been implemented through the *reverse elimination method* (*REM*) [**10**]. Before each iteration is executed, the entire list of moves performed throughout the search is traced in *reverse* order, by starting from the latest moves applied, to determine which moves from the current $X^{(t)}$ would reproduce a previously visited configuration, i.e., which moves are prohibited at iteration t. The space-time complexities of *REM* are of $O(1)$ space and $O(\max\{t, L\})$ time *per iteration.* While the space complexity is optimal, the time complexity per iteration increases with the number of iterations t, leading eventually to $O(t^2)$ space: a fact that makes the application of "pure" *REM* problematic if many iterations are executed.

Alternative implementations are studied in [**5**], where the *hashing* and *radix tree* (or "digital tree") methods are adopted, see [**7**] for a reference textbook. In *Reactive-TS*, the *radix tree* reduces the computational cost per iteration to $O(L)$, and therefore the cost per iteration is *constant* with respect to the number of iterations, but it increases the space requirements to $O(L)$. If *hashing* is used to store the entire configuration, the *average* time complexity is again $O(L)$ while the space cost is $O(L)$ per iteration.

One is therefore confronted with two different scenarios: either constant space is used per iteration but with increasing amounts of time (*REM*), or time constant with respect to t is used but the storage of the current configuration requires space $O(L)$ (*hashing, digital tree*). Because a very large number of iterations can be executed in practical runs of heuristics one is motivated to study schemes requiring time $O(L)$ constant with respect to t, *and* $O(1)$ space.

In this papers we assume that the answer to the queries should always be correct. It is of interest to note that a different approach consists of permitting a certain probability of *false alarms*: the dictionary structure gives a positive answer to a query about a state, while the state has never been encountered. In this second case an effective strategy already exists that stores only a hashed value [**5, 3**] associated to the state. A query gives a positive answer if and only if the hashed value of the current configuration is equal to the hashed value of a previously visited configuration. Depending on the number of bits one can bound the probability of false alarms (by bounding the probability that two different configurations have the same hashed value) and obtain an efficient realization of the memory structure for history-sensitive heuristics.

3. Persistent dynamic sets to support heuristics

The above desired time and space requirements can in fact be obtained through the use of *persistent dynamic sets*, see [**17, 8**] and references therein. Ordinary data structures are *ephemeral* [**8**] because when a change is executed the previous version is destroyed. Now, in many contexts like computational geometry, editing, implementation of very high level programming languages, and, last but not least, the context of history-sensitive heuristics considered in this paper, multiple versions of a data structure must be maintained and accessed. In particular, in heuristics one is interested in *partially persistent* structures, where all versions can be accessed but only the newest version (the *live* nodes) can be modified. A review of *ad hoc* techniques for obtaining persistent data structures is given in [**8**], a paper that is dedicated to a systematic study of persistence, continuing the previous work of [**16**].

3.1. Hashing combined with persistent red-black trees. The basic observation is that, because *Tabu Search* is based on *Local Search*, configuration $X^{(t+1)}$ differs from configuration $X^{(t)}$ only because of the addition or subtraction of a single index: a single bit is changed in the string. Let us define the operations $\textsc{Insert}(i)$ and $\textsc{Delete}(i)$ for inserting and deleting a given index i from the set. As cited above, configuration X can be considered as a set of indices in $[1, L]$ with a possible realization as a balanced red-black tree. Red-black trees are one of the many search-tree schemes that are balanced in order to guarantee that the basic dynamic-set operations take $O(\log L)$ time. See [**6, 11**] for two seminal papers about red-black trees, and [**7**] for a recent textbook. The binary string can be immediately obtained from the tree by visiting it in symmetric order, in time $O(L)$. $\textsc{Insert}(i)$ and $\textsc{Delete}(i)$ require $O(\log L)$ time, while at most a single node of the tree is allocated or deallocated at each iteration. Rebalancing the tree after insertion or deletion can be done in $O(1)$ rotations and $O(\log L)$ color changes [**19**]. In addition, the amortized number of color changes per update is $O(1)$, see for example [**15**].

Now, the *REM* method is closely reminiscent of a method studied in [**16**] to obtain partial persistence, in which the entire update sequence is stored and the desired version is rebuilt from scratch each time an access is performed, while a systematic study of techniques with better space-time complexities is present in [**17, 8**]. Let us now summarize from [**17**] how a partially persistent red-black tree can be realized. An example of the realizations that we consider is presented in Fig. 1.

The trivial way is that of keeping in memory all copies of the ephemeral tree (see the top part of Fig. 1), each copy requiring $O(L)$ space. A more efficient realization is based on *path copying*, independently proposed by many researchers, see [**17**] for references. Only the path from the root to the nodes where changes are made is copied: a set of search trees is created, one per update, having different roots but *sharing* common subtrees. The time and space complexities for INSERT(i) and DELETE(i) are now of $O(\log L)$.

The method that we will use is a space-efficient scheme requiring only linear space proposed in [**17**]. The approach avoids copying the entire access path each time an update occurs. To this end, each node contains an additional "extra" pointer (beyond the usual left and right ones) with a time stamp. When attempting to add a pointer to a node, if the extra pointer is available, it is used and the time of the usage is registered. If the extra pointer is already used, the node is copied, setting the initial left and right pointers of the copy to their latest values. In addition, a pointer to the copy is stored in the last parent of the copied node. If the parent has already used the extra pointer, the parent, too, is copied. Thus copying proliferates through successive ancestors until the root is copied or a node with a free extra pointer is encountered. Searching the data structure at a given time t in the past is easy: after starting from the appropriate root, if the extra pointer is used the pointer to follow from a node is determined by examining the time stamp of the extra pointer and following it iff the time stamp is not larger than t. Otherwise, if the extra pointer is not used, the normal left-right pointers are considered. Note that the pointer direction (left or right) does not have to be stored: given the search tree property it can be derived by comparing the indices of the children with that of the node. In addition, colors are needed only for the most recent (live) version of the tree.

In Fig. 1 the NULL pointers are not shown, the colors are correct only for the live tree (the nodes reachable from the rightmost root), and the extra pointers are dashed and time-stamped.

The worst-case time complexity of INSERT(i) and DELETE(i) remains of $O(\log L)$, but the important result derived in [**17**] is that the amortized space cost per update operation is $O(1)$. The amortized cost analysis executed in [**17**] for persistent red–black trees uses the *potential* paradigm [**20**].

Let us summarize from [**17**]. The nodes of the data structure are partitioned into two sets: *live* and *dead*. The live nodes form the version of the search tree at the current time. When changes are executed and the current time increases, live nodes can become dead and they will remain in this state forever. All nodes dead at a given time are not affected by future updates. Node-rebalancing operations are executed only on the live part of the structure. The *potential* of the structure is defined to be the number of live nodes minus $1/k$ times the number of free pointers in live nodes (k is the number of extra pointers available at each node, it will be

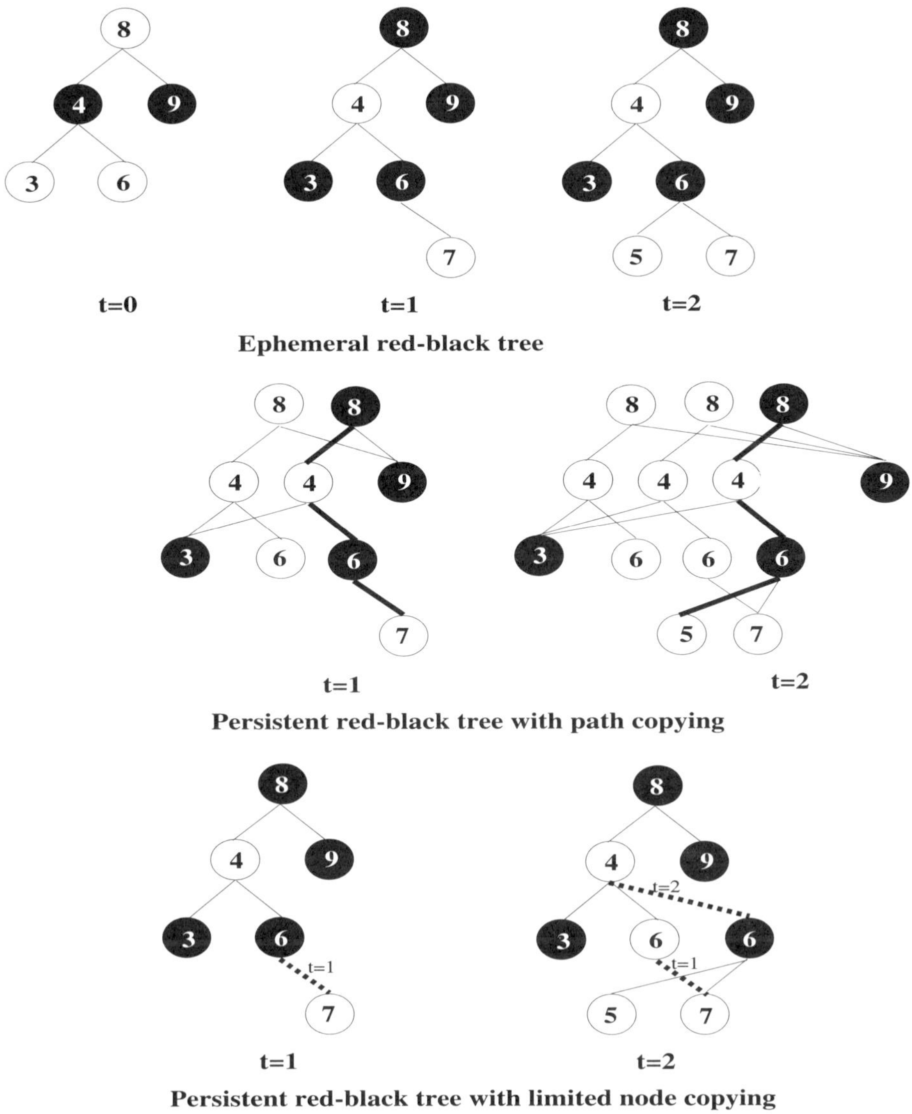

FIGURE 1. How to obtain a partially persistent red-black tree from an ephemeral one (top), containing indices 3,4,6,8,9 at t=0, with subsequent insertion of 7 and 5. Path copying (middle), with thick lines marking the copied part. Limited node copying (bottom) with dashed lines denoting the "extra" pointers with time stamp.

equal to one in our case). The *amortized space cost* of an update operation is defined as the actual number of nodes created plus the net increase in potential. With this definition, if one starts with an empty data structure (with zero potential) the total amortized space cost is an upper bound on the actual number of nodes created. With the given definition of potential, copying a node has an amortized space cost of zero, because a live node with no free pointers becomes dead and a new live node with k free pointers is created, for a net decrease in potential of one, balancing the new node created. Storing a new pointer in a node has an amortized space cost of $1/k$. The creation of a new node during an insertion has an amortized space cost of one. Because an insertion or deletion requires storing $O(1)$ new pointers not counting node copying, the amortized space cost of an update is $O(1)$. Additional details are present in the cited paper.

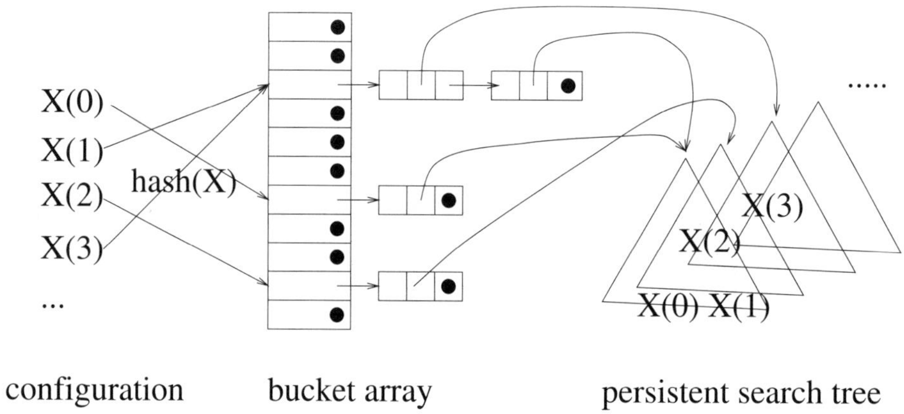

FIGURE 2. Open hashing scheme with persistent sets: a pointer to the appropriate root for configuration $X^{(t)}$ in the persistent search tree is stored in a linked list at a "bucket". Items on the list contain satellite data. The index of the bucket array is calculated from the configuration through a hashing function.

Let us now consider the context of history-sensitive heuristics. Contrary to the popular usage of persistent dynamic sets to search past versions at a specified time t, one is interested in checking whether a configuration has already been encountered in the previous history of the search, at *any* iteration.

A convenient way of realizing a data structure supporting X-SEARCH(X) is to combine *hashing* and *partially persistent dynamic sets*, see Fig. 2. From a given configuration X an index into a "bucket array" is obtained through a hashing function, with a possible incremental evaluation in time $O(1)$. Collisions are resolved through chaining: starting from each bucket header there is a linked list containing a pointer to the appropriate root of the persistent red-black tree and satellite data needed by the search (time of configuration, number of repetitions).

As soon as configuration $X^{(t)}$ is generated by the search dynamics, the corresponding persistent red-black tree is updated through INSERT(i) or DELETE(i). Let us now describe X-SEARCH($X^{(t)}$): the hashing value is computed from $X^{(t)}$ and the appropriate bucket searched. For each item in the linked list the pointer to the root of the past version of the tree is followed and the old set is compared with $X^{(t)}$. If the sets are equal, a pointer to the item on the linked list is returned.

Otherwise, after the entire list has been scanned with no success, a NULL pointer is returned.

In the last case a new item is linked in the appropriate bucket with a pointer to the root of the live version of the tree (X-INSERT(X, t)). Otherwise, the last visit time t is updated and the repetition counter is incremented.

After collecting the above cited complexity results, and assuming that the bucket array size is equal to the maximum number of iterations executed in the entire search, it is straightforward to conclude that a sequence of t iterations of *Reactive-TS* requires $O(L\ t)$ average-case time and $O(t)$ space for storing and retrieving the past configurations and for establishing prohibitions.

In fact, both the hash table and the persistent red-black tree require $O(1)$ space, amortized for the tree. Let us remember that $O(1)$ amortized space per iteration implies that $O(t)$ is an upper bound on the space needed for a sequence of t iterations. The worst-case time complexity per iteration required to update the current $X^{(t)}$ is $O(\log L)$, the average-case time for searching and updating the hashing table is $O(1)$. In detail, searches take time $O(1+\alpha)$, α being the load factor, in our case upper bounded by 1. The time is therefore dominated by that required to compare the configuration $X^{(t)}$ with that obtained through X-SEARCH$(X^{(t)})$, i.e., $O(L)$ in the worst case. Because $\Omega(L)$ time is needed during the neighborhood evaluation to compute the f values for all neighbors, the above complexity is optimal for the considered application to history-sensitive heuristics.

Let us note that the actual number of bytes used per iteration is very small. If the total number of iterations that will be executed by the search is not known from the beginning, a table with dynamic expansion (see [**7**], Sec. 18.4) can be used for hashing: for example by doubling its size when the load factor becomes equal to one. The space required for t iterations remains $O(t)$. Finally, let us note that the time complexity is pessimistic if the number of nonzero bits in the string is upper-bounded during the search. For example, in a Maximum Clique task, this number is less than or equal to the largest clique size [**3**], which is typically much smaller than L, the number of nodes in the graph.

4. C++ class and experiments

The partially persistent red-black tree previously described has been implemented in the C++ object-oriented language by creating a *class* called `per_rb_tree`, see Fig. 3.

Each node in the tree contains the "extra" pointer with a time stamp, as described in Sec. 3.1, and pointers to the appropriate roots of the partially persistent tree at the different times of its existence are stored in an array.

The "private" functions of the class are not described for brevity reasons. The constructor of the class `per_rb_tree(long max_roots)` takes as argument the maximum number of roots or, equivalently, the maximum life time of the structure. A default value is given if none is specified.

Let us note that the array of pointers is not needed when the pointers to the appropriate roots are stored through hashing, see Fig. 2. It is nonetheless used in the current implementation in order to study the space and time requirements of the persistent red-black tree structure in isolation.

To evaluate the different computational requirements of the ephemeral versus the persistent structure, a public function `enable_persistence()` is used to select

```
class per_rb_tree
 {
 private:
   ...
 public:
   per_rb_tree(long max_roots=1000000);
   ~per_rb_tree();

   void enable_persistence();

   void insert_key(ky_type key);

   per_rb_node * delete_item(per_rb_node* x);
   void delete_key(ky_type key);

   per_rb_node * lookup(ky_type key, long time= -1);

   void inorder_tree_walk(long time =-1);

   long size(long time =-1);
 }
```

FIGURE 3. C++ class realizing the partially persistent red-black tree.

the preferred option. The function is called when the user of the class wants to activate the persistency. Before calling the function the data structure implements an ordinary ephemeral red–black tree.

The operations `insert_key(ky_type key)` and `delete_item(per_rb_node* x)` have the usual meaning for dictionary data types: keys are inserted by creating a new node at the appropriate place in the tree and a pointer to a node is required to delete it. The operation `lookup(ky_type key, long time)` takes as additional parameter the time at which the structure is to be searched. The default value `time = -1` means that one is searching the current *live* version of the structure. The other possible values range from 1 to the current time, equal to the number of modifications (additions or deletions) executed on the structure after its creation. The operation `delete_key(ky_type k)` is realized by first calling `lookup(k)` to get a pointer and then calling `delete_item`, as in: `delete_item(lookup(k))`.

The operation `inorder_tree_walk(long time)` visits the tree at the given time. As usual, `time = -1` means that one is visiting the current structure.

All the experiments have been run on a HP 747i workstation at 100 MHz, with 128 Mb RAM. The GNU `gcc` compiler version 2.7.0 has been used with the `-O2` optimization level.

4.1. Memory usage tests: random numeric keys. In the special case of $k = 1$ the amortized space cost given in [**17**] is 6 for an insertion or deletion. It is therefore of interest to compare the above upper bound with the actual number of nodes in the tree created during its lifetime. The number of nodes is the relevant parameter in the experiments: it is then straightforward to derive the total number of bytes by multiplying that amount by the machine-dependent size of each node.

The first series of experiments is executed on the dictionary tests with random numeric keys proposed by DIMACS and collected by C. McGeoch. The `dimacs_test1` group consists of 27 dictionary trace files. These represent three random trials at each of 3 problem sizes (N=1k, 10k, 100k) with 3 kinds of problems (N inserts followed by N deletes, N inserts followed by N successful lookups, N inserts followed by N unsuccessful lookups). The `dimacs_test2` group consists of 27 more dictionary trace files for 3 different kinds of problems (N inserts followed by N repetitions of [ins del], N inserts followed by N repetitions of [ins successful del], N inserts followed by N repetitions of [ins unsuccessful delete]). Additional details and informations on the test problems are present in Appendix A of this volume.

The average values of the total number of cells created during the lifetime of the structure (both live cells of the current version and dead cells storing the information about previous versions) are plotted in Fig. 4 and Fig. 5. The growth behavior is well captured as a first approximation by a linear function. Therefore, in order to make the figures more informative and to highlight the differences between the various experiments what is charted is the total number of cells divided by the number of changes executed on the structure (the "time" of the persistent structure). To avoid cluttering the figures with too many details, standard error bars are shown only for one plot, the error bars in the other cases are comparable.

A best fit with a linear function executed on the complete set of data on the linear scale gives the following values for the slope of the growth curve: 2.558 ($\sigma = 0.003$) , for `dimacs_test1`, and 2.541 ($\sigma = 0.001$) for `dimacs_test2`.

The general conclusion that can be derived is that the upper bound of 6 is not tight: the actual number of cells as a function of the number of changes executed grows at a much smaller rate of about 2.5 for each change. What is more of interest is to analyze in detail the behavior of the different experiments. In particular, in the top plots of Fig. 4, one observes a convergence of the curves to a value of $2.68 - 2.69$ cells per change during the insertion phase and a slow decrease toward values of $2.53 - 2.54$ during the deletion phase. A qualitatively similar behavior is present also in Fig. 5.

The fact that insertions are executed in the first part and that deletions are executed in the second one suggests two possible hypotheses: i) more cells per change are created during insertions than during deletions, ii) the number of cells generated is influenced by the size of the live part of the persistent structure. In order to test these hypotheses, the number of *new* cells created during each operation for different sizes of the live structure has been collected on the `id` files. Because the raw data are very noisy, the numbers of new cells created when the size is within a suitable interval have been averaged (e.g., for the `id.a` files, the interval is 100).

Fig. 6 shows the results. Of course, because more points are averaged when the binning interval grows, the standard error on the average decreases for the bottom plots, corresponding to the experiments with more changes executed. It can be observed that there is a significant difference in the number of new cells created for insertions and for deletions (from about 2.7 cells to about 2.4 cells). The size of the data structure also influences the number of new cells but in a counter-intuitive way: in particular less cells are generated during the first deletions, when the size of the "live" structure is larger.

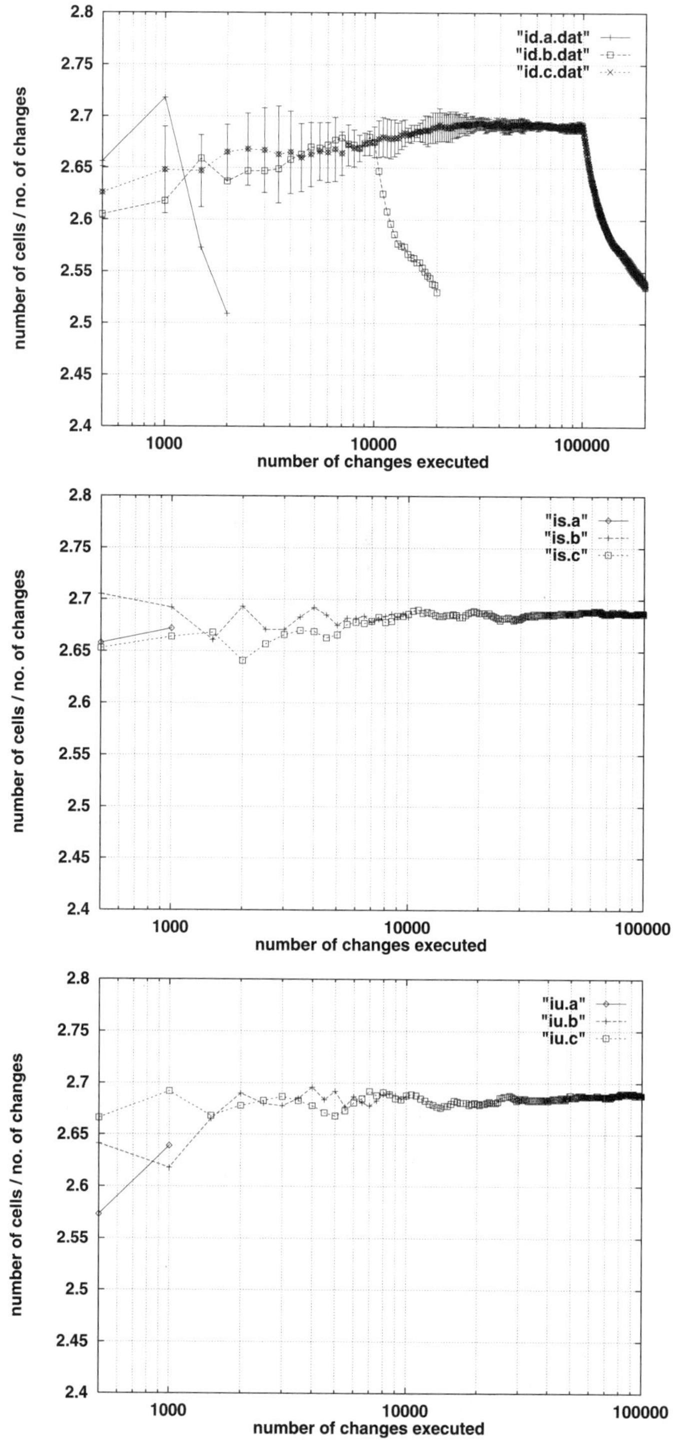

FIGURE 4. Memory usage (cells / number of changes) for DIMACS test1 dictionary tasks. `id` files (top) `is` files (middle) `iu` files (bottom).

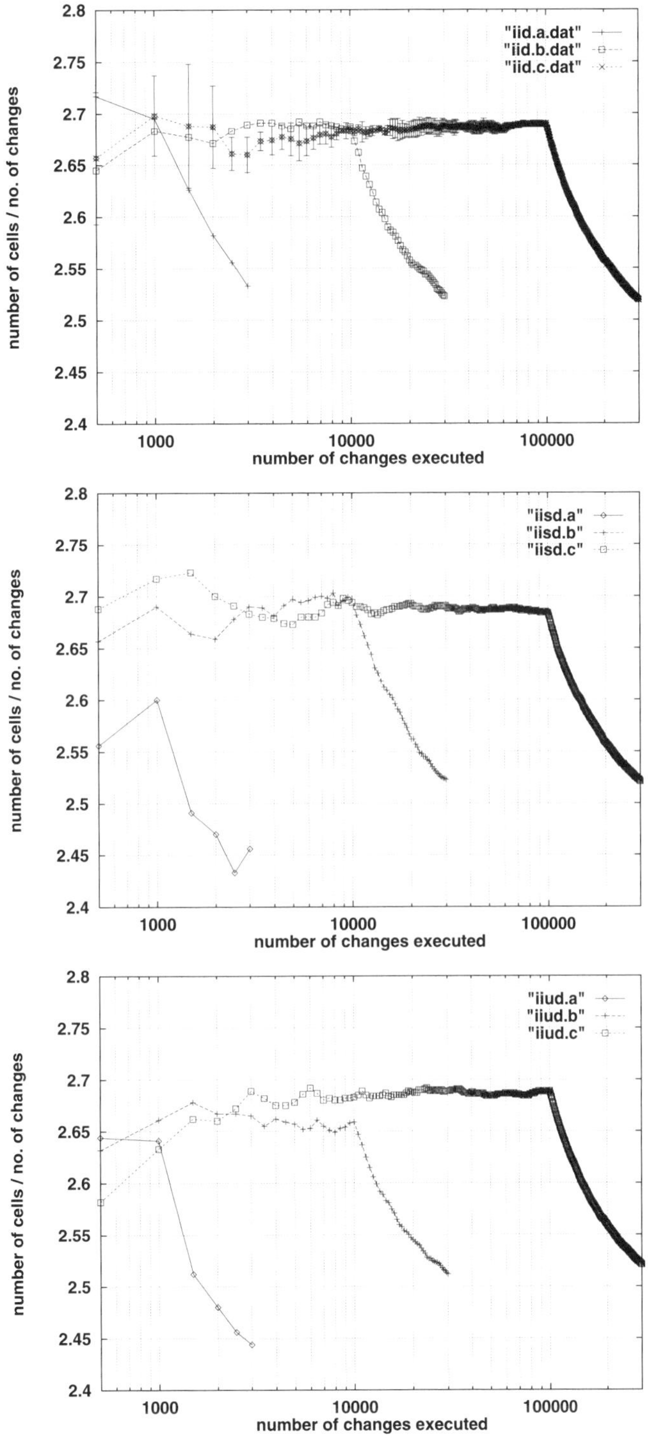

FIGURE 5. Memory usage (cells / number of changes) for DIMACS test2 dictionary tasks. `iid` files (top) `iisd` files (middle) `iiud` files (bottom).

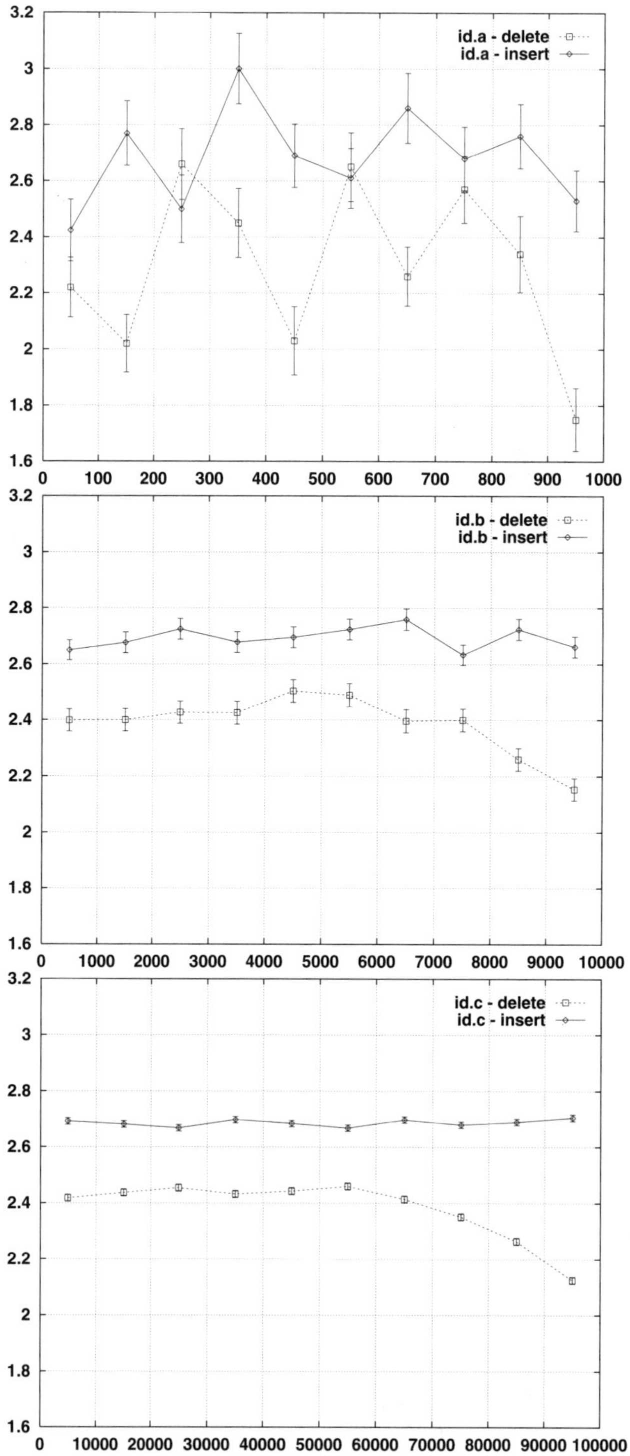

FIGURE 6. Average number of new cells created for each insert or delete operation as a function of the size of the live structure. Tests on `id.a` `id.b` `id.c` files, see text for details.

4.2. Memory usage tests: application to Reactive Search. The initial motivation for considering persistent dynamic sets was that of storing and retrieving the past history of *Local Search* based heuristic methods. In particular, we consider the case of a configuration space given by binary strings. Each binary string X is represented by a set containing the positions of the bits equal to one, where each index is in the range $[1, L]$.

The particular case considered in the experiments is that of solving the Maximum Clique problems in graphs with the *Reactive Local Search* method proposed in [**3**], to which the reader is referred for the algorithm details. Let $L = |V|$, the number of vertices. A clique is represented by a binary vector of length L in which a 1 is in position i if and only if the ith vertex is in the clique. In each run, one starts from a "seed" node and generates a search trajectory, where at each iteration a node is either added to or deleted from the current clique. The corresponding INSERT and DELETE operations are registered in a file with the format required by the DIMACS "driver" program, that is then used to test the dictionary data structure.

The memory usage results obtained by using the persistent red-black tree for different instances of the Maximum Clique problem are illustrated in Fig. 7. Standard error bars are shown only for a plot to make the figure more readable. The instances have been used in a benchmark organized by the second DIMACS implementation challenge [**13**], and they are electronically available at: `http://dimacs.rutgers.edu/Challenge/index.html`.

To better show the approximately linear growth, what is plotted is the number of cells divided by the number of changes executed on the structure. Again, it can be noted that the upper bound of 6 cells per change is not tight. Furthermore, the number of cells created after the initial transient phase shows an approximate convergence to values of 2.12 (for the random graphs with density 0.5), and 2.3 (for the random graphs with density 0.5 and for the two additional graphs).

The number of cells generated is lower than that for the dictionary tests. This fact is explained by the very small size of the current clique during the search and therefore by the very small size of the "live" part of the persistent structure. In fact, the heuristic Maximum Clique sizes found in [**3**] are in the range $14 - 16$ for the random graphs with density 0.5 (`DSJC500.5, DSJC1000.5, C2000.5`) in the range $34 - 75$ for the random graphs with density 0.9 (`C125.9, ... , C2000.9`). The `gen400_p0.9_55` graph has a clique of size 55, the `p_hat1500-2` graph has a clique of size 65.

To test the hypothesis that the reduced number of cells created is related to the small size of the live structure, the initial period of the `id` tasks has been analyzed in more detail. In particular, Fig. 8 shows that the number of new cells created during insertions grows rapidly as a function of the size of the live structure and stabilizes only after some hundreds of changes.

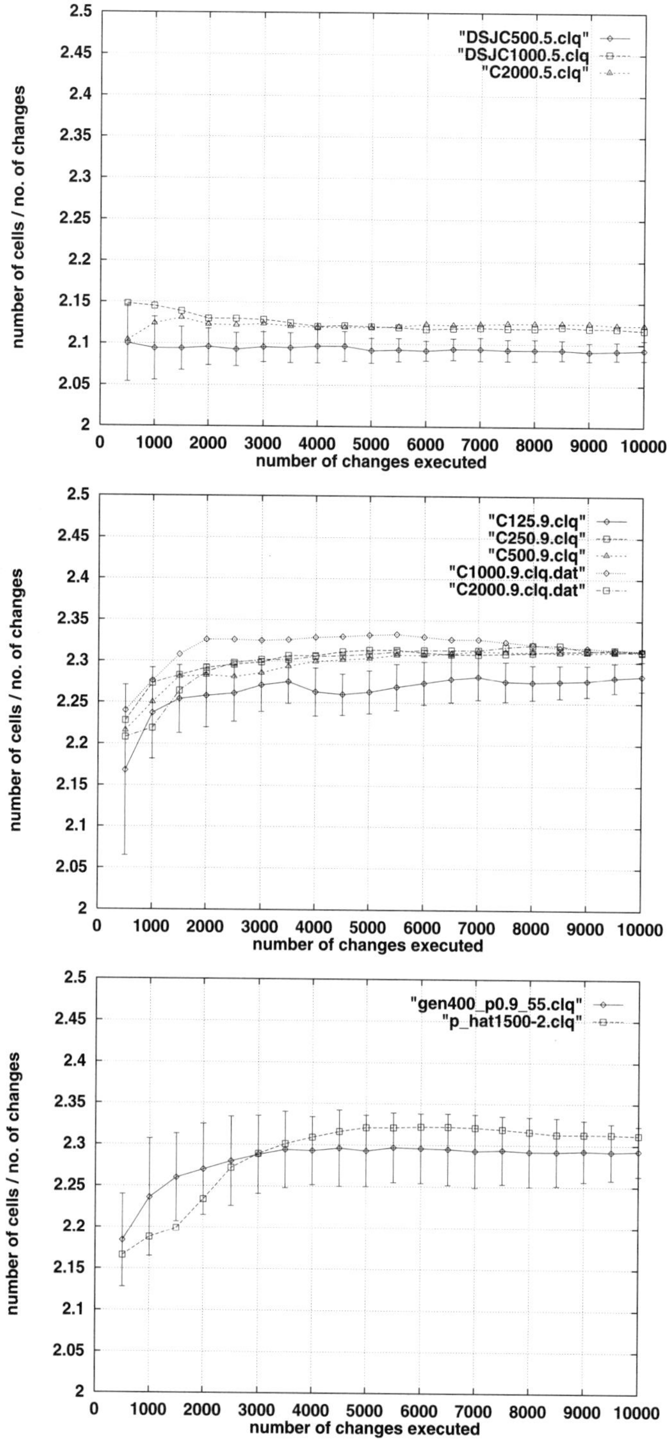

FIGURE 7. Memory usage (no. of cells) when persistent sets are used to support the Reactive *Local Search* algorithm for the MAX-CLIQUE problem.

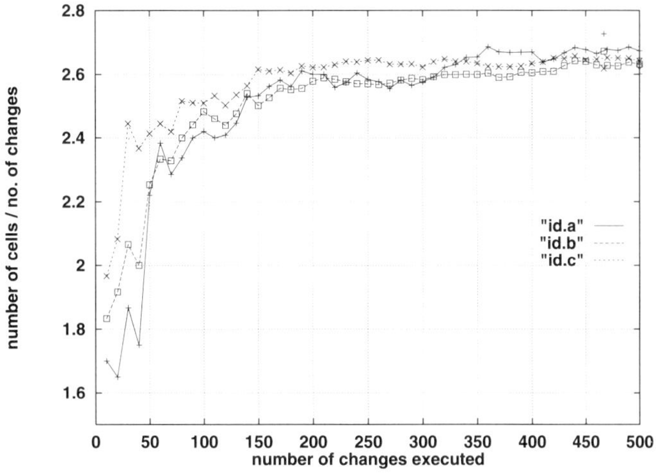

FIGURE 8. Memory usage (no. of cells / no. of changes) as a function of the number of changes: initial period for the `id` tasks.

4.3. Timing tests. Because our main interest is in the above described use of the persistent structure to support *history-sensitive heuristics*, in addition to providing timing results for a subset of the dictionary tests proposed by DIMACS (the same subset that was used in Sec. 4.1 to study the algorithm space complexity) we also provide timing results for the set of Maximum Clique problems described in Sec. 4.2.

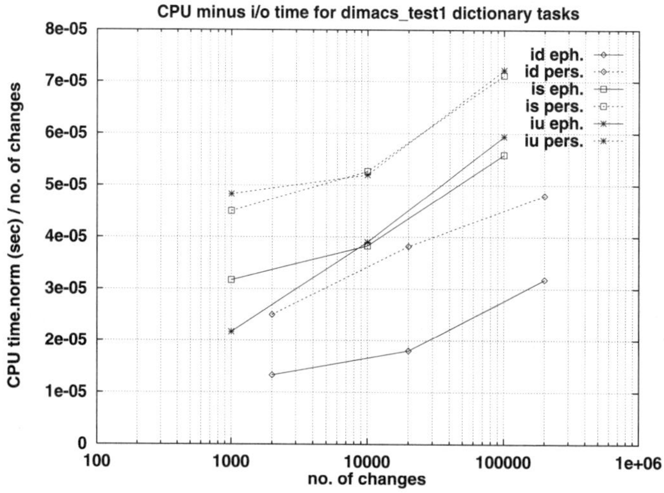

FIGURE 9. CPU time time for DIMACS test1 dictionary tasks as a function of the number of changes. Input-output time has been subtracted.

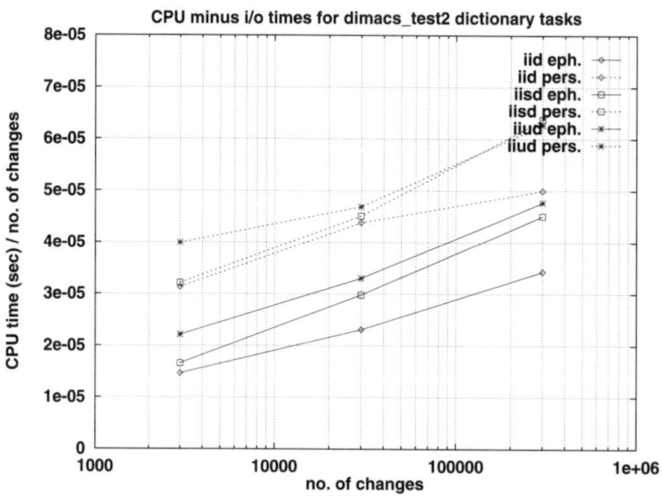

FIGURE 10. CPU time time for DIMACS test2 dictionary tasks as a function of the number of changes. Input-output time has been subtracted.

The CPU times in seconds obtained on the `dimacs_test1` and `dimacs_test2` dictionary tasks are illustrated in Fig. 9 and Fig. 10, respectively, as a function of the total number of changes executed at the end of each run. The plots correspond to the different tests and to the two versions (ephemeral or persistent) of the red-black tree structure. In order to subtract the input/output times, separate runs are executed where the driver program is calling the same input/output operations without calling any data structure operation. The average input/output time is not negligible: it is 22.5 microseconds per operation. Therefore the individual input-output times of the different tests have been subtracted to get accurate estimates of the CPU times.

The difference in the average time for operation for the different kinds of files is significant, because of the different sequences of operations executed. Therefore, separate averages are presented for the different files. After the input/output time is discounted, the average time per operation in the ephemeral structure is 21 microseconds for the `id` files, 42 microseconds for the `is` files, 40 microseconds for the `iu` files. For the persistent structure the average times in the same order are of 37, 56, and 57 microseconds. The incremental cost to pass from an ephemeral to a persistent red-black tree for the three different kinds of files is therefore of about 76%, 33% and 42%.

The average time per operation in the ephemeral structure is 24 microseconds for the `iid` files, 30 microseconds for the `iisd` files, 34 microseconds for the `iiud` files. The standard error is less than $\sigma = 1$ in all cases. For the persistent structure the average times in the same order are of 41, 47, and 49 microseconds. The incremental cost to pass from an ephemeral to a persistent red-black tree for the three different kinds of files is therefore of about 70%, 56% and 44%.

In general, the CPU time appears to increase more rapidly than a linear function of the number of changes, both because of the size of the data structure, the nature of the changes executed and, possibly, because of cache effects. A detailed analysis of the CPU time as a function of the different parameters and sequences is beyond the scope of this paper.

Graph	ephemeral CPU	persistent CPU	(pers. CPU - eph. CPU) / (eph. CPU)
C125.9.clq.b	11.7	24.4	1.08
C250.9.clq.b	13.1	25.0	0.90
C500.9.clq.b	12.4	25.6	1.06
C1000.9.clq.b	12.4	24.6	0.98
C2000.9.clq.b	12.9	24.2	0.87
DSJC500.5.clq.b	9.8	19.1	0.94
DSJC1000.5.clq.b	9.7	21.5	1.21
C2000.5.clq.b	11.	21.0	0.90
gen400_p0.9_55.clq.b	11.8	24.6	1.08
p_hat1500-2.clq.b	13.5	24.3	0.80

TABLE 1. CPU time per change (in microseconds) for the ephemeral and persistent version on the Maximum Clique problems.

The average CPU time per change for the ephemeral and persistent version on the files produced by Maximum Clique problems (averages on 10 runs for each task) are shown in Table 1. The last column shows the increase in CPU time when passing from an ephemeral to a persistent structure, divided by the ephemeral CPU time. The CPU time is approximately doubled but it remains acceptable for the application to history-sensitive heuristics.

5. Conclusions

History-sensitive heuristics require that the previous history of a *Local–Search*–based process be stored so that it can be accessed in an efficient way. In particular, we consider search problems where the configuration space can be represented by binary strings of length L.

Partially persistent dynamic structures like the persistent red–black tree considered in this paper give an optimal solution to store the entire previous history of a sequence of t iterations with $O(t)$ space requirements. A small number of bytes per iteration, constant with respect to the iteration number and to the binary string dimension, is sufficient to store *all previous versions* of the data structure. The worst-case time complexity per update operation is $O(logL)$.

In addition, hashing can be combined with partially persistent red-black trees so that one can check whether a given configuration has already been encountered during the previous phase of the search, as it is required in *Strict Tabu Search* and *Reactive Tabu Search* algorithms. The experiments confirm the applicability of the approach and the actual average number of cells needed per update operations is much less than the theoretical upper bound of 6: in fact it is upper bounded by about 2.5 in the considered tests. The time penalty incurred in passing from an ephemeral to a persistent structure, after input-output times are discounted, is from about 30% to about 100%.

Of course, the use of persistent data structure in history–sensitive heuristic schemes based on *Local Search* is not limited to *Reactive Search* schemes, but it can be extended to all cases where the information about the previously visited configurations is used to direct the future steps of the search.

To the best of our knowledge this is the first paper to consider the use of *persistent* structures in the framework of history-sensitive heuristics. The work has shown the applicability of the approach but many issues remain open for future research. In particular, a theme of interest is to see whether tighter bounds on the number of cells created during the history of a persistent structure can be derived by considering the detailed realization. A second theme is to see whether more efficient realizations of persistent dictionaries (not limited to the red-black tree) can be derived. Different realizations will also permit to compare the adopted "red-black tree plus hashing" implementations with different data structures.

The complete algorithms developed to make red-black trees persistent are rather complex and not amenable to a brief description. Because of this, the C++ implementation of the persistent red-black trees is available from the author for research purposes.

Acknowledgements

We wish to thank prof. A. Bertossi for reading and commenting a preliminary version of this work and the anonymous referees for their detailed comments.

References

[1] R. Battiti and A. A. Bertossi, Greedy, Prohibition, and Reactive Heuristics for Graph-Partitioning, *IEEE Transactions on Computers*, in press.

[2] R. Battiti, A. A. Bertossi, and R. Rizzi. Randomized Greedy Algorithms for the Hypergraph Partitioning Problem, *Proceedings of the DIMACS Workshop on Randomization Methods in Algorithm Design*, Princeton, Oct 20, 1997. Edited by: P. Pardalos, S.. Rajasekaran, and J. Rolim. American Mathematical Society, 1998, in press

[3] R. Battiti and M. Protasi, Reactive *Local Search* for the Maximum Clique problem, Tech. Rept. TR-95-052, International Computer Science Institute, Berkeley, CA, 1995, *Algorithmica*, to appear.

[4] R. Battiti and M. Protasi, Reactive Search, a history-sensitive heuristic for MAX-SAT, *ACM Journal of Experimental Algorithmics*, **2**, Article 2. Available at URL `http://www.jea.acm.org/` .

[5] R. Battiti and G. Tecchiolli, The Reactive Tabu Search, *ORSA Journal on Computing*, **6(2)** (1994) 126–140.

[6] R. Bayer, Symmetric binary B-trees: Data structure and maintenance algorithms, *Acta Informatica* **1** (1972) 290–306.

[7] T. H. Cormen, C. E. Leiserson, and R. L. Rivest, *Introduction to Algorithms* (McGraw-Hill, New York, 1990).

[8] J. R. Driscoll, N. Sarnak, D. D. Sleator, and R. E. Tarjan, Making data structures persistent, in: *Proc. 18th Ann. ACM Symp. on Theory of Computing*, Berkeley, CA (1986) 109–121.

[9] F. Glover, Tabu Search - part I, *ORSA Journal on Computing* **1(3)** (1989) 190–260.

[10] F. Glover, Tabu Search - part II, *ORSA Journal on Computing* **2(1)** (1990) 4–32.

[11] L. J. Guibas and R. Sedgewick, A dichromatic framework for balanced trees, in: *Proc. of the 19th Ann. Symp. on Foundations of Computer Science* (IEEE Computer Society, 1978) 8–21.

[12] P. Hansen and B. Jaumard, Algorithms for the maximum satisfiability problem, *Computing* **44** (1990) 279–303.

[13] D. S. Johnson and M. A. Trick, Introduction to the Second DIMACS Challenge: Cliques, Coloring and Satisfiability, in: *Cliques, Coloring, and Satisfiability, Second DIMACS Implementation Challenge*, DIMACS Series in Discrete Mathematics and Theoretical Computer Science, Vol. 26, AMS (1996), 1–7.

[14] S. Lin, Computer Solutions of the Traveling Salesman problems, *BSTJ* **44(10)** (1965) 2245–69.

[15] D. Maier and S. C. Salveter, Hysterical B-trees, *Inform. Process. Lett.* **12 (4)** (1981) 199–202.

[16] M. H. Overmars, Searching in the past II: general transforms, Tech. Rept. RUU-CS-81-9, Dept. of Computer Science, Univ. of Utrecht, Utrecht, The Netherlands, 1981.

[17] N. Sarnak and E. Tarjan, Persistent planar point location using persistent search trees, *Communications of the ACM* **27(7)** (1986) 669–679.

[18] K. Steiglitz and P. Weiner, Some improved algorithms for computer solution of the Traveling Salesman problem, in: *Proc. Sixth Allerton Conf. on Circuit and System Theory*, Urbana, Illinois (1968), 814–21.

[19] R. E. Tarjan, Updating a balanced search tree in $O(1)$ rotations, *Inform. Process. Lett.* **16 (5)** (1983) 253–257.

[20] R. E. Tarjan, Amortized computational complexity, *SIAM J. Alg. Disc. Meth.* **6 (2)** (1985) 306–318.

(R. Battiti) Dipartimento di Matematica, Università di Trento, Via Sommarive 14, 38050 Povo (Trento) Italy

E-mail address, R. Battiti: `battiti@science.unitn.it`

DIMACS Series in Discrete Mathematics
and Theoretical Computer Science
Volume **59**, 2002

A Practical Perfect Hashing Algorithm

Craig Silverstein

ABSTRACT. Hashing is a fundamental technique in Computer Science, and perfect hashing, which guarantees constant-time lookup, has particular theoretical and practical importance. The algorithm of Fredman, Komlós, and Szemerédi [**8**], augmented by Dietzfelbinger, *et al.* [**7**], is a simple perfect hashing scheme that has not seen extensive use due to poor practical performance. In this paper, we develop modifications to the previous techniques that result in a fast, space-efficient algorithm. We show the resulting algorithm is comparable to hash algorithms used in several popular dictionary libraries but is more flexible and has better theoretical performance.

1. Introduction

The *dictionary* abstract data type — which provides insertion, deletion, and lookup of arbitrary items — is one of the most important in computer science, having applications from databases to function optimization. Arguably the most popular implementation of the dictionary data type is via *hashing*, in which items are kept in an array of buckets, indexed by small integers, and a *hash function* is used to map items to buckets. Using hashing it is possible to get constant-time lookup and (amortized) constant-time insertion and deletion. Alternative implementations of the dictionary data type, such as B-trees, do not seem to be able to match these time bounds.

Early hashing algorithms could only guarantee *average case* constant-time lookup (see, e.g., [**9**]), assuming a friendly distribution of inputs. For instance, lookup in linear probing hashing schemes could take linear time for lookup if all the keys hashed to a small range of values. In the past decade research has focused on algorithms for *perfect* (i.e., collision-free) hash functions, which guarantee constant-time lookup even in the worst case. Fredman, Komlós, and Szemerédi developed a particularly appealing randomized hashing algorithm [**8**], combining $O(1)$ worst case lookup time with $O(n)$ worst case space use. This algorithm did not support insertion or deletion but only lookup on a static data set. However,

---

Supported by the Department of Defense, with partial support from NSF Award CCR-9357849, with matching funds from IBM, Schlumberger Foundation, Shell Foundation, and Xerox Corporation.

Dietzfelbinger, *et al.* [**7**] remedied this shortcoming, describing a modified algorithm with amortized expected constant time insertion and deletion. We call this modified algorithm *FKS hashing.*

FKS hashing is easy to implement; its major shortcoming is that the order notation hides some fairly large constants. The lookup algorithm, for instance, multiplies two large numbers and is therefore quadratic in the number of bits in the largest key. Furthermore, a naive implementation uses $37n$ space, which is unacceptably large in practice. A somewhat slower implementation uses only $2n + o(n)$ space, but even this bound hides some practically significant constants in the $o(n)$ term.

In this paper, we attack these time and space issues, attaining an algorithm that is comparable to hashing schemes that lack the theoretical guarantees of the FKS algorithm. In the rest of this section, we describe the canonical FKS algorithm. In Section 2 we describe how we evaluate the various algorithms discussed in this paper. In Section 3 we describe a series of modifications to the canonical FKS scheme that yields a faster, more compact variant of FKS. In Sections 4 and 5 we discuss various ways to make hashtables smaller, at the cost of speed: by using space-efficient tables (Section 4) and by adjusting load factor parameters (Section 5). Section 6 compares the FKS class of hash table algorithms to other hash table algorithms, including some in widely used applications such as Perl. Finally, in Section 7 we conclude with a discussion of the feasibility of using FKS-based hashing algorithms in practice.

1.1. Hashing with Linear Probing. We start by describing a simple, fast hashing algorithm similar to ones used in such publicly available dictionary libraries as LEDA [**4**] and AT&T System V's `hsearch` [**5**].[1] Assume for the moment we know we are going to insert n items. We construct the hashtable, which is an array of size $t > n$. We then choose an arbitrary hash function $h(x)$ that maps a key x to an integer in $\{1, \ldots, t\}$. $h(x)$ should be chosen so that, for most data, different keys will map to different values. Constructing a general, high quality hash function is a difficult task; [**2**] discusses some of the issues involved. For a good hash function, the time to compute $h(x)$ should be linear in the number of bits in x. Superlinear hash functions are too slow, while faster ones cannot look at all the input and are susceptible to collisions in keys that differ only on the unexamined bits.

To insert a key x, we first look at bucket $h(x)$ in the hashtable. If it is empty, we insert x at that position. If it is already occupied, we have a *collision*, and we instead try to insert x at position $h(x) + 1$. If that bucket is occupied we try $h(x)+2$, and so on, wrapping around if necessary, until we find an empty bucket. If $h(x)$ causes few collisions on the data set, and the table is not too full, the expected time to insert will be small.

Lookup proceeds similarly to insertion. To look up x, we first examine bucket $h(x)$. If it holds x, we terminate successfully. If it is empty, we terminate unsuccessfully. If it holds some key other than x, we examine bucket $h(x) + 1$, then $h(x) + 2$, and so on, until we find x or an empty bucket. The worst-case time to look up x is the same as the time to insert x, while the average-case time, if x actually is in the hashtable, is about half that.

[1]LEDA actually performs hashing with chaining, while `hsearch` performs double hashing. These approaches are qualitatively similar to hashing with linear probing. See [**9**] for a discussion of the relative merits of these approaches.

To delete x, we are tempted to merely look up x and empty the returned bucket. This may cause lookup to fail, however, since it will now terminate (incorrectly) when examining bucket $h(x)$ while before it would have continued to look at $h(x)+1$. This can cause lookup to miss a key y that had collided with x and is therefore in bucket $h(x)+1$. The solution is to insert a special "place holder" into bucket $h(x)$ indicating it holds deleted contents. Lookup treats the bucket as if it holds a non-matching key, while insert treats it as empty.

If the total number of insertions n is not known, the hashtable can be resized dynamically. When the number of filled buckets gets too close to t ($t/2$ is a good maximum value in practice, since as the number of empty buckets gets small, insertion and lookup times increase dramatically), the entire contents are rehashed into a hashtable of size $2t$. Likewise, if the number of filled buckets gets too small (say, $t/5$), the entire hashtable can be rehashed into a table of size $t/2$. (Such rehashing is necessary to keep the space use linear in n but does not improve future running time.) Rehashing takes amortized constant time.

For computational reasons, it is advantageous to have t be a power of 2; then the last step of computing $h(x)$ is merely a bit mask. Note that rehashing preserves the property that t is a power of 2.

1.2. Dynamic Perfect Hashing. If the hash function described above could guarantee no collisions for every data set and every potential value of t, it would be a *perfect* hash function. It is not hard to believe that there is no perfect hash function that works for all possible inputs, but it turns out there is a simple *family* of hash functions such that, for any data set and any value of t, most hash functions in the family result in a very small number of collisions. Fredman, Komlós, and Szemerédi, in [**8**], leveraged this into a perfect hashing algorithm, one in which there are no collisions and all dictionary operations are therefore guaranteed constant time.

Suppose our (static) input consists of n integers in the range $1 \ldots p-1$, where p is a prime.[2] Given a hashtable with t buckets, and an arbitrary parameter $k < p$, we define the hash function $h_k(x)$ to be $(kx \bmod p) \bmod t$. Let $C_k(i)$ be the set of input keys that hash into bucket i $(1 \leq i \leq t)$. From [**8**] we have that

$$\sum_{k=1}^{p-1}\sum_{i=1}^{t}\binom{|C_k(i)|}{2} < \frac{(p-1)n^2}{t} \tag{1.1}$$

This implies that, with probability $\frac{1}{2}$, a random k satisfies

$$\sum_{i=1}^{t}\binom{|C_k(i)|}{2} < \frac{2n^2}{t}$$

Clearly $\sum_{i=1}^{t}|C_k(i)| = n$, so a random k, with probability $\frac{1}{2}$, satisfies

$$\sum_{i=1}^{t}|C_k(i)|^2 < \frac{4n^2}{t} + n \tag{1.2}$$

If $t \in \Omega(n)$, this equation limits, but does eliminate, collisions: $|C_k(i)|$, the number of items in bucket i, can be greater than 1. Therefore we hash the items in each bucket a second time. With each bucket i we associate a second level hashtable

[2]We can easily handle arbitrary data by considering any series of bits to represent a (very large) integer.

of size $t_i = 2|C_k(i)|^2$. The inequality (1.2) again applies, with n set to $|C_k(i)|$ and t set to $2n^2$, and it can only be satisfied if each bucket holds at most one item. With probability $\frac{1}{2}$, then, our choice of k_i yields a perfect hash function for bucket i. It is easy to see that, in constant expected time, we end up with a perfect hash function for each second level hashtable. The space requirement is $t + \sum_{i=1}^{t} t_i$. If $t = n$, we can apply (1.2) to bound $\sum t_i$, giving a bound of $11n$ on the number of buckets.

To handle the dynamic case, with insertions and deletions, [**7**] starts with the static hashing scheme, but the authors make the top level hashtable larger than necessary. In particular, when hashing n_0 items they pretend there are really $(1+c)n_0$ items to be inserted. When the number of items actually grows to $(1+c)n_0$, or drops to $\frac{1+c}{1+2c}n_0$, they rehash the entire hashtable. This rehashing takes linear time but can be amortized over the cn_0 (or more) insertions and deletions that must have taken place since the previous rehashing. We can also rehash if the total number of low-level buckets grows too large, but this does not affect the time analysis. Note this is essentially the same rehashing technique as described in Section 1.1.

The second level hashtables are dealt with in a similar way. If bucket i has $n_0 = |C_k(i)|$ items, we size the second level hashtable as if it held $(1 + c')n_0$ items, and we rehash it when the number of items grows to $(1+c')n_0$ or shrinks to $\frac{1+c'}{1+2c'}n_0$. Unlike at the top level, each insertion may require that we re-choose k_i to preserve non-collision. However, with probability $\frac{1}{2}$ each choice of k_i can hash all $(1 + c')n_0$ items without collision, so we expect to have to look at only 2 possible k values between rehashings. As a result, overall insertion and deletion take amortized constant time. It is also easy to show the total space required is linear throughout the lifetime of the algorithm.

2. Experimental Setup

All of the modifications to FKS suggested in this paper are heuristics; how well they work, and indeed if they work at all, can only be determined by experiment. Before describing changes to the FKS algorithm, we describe the experimental setup used to test these changes. This is the setup provided by the DIMACS Challenge organizers, along with evaluation metrics appropriate to this study.

2.1. The Test Suite. The test set suite used is the one provided for the Dictionary portion of the DIMACS challenge (see [**3**]). It is summarized in Table 1. In our analysis we ignore the smaller test sets and only examine the following 34 test sets: `matchexact.*` (26 test sets; we omitted the 100-element subset of `matchexact.trace-3.2-Y-1`), `id.c`, `is.c`, `iu.c`, `iid.c`, `iisd.c`, `iiud.c`, `circ.100000`, and `joyce.dat`.

For those test sets that take a random number seed, we ran the test three times with different seeds, averaging the running times. We also averaged the results of the five `circ` test sets of a given size. In no case was the variance of the tests large enough to be a concern.

All tests were run on three separate machines:

Alpha: an AlphaServer 4100 5/300 with 4 EV5 300 MHz. processors and 4 Gig. memory running OSF1 V4.0 and including gcc 2.7.2;

Test Set	Key size	description
matchexact.*	4 bytes (int)	Dictionary traces of ML and Smalltalk programs.
circ.n	36 bytes	Library call data (n is number of records).
id.n	16 bytes	Inserts of random keys followed by deletion. n is one of `a` (1000 items), `b` (10000 items), or `c` (100000 items).
is.n	16 bytes	Inserts of random keys followed by successful lookups. n is as in `id`.
iu.n	16 bytes	Inserts of random keys followed by unsuccessful lookups. n is as in `id`.
iid.n	16 bytes	Inserts of random keys followed by insert-then-delete operations. n is as in `id`.
iisd.n	16 bytes	Inserts of random keys followed by insert-then-successful-lookup-then-delete operations. n is as in `id`.
iiud.n	16 bytes	Inserts of random keys followed by insert-then-unsuccessful-lookup-then-delete operations. n is as in `id`.
ed.t	20 bytes	`ed.`t is equivalent to t`.a` — where t is one of `id`, `iu`, etc. as above — for words in a book by Eddington. For example, *ed.iid* inserts 1000 words, then does 1000 insert-delete operations.
jy.t	20 bytes	Same as for `ed`, but using words from a book by Joyce.
*.dat	20 bytes	Lookup followed by insertion (if necessary) of words from various books.

TABLE 1. DIMACS standard suite of Dictionary test sets.

POWER: an RS/6000 604e with 4 POWER 166 Mhz. processors and 512 Meg. of memory running AIX 4.2 and including gcc 2.8.1; and

x86: a Pentium Pro with a 200 Mhz. processor and 96 Meg. of memory running Solaris x86 5.5.1 and including gcc 2.8.1.

In general, we will refer to each machine by the bold processor name. In each case, the code — written in C — was compiled using gcc with the `-O6` optimization option.

We chose these three configurations in order to test a variety of processor types, word sizes, and cache configurations. Such variety is particularly important in low-level data structures such as dictionaries, which can depend on specific properties of the architecture for improved performance.

Our implementation of the hash function, for instance, operates on a word-by-word basis. This has several consequences. Machines with 64-bit architectures can, in theory, hash more quickly than 32-bit machines because the same bit string will fit into fewer words. Furthermore, hashing strings will be different on big-endian and little-endian hardware, because the sequence of characters will be interpreted as different numbers in each case. In order to explore these issues, we chose test platforms that include both 32- and 64-bit architectures and both big- and little-endian word orders. In particular, the x86 is 32-bit and little-endian, the POWER is 32-bit and big-endian, and the Alpha is 64-bit and little-endian.

2.2. Evaluating Modifications of the FKS Algorithm. We would like to obtain a single number encapsulating how fast, or how small, a given variant of the FKS algorithm is. To do this with the 34 test sets we include in our analysis, we report the performance of each algorithm relative to the performance of the canonical FKS algorithm as described in Section 1.2. To measure time performance, for instance, we would, for each test, take the time of the new algorithm on that test and divide it by the time of the canonical algorithm on that test. We then average the 34 resulting ratios to get the relative performance of the new algorithm. On occassion, we also report the minimum and maximum ratio.

When measuring time, we record the user time spent by each process. User time is an imperfect measure of hash performance. It does not include the time spent paging, for instance, which is often the major time bottleneck for large dictionaries. On the other hand, user time does include such activities as making a copy of each hash command, converting strings to integers, and so forth — I/O-related operations which should not be counted as a cost of hashing. To account for this I/O time, we ran each test on a "dummy" hash routine, which parsed the commands in the same manner as all the other algorithms, but immediately returned FALSE on all inserts, lookups, and deletes. We subtracted the time taken by the dummy hash routine from all the times calculated. We subtracted this time even from the DIMACS demo hash and Perl code, even though they use different parsing routines, because we have no way of accurately measuring the time spent parsing for these implementations. The parsing code used by the dummy hash is not particularly efficient, so we believe the normalization is conservative, making the demo and Perl hashing routines perhaps seem faster than they actually are.

As a proxy for paging cost, we report the space used for the various algorithms. The less space an algorithm uses, the larger the dictionary problem that can be efficiently handled. When evaluating space use, we measure the maximum amount of memory allocated during any part of the algorithm. Because resizing the hashtable requires two copies of the hashtable to be in use simultaneously, the high-water memory need will typically be higher than that of the final hashtable, even if no hash table items are ever deleted.

3. Improving the FKS algorithm

There are several reasons the algorithm described in Section 1.2 is impractical. One is the space use, which is linear in the number of items but has large constants. For instance, we must store a value of k_i with each bottom-level bin, and each k_i requires as much space to store as the longest key. While space/time trade-offs are possible — the user can modify c and c', the overestimation parameters used in the dynamic FKS algorithm — they cannot improve the algorithm enough to make it space efficient.

Time inefficiencies are even more problematic. Computing $h_k(x)$ requires time quadratic in the number of bits in x. If x is actually a string, this means that hash computations are quadratic in the length of the string. Furthermore, every insert and lookup requires computing two hash values. In addition, while the number of times a low-level bin is grown may be linear in the number of operations, it is certainly mcuh larger than the number required by, say, hashing with linear probing, and every bin-growth operation requires a slow memory-allocation step. Finally, the two-level scheme requires accessing more parts of memory than does hashing with linear probing. In modern machines, the cost of random (as opposed to sequential) memory access can be a significant part of the cost of a hashing algorithm.

In the remainder of this section, we propose a series of modifications to the FKS algorithm that improve its time and space profiles. Each modification is added to the previous ones, so the final algorithm includes all the proposed modifications. The major benefits come from two of the optimizations: (1) storing some data directly in the top level bin, thus dramatically decreasing the number of hashes that need be performed, and (2) modifying the algorithm in such a way that almost all k values can be 1, significantly speeding up the hash function.

3.1. Storing Items in the Top-Level Bin. One easy optimization, noted by the original authors of the algorithm in [**8**], is to store singleton items of low-level bins in the top level. That is, instead of having, in the top-level bucket, a pointer to a bin with only one item in it, store the item itself in lieu of the pointer. This saves space because there is no need to allocate space for a low-level bin. In addition, since the value of k_i is already stored in the top-level bin, along with the pointer, there is no need to make the top-level buckets larger to accomodate holding an item instead of merely a pointer. Finally, lookup on singleton items requires only one hash, instead of two.

As can be seen in Section 3.7, this simple modification greatly improves the performance of the FKS algorithm.

3.2. Making Small Low-level Bins Smaller. In modifying FKS for the dynamic case, Dietzfelbinger et al. required that an extra factor of $(1 + c')$ space be alloted when allocating low-level bins. In this way, when a third item is inserted there is no need to regrow the table.

However, if the hash values are evenly distributed, very few low-level bins will ever see three items. Therefore, we can save space by not allocating the extra space when inserting a second item into a low-level bin. (Because of the previous optimization, low-level bins are never even allocated until the second item is inserted into the same top-level buckets.) Only when three items find their way into the same bin, indicating that perhaps the distribution of hash values is not uniform, is the extra space allocated.

This optimization obviously saves space, but by doing so it also saves time. This is because the smaller each low-level bin, the more bins can fit on a single page of memory. This makes caching more effective. It also decreases the number of buckets that must be examined for recopying when growing or shrinking the hashtable.

3.3. Making All Low-level Bins Smaller. An extension of the above modification is to never allocate the extra space on a low-level bin, under the theory that if adding a third item in a bin is rare, adding a fourth must be even rarer, so there is even less cause to allocate extra space for the eventuality.

Note that with this modification, the algorithm no longer has amortized constant-time bounds since if n items get put in one low-level bin, we will grow the bin n times. (The previous scheme, which refrained from resizing only a constant number of times — namely once — remains theoretically optimal.) The modification does not noticeably affect either the running time, but we include it in our modified algorithm since, according to our analysis, it improves the space usage.

3.4. Preferring $k = 1$. With the modification of Section 3.1, this is the single most effective modification to the FKS algorithm: When choosing a value for k, at both the top and low levels, try $k = 1$ before picking k at random.

Having $k = 1$ provides several advantages. The most obvious is that it speeds up the algorithm: calculating kx, usually the most expensive operation in the hash function, is particularly straighforward when $k = 1$. It also saves space; normally we require many bits to store k, particularly if the keys can be large. By storing a short code for the common $k = 1$ case, however, we can reduce the memory requirement needed to store k values.[3]

Note that having $k = 1$ is a particular benefit at the top level, since every hash operation requires a hash at the top level, but only those items stored in low-level bins require a second hash. However, we have found that if $k = 1$ at the top level, it is advantageous to have the top bin size not be a power of 2. This is because if both the top bin and low bins are powers of 2, as might often happen, items that hash to the same bucket in the top level will hash to the same bucket in the low level as well, unless $k \neq 1$ for one of the bins (since both levels are looking at the same low-order bits of the item keys). The most time-efficient way of avoiding this problem is to have the top bin be slightly smaller than a power of 2.

The theoretical effect of trying $k = 1$ before trying a random k is to increase the average number of k that may need to be examined in each resizing step. The constant time bounds, however, remain unchanged.

3.5. Resizing When $k \neq 1$. While having $k = 1$ is advantageous, it is not always possible. On the low level, $k = 1$ may cause a collision, while on the top level it may result in an uneven distribution of items into low-level bins. One solution to this problem is to modify the hash function h, not by changing k, but by changing t, the size of the hash table. In practice, we grow t so the theoretical properties governing the number of collisions continue to hold. The new hash function, with the larger t, hopefully will be collision-free for $k = 1$. If necessary, several values of t can be tried. In our implementation, we try 10 different values of t before settling for a non-unit k.

This modification is not cost-free. Besides the cost of a few extra words of memory, changing the size of the hash table requires a new memory allocation. It also makes the hash table slower, since t is no longer a power of 2 and hence the final mod cannot be implemented as a bitmask. However, the cost of these operations is dwarfed by the cost of hashing with a non-unit k. As we see from the figure in Section 3.7, this modification improves the performance of the algorithm.

In the experiments described in Section 3.7, the version of the algorithm incorporating all the above modifications needed to allocate very few non-unit k values, typically zero or one per test set. As a result, we get an additional space savings in our implementation. We store k values as pointers to memory locations, with the NULL pointer indicating $k = 1$. With few non-zero k values, it suffices to use a single byte, rather than a full word, to store the pointer. This saves 3 bytes per bucket on a 32 bit machine.

[3]In practice, we store each k as a pointer to memory that's allocated on demand. Thus, we have one word of overhead for each k. However, we use the NULL pointer to indicate $k = 1$, saving memory in that case.

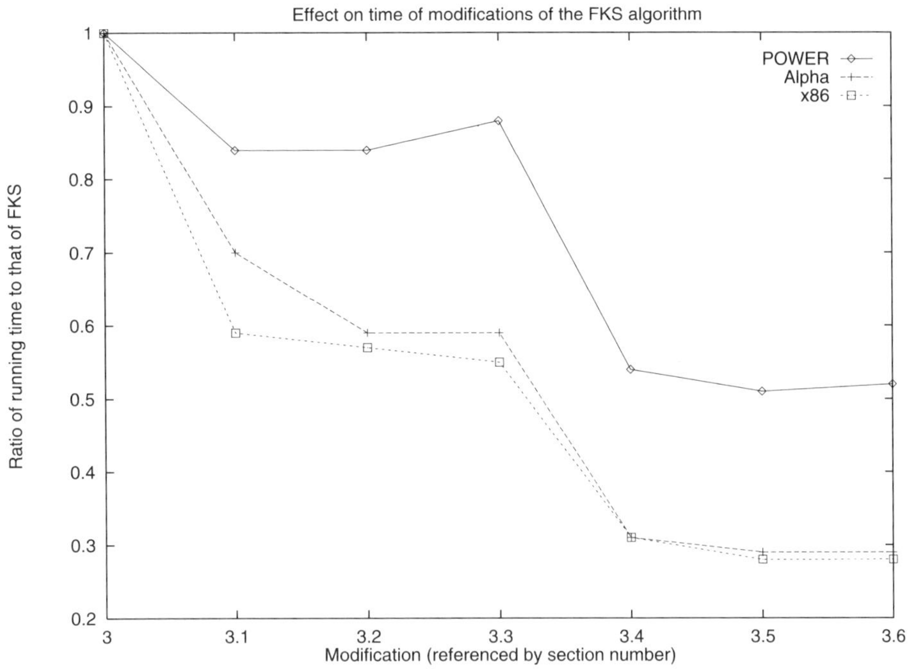

FIGURE 1. The improvement in running time as the FKS algorithm is modified, for three different computer architectures. The numbers along the x-axis refer to the section of the paper in which the modification is proposed.

3.6. Using Non-Prime p. An expensive operation in computing the hash function h is taking kx mod a prime p. While this operation is crucial for the theoretical correctness of the time bound, it is onerous. On the other hand, calcuating $kx \bmod 2^i + 1$, for some i, can be done quite efficiently (see [**10**, p. 272]). Note that if $k = 1$, then the value of p does not matter, since $kx < p$ in this case. Since, as we've noted, $k = 1$ almost always in practice, setting $p = 2^i + 1$ will probably not destroy the correctness of the algorithm — though in theory there could be two keys that collide on every value of k for a swath of t values. On the other hand, making p non-prime probably will not improve the algorithm very much either, even in the best case. As we see in Section 3.7, this modification has little effect on the running time.

One reason being able to use non-prime p is important is because finding a large prime, while a one-time cost, is expensive and can dominate the time of FKS hashing. Assuming the range of keys is always a power of 2, it is possible to precompute a table listing the smallest prime larger than every power of 2, but this limits the maximum key size that may be used. One compromise is to use a prime p if there is an appropriate table entry and to use $2^i + 1$ otherwise.

The version of the algorithm with all of the above modifications included is called the *mFKS* algorithm, for "modified FKS."

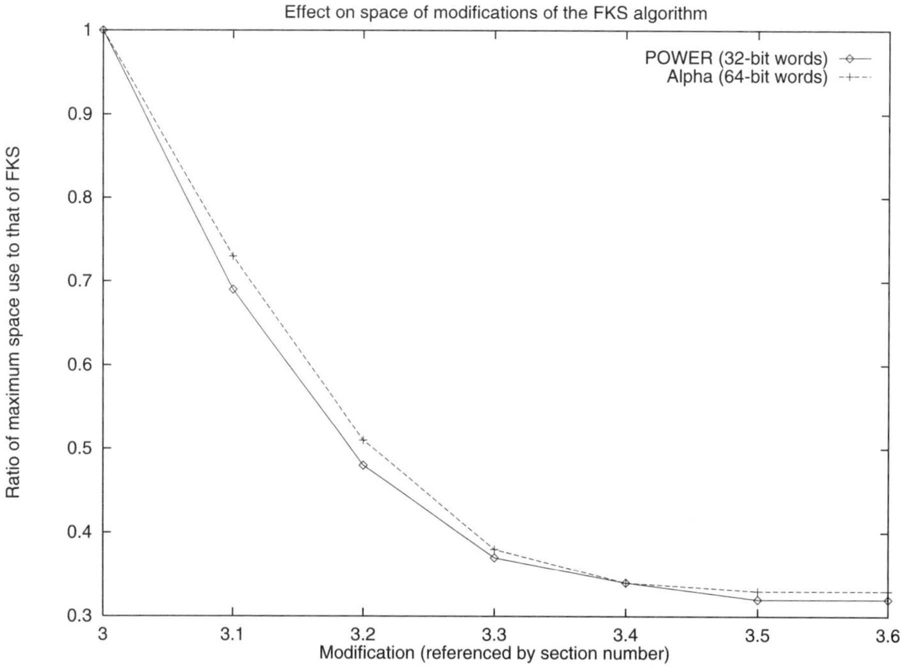

FIGURE 2. The improvement in space use as the FKS algorithm is modified, for three different computer architectures. The numbers along the x-axis refer to the section of the paper in which the modification is proposed.

3.7. Experimental Results. Figure 1 shows the reduction in average time per test set as each modification is added to the basic FKS algorithm. The modifications are labeled on the x-axis by the section in which they are discussed. The times are shown relative to the unmodified FKS algorithm — which therefore has a time ratio of 1. We show results for all three architectures we examined.

The fully modified FKS scheme, mFKS, is almost 4 times faster than the unmodified scheme on the x86 and Alpha processors. It is about twice as fast on the POWER. The data support the hypothesis that the POWER machine is relatively faster at memory access, and relatively slower at bit-level operations such as multiplying large words: the improvement in time for the POWER machine is relatively small when adding top-level buckets (3.1), but relatively large when adding preference for $k = 1$ (3.4).

In Figure 2 we show the improvement in space use as the FKS algorithm is modified. We show results both for 32- and 64- bit machines. The space performance on both architectures is the same.

It is worth noting that making all low-level bins static (3.3) yields a substantial improvement in space use, though, as Figure 1 indicates, it made the algorithm slower on many architectures. Deciding whether to incorporate this modification therefore involves making a time/space trade-off, one of several available with the FKS algorithm (see Section 5).

4. The Table Data Structure

The primary data structure used for hash tables is the table. The obvious representation of a table is an array. Access is straightforward and takes constant time. On the other hand, an array is profligate with memory use if many of the cells of the table are empty.[4]

There are several data structures that can represent empty table cells more efficiently than the array. These variants, typically called *sparse arrays*, only store non-empty cells. In addition, they store a small number of bits indicating which cells are empty and which are full. It is possible, using sparse arrays, to look up a cell's contents in constant time, though the constants are larger than they are using a *dense* (i.e., not sparse) array. Thus, choosing whether to use a sparse or a dense array involves a time/space trade-off.

Note: The time/space trade-off in using dense or sparse arrays for hash tables is not as clear-cut as the previous discussion indicates. While dense arrays are faster than sparse arrays for lookup and (particularly) for insert, they are actually slower in performing another common hash table operations: traversing a hash table (that is, examining each item of the hash table in turn). This is because a dense array must skip over empty cells. A sparse array, which only allocates memory for non-empty cells, does not suffer from this time sink. In addition, sparse arrays have better spatial locality than dense arrays due to their smaller size, yielding time advantages over dense arrays with respect the memory subsystem.

In the following sections we describe two implementations of sparse arrays, one proposed in [**8**] and one a modified version that uses less memory. We then compare the performance of the mFKS algorithm under the different table implementations.

4.1. Sparse Arrays Using Offsets. This method of efficiently reprsenting a table is from [**8**]. The idea is to consider the table of size t as consisting of t/M blocks of M cells each, for some value M. Cell x can be found in cell $x \bmod M$ of block $\lfloor x/M \rfloor$.

Memory is saved by storing each block sparsely: Only occupied buckets in the block are allocated. Occupied buckets are stored in a dense array, which we call the *store*. When a previously unoccupied bucket becomes occupied, the store is grown and the item is stored in the empty cell now available at the end of the store. An array A is used to map from the position in the sparse array, i.e. $x \bmod M$, to the position in the store. $A[i] = j$ if cell i is the jth item in the store. If cell i is empty, $A[i] = -1$. When a cell is deleted, the appropriate entry in A is set to -1, but the space in the store is not reclaimed. Periodically recopying the sparse array can keep memory use from growing excessively with many deletes. This recopying can be amortized over the cost of the deletes, so maintaining the sparse array takes constant time per operation.

This technique saves space because we require only $t \log M$ bits to store all the A's, not $t \log t$. In [**8**], the authors recommend setting $\log M$ to $\sqrt{\log n}$, meaning all the arrays A, as well as the top and low level hash tables, can be stored in $O(n)$ space. In practice, we find setting M to a convenient power of 2, such as 256,

---

[4] In the context of hash tables, we have been referring to "bins" and "buckets." These terms are equivalent to "tables" and "cells," respectively. We use new terminology here to distinguish discussion that applies to all tables from that applying only to hash tables.

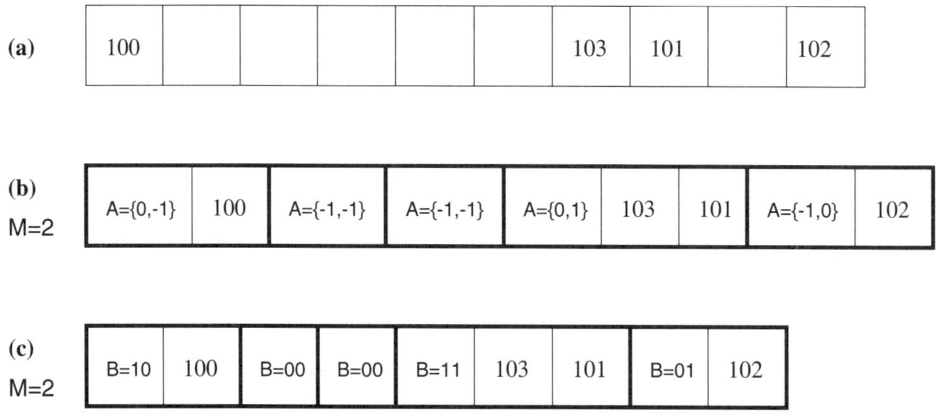

FIGURE 3. **(a)** The dense array scheme. **(b)** The sparse array scheme using offsets. The thicker lines separate groups. In practice, M would be much larger than 2. **(c)** The sparse array scheme using bitmaps.

provides good space savings while being easy to implement. Only for $n > 2^{64}$ will $\log 256 = 8$ be smaller than $\sqrt{\log n}$.

4.2. Sparse Arrays Using Bitmaps. The technique described above can be modified to yield even more space savings by using a bitmap B instead of an offset array A. B consists of M bits; bit i is 1 if and only if cell i of the group is occupied. If there are b bits set in $B[0, \ldots, i-1]$, then item i is the bth item in the store.

Unlike in the offset sparse array, in which newly inserted items are appended to the end of the store, in the bitmap sparse array inserted items must stay in place relative to other non-empty cells. If the calculations place the item as the bth item in the store, all items currently in position $b+1$ and larger must be moved one space down in the store. Likewise, when an item is deleted all items after it in the store must be moved one space up. Both move steps can be done efficiently if the store is implemented as a linked list, but such an implementation defeats the purpose of saving memory. Instead, the store is recopied. If M is a constant, the recopying is a constant-time operation.

Besides copying the store, an event that is only necessary on insert and delete, the most expensive operation for sparse arrays is counting the number of bits set in $B[0, \ldots, i-1]$. This can be done reasonably efficiently — in particular, in time proportional to the number of bits set — in the RAM model. By treating B as a computer word, and using tables, it is possible to calculate the number of bits set even more efficiently. In any case, even the naive implementation takes constant time if M is constant.

Figure 3 illustrates the three implementations of the table data structure.

4.3. Experimental Comparison. The FKS data structure includes more than one table. It is possible to use one representation of a table for the top level bin and another representation for the low level bins. For instance, since the top level bin is accessed on every query, it might make sense to use the fast dense array for the top level. Each low level bin, on the other hand, might be represented using a sparse array. If many items are held on the top level, this implementation

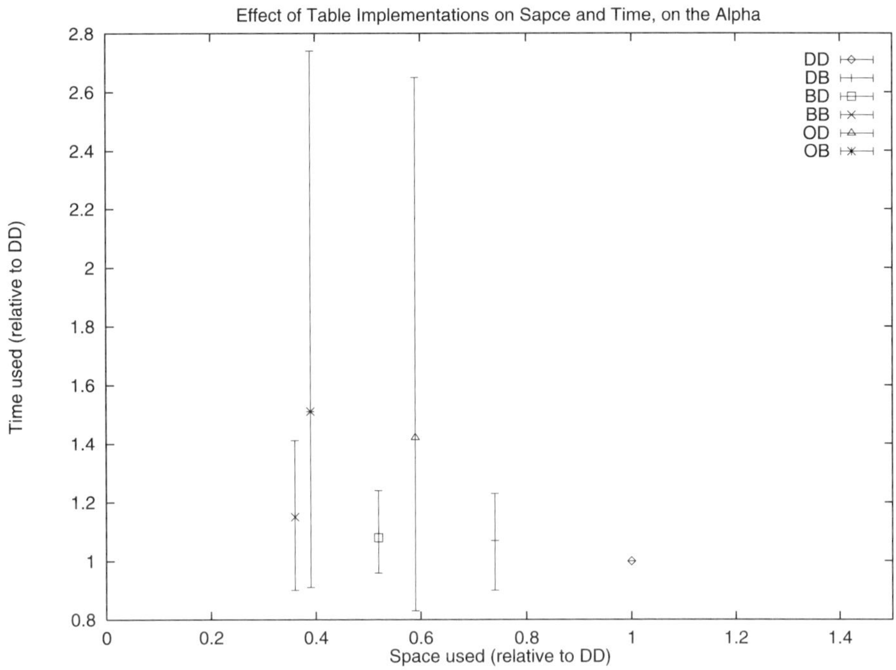

FIGURE 4. A scatterplot comparing space and time use for various table implementations on the Alpha. D = dense arrays, B = sparse arrays with bitmaps, and O = sparse arrays with offsets. The first letter of the implementation name is for the top-level bin; the second is for the low-level bins. The vertical lines indicate the minimum and maximum time ratio among the 34 test sets.

gives a space savings over the canonical, dense-only implementation without unduly affecting running time.

We explored six different implementations of the FKS data structure:

`DD` dense array at top level, dense array at low level,
`DB` dense array at top level, bitmap sparse array at low level,
`BD` bitmap sparse array at top level, dense array at low level,
`BB` bitmap sparse array at both levels,
`OD` offset sparse array at top level, dense array at low level, and
`OB` offsedt sparse array at top level, bitmap sparse array at low level.

The `DD` implementation is the canonical one; we represent every other implementation by the ratio of the running time, or space used, of the implementation to `DD`. We plot each implementation in a scatterplot, with time ratio along one axis and space ratio along the other. In addition to plotting the average time ratio, as described in Section 2, we use vertical lines to indicate the minimum and maximum time ratio among the 34 tests. The length of the vertical lines is an indication of how consistently the choice of table implementation affects running time.

In Figure 4 we show results for the Alpha architecture, while Figure 5 shows results for the POWER. The performance on the x86 was similar to that of the Alpha. We see that the bitmap schemes performed much worse on the POWER

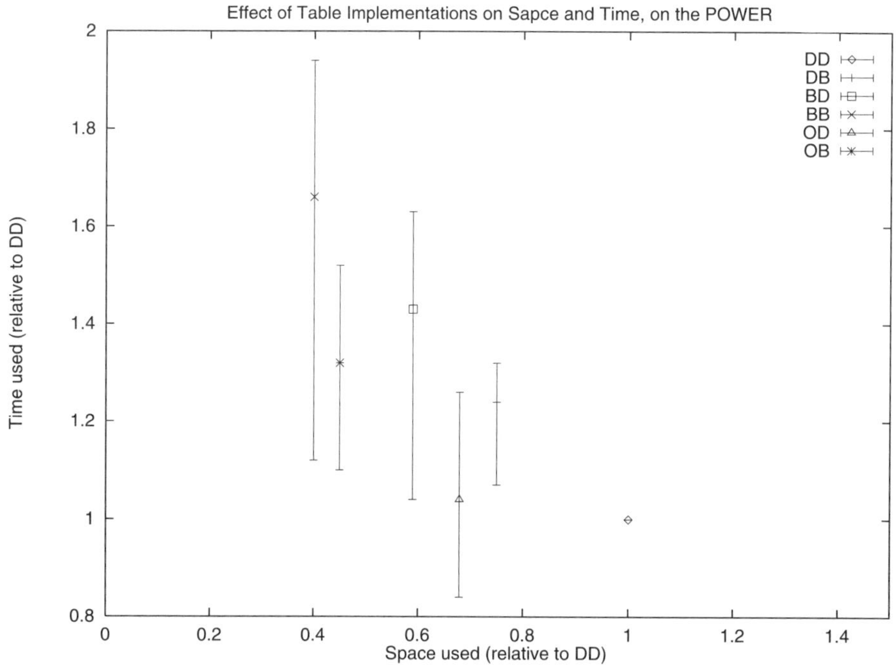

FIGURE 5. A scatterplot comparing space and time use for various table implementations on the POWER. `D` = dense arrays, `B` = sparse arrays with bitmaps, and `O` = sparse arrays with offsets. The first letter of the implementation name is for the top-level bin; the second is for the low-level bins. The vertical lines indicate the minimum and maximum time ratio among the 34 test sets. Unlike on the Alpha and x86, offset arrays are faster than bitmap arrays on the POWER.

than the other architectures, and also the range of time ratios (among the 34 DIMACS test sets) was higher on the POWER. This is not surprising, since the bitmap implementations depend on efficient bit manipulation for good performance, and the POWER processor was already seen to be relatively weak in this area.

While the sparse arrays generally lead to longer running times, on several test sets, particularly on the Alpha, the sparse array variants were faster than the canonical mFKS algorithm. This perhaps indicates these test sets benefitted from the improved memory locality a sparse implementation provides.

5. Parameters for Trading Off Time and Space

There are several parameters that can be tweaked to obtained a time/space trade-off for FKS hashing. One is available only for the bitmap sparse array implementations: modifying M, the size of the array groups. (Modifying M is theoretically possible in the offset array case as well, but in practice M is efficient only if stored in a series of bytes. Thus, the next-highest value above $M = 256$ is the impractical 65,536.) Larger values of M decrease the size by reducing the number of groups, and therefore the per-group overhead. At the same time, they make lookup slower by increasing the size of each bitmap array.

In Section 1.2, several constants are introduced that can be modified. Each of them, coincidentally, has a recommended value of 2 that is used in the canonical version of FKS.

$1 + c$: — top-level size multiplier for dynamic hash tables
Effect of increase on **space**: top level hash table gets larger
Effect of increase on **time**: fewer rehashes needed
Recommended value [7]: 2

$1 + c'$: — low-level size multiplier for dynamic hash tables
Effect of increase on **space**: each low-level hash table gets larger
Effect of increase on **time**: fewer rehashes needed
Recommended value [7]: 2

c in $4cn^2/t + n$: — maximum allowable sum of squares of top level collisions
Effect of increase on **space**: increases the low-level hash tables' cumulative size
Effect of increase on **time**: decreases the expected number of k's examined
Recommended value [8]: 2

c in $c|C_k(i)|^2$: — size of low-level hash tables
Effect of increase on **space**: each low-level hash table is larger
Effect of increase on **time**: decreases the expected number of k_i's examined
Recommended value [8]: 2

As a group, these constants affect the *load factor*, that is, the percent of hash table buckets are occupied. A higher load factor on the top level tends to cause larger low-level bins. A higher load factor on the bottom level tends to complicate the search for a perfect hash function.

There is one constant that can be solved optimally: the size t of the top hash table versus the (cumulative) size of the low level hash tables. While theory requires that $t \in \Omega(n)$, we can pick the constant. If we assume that the keys are distributed randomly in the hash table,[5] we can predict the number of collisions, and thus the size of the hash table, before inserting any elements. Under this model, the total hash table size is a second-order function of t, and we can use bisection or other methods to find the value of t that minimizes expected space use. Note that the value thus obtained is merely an estimate, since keys may not in fact be distributed randomly, and it will work better on some data sets than others.

In the following sections we experiment with modifying the values of M and of the constants affecting the load factor.

5.1. Modifying M. We experimented with letting M range from 1 to 32 words. (In all previous experiments, M had been set to 1 word.) Most of the results we show are for the Alpha, where one word has 64 bits. On all other architectures, one word has 32 bits.

[5]This is, of course, not the same as saying they are distributed randomly throughout the possible key space.

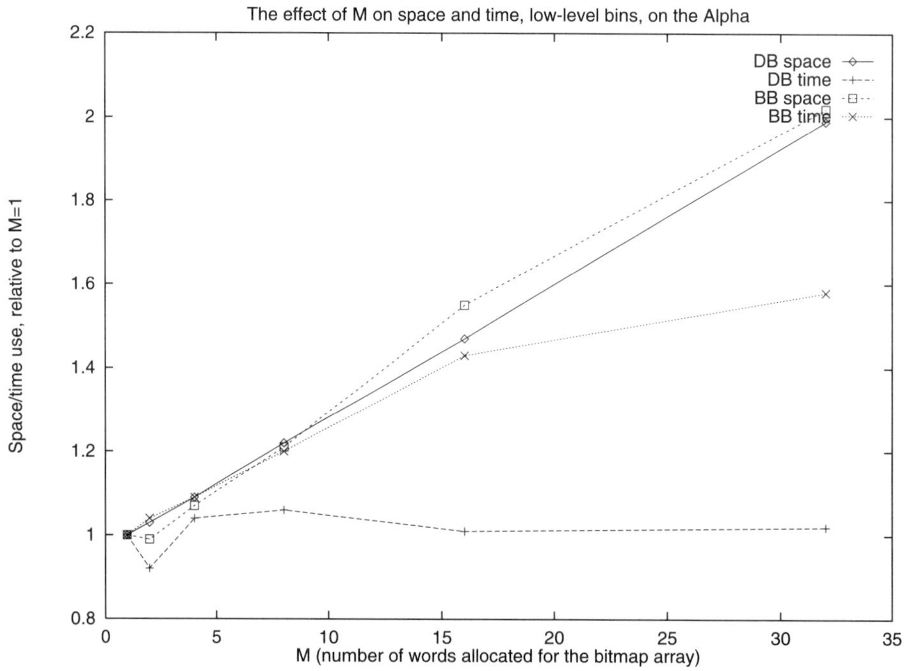

FIGURE 6. The effect of increasing M on space and time use when the low-level bins are sparse arrays, on the Alpha. The space use increases for large M because the number of buckets in a low-level bin is small, so increasing M increases the overhead without improving the addressing capability of the bitmap scheme.

In Figure 6 we explore the effect of increasing M on space and time use for those implementations where the *low-level* bins are sparse. Results are only shown for the Alpha, but the effect on other machines is similar. Perhaps surprisingly, the space use increases with M, rather than decreasing. This is because low-level bins tend to be small; large M provides a space savings by requiring fewer array groups, but for low-level bins all the buckets fit into one group even for small M. Since there are no time savings from using larger M in this case, it makes sense to use $M = 1$ or 2 for low-level bins.

Changing M for the top-level bin shows the expected time/space trade-off, as Figure 7 shows. We only show show memory use for the Alpha, but the pattern of memory use on the other, 32-bit machines is the same. The pattern of time use, however, differs remarkably among machines. For all the machines, the running time grows approximately linearly with M as M gets large. However, for small M, the time actually improves with increasing M. This seems to be due to the improved memory locality of larger M. In the mFKS implementation, each group of M buckets is stored in a separate location in memory, though all the buckets in a group are stored contiguously. Since only buckets in the same group are guaranteed to be on the same page of memory, as M increases the memory locality of the buckets is likely to increase as well, decreasing the number of cache misses. Fewer cache misses results in a time decrease since, unlike time spent handling page misses, time spent handling cache misses is attributed to the application.

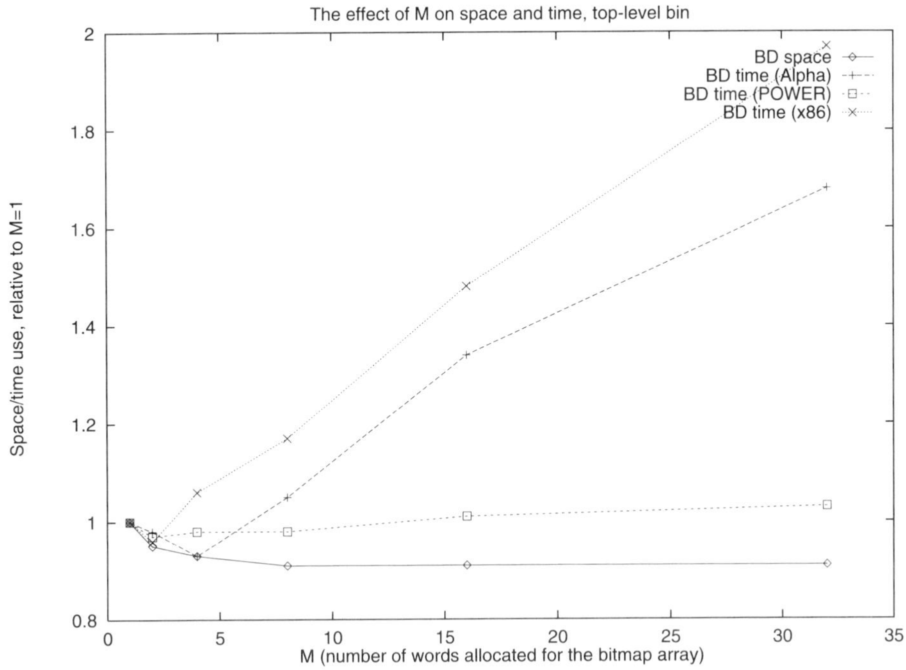

FIGURE 7. The effect of increasing M on space and time use when the top-level bins is a sparse array. The space improves only marginally — we only show data for the Alpha, but that for the other architectures is similar — while the running time increases significantly for large M.

Another potentially surprising observation from Figure 7 is that the running time increases very slowly on the POWER as M increases. Given our theory that the POWER processor is relatively slow with bit operations, we might expect the opposite: that as the bitmaps get larger, the performance of the POWER machine would degrade. We have no explanation for why the running time instead stays relatively constant.

In general, as M grows the running time increases much faster than space use decreases. There does not seem to be much reason to ever use $M > 8$. $M = 4$ words seems optimal on the Alpha, while $M = 2$ words is fastest on the POWER and x86 architectures.

5.2. Modifying the Load Factor Constants. For all four of the load factor parameters in Section 5, the values suggested in the original text is 2. We experimented with letting these values range, in concert, from 1.1 to 6.

As Figure 8 shows, the load factor has a consistent effect on running time regardless of machine architecture and table implementation. However, as we see in Figure 9, the space performance depends heavily on the table implementation. The space use does not depend very much on architecture, so we concentrate only on the Alpha architecture.

One observation is that space use actually increases for small load factor parameters when the top-level bin is sparse. This is because small load factor parameters

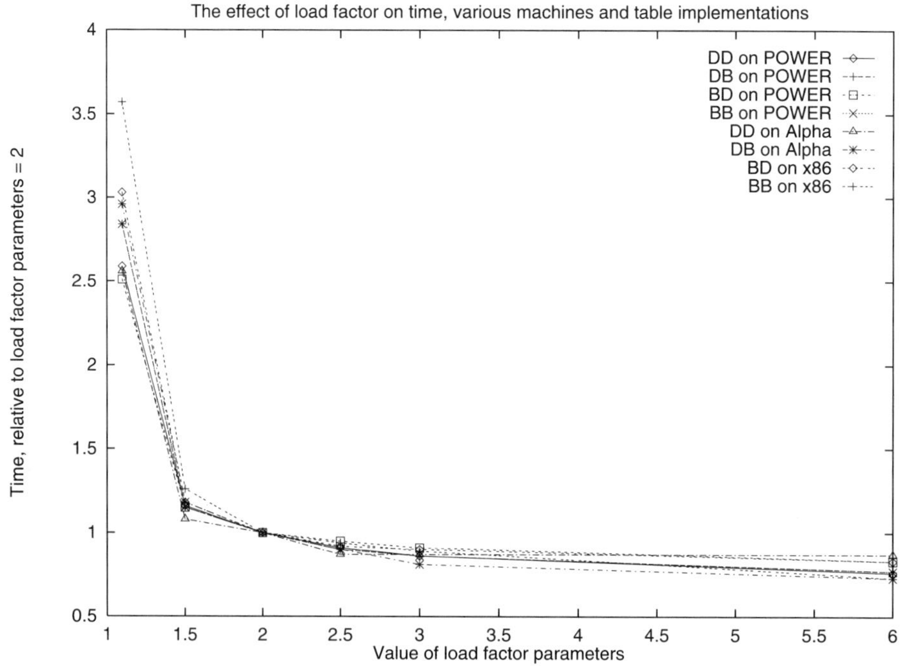

FIGURE 8. The effect of load factor parameter on running time. To keep clutter to a minimum, only a subset of all the architecture/table implementation pairs is shown. Behavior is similar for those pairs omitted.

make the top-level bin more full, reducing the number of empty top-level buckets while increasing the number of low-level buckets. For a sparse array, however, the cost of empty top-level buckets is much lower than the added cost of the low-level buckets. Combining a sparse top-level bin with a dense low-level bin provides the worse performance of all: not only is space use inefficient for small values of the constants, it is inefficient for large values of the constants as well, since in this case the (dense) low-level bins, though they have fewer items in them because of the low load, are all exceedingly large since c' is high.

5.3. Putting It All Together. In Figure 10 we show a scatterplot of the time/space trade-off for the following parameters: $M = 1$, 2, 4, 8, 16, and 32 words for `DB`, `BD`, and `BB` tables, and load factor parameters $= 1.1$, 1.5, 2.0, 2.5, 3.0, and 6.0, for `DD`, `DB`, `BD`, and `BB` tables. Space and time are calculated relative to the canonical implementation: $M = 1$, all load time parameters at 2, and dense tables at both levels. Results are shown for the Alpha architecture. Results for other architectures are comparable.

While for reasons of space we cannot label each point with the parameter/table pair that produced it, which would allow us to study how individual choices affect the time and space use, the figure provides an indication of the capability to trade off time and space in the mFKS algorithm. The canonical algorithm, with its small M, relatively small values for load factor constants, and dense tables, yields a particularly fast but space-inefficient variant of mFKS. By increasing the value

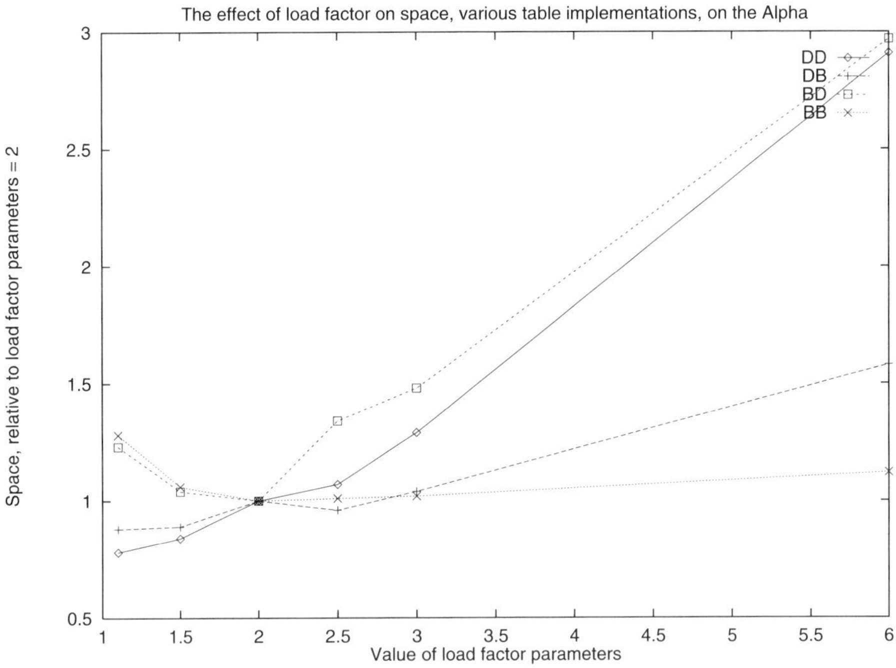

FIGURE 9. The effect of load factor parameter on space use, for the Alpha. Behavior is similar for other architectures, though these results are not shown.

of the constants and using sparse arrays, it is possible to significantly reduce the space use. It is much more difficult, however, to attain a faster implementation of the mFKS algorithm using techniques in this and the previous sections.

6. FKS Hashing vs. Other Hashing Algorithms

While we have shown how to improve the the performance of FKS hashing via modifications, and how to effect a time/space trade-off through parameter tuning, we have not shown that the resulting algorithms are competitive with other hashing schemes in terms of either time or space. It is not necessary that FKS-style hashing be superior in all circumstances, as it might still be useful in situations where the guarantee of constant-time operations is essential. But if the performance is not competitive, the FKS hashing technique will remain an object of only theoretical interest.

We compare mFKS against two other dictionary schemes: an implementation of hashing with linear probing based on discussion in Knuth [**9**], and the dictionary implemetation used for associative arrays in Perl 5.[6] Linear probing yields a fast and compact hash table implementation. As we demonstrate below, on the DIMACS test set it is strictly superior to the more common hashing with separate chaining, which is used for instance in LEDA. The Perl implementation, while not intended for the large data sets used in the DIMACS Challenge, gives a feel for how the FKS variants compare to an off-the-shelf hashing routine. The Perl

[6]Perl 5.003 was used on the Alpha machine. The other machines used Perl 5.004_04.

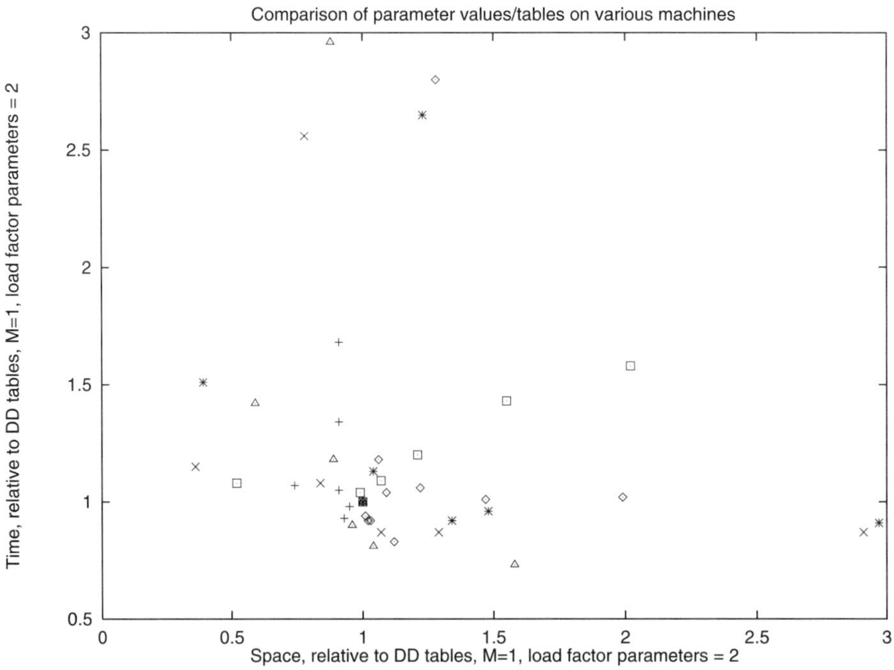

FIGURE 10. Space use versus running time, on the Alpha, relative to the canonical implementation of the mFKS algorithm (DD tables, $M = 1$, and load factor constants $= 2$). The data points represent different values and implementations for these three facets of the mFKS algorithm.

implementation compares favorably to other off-the-shelf implementations such as those found in LEDA and the C++ Standard Template Library [**6**] because it is written in C rather than the significantly slower C++ with templates. Also, unlike the LEDA implementation, the Perl implementation is optimized for performance over readability and rigorous error handling.

The perl code for testing the dictionary data structure is very straightforward, since the dictionary data type is a basic one in perl. We present the entire code in Table 2.

For comparison purposes, on some of the test sets we also ran a demo hashing algorithm, provided by the DIMACS Challenge organizers [**1**], that uses a binary tree to hold hashing information. Because the demo hash took an unacceptably long time to run on the large `matchexact` data sets, we did not test it on these data sets, leaving only eight data sets for hashing the demo algorithm. Thus, the variance of the time use of this algorithm is higher than that of the other algorithms.

Hashing with linear probing was described in Section 1.1. We use the hash function described in [**2**] — it includes versions for both 32- and 64-bit architectures —, and for the table implementation we explore all three options described in Section 4. We also explore quadratic probing in addition to linear probing. In quadratic probing, instead of trying bucket $h(x)+i$, as i ranges from 1 to t, until an empty bucket is found, the lookup function tries $h(x)+i(i+1)/2$. If the table size is a power of 2, this quadratic probing scheme examines all t buckets in the first t

```
line: while ( <> )
{
   /^ins (\S*)/ && do { $count++ if $dict{$1}++ == 0;                  next line};
   /^lkp (\S*)/ && do { ($lastkey, $lastvalue) = ($1, $dict{$1}); next line};
   /^dlk (\S*)/ && do { $count-- if delete($dict{$1});                next line};
   /^dli /      && do { $count-- if delete($dict{$lastkey});          next line};
   /^kyv /      && do { $lastkey;                                     next line};
   /^inv /      && do { $lastvalue;    next line};
   /^siz /      && do { $count;    next line};
   /^clr /      && do { undef %dict; $count = 0;                      next line};
   # dch and com can be ignored
}
print "$count items in the hashtable at algorithm's end.\n";
```

TABLE 2. A perl dictionary implementation that accepts DIMACS dictionary commands.

probes. While, for large i, quadratic probing has poor locality when compared to linear hashing, it avoids problems with item clustering and should therefore prove superior in most situations.

Hashing with linear probing uses tables and thus has dense and sparse array variants. We consider three variants of tables — dense (`D`) sparse with offsets (`O`), and sparse with bitmaps (`B`) — for hashing with linear probing. Results for quadratic probing are virtually identical. We also consider `DD` and `BB` mFKS algorithms, which show the extremes of the table implementations, with $M = 1$ and the canonical values for the load factor parameters. Finally, we consider the Perl and demo implementations.

Figure 11 shows the performance of each algorithm relative to the canonical mFKS algorithm (with `DD` tables), in terms of both time and space, on the Alpha. Figure 12 shows the same algorithms on the POWER, and Figure 13 on the x86.

Since we do not have space measurements for the demo and Perl implementations, we assign a space ratio of 0 to these tests. The times for the Perl implementation did not fit on the graph: 10.56 times as much time as mFKS for Alpha, 4.35 for POWER, and 13.95 for x86.

As the figures show, the hashing with linear probing is the fastest and the smallest on all three architectures. The reasons for this are discussed below. Nevertheless, the mFKS algorithms are competitive in performance. They are within a factor of two in terms of both time and space. The mFKS schemes are also significantly better than the demo hash on all the machines but the POWER, where the demo hash presumably benefits from not having to do any arithmetic to compute a hash function. The Perl implementation is at least five times slower than either the mFKS or probing schemes on all architectures.

Hashing with linear probing was the best performer in terms of both time (with dense arrays) and space (with sparse bitmap arrays) on all architectures. The reason for the space advantage is straightforward: by having only one level of tables instead of two, hashing with probing avoids much of the overhead of the FKS-based algorithms. It is possible to modify load factor parameters, as it is in the FKS case, to trade off running time and space use. See **[9]** for details.

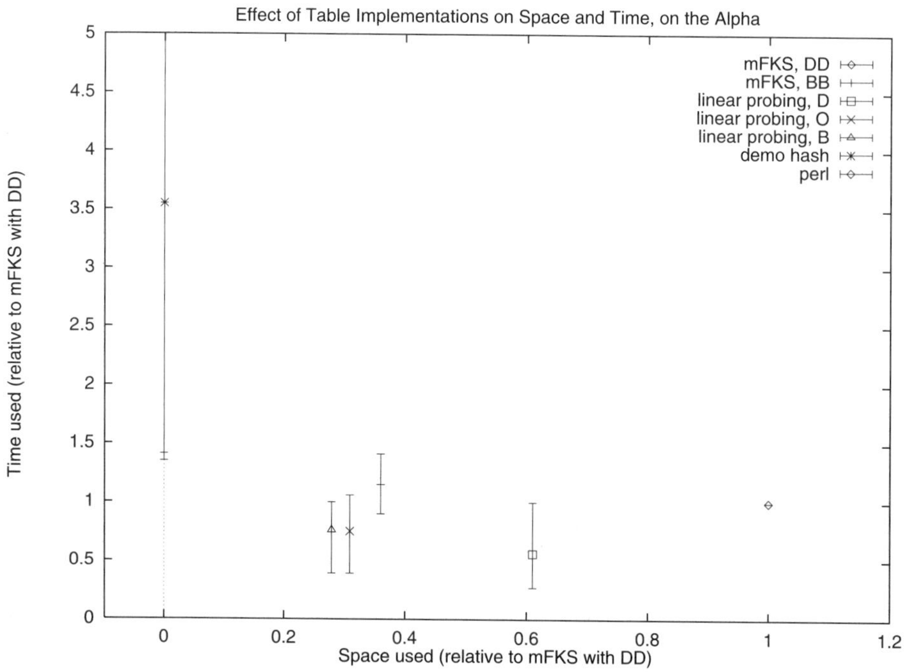

FIGURE 11. A comparison of various non-mFKS-based hashing schemes against various mFKS-based schemes, on the Alpha. While mFKS is faster and smaller than the demo hashing routine and also than Perl's dictionary code, it is slower and larger than hashing with linear probing.

The time advantage of hashing with linear probing is dependent on the distribution of key hash values. If many hash keys clump together in the table, causing items to be inserted far from their hashed-to buckets, each lookup and insert will have to examine many buckets. While there will be only one hash performed, with poorly distributed keys there will be many probes into the hash table until an empty bucket is found. On the other hand, if the hash function distributes keys well, and at least half the table cells stay empty, the average-case time for lookup and insert will remain constant, with only a few probes per hash. Furthermore, since linear probing is a simple technique, the constants will be small.

For the DIMACS data set, using the hash function from [**2**], the distribution of keys does in fact turn out to be almost ideal. As we see in Figure 14, the number of probes per hash for the 34 test sets in the DIMACS suite is very close to the optimal value of 1 and only rarely tops 2. The values for hashing with quadratic probing are similar, improving on the linear probing values by an average, over the 34 test sets, of 0.06 probes per hash.

Because the number of probes per hash is low, hashing with linear probing is superior to hashing with separate chaining on this data set. Hashing with separate chaining uses a linked list of items in each bucket; all items that hash to bucket i are appended to bucket i's linked list. When there are many hash collisions, hashing with separate chaining is faster than hashing with probing, since items that hash to distinct buckets cannot collide as they can in the probing case. For the DIMACS

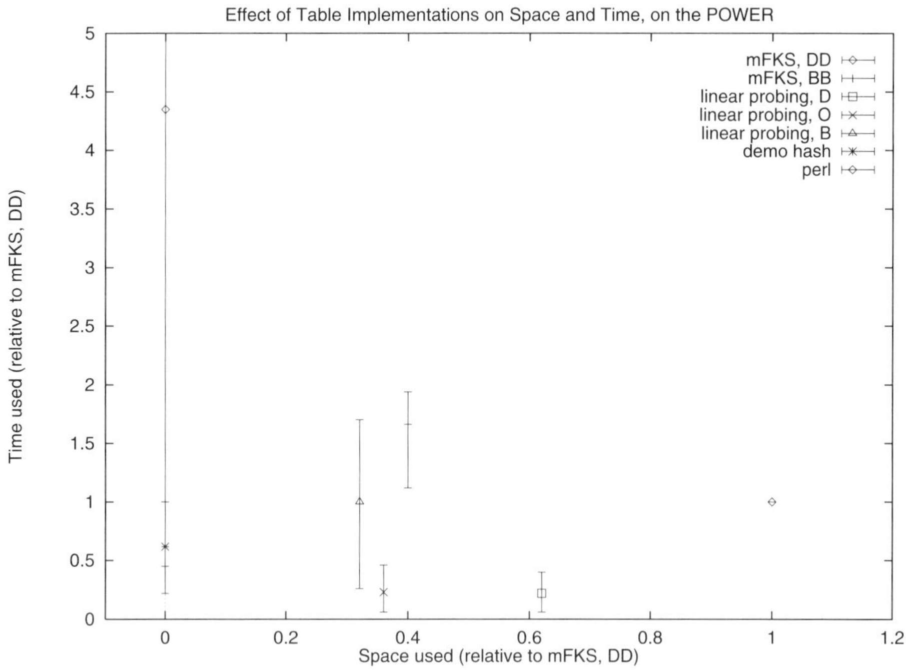

FIGURE 12. A comparison of various non-mFKS-based hashing schemes against various mFKS-based schemes, on the POWER. As with the Alpha, the probing schemes are the fastest and smallest, while the Perl implementation is the slowest. The demo implementation does well, presumably because it involves no hashing, which the POWER implements relatively slowly.

test set, however, no such time advantage accrues. On the other hand, hashing with separate chaining requires more memory than hashing with probing, since it requires overhead of at least one pointer per non-empty bucket to store the linked lists. We expect that, because of the low collision rate, hashing with linear probing is near the optimal hashing algorithm for the test sets in the DIMACS suite.

7. Conclusion

The perfect hashing algorithm as described in [**8**] may not be practical due to the cost of multiplying and dividing large numbers. However, a slightly modified algorithm is not only fast in practice but also parsimonious in terms of its space requirements. The modified algorithm retains the guarantee of constant time lookup, and can also easily be made to retain the guarantee of constant time insertion and deletion as well.[7]

Experimental results on the DIMACS data set indicate that FKS hashing is within a factor of two of a much simpler algorithm in terms of both time and space utilization. This is significant, because the data set was, in general, very well behaved with respect to the simple algorithm, indicating that the added complexity

[7]It would be necessary to remove the relatively unimportant modifications in Sections 3.3 and 3.6.

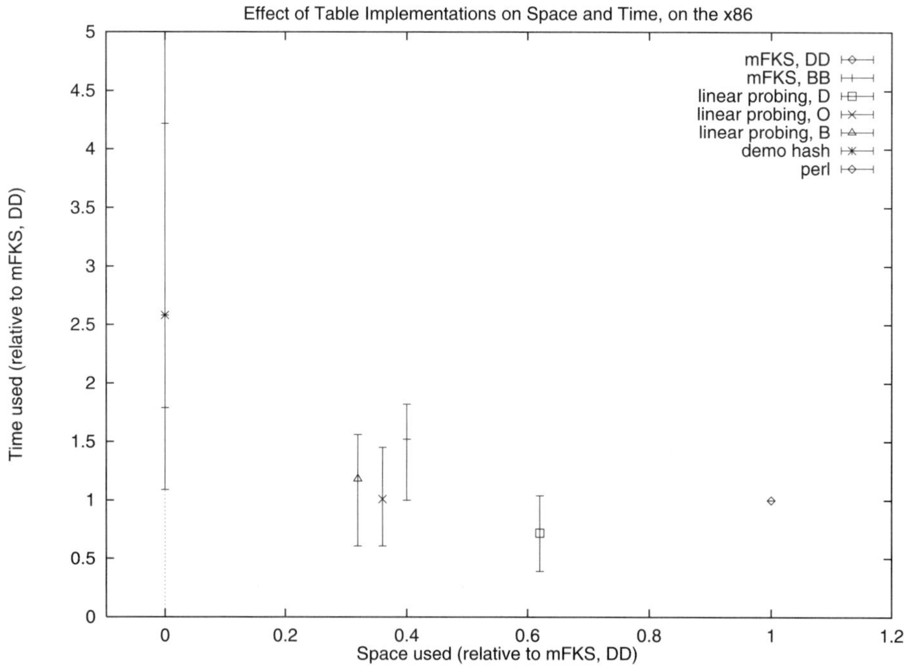

FIGURE 13. A comparison of various non-mFKS-based hashing schemes against various mFKS-based schemes, on the x86. Again the probing schemes are the smallest and fastest, but the mFKS schemes are competitive.

of FKS hashing does not necessarily make it impractical. At the same time, its theoretical guarantees allow it to outperform simpler algorithms in cases where the data is not as well behaved. Furthermore, with several parameters controlling the load factor and the sparse array constant M, the FKS algorithm can be tuned to favor space use over time or *vice versa*.

For general applications, hashing with linear probing, or perhaps with separate chaining, makes the most sense. These algorithms are fast when the keys hash uniformly over the bucket space, a situation which can often be achieved through either high-quality, general purpose hashing functions or hashing functions tuned for the specific application. In other circumstances, however, the average-case guarantees of hashing with linear probing may not be strict enough. In such situations, if a loss of a factor of two in running time and space use is acceptable, a modified version of FKS gives superior theoretical guarantees with an acceptably small degradation in performance.

References

[1] `ftp://cs.amherst.edu/pub/dimacs/dc_demo.tar.Z.`
[2] `http://ourworld.compuserve.com/homepages/bob_jenkins/evahash.htm.`
[3] `http://www.cs.amherst.edu/ ccm/challenge5/.`
[4] `http://www.mpi-sb.mpg.de/LEDA/.`
[5] AT&T. Hsearch(ba_lib). *Unix System User's Manual, System V.3*, pages pp. 105–109, 1985.
[6] Javier Barreiro and David R. Musser. An stl hash table implementation with gradual resizing, February 1995. Available by anonymous ftp from `ftp.cs.rpi.edu` in `pub/stl/hashimp2.Z`.

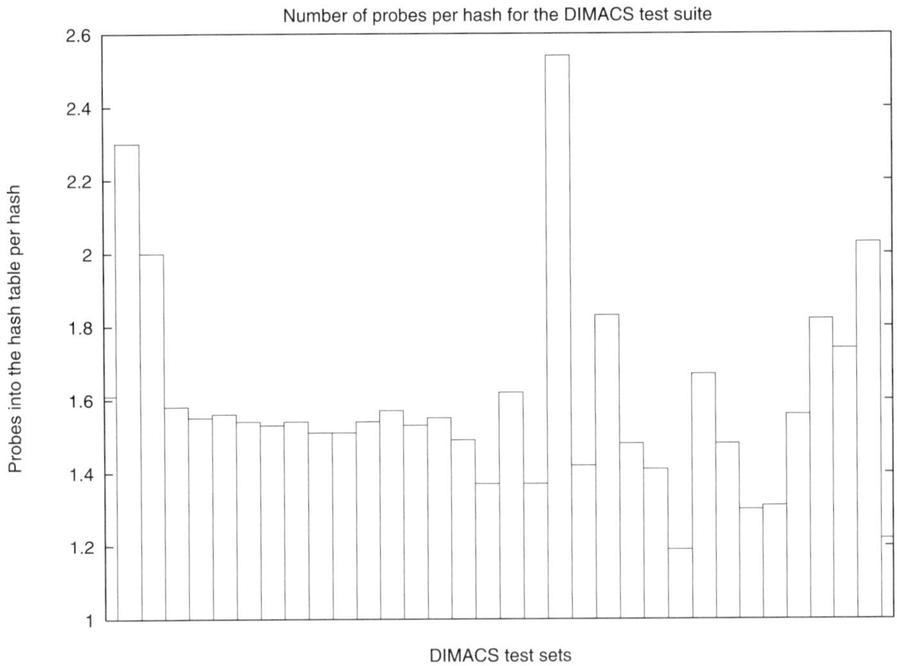

FIGURE 14. The number of probes per hash for hashing with linear probing, on the 34 test sets in the DIMACS test suite. The closer this value is to 1, the faster are lookup, insertion, and deletion.

[7] M. Dietzfelbinger, A. Karlin, K. Mehlhorn, F. Meyer auf der Heide, H. Rohnert, and R. Tarjan. Dynamic perfect hashing: Upper and lower bounds. *Symposium on the Theory of Computing*, 18:524–531, 1988.

[8] M. Fredman, J. Komlós, and E. Szemerédi. Storing a sparse table with $O(1)$ worst case access time. *Journal of the ACM*, 31(3):538–544, July 1984.

[9] D. Knuth. *The Art of Computer Programming*, volume III. Addison-Wesley, second edition, 1981.

[10] D. Knuth. *The Art of Computer Programming*, volume II. Addison-Wesley, second edition, 1981.

COMPUTER SCIENCE DEPARTMENT, STANFORD UNIVERSITY, STANFORD, CA 94305
E-mail address: `csilvers@cs.stanford.edu`

DIMACS Series in Discrete Mathematics
and Theoretical Computer Science
Volume **59**, 2002

Computational Evaluation of Hot Queues

Andrew V. Goldberg and Craig Silverstein

ABSTRACT. The heap-on-top (hot) queue data structure [**7**] is an implementation of monotone priority queues developed and tested in the context of Dijkstra's shortest path algorithm. Hot queues proved to be efficient and robust in that context. In this paper, we show that hot queues are efficient and robust in a more general context of monotone priority queue applications.

1. Introduction

A priority queue is a data structure that maintains a set of elements and supports operations `insert`, `decrease-key`, and `extract-min`. Priority queues are fundamental data structures with many applications. Typical applications include graph algorithms (*e.g.* [**11**]) and event simulation (*e.g.* [**4**]).

An important subclass of priority queues used in applications such as event simulation and in Dijkstra's shortest path algorithm [**10**] is the class of monotone priority queues. Intuitively, a priority queue is *monotone* if at any time keys of elements on the queue are at least as big as the key of the element most recently extracted from the queue. In this paper we deal with monotone priority queues.

Unless mentioned otherwise, we refer to priority queues whose operation time bounds depend only on the number of elements on the queue as *heaps*. The fastest implementations of heaps are described in [**3, 11, 15**]. Alternative implementations of priority queues use buckets (*e.g.* [**1, 6, 8, 9**]). Operation times for bucket-based implementations depend on the maximum event duration C, defined in Section 2. See [**2**] for a related data structure.

Heaps are particularly efficient when the number of elements on the heap is small. Bucket-based priority queues are particularly efficient when the maximum event duration C is small. Furthermore, some of the work done in bucket-based implementations can be amortized over elements in the buckets, yielding better bounds if the number of elements is large. In this sense, heaps and buckets complement each other.

Heap-on-top queues (hot queues) [**7**] combine the multi-level bucket data structure of Denardo and Fox [**8**] and a heap. These queues use the heap instead of

Supported by the Department of Defense, with partial support from NSF Award CCR-9357849, with matching funds from IBM, Schlumberger Foundation, Shell Foundation, and Xerox Corporation.

buckets when buckets would be sparsely occupied. The resulting implementation takes advantage of the best performance features of both data structures.

Hot queues, multi-level buckets, and k-heaps have been compared in the context of Dijkstra's algorithm, on several types of graphs (see [**7**]). In these tests, the hot queue was always competitive with, and overall more robust than, the other two implementations. However, Dijkstra's algorithm tends to stress only certain aspects of a priority queue implementation. For instance, the number of `decrease-key` operations tends to be small compared to the number of `extract-min` operations. Also, Dijkstra's algorithm tends to have a certain pattern of insertions and deletions: since items in the queue form the "border" of the explored graph, items tend not to stay in the queue for as long as in some other applications.

We evaluate hot queues in a more general context, including problem families that model sorting and event simulation applications. We compare hot queues to k-heaps and multi-level buckets, as well as to the demo code provided by the DIMACS Challenge organizers.

Note that a good implementation of simple heaps [**16**] (like binary heaps or 4-heaps) has very small constant factors and worst-case operation times of $O(\log N)$. It is unrealistic to expect large wins over these heaps unless the number of elements in the data structure, N, is very large. However, because priority queues are fundamental data structures with many applications, they are a natural candidate for data structure libraries such as LEDA [**13**]. As a result, priority queue users need not write their own algorithm but can readily find one in off-the-shelf packages. Because of this capability for code reuse, the simplicity of the algorithm is not as important as it might otherwise be. Furthermore, since the code is so widely used, even modest improvements in running time, e.g. 25%, are interesting. Our experiments suggest that if a good hot queue code is available, it should be considered for an application that uses monotone priority queues with integer keys.

2. Preliminaries

A *priority queue* is a data structure that maintains a set of elements and supports operations `insert`, `decrease-key`, and `extract-min`. We assume that elements have *keys* used to compare the elements and denote the key of an element u by $\rho(u)$. Unless mentioned otherwise, we assume that the keys are integers. By the value of an element we mean the key of the element. The `insert` operation adds a new element to the queue. The `decrease-key` operation assigns a smaller value to the key of an element already on the queue. The `extract-min` operation removes a minimum element from the queue and returns the element. We denote the number of `insert` operations in a sequence of priority queue operations by N.

To gain intuition about the following definition, think of event simulation applications where keys correspond to processing times. Let u be the latest element extracted from the queue. An *event* corresponds to an `insert` or a `decrease-key` operation on the queue. Given an event, let v be the corresponding element inserted into the queue or the element whose key was decreased. The *event duration* is $\rho(v) - \rho(u)$. We denote the maximum event duration by C, and assume that C is known in advance. An application is *monotone* if all event durations are nonnegative. A *monotone* priority queue is a priority queue for monotone applications. To make these definitions valid for the first insertion, we assume that during initialization, a special element is inserted into the queue and deleted immediately afterwards. Without loss of generality, we assume that the value of this element is zero. (If it is not, we can subtract this value from all element values.)

We assume that heaps also support the `find-min` operation, which returns the minimum element on the heap.

We call a sequence of operations on a priority queue *balanced* if the sequence starts and ends with an empty queue. In particular, implementations of Dijkstra's shortest path algorithm produce balanced operation sequences.

3. Multi-Level Buckets

In this section we describe the k-level bucket data structure of Denardo and Fox [**8**]. Our description follows that of [**7**]. Consider a bucket structure B that contains k levels of buckets, where k is a positive integer. We number the levels from k (top) to 1 (bottom). Except for the top level, a level contains an array of Δ buckets. The top level contains infinitely many buckets. Each top level bucket corresponds to an interval $[i\Delta^{k-1}, (i+1)\Delta^{k-1} - 1]$. We choose Δ so that at most Δ consecutive buckets at the top level can be nonempty (*i.e.*, $\Delta^k > C$); we need to maintain only these buckets.[1]

We denote bucket j at level i by $B(i,j)$. A bucket contains a set of elements in a way that allows constant-time additions and deletions, *e.g.* in a doubly linked list.

Given k, we choose Δ as small as possible subject to two constraints. First, as mentioned above, $\Delta^{k+1} > C$. Second, Δ must be a power of two so that we can manipulate base-Δ numbers efficiently using RAM operations on words of bits. With these constraints in mind, we set Δ to the smallest power of two greater than $C^{1/k}$.

We maintain μ, the key of the latest element extracted from the queue. Consider the base-Δ representation of the keys and an element u in B. By definitions of C and Δ, μ and the k least significant digits of the base-Δ representation of $\rho(u)$ uniquely determine $\rho(u)$. If $\overline{\mu}$ and $\overline{\rho}$ are the numbers represented by the k least significant digits of μ and $\rho(u)$, respectively, then $\rho(u) = \mu + (\overline{\rho} - (\overline{\mu}))$ if $\overline{\rho} \geq \overline{\mu}$ and $\rho(u) = \mu + \Delta^k + (\overline{\rho} - \overline{\mu})$ otherwise. For $1 \leq i < k$, we denote by μ_i the i-th least significant digit of the base-Δ representation of μ. We denote the number obtained by deleting the $k-1$ least significant digits of μ by μ_k. Similarly, for $1 \leq i < k$, we denote the i-th least significant digit of $\rho(u)$ by u_i and we denote the number obtained by deleting $k-1$ least significant digits of $\rho(u)$ by u_k.

The levels of B are numbered from k (top) to 1 (bottom) and the buckets at each level are numbered from 0 to $\Delta - 1$. Let i be the index of the most significant digit in which $\rho(u)$ and μ differ or 1 if $\rho(u) = \mu$. Given μ and u with $\rho(u) \geq \mu$, we say that the *position of u with respect to μ* is (i, u_i). If u is inserted into B, it is inserted into $B(i, u_i)$. For each element in B, we store its position. If an element u is in $B(i,j)$, then all except for $i+1$ least significant digits of $\rho(u)$ are equal to the corresponding digits of μ and $u_i = j$.

The following lemma follows from the fact that keys of all elements on the queue are at least μ.

LEMMA 3.1. *For every level i, buckets $B(i,j)$ for $0 \leq j < \mu_i$ are empty.*

---

[1] The simplest way to implement the top level is to "wrap around" modulo Δ.

At each level i, we maintain the number of elements at this level. We also maintain the total number of elements in B.

The `extract-min` operation can change the value of μ. As a side-effect, positions of some elements in B may change. Suppose that a minimum element is deleted and the value of μ changes. Let μ' be the value of μ before the deletion and let μ'' be the value of μ after the deletion. By definition, keys of the elements on the queue after the deletion are at least μ''. Let i be the position of the least significant digit in which μ' and μ'' differ. If $i = 1$ (μ' and μ'' differ only in the last digit), then for any element in B after the deletion its position is the same as before the deletion. If $i > 1$, than the elements in bucket $B(i, \mu''_i)$ with respect to μ' are exactly those whose position is different with respect to μ''. These elements have a longer prefix in common with μ'' than with μ' and therefore they belong to a lower level with respect to μ''.

The *bucket expansion* procedure moves these elements to their new positions. The procedure removes the elements from $B(i, \mu''_i)$ and puts them into their positions with respect to μ''. The two key properties of bucket expansions are as follows:

- After the expansion of $B(i, \mu''_i)$, all elements of B are in correct positions with respect to μ''.
- Every element of B moved by the expansion is moved to a lower level.

Now we are ready to describe the multi-level bucket implementation of the priority queue operations.

- `insert`

  To insert an element u, compute its position (i, j) and insert u into $B(i, j)$.
- `decrease-key`

  Decrease the key of an element u in position (i, j) as follows. Remove u from $B(i, j)$. Set $\rho(u)$ to the new value and insert u as described above.
- `extract-min`

  (We need to find and delete the minimum element, update μ, and move elements affected by the change of μ.)

  Find the lowest nonempty level i.

  Find the first nonempty bucket $B(i, j)$ at level i by examining buckets starting from $B(i, \mu_i)$.

  If $i = 1$, delete an element from $B(i, j)$, set $\mu = \rho(u)$, and return u. (In this case old and new values of μ differ in at most the last digit and all element positions remain the same.)

  If $i > 1$, examine all elements of $B(i, j)$ and delete a minimum element u from $B(i, j)$. Set $\mu = \rho(u)$ and expand $B(i, j)$. Return u.

Next we deal with efficiency issues.

LEMMA 3.2. *Given μ and u, we can compute the position of u with respect to μ in constant time.*

Iterating through the levels, we can find the lowest nonempty level in $O(k)$ time. Using binary search, we can find the level in $O(\log k)$ time. We can do even better using the power of the RAM model:

LEMMA 3.3. *If $k \le \log C$, then the lowest nonempty level of B can be found in $O(1)$ time.*

As we will see, the best bounds are achieved for $k \leq \log C$.

A simple way of finding the first nonempty bucket at level i is to go through the buckets. This takes $O(\Delta)$ time.

LEMMA 3.4. *We can find the first nonempty bucket at a level in $O(\Delta)$ time.*

By giving insertion an amortized cost k, even though its actual cost is $O(1)$, we obtain the following amortized bounds:

THEOREM 3.5. *Amortized bounds for the multi-level bucket implementation of priority queue operations are as follows: $O(k)$ for* `insert`, *$O(1)$ for* `decrease-key`, *$O(C^{1/k})$ for* `extract-min`.

Note that in any sequence of operations the number of `insert` operations is at least the number of `extract-min` operations. In a balanced sequence, the two numbers are equal, and we can modify the above proof to obtain the following result.

THEOREM 3.6. *For a balanced sequence, amortized bounds for the multi-level bucket implementation of priority queue operations are as follows: $O(1)$ for* `insert`, *$O(1)$ for* `decrease-key`, *$O(k + C^{1/k})$ for* `extract-min`.

For $k = 1$, the `extract-min` bound is $O(C)$. For $k = 2$, the bound is $O(\sqrt{C})$. The best bound of $O\left(\frac{\log C}{\log \log C}\right)$ is obtained for $k = \lceil \frac{\log C}{\log \log C} \rceil$.

REMARK 3.7. The k-level bucket data structure uses $\Theta(kC^{1/k})$ space.

4. Hot Queues

A *hot queue* [**7**] uses a heap H and a multi-level bucket structure B. Intuitively, the hot queue data structure works like the multi-level bucket data structure, except we do not expand a bucket containing less than t elements, where t is a parameter set to optimize performance. Elements of the bucket are copied into H and processed using the heap operations. If the number of elements in the bucket exceeds t, the bucket is expanded. In the analysis, we charge scans of buckets at the lower levels to the elements in the bucket during the expansion into these levels and obtain an improved bound.

A k-level hot queue uses the k-level bucket structure with an additional *special* level $k + 1$, which is needed to account for scanning of buckets at level k. These buckets correspond to the same ranges as the top level buckets of a $k + 1$ level bucket structure, but we set Δ as for a k-level bucket structure. Thus, only two buckets at the top level can be nonempty at any time, μ_{k+1} and $\mu_{k+1}+1$. Note that if the queue is nonempty, then at least one of the two buckets is nonempty. Thus bucket scans at the special level add a constant amount to the work of processing an element found. We use wrap-around at level $k + 1$ instead of k.

An *active* bucket is the bucket whose elements are in H. At most one bucket is active at any time, and H is empty if and only if there is no active bucket. We denote the active bucket by $B(a, b)$. We make a bucket active by making H into a heap containing the bucket elements, and inactive by resetting the heap to an empty heap. (Elements of the active bucket are both in the bucket and in H.)

To describe the details of hot queues, we need the following definitions. We denote the number of elements in $B(i, j)$ by $c(i, j)$. Given μ, $i : 1 \leq i \leq k + 1$, and

$j : 0 \le j < \Delta$, we say that an element u is *in the range of* $B(i, j)$ if $\underline{\mu}_i \le \rho(u) \le \overline{\mu}_i$, where $\underline{\mu}_i$ ($\overline{\mu}_i$) is obtained by replacing each of the $i - 1$ least significant digits of μ by 0 ($\Delta - 1$). Using RAM operations, we can check if an element is in the range of a bucket in constant time.

We maintain the invariant that μ is in the range of $B(a, b)$ if there is an active bucket.

The detailed description of the queue operations is as follows.

- `insert`

  If H is empty or if the element u being inserted is not in the range of the active bucket, we insert u into B as in the multi-level case.

  Otherwise u belongs to the active bucket $B(a, b)$. If $c(a, b) < t$, we insert u into H and $B(a, b)$. If $c(a, b) \ge t$, we make $B(a, b)$ inactive, add u to $B(a, b)$, and expand the bucket.
- `decrease-key`

  Decrease the key of an element u as follows. If u is in H, decrease the key of u in H. Otherwise, let (i, j) be the position of u in B. Remove u from $B(i, j)$. Set $\rho(u)$ to the new value and insert u as described above.
- `extract-min`

  If H is not empty, extract and return the minimum element of H. Otherwise, proceed as follows.

  Find the lowest nonempty level i. Find the first nonempty bucket at level i by examining buckets starting from $B(i, \mu_i)$.

  If $i = 1$, delete an element from $B(i, j)$, set $\mu = \rho(u)$, and return u.

  If $i > 1$, examine all elements of $B(i, j)$ and delete a minimum element u from $B(i, j)$. Set $\mu = \rho(u)$. If $c(i, j) > t$, expand $B(i, j)$. Otherwise, make $B(i, j)$ active. Return u.

Correctness of the hot queue operations follows from the correctness of the multi-level bucket operations, Lemma 3.1, and the observation that if u is in H and v is in B but not in H, then $\rho(u) < \rho(v)$.

The following theorem is proved in [**7**].

THEOREM 4.1. *Let $I(N)$, $D(N)$, $F(N)$, and $X(N)$ be the time bounds for heap* `insert`, `decrease-key`, `find-min`, *and* `extract-min` *operations. Then amortized times for the hot queue operations are as follows: $O(k+I(t))$ for* `insert`, *$O(D(t)+I(t))$ for* `decrease-key`, *and $O(F(t) + X(t) + \frac{kC^{1/k}}{t})$ for* `extract-min`.

Similarly to Theorem 3.6, we can get bounds for a balanced sequence of operations.

THEOREM 4.2. *Let $I(N)$, $D(N)$, $F(N)$, and $X(N)$ be the time bounds for heap* `insert`, `decrease-key`, `find-min`, *and* `extract-min` *operations, and consider a balanced sequence of the hot queue operations. The amortized bounds for the operations are as follows: $O(I(t))$ for* `insert`, *$O(D(t) + I(t))$ for* `decrease-key`, *and $O(k + F(t) + X(t) + \frac{kC^{1/k}}{t})$ for* `extract-min`.

REMARK 4.3. Consider the 1- and 2-level implementations. Although the time bounds are the same, the two-level implementation has two advantages: It uses less space and its time bounds remain valid for a wider range of values of C.

5. Experimental Setup

We present data for experiments conducted on a Pentium Pro with a 200 Mhz. processor running Solaris x86 5.5.1. The machine has 96 Meg. of memory and all problem instances fit into main memory. Our code was written in C++ and compiled with `gcc` version 2.7.2.1 using the `-O6` optimization option. We also experimented with two different architectures; see Section 6.5.

We made an effort to make our code efficient. As mentioned earlier, we set the bucket array sizes to be powers of two. This allows us to use word shift operations when computing bucket array indices.

Our study compares six implementations of monotone priority queues: k-ary heaps, with k=4; 2- and 3-level buckets; and 2- and 3-level hot queues; and (for calibration purposes) a simple heap-based demo algorithm provided by DIMACS Challenge organizers. Some of these have parameters to tune, and the results we show are for the best parameter values we tested.

We do not show results for 3-level algorithms because the results never significantly differ from those of the 2-level implementations. In our figures, we refer to the implementation as follows:

- `demo`: the demo implementation,
- `heap`: our implementation of 4-heaps,
- `bck2`: our implementation of 2-level buckets,
- `hotq2`: our implementation of 2-level hot queues.

The demo data is presented only to facilitate comparison of our results with those of other Challenge participants.

Our implementation of multi-level buckets and hot queues is described in detail in [**7**]. That paper also indicates which values of the tunable parameters of the hot queue implementation worked best for the Dijkstra tests. Surprisingly, the same parameter values proved best for the additional tests of the current study. This suggests that good parameter values are robust over a wide range of applications.

We plot and tabulate the data. We provide running times (user time spent by the application, in seconds), and statistics that contribute the most to the running time. For `heap`, we give the number of heap swap operations performed, a swap being the basic operation used to preserve the heap property. For `bck2`, we give the number of empty buckets examined. For `hotq2`, we give both statistics; the heap operations are calculated in the case the active bucket is implemented as a heap.

To calculate the running time, we ran each test three times, each time using a different random number seed. The times we report are the average of the three tests.

In addition to some Dijkstra-based problem families taken from [**7**], we study three new problem families: a simple problem family that uses a priority queue to perform sorting, an event simulation family and a family based on monotone sequences with many `decrease-key` operations.

Dijkstra-based families. We study three families that generate a series of events from a run of Dijkstra's algorithm. They differ in the construction of the graph that Dijkstra's algorithm is run on. The first graph is a grid, where the width of the grid is 16 vertices and the length ranges from 8192 to 32768 vertices. An additional source vertex is connected to all 16 vertices at the left side of the grid. Path lengths in this graph are $O(n)$.

The second graph is a random graph. This graph has N vertices — we considered $N = 262144$ and 524288 —, and $4N$ edges. Each edge connects two vertices chosen uniformly at random.

The third graph is designed, unlike typical graphs, to result in many `decrease-key` operations for the priority queue. The graph consists of a cycle, connecting all vertices, of length 1 arcs. In addition, each vertex has 8 random arcs. The length of each arc is proportional to the square of the distance between the two endpoints (as measured along the cycle). As a result, paths with many vertices are invariably longer than paths with few vertices, resulting in many `decrease-key` operations. We consider graphs with 512, 1024, and 2048 vertices.

Sorting. The only parameter is N, the number of items to be sorted; it ranges from 1000 to 100000. N items are randomly generated in the range 1–$10N$ and inserted into the queue. Then N `extract-min` operations are performed.

Event simulation sequences. Parameters are C (maximum event duration), K (approximate queue size), and E ("clusterdness" of keys; the smaller E is, the more clustered the data, but E must be less than $C/2$). Let T denote the current "time" — the key of the last extracted element or zero if no elements have been extracted. Let tC be the smallest integer multiple of C greater than T. To generate an insert operation, we select an integer i uniformly at random from the interval $[0, E]$ and set the key of the new element to $(tC+i)$ if $tC+i \leq T+C$ and to $(tC-i)$ otherwise. The generator starts with K insert operations. Then it alternates insert and extract-min operations, maintaining queue size of K or $K+1$.

We tested nine families of event simulation:

(1) C ranges from 99 to 9999999 as $E = 1$ and $K = 100$
(2) C ranges from 99 to 9999999 as $E = 1$ and $K = n/10$
(3) C ranges from 99 to 9999999 as $E = C/3$ and $K = 100$
(4) C ranges from 99 to 9999999 as $E = C/3$ and $K = n/10$
(5) E ranges from 1 to $C/3$ as $C = 99999$ and $K = 10000$
(6) K ranges from 100 to $n/10$ as $C = 99$ and $E = 1$
(7) K ranges from 100 to $n/10$ as $C = 99$ and $E = C/3$
(8) K ranges from 100 to $n/10$ as $C = 9999999$ and $E = 1$
(9) K ranges from 100 to $n/10$ as $C = 9999999$ and $E = C/3$

For each family we made $n = 300000$, which was the largest value that would comfortably fit into memory. Note that n is not an interesting parameter for this family: the algorithm performs the same set of operations approximately $n/2$ times, and so running time should scale linearly with n no matter what the values of the other parameters. Indeed, experiments confirmed this behavior. We chose to make n large enough to make clear the differences in running times between the various algorithms, but not so large the machines had to page when running the tests.

General monotone sequences. Parameters are C and K (as in event simulation), and D, the approximate number of decrease-key operations per element. Let T denote the current "time" — the key of the last extracted element or zero if no elements have been extracted. Let tC be the smallest integer multiple of C greater than T. A new element is assigned the key of tC and immediately inserted. The number of elements on the queue after the initial inserts is K or $K+1$. Let S denote the set of elements with keys greater than T. The generator maintains S. Decrease-key operations are produced only if S is not empty. We pick a random element s from S and denote its key by $k(s)$. Then we select, uniformly at random, an integer i from $[0, \lfloor\sqrt{(k(s))}\rfloor]$ and decrease the key of s to $k(s)-(i+1)$. The body of the sequence consists of an `insert`, followed by D `decrease-key` operations, and an `extract-min`. This series of $D+2$ operations is repeated $N/(D+2)$ times. Note the series may actually have fewer than $D+2$ operations if $|S|$ is smaller than D.

For general monotone sequences, we tested four families, with $C = 99$ or 9999999 and $K = 100$ or $n/10$. In each case we let D range from 1 to 10000. Not all of these tests were physically feasible: D must be less than C, for instance, since otherwise the event expires before all the requested `decrease-key` operations can be performed.

The cost of `decrease-key` should dominate the running time, so this family can be used to compare the cost of this operation.

6. Experimental Results

6.1. Sorting Tests. In Figure 1 we show results for the sorting tests. The heap algorithm starts to perform somewhat worse than the other two as n — and C — grow.

6.2. Dijkstra-Based Tests. In this section we show results for the operation sequences from Dijkstra's shortest path algorithm (Figures 2, 3, and 4). See [**7**] for a detailed study of how hot queues perform in Dijkstra's algorithm.

Operation sequences corresponding to long grids have small queue size and large gaps in key values. This makes the sequences good for heaps and bad for a 1-level bucket implementation. Figure 2 shows that indeed our heap implementation is the fastest; hot queues perform the same because it emulates the heap implementation. The two-level bucket implementation is slower, but not by much.

On random graph sequences (Figure 3), the key distribution is uniform with no big gaps in key values, and a large queue size. This favors bucket-based implementations, which are the best on this family. The heap implementation is a little slower.

Most shortest path problems yield operation sequences with a relatively small number of decrease-key operations. Figure 4 shows data for a problem family designed to yield many `decrease-key` operations. From the worst-case bounds, one would expect the heap implementation to be the slowest on this family, because this is the only implementation with a nonconstant `decrease-key` bound. However, on this problem family heap `decrease-key` performs better than the worst case would predict, presumably because elements did not have to traverse the entire height of the tree as a result of each `decrease-key` operation. As a result, the heap's performance is very close to that of hot queues and multi-level buckets.

6.3. Event Simulation. The first four event simulation families test the behavior of the algorithms as C, the maximum event duration, increases. It is expected that the heap should be immune to changes in C, while bucket-based algorithms should degrade slightly as C increases due to the increased number of empty buckets. With multi-level buckets, the performance should degrade less when the data points are more clustered, because with clustered data there are likely to be large stretches of empty buckets, which multi-level bucket implementations handle particularly efficiently.

These expectations are borne out in Figures 5 and Figures 6. In each case, hot queues performs best, and the heap's somewhat erratic behavior does not seem

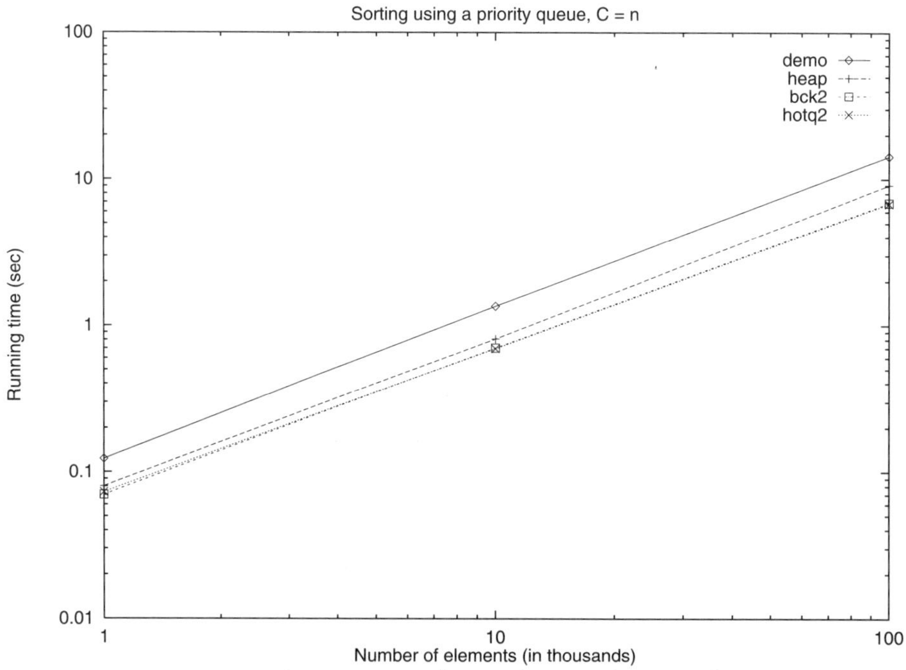

alg.	N	1	10	100
demo	**time**	**0.12**	**1.35**	**14.32**
heap	**time**	**0.08**	**0.81**	**9.13**
	heap swaps	6493	81869	982138
bck2	**time**	**0.07**	**0.70**	**6.91**
	empty	371	3709	36670
hotq2	**time**	**0.07**	**0.70**	**6.82**
	heap swaps	145	144	144
	empty	363	3715	37007

FIGURE 1. Sorting tests. The sort keys are integers in the range 1 to n, where n is the number of elements being sorted. For the largest n, the heap is about one-third slower than the other two algorithms.

to depend on C. When $E = 1$ and data is very clustered, bucket-only algorithms perform well, but when $E = C/3$ and data is less clustered, their performance degrades for large C.

Though we do not show the data here, results are similar when the queue size K is increased up to 30000. However, as K increases, the bucket-based algorithms stay competitive with heaps for larger values of C. This is because as K increases, the buckets become increasingly densely occupied, allowing us to amortize the cost of looking at empty buckets — even if they are evenly distributed — over the large number of non-empty buckets.

Though the queue size K thus has some effect on bucket implementations, we would expects its major impact to be on the heap implementation, since operation times grow with the queue size for that data structure. In Figure 7, we do in fact

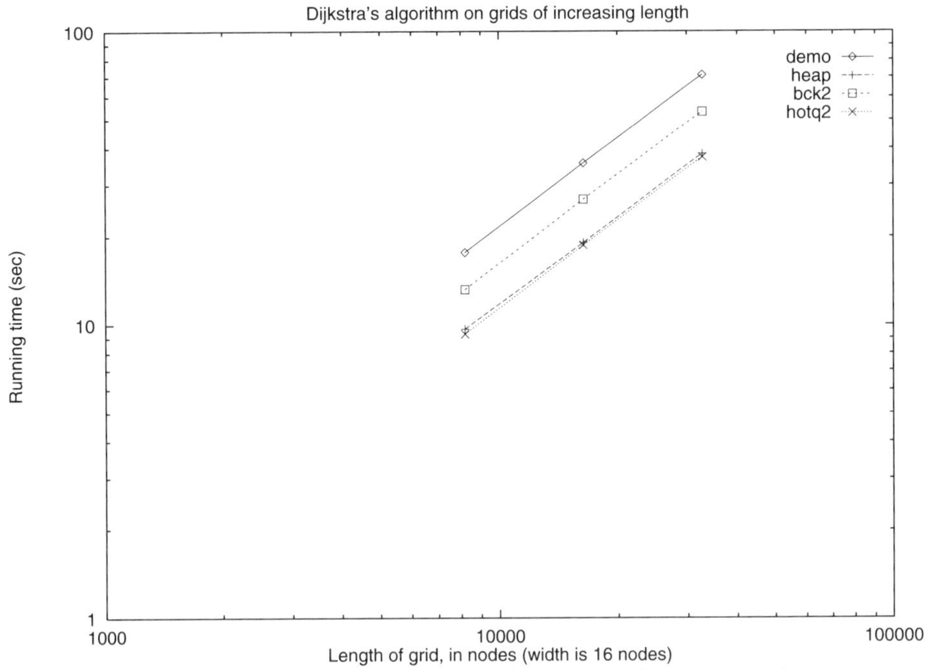

alg.	length	8192	16384	32768
demo	**time**	**17.69**	**35.57**	**71.10**
heap	**time**	**9.66**	**19.08**	**38.29**
	heap swaps	573401	1146904	2294574
bck2	**time**	**13.19**	**26.79**	**53.25**
	empty	31528853	62970119	126057763
hotq2	**time**	**9.29**	**18.71**	**37.24**
	heap swaps	571983	1145479	2293206
	empty	0	0	0

FIGURE 2. The performance for Dijkstra's algorithms on long grids. Buckets do worst — about 40% slower than the other algorithms — because the average queue size is small.

see this behavior, but the effect is slight. Since heap times grow only with the log of the queue size, it is expected the queue will have to grow much larger than 10000, the largest value we tested, before we see significant degradation in performance. Hot queues and buckets seem unaffected by the queue size. Though we do not present the data, the trends in Figure 7 remain for larger values of C and E.

6.4. Monotone event generation with many `decrease-key` operations. The intent of this family of tests is to examine the behavior of algorithms as the number of `decrease-key` operations per key increases.

Figure 8 shows that none of the algorithms have a running time that depends on the number of `decrease-key` operations per key. Hot queues perform slightly better than buckets when the number of `decrease-key` operations is small, but we attribute this to the fact this test has a large event duration combined with small

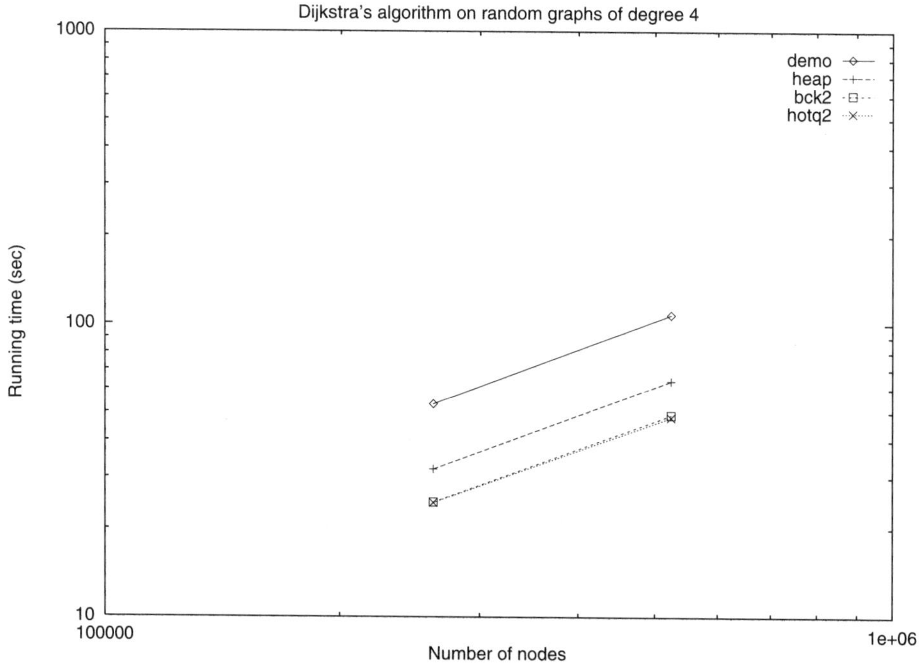

alg.	N	262144	524288
demo	**time**	**53.34**	**107.55**
heap	**time**	**31.95**	**63.98**
	heap swaps	3211850	6703905
bck2	**time**	**24.67**	**48.90**
	empty	0	0
hotq2	**time**	**24.56**	**48.00**
	heap swaps	190	194
	empty	0	0

FIGURE 3. The performance for Dijkstra's algorithms on random graphs. `heap` is 30% slower than the other algorithms because there are no empty buckets in the bucket-based implementation, making them particularly efficient.

event queue. This is the same situation as in Figure 6, in which the bucket algorithms performed worse than hot queues, and it is caused by the relative expense of `extract-min` for bucket based algorithms when there are many empty buckets. This disparity in performance is attenuated as the number of `decrease-key` operations increases, because in that case the relative number of `extract-min` operations decreases. Figure 9 supports this explanation, since in this test the buckets are denser, and in fact we see the bucket algorithm and the hot queue algorithm performing similarly. We have no explanation for the spike in running time for the heap code for large D. A similar spike was present in experiment conducted on `MIPS` and `POWER` architectures as well (see Section 6.5).

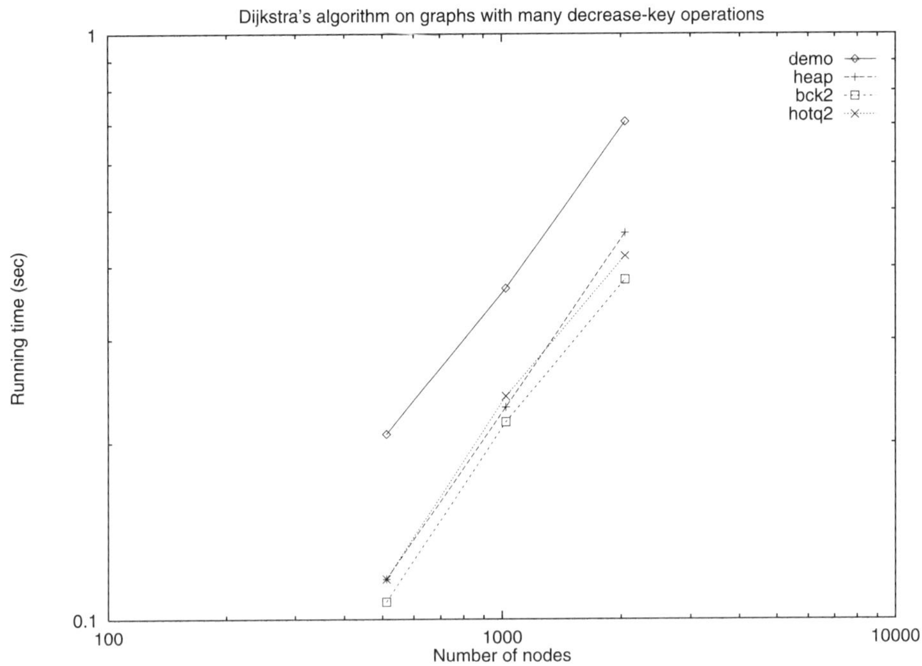

alg.	N	512	1024	2048
demo	**time**	**0.21**	**0.37**	**0.71**
heap	**time**	**0.12**	**0.23**	**0.46**
	heap swaps	3458	5475	12252
bck2	**time**	**0.11**	**0.22**	**0.38**
	empty	0	0	0
hotq2	**time**	**0.12**	**0.24**	**0.42**
	heap swaps	3010	4974	11886
	empty	0	0	0

FIGURE 4. The performance for Dijkstra's algorithms on graphs with many `decrease-key` operations. All algorithms perform approximately equally.

6.5. Tests on Different Architectures. Because the relative time difference between the competing codes is usually small, we conducted additional tests on different architectures and with different compiler optimization levels.

We ran our tests on two additional machines with different architectures: an SGI Onyx Reality Engine/2 with 8 250 MHz. `MIPS`R4400 processors and 1 Gigabyte of main memory, and an IBM RS6000 with 4 166 MHz. `POWER` 604e processors and 512 Megabytes of main memory. The results of these two sessions confirm our conclusions based on the main `x86` experiments. The main differences in the relative algorithm performance are as follows:

- For the `POWER` architecture, on some problem families the relative speed of the heap and demo codes were lower, but not drastically so.

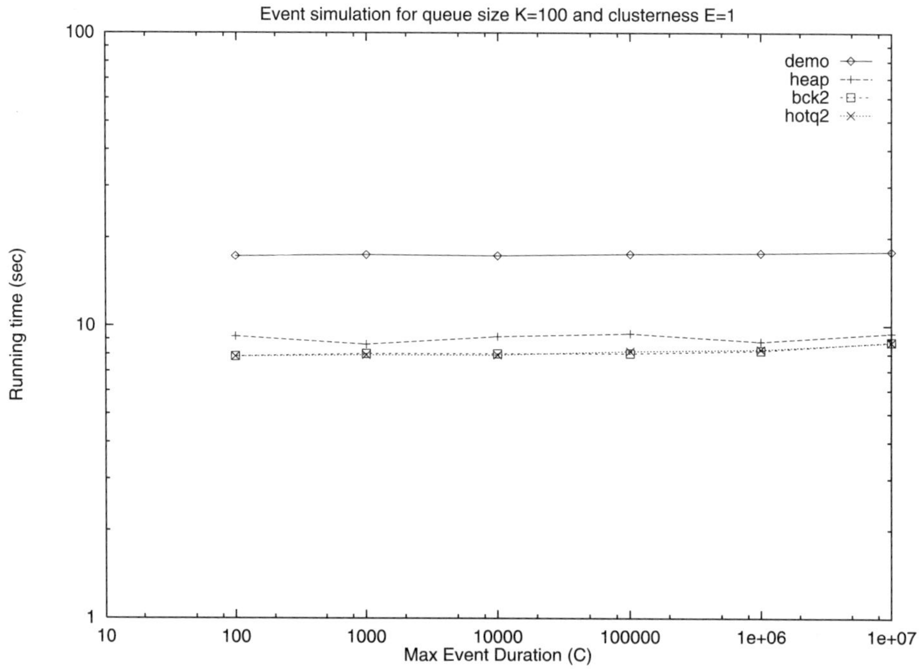

alg.	C	99	999	9999	99999	999999	9999999
demo	**time**	**17.30**	**17.45**	**17.32**	**17.55**	**17.67**	**17.92**
heap	**time**	**9.19**	**8.63**	**9.17**	**9.39**	**8.82**	**9.43**
	heap swaps	596961	353919	503521	597445	362369	311687
bck2	**time**	**7.86**	**8.02**	**8.02**	**8.04**	**8.22**	**8.81**
	empty	4682	1110	44566	178376	66335	1461790
hotq2	**time**	**7.85**	**7.94**	**7.94**	**8.19**	**8.29**	**8.78**
	heap swaps	3	3	3	5	10	40
	empty	4682	1110	44566	178376	66335	1461790

FIGURE 5. The performance on event simulation as event duration increases, with events very clustered. `bck2` and `hotq2` perform similarly; statistics show the hot queue uses its buckets almost exclusively. `heap` is slower by about 5–15%.

- For both `POWER` and `MIPS` architectures, on a small number of problem families the relative speed of the two-level bucket code was lower, but again not drastically so.

We also ran the experiments with optimization turned off, that is, compiling with the `-O0` option instead of `-O6`. We ran this session on the `POWER` machine. Results were qualitatively identical to the optimized versions of the tests.

While our experiments with the additional architectures are fairly limited, they suggest that our conclusions remain valid for a variety of architectures and systems.

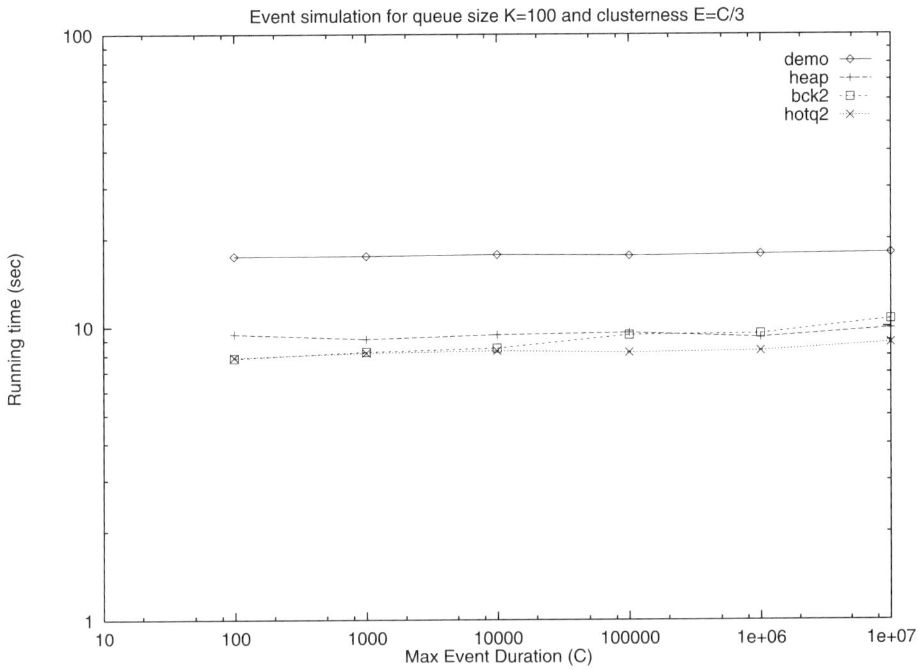

alg.	C	99	999	9999	99999	999999	9999999
demo	**time**	**17.41**	**17.44**	**17.65**	**17.54**	**17.78**	**17.96**
heap	**time**	**9.45**	**9.10**	**9.41**	**9.56**	**9.23**	**9.88**
	heap swaps	724012	648179	697758	727922	652057	447446
bck2	**time**	**7.83**	**8.23**	**8.48**	**9.40**	**9.50**	**10.63**
	empty	3417	282754	2454667	9640212	7320689	13538634
hotq2	**time**	**7.88**	**8.17**	**8.30**	**8.20**	**8.31**	**8.84**
	heap swaps	272	2937	45059	72336	20624	8703
	empty	3415	271797	1149440	144419	676859	2020686

FIGURE 6. The performance on event simulation as event duration increases, with events not clustered. Unlike for small E, `bck2` is up to 20% slower than `hotq2` for large C. `heap` is about 15% slower than the hot queue.

7. Concluding Remarks

Some heaps with good theoretical bounds, including [**3, 15**], seem to complicated to be practical. The situation is less clear with Fibonacci heaps [**11**] and pairing heaps [**14**]. The `insert` operation on these heaps is relatively expensive, but the `decrease-key` operation is cheap. In an application involving minimum-cut problems on large dense graphs, which have a large number of `decrease-key` operations, Fibonacci heaps outperformed the simple heaps in the computational studies of [**5, 12**]. A computational study of Fibonacci and pairing heaps may

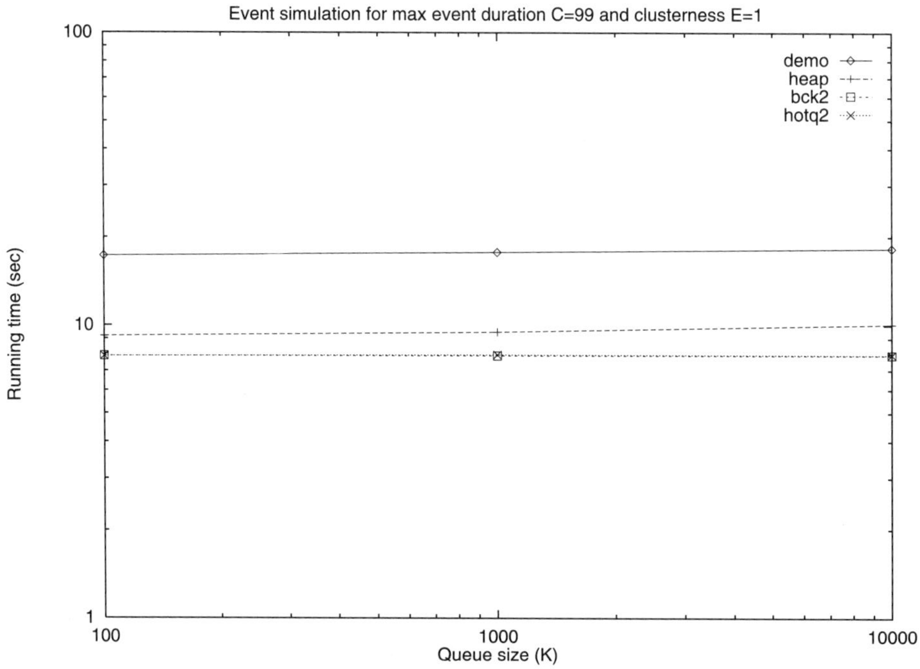

alg.	K	100	1000	10000
demo	**time**	**17.30**	**17.71**	**18.27**
heap	**time**	**9.19**	**9.48**	**10.07**
	heap swaps	596961	788051	985371
bck2	**time**	**7.86**	**7.87**	**7.89**
	empty	4682	469	45
hotq2	**time**	**7.85**	**7.92**	**7.92**
	heap swaps	3	3	3
	empty	4682	469	45

FIGURE 7. The performance on event simulation as the queue size grows. The heap-based demo algorithm cannot support large values of K since the heap size is directly proportional to K. For the largest value of K, `heap` is about 25% slower than the other algorithms.

provide interesting insights. Such a study would require a highly efficient implementation of these data structures, probably better then those currently available in LEDA [**13**].

In [**7**], hot queues have been shown to be fast and robust when used in Dijkstra's algorithm. In the current paper, we have seen that hot queues are equally effective for several other applications that use a priority queue, such as sorting and event simulation. Tests with an artificially large number of `decrease-key` operations confirm that hot queues do not underperform in this context.

Hot queues showed themselves to be more robust than the alternative algorithms based on heaps and buckets alone. The heap algorithm was sensitive —

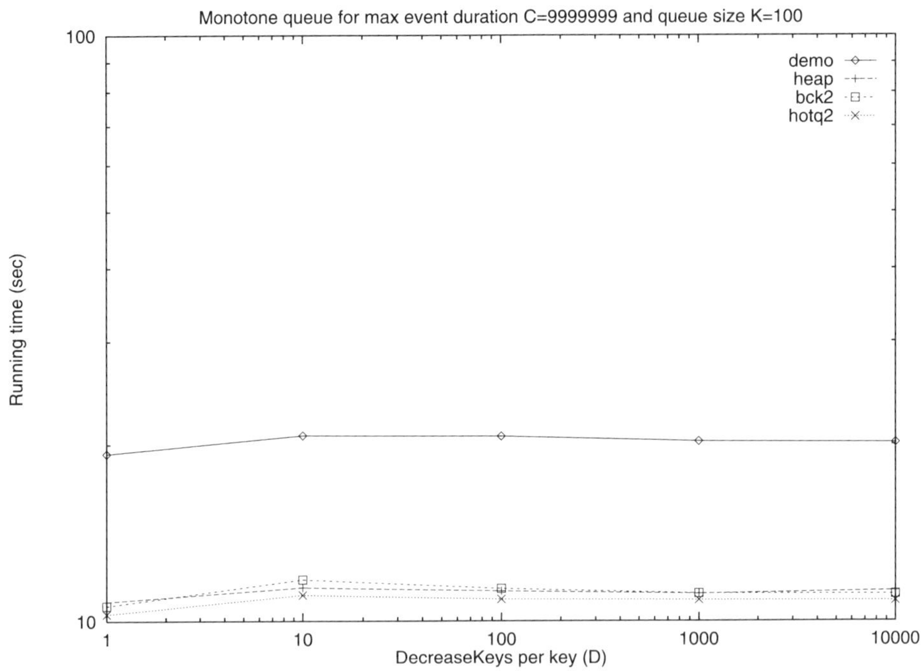

alg.	D	1	10	100	1000	10000
demo	**time**	**19.29**	**20.71**	**20.65**	**20.24**	**20.14**
heap	**time**	**10.79**	**11.40**	**11.24**	**11.13**	**11.27**
	heap swaps	334301	265666	252080	299839	
bck2	**time**	**10.62**	**11.77**	**11.36**	**11.14**	**11.11**
	empty	4217456	3759953	1551047	42177	0
hotq2	**time**	**10.28**	**11.07**	**10.89**	**10.86**	**10.84**
	heap swaps	12216	48578	5093	3299	3682
	empty	2481904	316255	27846	2400	0

FIGURE 8. The performance on monotone simulation as the number of `decrease-key` operations grows. We show results for large C since D must be less than C. `heap` and `bck2` perform the same, 5% slower than `hotq2`.

though, admittedly, not very sensitive — to the event queue size K. Bucket algorithms did badly when data was sparse but not clustered. Hot queues performed well in both situations.

Hot queues are harder to implement efficiently than simple heaps, and and the performance difference is relatively small. A simple heap data structure, such as a 4-heap, is reasonable for a self-contained application. On the other hand, the overall performance of hot queues is better than that of simple heaps. Furthermore, the implementation complexity is not an issue if an implementation of hot queues is already available.

We conclude that the hot queue structure with two or three bucket levels should be considered for a wide range of applications with different mixes of priority queue

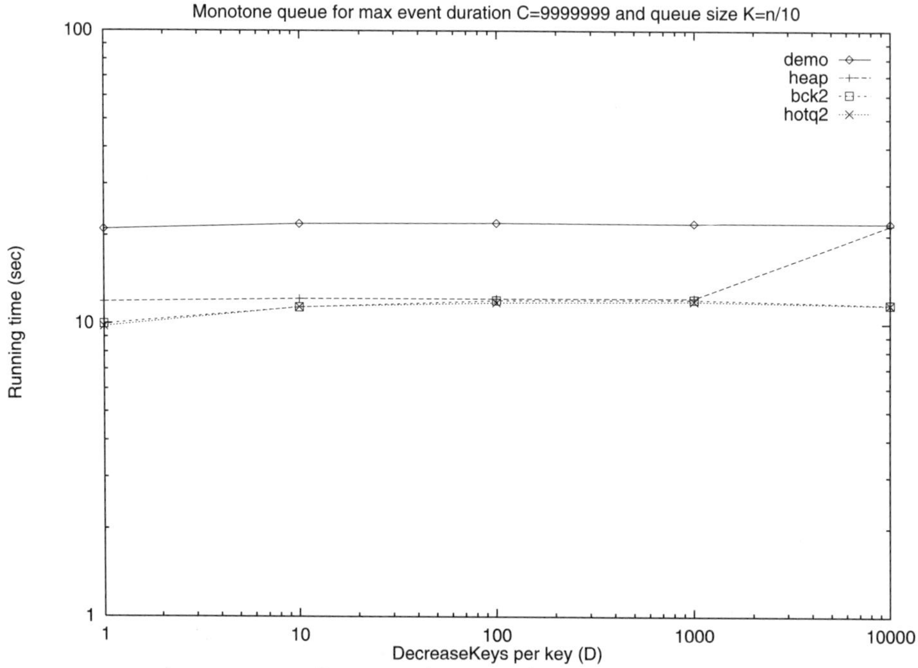

alg.	D	1	10	100	1000	10000
demo	**time**	**21.03**	**21.94**	**22.07**	**21.98**	**21.99**
heap	**time**	**11.86**	**12.14**	**12.14**	**12.21**	**21.65**
	heap swaps	855455	543238	354190	349550	300446
bck2	**time**	**9.96**	**11.36**	**11.98**	**12.07**	**11.63**
	empty	18801	2135	2020	1861	2414
hotq2	**time**	**9.76**	**11.39**	**11.78**	**11.90**	**11.59**
	heap swaps	41	40	40	45	40
	empty	17072	2135	2020	665	2414

FIGURE 9. The performance on monotone simulation as the number of `decrease-key` operations grows, with a large queue size. We show results for large C since D must be less than C. Heap is about 5–10% slower than the other two algorithms.

operations. Reusable data structure libraries containing hot queue codes would facilitate their use.

References

[1] R. K. Ahuja, K. Mehlhorn, J. B. Orlin, and R. E. Tarjan. Faster Algorithms for the Shortest Path Problem. *J. Assoc. Comput. Mach.*, 37(2):213–223, April 1990.

[2] P. Van Emde Boas, R. Kaas, and E. Zijlstra. Design and Implementation of an Efficient Priority Queue. *Math. Systems Theory*, 10:99–127, 1977.

[3] G. S. Brodal. Worst-Case Efficient Priority Queues. In *Proc. 7th ACM-SIAM Symposium on Discrete Algorithms*, pages 52–58, 1996.

[4] R. Brown. Calendar Queues: A Fast $O(1)$ Priority Queue Implementation for the Simulation Event Set Problem. *Comm. ACM*, 31:1220–1227, 1988.

[5] C. S. Chekuri, A. V. Goldberg D. R. Karger, M. S. Levine, and C. Stein. Experimental Study of Minimum Cut Algorithms. In *Proc. 8th ACM-SIAM Symposium on Discrete Algorithms*, pages 324–333, 1997.
[6] B. V. Cherkassky, A. V. Goldberg, and T. Radzik. Shortest Paths Algorithms: Theory and Experimental Evaluation. *Math. Prog.*, 73:129–174, 1996.
[7] B. V. Cherkassky, A. V. Goldberg, and C. Silverstein. Buckets, Heaps, Lists, and Monotone Priority Queues. In *Proc. 8th ACM-SIAM Symposium on Discrete Algorithms*, 1997.
[8] E. V. Denardo and B. L. Fox. Shortest–Route Methods: 1. Reaching, Pruning, and Buckets. *Oper. Res.*, 27:161–186, 1979.
[9] R. B. Dial. Algorithm 360: Shortest Path Forest with Topological Ordering. *Comm. ACM*, 12:632–633, 1969.
[10] E. W. Dijkstra. A Note on Two Problems in Connexion with Graphs. *Numer. Math.*, 1:269–271, 1959.
[11] M. L. Fredman and R. E. Tarjan. Fibonacci Heaps and Their Uses in Improved Network Optimization Algorithms. *J. Assoc. Comput. Mach.*, 34:596–615, 1987.
[12] M. Juenger, G. Rinaldi, and S. Thienel. Practical performance of efficient minimum cut algorithms. In *Proc. 1st Workshop on Algorithm Engineering, Venice, Italy*, 1997. Available via URL http://www.dsi.unive.it/ wae97/proceedings/.
[13] K. Mehlhorn and S. Naher. LEDA: A Platform for Combinatorial and Geometric Computing. *Comm. ACM*, 38:96–102, 1995.
[14] J.T. Stasko and J.S. Vitter. Pairing Heaps: Experiments and Analysis. *Comm. ACM*, 30:234–249, 1987.
[15] M. Thorup. On RAM Priority Queues. In *Proc. 7th ACM-SIAM Symposium on Discrete Algorithms*, pages 59–67, 1996.
[16] J. W. J. Williams. Algorithm 232 (Heapsort). *Comm. ACM*, 7:347–348, 1964.

NEC Research Institute, 4 Independence Way, Princeton, NJ 08540
E-mail address: avg@acm.org

Computer Science Department, Stanford University, Stanford, CA 94305
E-mail address: csilvers@cs.stanford.edu

DIMACS Series in Discrete Mathematics
and Theoretical Computer Science
Volume **59**, 2002

Nearest Neighbor Search for Data Compression

Kevin Zatloukal, Mary Holland Johnson, and Richard E. Ladner

ABSTRACT. Vector Quantization is a lossy data compression method whose running time is dominated by a series of nearest neighbor searches. In this paper, we empirically compare six nearest neighbor search algorithms for performing vector quantization. Three of these algorithms were designed specifically for vector quantization. One is the traditional *k-d* tree algorithm. The other two are new algorithms based on the idea of principal component partitioning.

1. Introduction

Vector Quantization (VQ) is a standard method for lossy data compression [**10, 6, 5**]. The running time of VQ is dominated by a series of nearest neighbor searches of a set a *d*-dimensional vectors called a *codebook*. Hence, the choice of nearest neighbor search algorithm is of critical importance in producing a fast implementation of VQ.

In this paper, we compare six nearest neighbor search algorithms for performing VQ. Orchard's Method [**11**], the Annulus Method [**7**], and the Double Annulus Method [**9**] are algorithms that were specifically designed for VQ. The *k-d* tree nearest neighbor search algorithm [**3**] is a traditional, general–purpose algorithm. The PCP tree nearest neighbor search algorithm is based on a partitioning of the codebook by hyperplanes perpendicular to principal components of subsets of the codebook. In prior work the PCP tree was used for progressive transmission of compressed images [**12**] and for approximate nearest neighbor search [**16, 15**]. We use the same PCP tree for nearest neighbor search. The last algorithm is the PCP/*k-d* tree nearest neighbor search algorithm which combines the PCP tree with the *k-d* tree. The PCP and PCP/*k-d* tree nearest neighbor search algorithms are presented for the first time in this paper.

These six algorithms are compared empirically using data from standard images. We will see that no one algorithm is the best for all situations. Each of

1991 *Mathematics Subject Classification.* 68W05.

Key words and phrases. Nearest Neighbor Search, Vector Quantization, Principal Components.

The first author was supported in part by a Mary Gates Research Award at the University of Washington.

The third author was supported in part by NSF grant No. CCR-9732828.

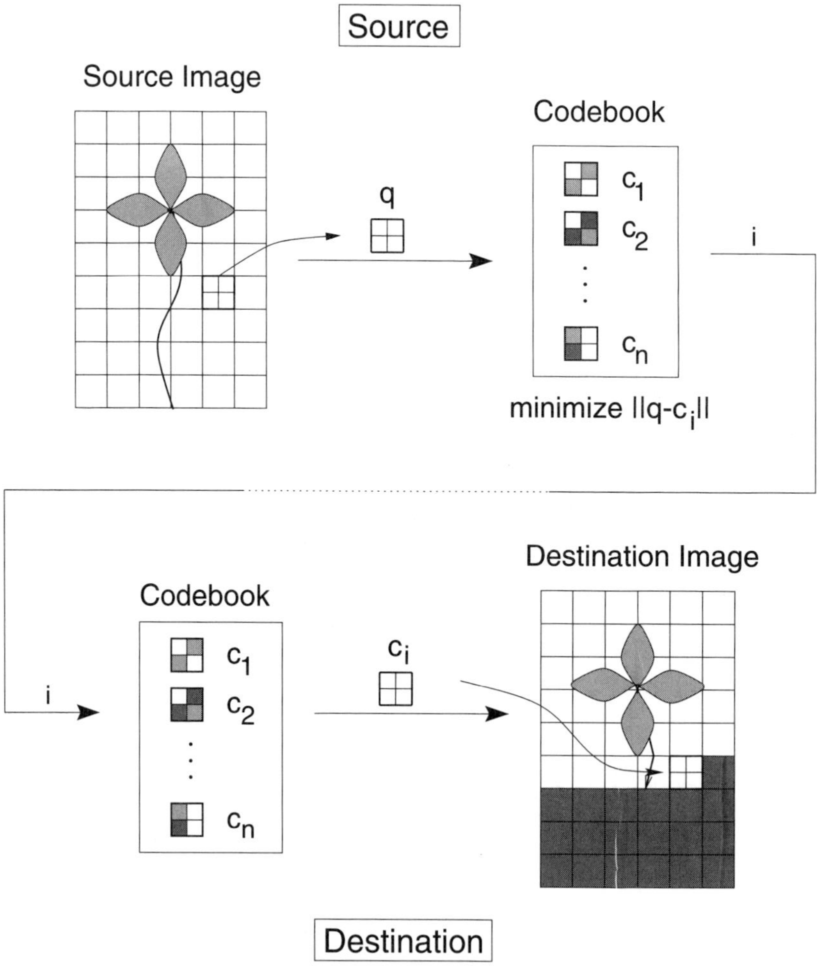

FIGURE 1. VQ algorithm

the algorithms has strengths and weaknesses and their relative running times depend on the vector dimension and size of the codebook. The paper is organized as follows. In section 2 we describe the vector quantization method for image compression. In section 3 we describe all the algorithms we will compare except for the PCP/*k-d* tree nearest neighbor search algorithm. In section 4 we give the results of experiments comparing the first five algorithms for various vector dimensions and codebook sizes. In section 5 we present the PCP/*k-d* tree nearest neighbor search algorithm and compare it with the best of the other five. Finally, in section 6 we summarize what we can conclude from the experiments.

2. Vector Quantization

The Vector Quantization algorithm can be used to compress data stored in an array of any dimension [**10, 6, 5**]. However, in this paper, we are only concerned with 2D arrays. In particular, our input is a gray–scale image, i.e., a 2D array of pixel data.

Figure 1 demonstrates how VQ is used to compress an image being sent across a communication channel. The algorithm processes the source image in small 2D blocks (typically between 2×2 and 8×8 pixels). Both the source and destination have a copy of the codebook, a collection of representative blocks. (The blocks in the codebook are called *codewords*.) For each block q of the source image, we find the codeword $\mathsf{c_i}$ that is "most similar" and transmit the index i across the channel. When the index i is received at the destination, the block $\mathsf{c_i}$ is placed into the appropriate position in the destination image. Provided that the codewords chosen are suitably similar to the blocks of the source image, this will produce a destination image very similar to the source image.

One question that remains is how to measure the similarity between two blocks. First, note that any 2D block can be considered to be a mathematical vector by enumerating the pixels in some order. For example, 2×2 blocks are 4D vectors, and 4×4 blocks are 16D vectors. In VQ blocks are not always square, but are typically a power of two on a side. For example, 2×4 blocks are 8D vectors. We can consider a block q from the source image to be a vector $\mathbf{q}$, and we can consider each codeword $\mathsf{c_i}$ to be a vector $\mathbf{c}_i$. Vector quantization defines the "most similar" codeword to be the $\mathbf{c}_i$ that minimizes

$$\|\mathbf{q} - \mathbf{c}_i\| = \sqrt{\sum_{j=1}^{k}((\mathbf{q})_j - (\mathbf{c}_i)_j)^2},$$

the Euclidean distance from $\mathbf{c}_i$ to $\mathbf{q}$, where k is the dimension of the vectors. Finding this $\mathbf{c}_i$ is a nearest neighbor search.

Vector Quantization achieves compression because the number of bits in an index is usually much smaller than the number of bits in a block. The compression ratio is $b : \log_2 n$ where b is the number of bits in a block and n is the number of codewords. Vector Quantization commonly yields compression ratios better than $10 : 1$ while producing a destination image that is nearly indistinguishable from the source image. For example, suppose we compressed a gray-scale image using 1,024 codewords each 4×4 pixels of 8 bits each. A block would require $b = 4 \cdot 4 \cdot 8 = 128$ bits, whereas an index would require only $\log_2 1024 = 10$ bits. This gives us a compression ratio of $12.8 : 1$. We should note that we are not counting the size of the codebook because we make the reasonable assumption that many images are compressed using the same codebook.

Vector Quantization can also be used to compress data stored in files. The compressed file is simply the stream of indices that would be sent across the channel.

Another question that has not been answered is how to produce the codebook. The goal is to have the codebook contain vectors that are close to vectors that will be coded. Typically, the codebook is created by the Generalized Lloyd Algorithm (GLA) which is a variant of the k-means algorithm [**10**]. The GLA produces a codebook from a large set of training data that is similar to data to be coded. For example, if the images are photographs of people then so should be the set of training images. In this way vectors in the source image are likely to be closely approximated by vectors in the codebook. The GLA starts with some initial codebook and iteratively improves the codebook until the improvements become sufficiently small. This process can take many minutes to produce the final codebook. However, this is an offline cost since the same codebook is used to compress many images.

We see that encoding an image using VQ is simply a series of nearest neighbor searches. There are several properties of VQ codebooks and the searching process that influence the organization of codebooks for fast search. First, neighboring pixels in a vector in an image tend to be highly correlated. For example, if a pixel is dark then the pixel to its right is likely to be dark. Hence, the vectors that form an image tend to cluster on the diagonal rather than be more uniformly distributed. As the vector dimension grows this tendency to be clustered on the diagonal becomes less because the pixels in the vector are further apart in the image. Second, typically vectors are encoded one row at a time from top to bottom. This means that the nearest neighbor in the codebook to one vector is likely to be close to the nearest neighbor for the next vector. Again, this tendency is less as the dimension grows.

In all algorithms below we let n be the number of codewords in the codebook and let k be the dimension of the codewords. In order to achieve data compression it is necessary to have $\log n = O(k)$. For example, a k-dimensional codeword of 8 bit pixels uses $8k$ bits. A codeword requires $\log_2 n$ bits. Hence, VQ achieves a compression ratio of $8k : \log_2 n$. Unless $\log_2 n < 8k$ there is no compression. To be more concrete, if $k = 4$ then we should only consider codebooks of size $< 2^{32}$. Consequently asymptotic analyses of nearest neighbor search algorithms with n becoming arbitrarily large and fixed dimension may be inappropriate.

3. Nearest Neighbor Search Algorithms

As we saw above, the nearest neighbor search problem that arises in VQ is to find the codeword $\mathbf{c}_i$ with minimal Euclidean distance to the query vector $\mathbf{q}$. The "brute–force" solution to the nearest neighbor search problem is simply to compute the distance between $\mathbf{q}$ and each codeword $\mathbf{c}_i$ and keep track of which was the closest. The idea of each of the algorithms below is to try to search only a subset of the codewords. In the worst case, this subset could include every codeword; however, in the average case, this subset will include only a small fraction of them.

For all of these algorithms, including "brute–force," there are two standard optimizations that should be used [**2**]. The first is to notice that minimizing $\|\mathbf{q} - \mathbf{c}_i\|$ is equivalent to minimizing $\|\mathbf{q} - \mathbf{c}_i\|^2$, and thus we can avoid performing most square root computations by using squared distances rather than distances. The second comes from noticing that most often when we are computing the quantity $\|\mathbf{q} - \mathbf{c}_i\|^2 = \sum_{j=1}^{k}((\mathbf{q})_j - (\mathbf{c}_i)_j)^2$, we only want to know whether it is less than smallest squared distance found thus far. Thus, if at some point the partial sum becomes larger than the smallest squared distance found thus far, we can stop the computation.

We will use two metrics in measuring the performance of the algorithms. The first is the execution time of the algorithm. The second, which is a major component of the first, is the *number of codewords searched* which is the number of distance computations made.

3.1. Orchard's Method. Orchard's Method is a nearest neighbor search algorithm designed specifically for Vector Quantization [**11**]. It is based on the geometric observation shown in Figure 2. (This picture is drawn in 2D; however, the result is true in any dimension.) Suppose that $\mathbf{c}_g$ is the closest codeword seen thus far, with $r = \|\mathbf{q} - \mathbf{c}_g\|$. Any codeword $\mathbf{c}_i$ that is closer to $\mathbf{q}$ than $\mathbf{c}_g$ must be no further than $2r$ from $\mathbf{c}_g$, or in symbols, $\|\mathbf{c}_i - \mathbf{c}_g\| \leq 2r$.

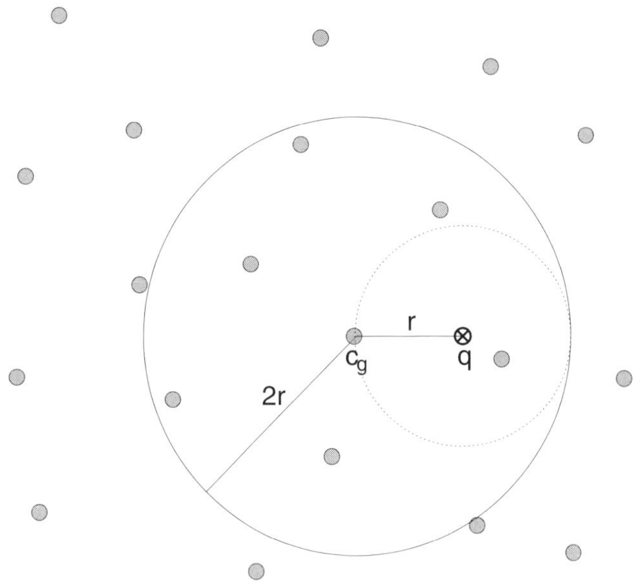

FIGURE 2. Orchard's Method

If we had a list of all the codewords sorted by their distance to $\mathbf{c}_g$ then we could simply enumerate those whose distance to $\mathbf{c}_g$ was less than $2r$ (which would be at the front of the list). Unfortunately, since $\mathbf{c}_g$ could be any codeword, we must maintain such a list for every codeword. More properly, the indices of the sorted codewords can be stored in these lists requiring $O(n^2)$ space.

Since $O(n^2)$ space is impractical for all but the smallest codebooks, a variation has been suggested which uses less space. The idea is to keep only the first m entries in each list for some number m. This requires $O(mn)$ space. If during our search we need to reference past the mth item in one of the lists, then we resort to a full search of every codeword. A smaller value of m will save space; however, it will also decrease performance.

One question that arises when implementing Orchard's Method is what to do when we encounter a codeword that is closer than the closest seen so far: do we keep enumerating through the current list or do we switch to the list of the codeword just discovered? Orchard's original paper [**11**] implemented the latter and we empirically verified that the latter is definitely the right thing to do. However, when this is done, care must be taken not to examine the same codeword more than once. This can be dealt with by marking codewords as they are examined. The marking process can be accomplished by maintaining an array of length n, indexed 1 to n for each codeword. Each member of the marking array has a bit indicating if the codeword has been searched and a pointer (index) to the last codeword that had been searched. Initially all the bits are zero and all the pointers are null. Before searching a codeword its bit is checked to see if it was already searched. When a codeword is searched its bit is switched from 0 to 1 and its pointer points to the last codeword searched. In the end, when the nearest codeword is found, the searched codewords are located by following the linked list, switching each 1 to 0 and setting each pointer to null. This returns the marking array to its initial state for the

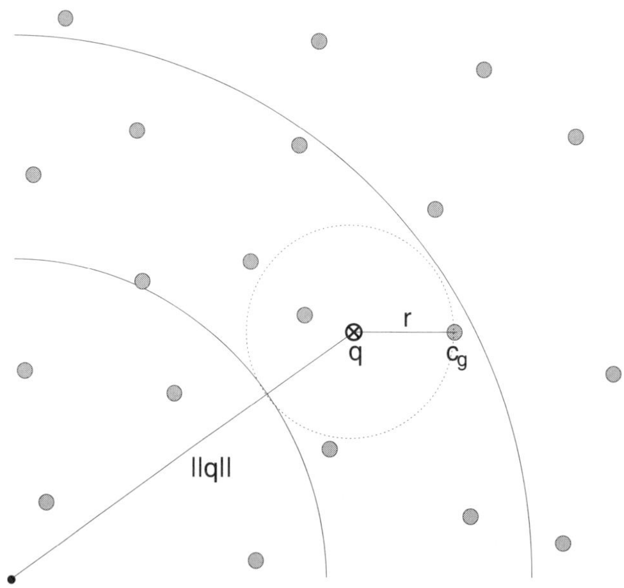

FIGURE 3. Annulus Method

next nearest neighbor search. In this way the time to find the nearest codeword is proportional to the number of codewords searched.

Another question that arises is which list to start processing initially. This choice has a large impact on the running time of this algorithm. To see this, note that the codewords enumerated are those that lie in the circle centered at $\mathbf{c}_g$ with a radius of twice the distance from $\mathbf{c}_g$ to $\mathbf{q}$. Thus, the number of codewords enumerated should grow as the distance between $\mathbf{c}_g$ and $\mathbf{q}$ grows. This means that we should try to pick an initial $\mathbf{c}_g$ that it is as close to $\mathbf{q}$ as possible. In other words, $\mathbf{c}_g$ should be a good guess of the closest codeword.

It remains for us to determine how to pick this guess codeword $\mathbf{c}_g$. It turns out that in VQ there is a very natural way to pick it: use the codeword that was closest to the last block processed. As mentioned earlier these two blocks are most likely adjacent to each other in the source image, they will probably be made up of very similar pixels. Thus, any codeword that is close to one will probably be close to the other. This prediction mechanism is very good in practice. Note that even if the prediction is correct other codewords inside the circle of radius $2r$ centered at the correct codeword must be searched to make sure it is the nearest.

3.2. Annulus Method. The Annulus Method is another nearest neighbor search algorithm designed specifically for VQ [**7**]. It is also based on a geometric observation. As is shown in Figure 3, any codeword $\mathbf{c}_i$ that is closer to $\mathbf{q}$ than $\mathbf{c}_g$ must satisfy $\|\mathbf{q}\| - r \leq \|\mathbf{c}_i\| \leq \|\mathbf{q}\| + r$, where $r = \|\mathbf{q} - \mathbf{c}_g\|$. This constraint defines an annular region.

To implement this algorithm, we maintain a list of the codewords sorted by their norm. We use the same guess codeword $\mathbf{c}_g$ as in Orchard's Method. To find the closest codeword, we enumerate those codewords whose norms lie in the range $[\|\mathbf{q}\| - r, \|\mathbf{q}\| + r]$. As with Orchard's Method, we can shrink the radius r

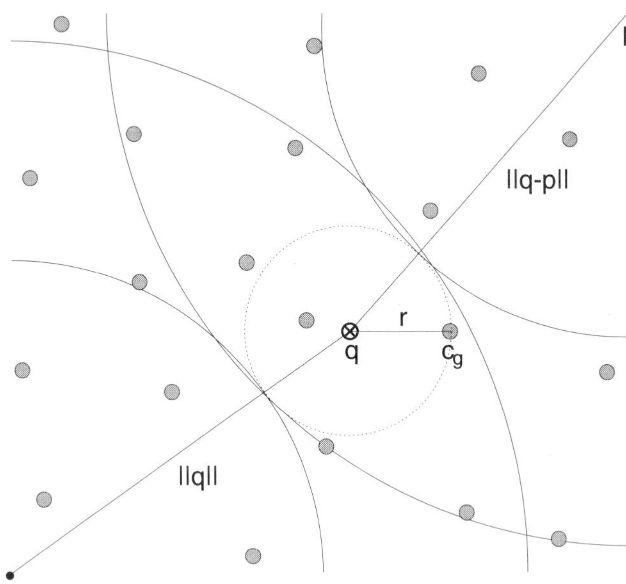

FIGURE 4. Double Annulus Method

of this search as we find closer codewords. However, we discovered as part of our experiments that this has little impact on performance.

The running time of this algorithm can be made proportional to the number of codewords which lie in the annulus. We can enumerate the codewords whose norms lie in this range without any additional work by taking advantage of the fact that we already know the index of $\mathbf{c}_g$ in the array. Starting with $\mathbf{c}_g$ we can traverse the list of codewords in both directions until the distance from the searched codewords to $\mathbf{q}$ exceeds r.

The main advantage of the Annulus Method over Orchard's Method is that the additional storage requirement is $O(n)$ rather than $O(n^2)$. The total storage requirement for the Annulus Method is $O(kn)$ which is the storage needed for the codebook itself.

3.3. Double Annulus Method. The Double Annulus Method is our third nearest neighbor search algorithm designed specifically for VQ [**9**]. The idea is to have two annular constraints and to try to search only those vectors lying in their intersection (see Figure 4). The second annulus is centered at a fixed vector $\mathbf{p}$ that is suitably chosen. Since the first annulus is centered at the origin, a good choice for $\mathbf{p}$ is where $(\mathbf{p})_j$ is the maximum pixel value for $1 \le j \le k$. Since the codewords tend to be clustered on the diagonal this choice of centers tends to eliminate from the intersection codewords that are in one annulus but far from the query vector. The two annuli require maintaining two sorted lists one for $\|\mathbf{c}_i\|$ and one for $\|\mathbf{c}_i - \mathbf{p}\|$ for $1 \le i \le n$. The the number of codewords searched by this algorithm can be made proportional to the number of codewords which lie in the intersection of the two annuli plus $\log n$. To accomplish this first do two binary searches on the first list to find the first and last codewords inside the first annulus. Similarly, find the first and last codewords in the second annulus. This requires $O(\log n)$ distance

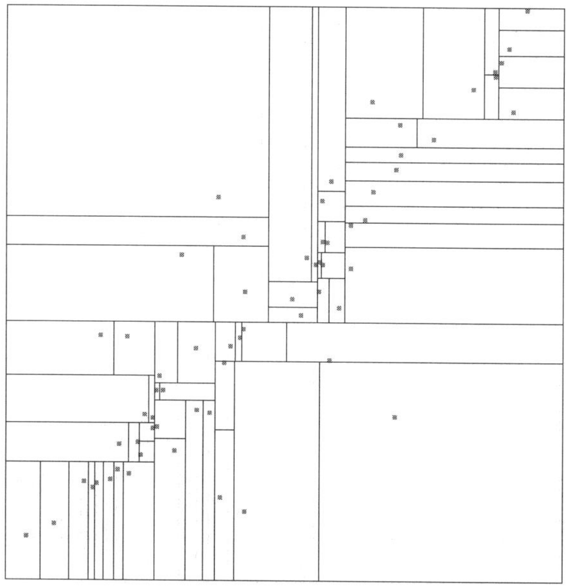

FIGURE 5. *k-d* Tree Splitting Lines

computations (searches). Next, find the intersection of the two lists, which contains at least $\mathbf{c}_g$. Finally, find the closest codeword to $\mathbf{q}$ in the intersection. Technically, the running time is proportional to the number of codewords in the union (not the intersection) of the annuli plus $\log n$, while the number of codeword searched is proportional to the number of codewords in the intersection (not the union) of the annuli plus $\log n$. The Double Annulus Method, like the Annulus Method, also uses storage $O(kn)$.

3.4. *k-d* Tree Search. The *k-d* tree is a multidimensional binary tree data structure that supports nearest neighbor and other spatial searches [**3, 4**]. Improvements to nearest neighbor search in *k-d* trees have been made [**13, 1**], but for this study we adhere to the basic algorithm described below.

A leaf of the *k-d* tree stores a k-dimensional vector (a codeword in our case). An internal node stores an index j and a value v that are used to define its left and right subtrees. The left subtree contains those nodes whose jth component is less than or equal to v, and the right subtree contains those nodes whose jth component is greater than v. For 2D vectors, each internal node partitions the data along a line which is perpendicular to one of the axes as shown in Figure 5. For example, an internal node with $j = 2$ and $v = 15$ partitions the vectors along the horizontal line $y = 15$. All vectors below the line have y–components less than or equal to 15, so they are in the left subtree, and all vectors above the line have y–components greater than 15, so they are in the right subtree. In higher dimension, each internal node partitions the data along a *splitting plane* that is perpendicular to some axis. A balanced *k-d* tree of height $\lceil \log_2 n \rceil$ can be built in $O(kn \log n)$ time and uses $O(kn)$ space.

The nearest neighbor search algorithm for *k-d* trees starts at the root of the tree and proceeds down toward the leaves recursively. At a leaf node, we simply compute the distance between the query vector and the vector stored in the leaf. At an internal node, we first search recursively down whichever subtree the query vector falls in. If the jth component of the query vector is less than or equal to v, then we search down the left subtree; otherwise, we search down the right subtree. When that recursive call returns, we check to see whether we must search the other subtree as well. If the distance between the query vector and the splitting plane is less than distance between the query vector and the closest codeword found thus far, then it is possible that there is a closer vector in the other subtree, so we must search there as well.

Unlike the previous algorithms that were designed specifically for VQ, the k-d tree nearest neighbor algorithm does not take advantage of the guess codeword from a previous nearest neighbor search. For this study we decided to keep to the basic algorithm as defined in the literature in order to compare a general purpose nearest neighbor search algorithm with those that were designed specifically for VQ. Even if we were to try to use the guess codeword in a new k-d tree nearest neighbor search algorithm, the new algorithm must eventually search the first codeword searched in the standard algorithm. This is because the query vector is in the leaf rectangle containing this first codeword searched, thereby creating the possibility that the distance between them is zero.

Friedman, Bentley, and Finkel [**4**] have shown that, in a reasonable model, the number of vectors searched in k-d tree nearest neighbor search is independent of n and the execution time is $O(\log n)$. In their model queries are given by a probability distribution and the codewords (keys in their terminology) are chosen from the same distribution. This situation is similar to the codebook being derived from a good training set by the GLA. They report, based on their own empirical studies, that the asymptotic result of a constant number of codewords searched per nearest neighbor search only applies to very large codebooks. Hence, their result has limited applicability to VQ because of the constraint that $\log n = O(k)$ to achieve data compression.

3.5. PCP Tree Search. The Principal Component Partitioning (PCP) tree [**12, 16, 15**] is a variation on a k-d tree that uses splitting planes which are usually not perpendicular to the axes. Each splitting plane is perpendicular to the principal component of the data it is partitioning. The principal component is an affine vector that points along the line which minimizes the sum of the squared distances to each vector (this is the "best fit" line of the vectors). Figure 6 shows the splitting planes (lines in 2D) of a PCP tree used to partition a set of codewords taken from a typical codebook.

The PCP tree was not originally designed for nearest neighbor search so why is the PCP tree a good vehicle for nearest neighbor search?

Suppose that we were allowed to choose a splitting line for a set of codewords. How would we characterize a good choice? First, we would like this line to split the codewords in half. If we do this at every internal node, then the resulting tree will be perfectly balanced. Second, we would like to choose our line so as to minimize the number of times that we have to search both sides when performing a nearest neighbor search. We are forced to search both sides when the distance from the query vector to the closest codeword is greater than the distance from the query vector to the splitting line. Thus, if we increase the expected distance from the

FIGURE 6. PCP Tree Splitting Lines

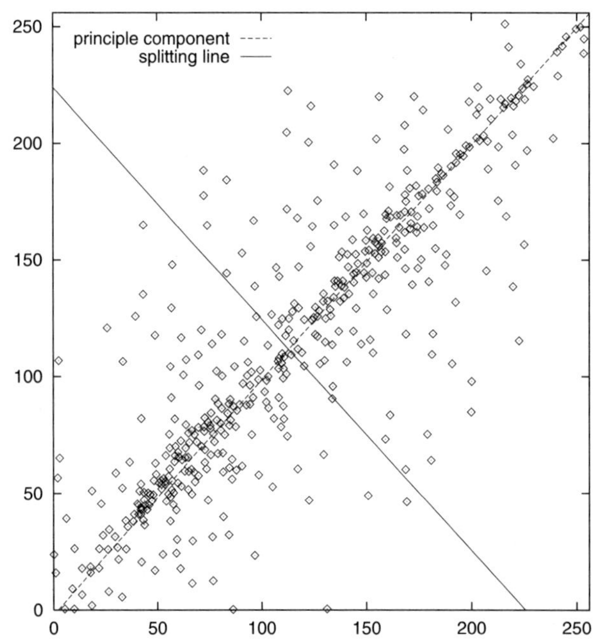

FIGURE 7. Principal Component Partitioning

query vector to the splitting line, we would expect to decrease the number of times that we are forced to search both sides.

It remains to determine how we can increase the expected distance from the query vector to the splitting line. First, we should note that we can expect the query vectors to be distributed very similarly to the codewords: the codewords are supposed to represent well the blocks that will occur in the source image. Therefore, we can increase the expected distance from the query vector to the splitting line by increasing the expected distance from a codeword to the splitting line. For example, Figure 7 shows a set of real 2×1 codewords taken from a typical codebook. The dotted line, along which the vectors are highly clustered, passes through the principal component. The solid line is perpendicular to the principal component. This is the line that principal component partitioning would choose, and as we can see, only a small number of vectors are very close to it. The *k-d* tree would choose a horizontal or vertical splitting line that partitions the vectors in half. In either case, this line would have more vectors close to it than the one chosen by principal component partitioning.

Building a PCP tree requires more time than building a *k-d* tree. To create each internal node, we must find the principal component of the codewords in that subtree. This is done by solving a small eigenvalue problem. To be specific, let $X = \{\mathbf{x}_1, \ldots, \mathbf{x}_m\}$ be a set of k-dimensional vectors (codewords in a subtree). To compute the principal component of X we compute the dominant eigenvalue of the symmetric $k \times k$ matrix $C = A^T A$, where A is the $m \times k$ matrix with entries $a_{ij} = (\mathbf{x}_i)_j - (\overline{\mathbf{x}})_j$. The vector $\overline{\mathbf{x}}$ is the centroid of X, defined by $(\overline{\mathbf{x}})_j = \sum_{i=1}^{m} (\mathbf{x}_i)_j / m$. The principal component of X is the affine vector that is in the direction of the dominant eigenvector of C and goes through the centroid $\overline{\mathbf{x}}$ of X. Computing dominant eigenvector of a $k \times k$ matrix can be done with the power method, which used negligible execution time in our studies. The power method is an iteration method for finding eigenvectors whose number of iterations depends on properties of the matrix and the desired accuracy [**14**]. Once the principal component of the set X is found, then a splitting plane is determined by choosing a plane perpendicular to the principal component of X that partitions X in half. A balanced PCP tree can be built in $O(k^2 n \log n)$ time ignoring the cost of computing the dominant eigenvectors. This bound comes from computing $A^T A$ for 2^i different matrices at level i of the tree where A is a $n/2^i \times k$ matrix. The PCP tree requires $O(kn)$ space with all the nodes, internal and leaves, using $O(k)$ storage. This is in contrast to the *k-d* tree where the internal nodes use constant size and only the leaves have size $O(k)$.

The nearest neighbor search algorithm for the PCP tree is conceptually the same as for *k-d* trees. The only differences are in how we determine which side of the splitting plane the query vector is on and how we compute the distance from the query vector to the splitting plane. For PCP trees, both operations require $O(k)$ time, whereas with *k-d* trees, both operations require only constant time. Since these two operations are more expensive in PCP trees, the nearest neighbor search algorithm will have to examine fewer codewords if it is to be faster than the *k-d* tree algorithm. Like the *k-d* tree algorithm, the PCP tree nearest neighbor search algorithm does not use the guess vector from a previous nearest neighbor search.

4. Experimental Results

In our study, we compare the six algorithms described above using two metrics. Since our ultimate goal is to find the fastest algorithm, our first metric is execution

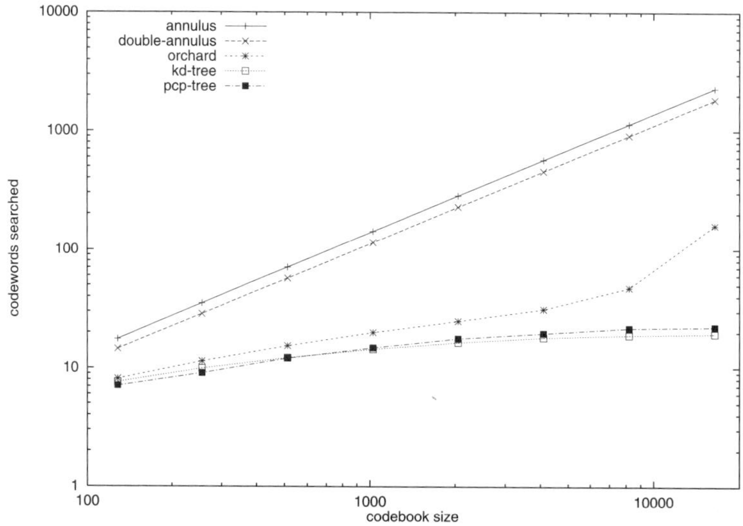

FIGURE 8. Codewords Searched in 4D

time. Our second metric is the number of codewords searched. This second metric should be a good predictor of execution time because distance computations account for the bulk of the processing done by most algorithms. In addition, this second metric will give us extra insight into the behavior of the algorithm.

The execution times and codewords searched that are presented include only the nearest neighbor searches. Preprocessing is not included. This is because the preprocessing time is greatly dominated by the GLA. In addition, as was mentioned earlier, the same codebook will be used to compress many images, so the preprocessing is an offline cost.

The algorithms were run on a total of up to 7 images (baboon, man, airport, couple, lena, and tiffany, grass) from the USC-SIPI Image Database [**8**]. All the images are 512×512 8 bit gray-scale. For the 4D and 16D we used one of the images, Lena, for training and the other 6 for testing. For 64D one image does not provide enough training data so we used all seven images for both training and testing. The experiments were performed on a 500 MHz DEC Alpha with 128MB of memory and running the Linux operating system[1]. Execution times reported in Figures 9, 11, 13, and 16 are the average execution times per nearest neighbor search for VQ encoding all the test images. The codewords searched in Figures 8, 10, and 12 are the average numbers of codewords searched per nearest neighbor search for VQ encoding all the test images.

Let's start by looking at the results in a low dimension, 4D (2×2 blocks). Figure 8 shows the number of codewords searched by the different algorithms. At the bottom are the two tree methods, *k-d* and PCP trees, which searched about the same number of codewords. Just above is Orchard's Method. At the top are Annulus Method and Double Annulus Method. Notice that all of the algorithms search far fewer codewords than would the "brute–force" algorithm. For example,

[1]The experiments were also run on the same machine using the Windows NT operating system and produced nearly identical results.

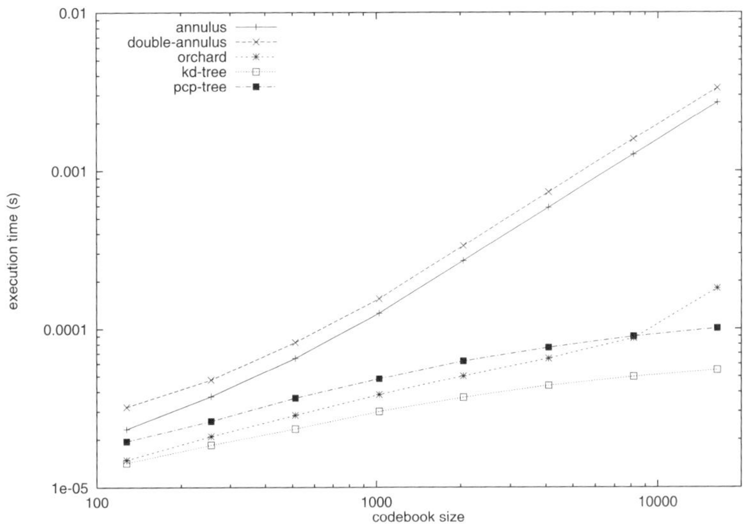

FIGURE 9. Execution Time in 4D

with a codebook containing 16,384 codewords (the last data point), these algorithms all search fewer than 10% of the codewords.

Notice that the plot of Orchard's Method bends up sharply at the larger codebook sizes. For large n a full $O(n^2)$ matrix would exceed the computer's memory causing the virtual memory system to do excessive paging. To avoid this the length of the sorted lists had to be decreased when searching larger codebooks. We restricted the list length so that the total memory usage was no more than 16 MB (still far more memory than was used by any other algorithm) to avoid paging. For all codebooks with up to 1,024 codewords, full length lists were used in all dimensions.

In Figure 8, we can see that Double Annulus Method searches only slightly fewer codewords than Annulus Method. The reason for such a mild increase is that the codewords tend to be clustered along the diagonal and the centers of the two annuli are at each end of the diagonal. The intersection primarily eliminates those few codewords in one annulus but far from the diagonal.

Figure 9 shows the execution time for the different algorithms in 4D. The results look quite similar to the those in the previous figure. This shows us that the number of codewords searched is a reasonably good predictor of execution time. However, there are two key differences between the two plots. The first difference is that PCP tree search was slower than k-d tree search while they searched about the same number of codewords. This is a result of the fact that the PCP tree algorithm did more work at each internal node: $O(k)$ instead of $O(1)$ work. The other difference is that is that Double Annulus Method was slower than Annulus Method while Double Annulus Method searched fewer codewords.

Next, let's look at the results in higher dimension, 16D (4×4 blocks). Figure 10 shows the number of codewords searched for the different algorithms. The only major difference from 4D is that the k-d tree algorithm moved up quite a bit compared to the other algorithms. When we look at Figure 11, which shows the

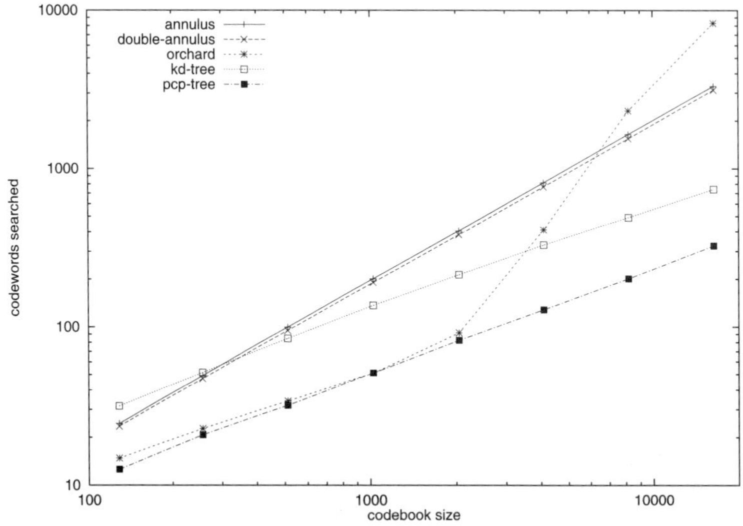

FIGURE 10. Codewords Searched in 16D

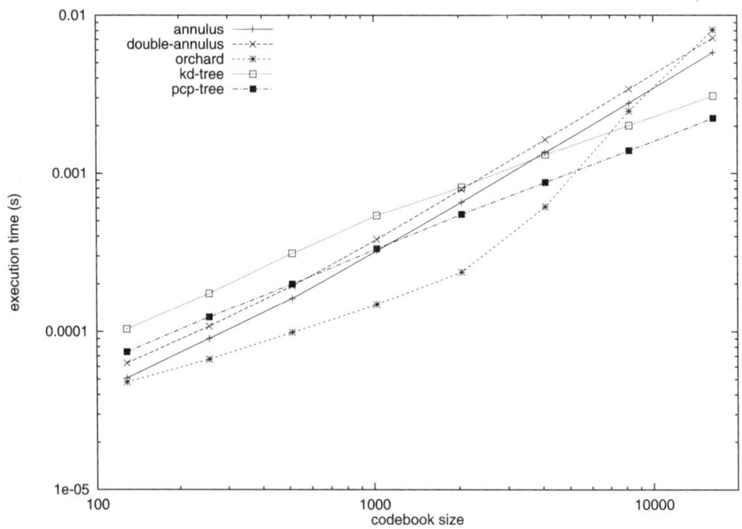

FIGURE 11. Execution Time in 16D

execution time of the different algorithms in 16D, we see that this resulted in a faster execution time for the PCP tree algorithm than the *k-d* tree algorithm. For small codebooks, both were greatly out done by Orchard's Method. However, Orchard's Method slows down considerably, once again, as the lists are shortened. Annulus Method and Double Annulus Method also gained a little ground compared to the other algorithms.

Lastly, Figure 12 and Figure 13 show the number of codewords searched and execution time, respectively, of the different algorithms in 64D (8×8 blocks). Again, it appears that the *k-d* tree algorithm is losing ground in higher dimension, while

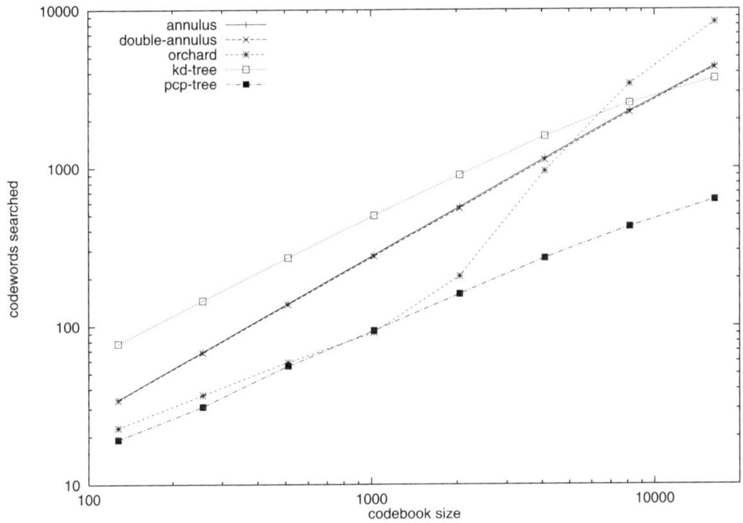

FIGURE 12. Codewords Searched in 64D

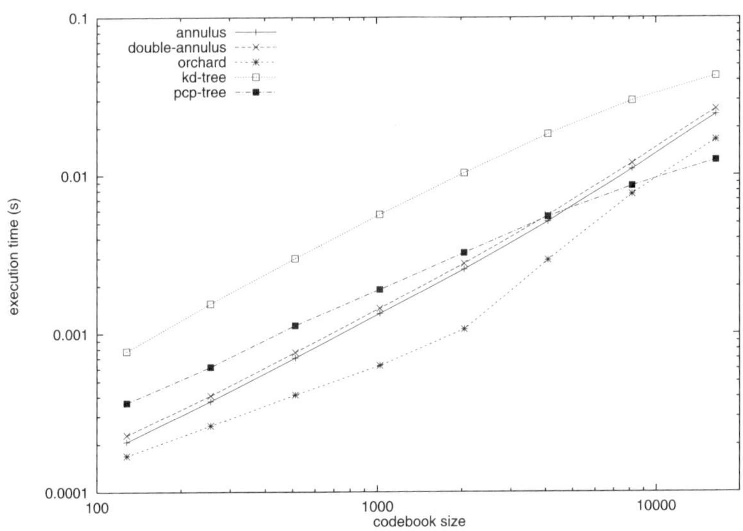

FIGURE 13. Execution Time in 64D

the Annulus Method and Double Annulus Method gain ground. Again, Orchard's Method performs extremely well for small codebooks, but slows down as the lists are shortened.

5. PCP/k-d Trees

The PCP tree was used in order to take advantage of the fact that the data are clustered along a line. Unfortunately, this fact is only true on the large scale: a small collection of neighboring vectors do not exhibit such clustering (in fact, they

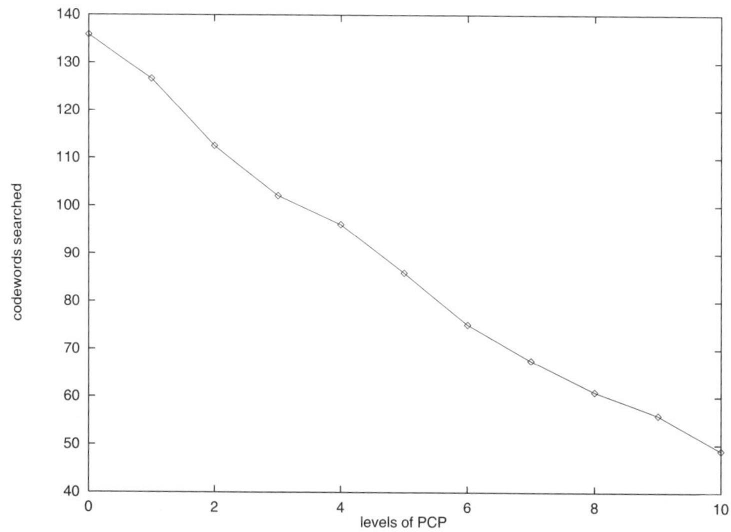

FIGURE 14. Levels of PCP v. Codewords Searched

appear to be almost uniformly random). The PCP nodes near the top of the tree are worth the extra expense, but the PCP nodes near the bottom of the tree are not earning their keep.

One solution is to use a mixed PCP/k-d tree. The first m levels of the tree are made up of the expensive PCP nodes and the rest of the levels are made up of lightweight k-d nodes. The number m is a parameter which we can vary.

Figure 14 shows the number of codewords searched as m, the number of levels of PCP nodes, is varied. (This figure is using 1024 16D codewords.) We can see that every extra level of PCP nodes causes fewer codeword to be searched. However, the levels near the bottom of the tree cause less of a decrease than those at the top. Figure 15 shows the execution time as m is varied. We can see that at some point adding extra levels of PCP nodes does not increase performance: the decrease in codewords searched does not make up for the extra expense of the PCP nodes. This is the point where the curve bottoms out.

The value of m for which the PCP/k-d tree performs best appears to depend on the dimension. In lower dimension, where the k-d tree performs well, the best value of m will be smaller. In higher dimension, where the PCP tree performs well, the best value of m will be larger. In general, the best value of m should remain strictly less than the height of the tree: it is almost never beneficial to use a PCP node to partition 2 vectors.

Figure 16 shows the running times of the algorithms in 4, 16, and 64 dimensions for a codebook of size 4,096. (Double–Annulus Method was left out as it always performed worse than Annulus Method.) We can see that PCP/k-d tree performs well in all cases. In 4D, the best PCP/k-d tree is a k-d tree, so its running time is equal to that of k-d tree which is the fastest. In 16D, the PCP/k-d tree is around 45% faster than k-d tree and around 15% faster than PCP Tree. In 64D, the PCP/k-d tree is around 75% faster than k-d tree and around 20% faster than PCP tree.

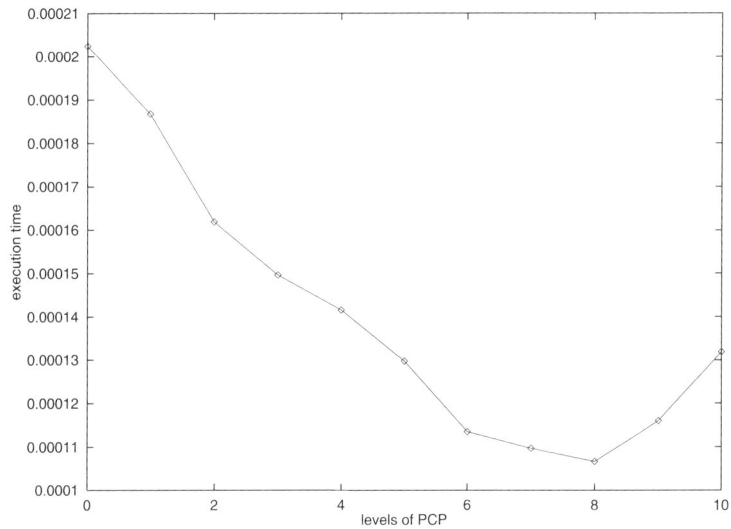

FIGURE 15. Levels of PCP v. Execution Time

	Orchard	Annulus	k-d	PCP	PCP/k-d
4D	0.065	0.585	0.044	0.076	0.044
16D	0.61	1.36	1.31	0.87	0.73
64D	2.9	5.1	18.2	5.4	4.3

FIGURE 16. Running Times of the Algorithms for 4,096 Codewords (in msec)

6. Summary

In this paper, we saw six nearest neighbor search algorithms for performing Vector Quantization, all of which greatly outperform "brute-force" search. We summarize our conclusions as follows.

- Orchard's Method has wonderful performance, especially in high dimension. Unfortunately, its $O(n^2)$ memory requirement make it impractical for large codebooks. We can lessen its memory requirement by using shorter lists; however, this quickly decreases performance.
- The Annulus Method is a simple algorithm that works well for small codebooks in high dimension.
- The Double Annulus Method is a variation on Annulus Method that does not appear to have better performance than the simpler Annulus Method in most situations.
- The k-d tree nearest neighbor search algorithm is the fastest algorithm in low dimension.
- The PCP tree nearest neighbor search algorithm is faster than the k-d tree algorithm in higher dimension. However, the nodes near the bottom of the tree provide little benefit over k-d nodes despite their extra expense.

- The PCP/k-d tree combines the strengths of PCP and k-d trees to obtain good performance in all dimensions and codebook sizes.

References

[1] S. Arya and D.M. Mount. Algorithms for fast vector quantization. In *Proceedings Data Compression Conference*, pages 381–390. IEEE, March 1993.
[2] C. D. Bei and R. M. Gray. An improvement of the minimum distortion encoding algorithm for vector quantization. *IEEE Transactions on Communications*, pages 1132–1133, October 1985.
[3] J. L. Bentley. Multidimensional binary search trees used for associative searching. *Communications of the ACM*, 18:509–517, September 1975.
[4] Jerome H. Friedman, Jon Louis Bentley, and Raphael Ari Finkel. An algorithm for finding best matches in logarithmic expected time. *ACM Transactions on Mathematical Software*, 3(3):209–226, September 1977.
[5] A. Gersho and R.M. Gray. *Vector Quantization and Signal Compression*. Kluwer, Boston, MA, July 1992.
[6] R. M. Gray. Vector quantization. *IEEE ASSP Magazine*, 1:4–29, April 1984.
[7] C. M. Huang, Q. Bi, G. S. Stiles, and R. W Harris. Fast full search equivalent encoding algorithms for image compression using vector quantization. *IEEE Transactions on Image Processing*, 1(3):413–416, July 1992.
[8] USC-SIPI Image Database. http://sipi.usc.edu/services/database/database.html.
[9] M. H. Johnson, R. Ladner, and E. A. Riskin. Fast nearest neighbor search of entropy-constrained vector quantization. *IEEE Transactions on Image Processing*, 9:1435–1437, August 2000.
[10] Y. Linde, A. Bruzo, and R. M. Gray. An algorithm for vector quantizer design. *IEEE Transactions on Communication*, 28:84–95, January 1980.
[11] Michael T. Orchard. A fast nearest-neighbor search algorithm. In *ICASSP 91: 1991 International Conference on Acoustics, Speech and Signal Processing*, volume 4, pages 2297–3000, New York, NY, USA, April 1991. IEEE.
[12] E. A. Riskin, R. Ladner, R.-Y. Wang, and L. E. Atlas. Index assignment for progressive transmission of full-search vector quantization. *IEEE Transactions on Image Processing*, 3(3):307–312, May 1994.
[13] R.L. Sproull. Refinements to nearest-neighbor searching in k dimensional trees. *Algorithmica*, 6:579–589, 1991.
[14] G.W. Stewart. *Introdution to Matrix Computations*. Academic Press, New York, NY, July 1973.
[15] R.-Y. Wang. *Organization of Fixed Rate Vector Quantization Codebooks*. Dissertation, University of Washington, July 1994.
[16] X. Wu and K. Zhang. A better tree-structured vector quantizer. In *Proceedings Data Compression Conference*, pages 392–401. IEEE, April 1991.

Department of Computer Science and Engineering, University of Washington, Seattle, WA 98195, USA
E-mail address: kevinz@cs.washington.edu

Department of Electrical Engineering, University of Washington, Seattle, WA 98195, USA
E-mail address: mhjohns@cs.washington.edu

Department of Computer Science and Engineering, University of Washington, Seattle, WA 98195, USA
E-mail address: ladner@cs.washington.edu

DIMACS Series in Discrete Mathematics
and Theoretical Computer Science
Volume **59**, 2002

Experimental Evaluation of Disk-Based Data Structures for Nearest Neighbor Searching

Norio Katayama and Shin'ichi Satoh

ABSTRACT. Nearest neighbor search attracts much interest of database researchers, since it plays an important role in multimedia database systems. Database researchers have tackled this problem by devising disk-based data structures for the acceleration of nearest neighbor searching. These data structures are similar to the well-known main-memory data structure, the k-d tree. However, they have two distinct features that are especially advantageous to large-scale persistent databases: one is the variance-based tree construction algorithm and the other is data-space partitioning with minimum bounding rectangles. Both features are advantageous for the reduction of disk I/O. This paper demonstrates these significant advantages through experimental evaluation. The contribution of this paper is twofold. Firstly, the effectiveness of the disk-based data structures are examined by applying them to practical multimedia applications, namely similarity retrieval of images and video scenes. Secondly, the merit and the demerit of disk-based data structures are clarified through the comparison with the main-memory data structures.

1. Introduction

Nearest neighbor search attracts much interest of database researchers, since it plays an important role in multimedia database systems. Nearest neighbor search is the principal component of the similarity retrieval of multimedia information. Each piece of multimedia information is mapped to a vector in a multi-dimensional space where the distance between two vectors corresponds to the similarity of multimedia information. These vectors and the space are called feature vectors and feature space respectively. Once the feature space is obtained, the similarity retrieval of multimedia information is reduced to nearest neighbor search in the feature space. One of the typical examples of the feature space is the color histogram of an image, which indicates what portion of an image has a specific color (e.g., red, blue, green, etc.). One of the important properties of the feature space is high dimensionality. It is very common to use 10 or higher dimensional space for the feature space. For example, colors are often classified into 16 or more colors for color histograms. This generates 16 or more dimensional feature vectors.

Thus, nearest neighbor search in high-dimensional space is one of the key components of multimedia database systems, and database researchers have tackled this

1991 *Mathematics Subject Classification.* Primary 68P05, 68P10, 68P20.
Key words and phrases. Nearest neighbor search, similarity retrieval.

problem by devising disk-based data structures for the acceleration of nearest neighbor searching. These data structures are similar to the well-known main-memory data structure, the k-d tree[**1**]. However, they have two distinct features that are especially advantageous to large-scale persistent databases: one is the variance-based tree construction algorithm and the other is data-space partitioning with minimum bounding rectangles. Both features are advantageous for the reduction of disk I/O (i.e., input from and output to disk storage). This paper demonstrates these significant advantages through experimental evaluation. The contribution of this paper is twofold. Firstly, the effectiveness of the disk-based data structures are examined by applying them to practical multimedia applications, namely similarity retrieval of images and video scenes. Secondly, the merit and the demerit of disk-based data structures are clarified through the comparison with the main-memory data structures.

This paper is organized as follows. Section 2 gives the brief introduction of disk-based data structures for nearest neighbor searching. Section 3 shows the results of the experimental evaluation by applying the data structures to multimedia applications, namely similarity retrieval of images and video scenes. Section 4 compares the disk-based data structures with the k-d tree. Section 5 contains conclusions.

2. Disk-Based Data Structures for NN-Search

2.1. Properties of Disk-Based Data Structures. Quite a few disk-based data structures have been proposed for high-dimensional nearest neighbor search: k-d-tree-like tree structures[**2, 3, 4, 5, 6**], a new space-partitioning method[**7**], an information compression technique[**8**], etc. Among these methods, some of the most promising techniques are the k-d-tree-like tree structures, because they allow us to expect the sub-linear search time in the practical cases. Nearest neighbor search using tree structures might fall into linear search in the worst case, e.g., in the case where the point density is too low. There is no guarantee that a search completes in sub-linear time. However, in the practical use, we can expect sub-linear search time. Therefore, this paper focuses on the evaluation of these k-d-tree-like tree structures.

The k-d-tree-like tree structures are based on space partitioning like the k-d tree. However, they have different properties from the k-d tree since they are disk-based data structures and aimed at large-scale persistent databases. The difference between the disk-based data structures and the main-memory data structures is as follows:

- While main-memory data structures are located on primary memory, disk-based data structures are located on secondary storage.
- Since reading from and writing to secondary storage is much slower than main memory, the reduction of disk access is crucial for disk-based data structures.
- Since secondary storage is usually organized by fixed-size data blocks (their typical sizes are 4,096 and 8,192 bytes), disk-based data structures need to be optimized for block input and output in order to exploit efficient disk I/O.
- Since persistent databases are usually maintained with the online addition and removal of data, disk-based data structures should support dynamic

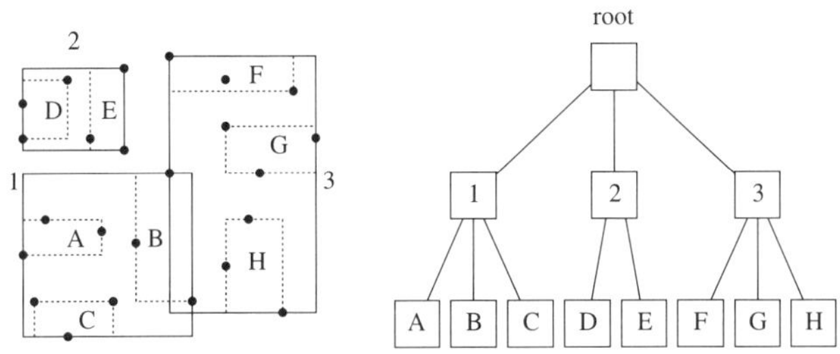

FIGURE 1. Structure of the R-tree.

update efficiently. Reorganization of an entire tree is significantly expensive for disk-resident persistent databases.

Thus, the reduction of disk I/O and the efficient support of dynamic update is the prominent property of disk-based data structures. The k-d tree is not necessarily suitable for disk-based data structures, since it does not support dynamic update efficiently. It might need entire reconstruction if it were seriously unbalanced with dynamic update[**9**].

2.2. The R-tree. The R-tree[**10**] is the most successful multidimensional data structure in database applications. The difference between the k-d tree and the R-tree is the way of managing internal nodes. The internal node of the k-d tree keeps the information of how the data space is split. On the other hand, the internal node of the R-tree keeps the information of partitioned sub-regions. In addition, the R-tree is an n-ary tree and each node is stored in a disk block. The size of a disk block determines how many children can be adopted by a single internal node. Each internal node of the R-tree stores bounding rectangles of child regions as follows:

$$InternalNode_{R\text{-}tree} := \langle\ \langle MBR_1, \mathit{offset}_1\rangle,\ \ldots\ ,\ \langle MBR_n, \mathit{offset}_n\rangle\ \rangle$$

where n is the number of children, MBR_i $(1 \le i \le n)$ denotes the minimum bounding rectangle of the ith child node, and offset_i $(1 \le i \le n)$ denotes the offset address of the ith child node in the disk storage. Thus, the R-tree is an n-ary tree and its tree structure corresponds to the hierarchy of rectangular regions (Figure 1). The upper bound of n is determined by the size of a disk block. A non-internal node, or a leaf node, stores the same information as the bucket node of the k-d tree:

$$NonInternalNode_{R\text{-}tree} := \langle\ \langle \boldsymbol{p}_1, attribute_1\rangle,\ \ldots\ ,\ \langle \boldsymbol{p}_n, attribute_n\rangle\ \rangle$$

where $\boldsymbol{p}_i$ $(1 \le i \le n)$ denotes a data point in the data space, and $attribute_i$ $(1 \le i \le n)$ denotes an arbitrary attribute associated to the data point, e.g., the pointer to a data record.

Although the employment of the minimum bounding rectangles increases the amount of information and the processing cost of internal nodes, this is the key to the efficient support of dynamic update. The R-tree supports dynamic update efficiently by allowing overlap among sub-regions, while the k-d tree partitions the data space into disjoint sub-regions. By relaxing the restriction on the region overlap, the R-tree successfully keeps being balanced and circumvents the reorganization of the entire tree on dynamic update. Besides, this relaxation enables the R-tree to store

TABLE 1. Properties of the SS-tree, SR-tree, and VAMSplit R-tree.

	SS-tree	SR-tree	VAMSplit R-tree
dynamic construction	variance-based algorithm	the same with the SS-tree	N.A.
static construction	N.A.	N.A.	variance-based algorithm
internal node entry	1. centroid 2. weight 3. bounding sphere radius 4. child node offset	1. centroid 2. weight 3. bounding sphere radius 4. minimum bounding rectangle 5. child node offset	1. minimum bounding rectangle 2. child node offset (the same with the R-tree)
size of internal node entry	sizeof(float)$\times(d+1)$ + sizeof(integer) + sizeof(offset)	sizeof(float)$\times(3d+1)$ + sizeof(integer) + sizeof(offset)	sizeof(float)$\times 2d$ + sizeof(offset) (the same with the R-tree)

not only points but also spatial objects, i.e., objects with extent. In this case, non-internal nodes store rectangles $\boldsymbol{R}_i$ instead of points $\boldsymbol{p}_i$ (This is the generic design of the R-tree. The R-tree is originally designed as a data structure for spatial objects). Apparently, the overlap among sub-regions degrades the search performance, since overlapped regions are likely to increase the number of nodes to be visited during the search operation. Therefore, elaborate algorithms have been proposed for the construction of the R-tree. The most successful one is the R*-tree[**11**]. We omit the description of the construction algorithm of the R*-tree, since it is beyond the scope of this paper.

2.3. R-tree Variants for Nearest Neighbor Search. Originally, the R-tree has been proposed for geometric database systems and mainly aimed at the acceleration of range search, i.e., searching for such spatial objects that resides in the specified search range which is usually given as a rectangular area. The recent research results[**4, 5**] show that the R-tree does not have good performance with respect to nearest neighbor search in high-dimensional space. Therefore, variants of the R-tree have been proposed for the acceleration of high-dimensional nearest neighbor search[**2, 3, 4, 5**]. Among such data structures, the SS-tree[**2**], the SR-tree[**5**], and the VAMSplit R-tree[**3**] demonstrate good performance in high-dimensional nearest neighbor search by employing variance-based construction algorithms.

Table 1 shows the properties of the SS-tree, the SR-tree, and the VAMSplit R-tree. The SS-tree and the SR-tree are designed for the dynamic construction, i.e., building a tree with dynamic update. Both the SS-tree and the SR-tree employ the construction algorithm originally proposed for the SS-tree by D. A. White and R. Jain[**2**], which will be described in Section 2.5. On the other hand, the VAMSplit R-tree is designed for the static construction, i.e., building a tree for given points all at

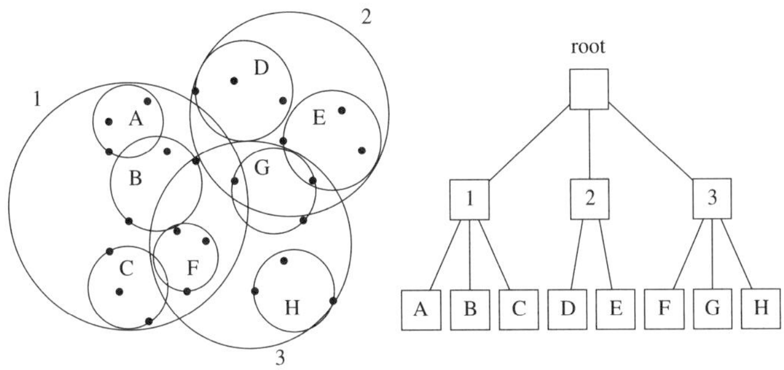

FIGURE 2. Structure of the SS-tree.

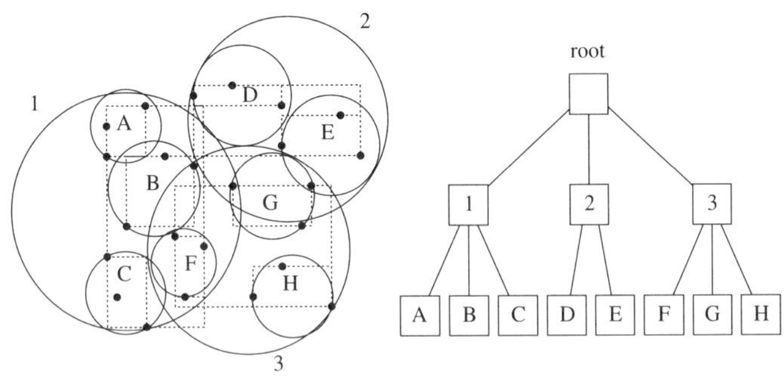

FIGURE 3. Structure of the SR-tree.

once. The VAMSplit R-tree is an R-tree built with a static construction algorithm called the VAMSplit which is also proposed by D. A. White and R. Jain[**3**]. Hence, the structure of the VAMSplit R-tree is identical to the R-tree. The construction algorithm of the VAMSplit R-tree will be described in Section 2.6.

The difference between the SS-tree and the SR-tree is entries of internal nodes. An internal node of the SS-tree has the following entries:

$$InternalNode_{SS\text{-}tree} := \langle\, \langle \boldsymbol{c}_1, w_1, r_1, \mathit{offset}_1\rangle,\ \ldots\ ,\ \langle \boldsymbol{c}_n, w_n, r_n, \mathit{offset}_n\rangle \,\rangle\,,$$

where $\boldsymbol{c}_i$ $(1 \le i \le n)$ denotes the centroid of the ith child node, i.e., the centroid of the points contained in the subtree whose root node is the ith child node, w_i $(1 \le i \le n)$ denotes the weight of the ith child node, i.e., the number of the points in the subtree, and r_i $(1 \le i \le n)$ denotes the radius of the minimum bounding sphere that covers all points in the subtree and whose center is $\boldsymbol{c}_i$. Thus, the SS-tree employs minimum bounding spheres instead of minimum bounding rectangles. The tree structure of the SS-tree corresponds to the hierarchy of spherical regions (Figure 2). The centroids $\boldsymbol{c}_1, \ldots, \boldsymbol{c}_n$ and the weights $w_1, \ldots, w_n$ play an important role in the variance-based construction algorithm. They make it possible to estimate the variance of the data distribution at each internal node. The SS-tree outperforms the R-tree by virtue of the variance-based algorithm as will be shown in the experimental evaluation.

The SR-tree is an enhancement of the SS-tree. It employs both the bounding sphere and the bounding rectangle as follows:

$$InternalNode_{SR\text{-}tree} :=$$
$$\langle\ \langle \boldsymbol{c}_1, w_1, r_1, MBR_1, \mathit{offset}_1 \rangle,\ \ldots\ ,\ \langle \boldsymbol{c}_n, w_n, r_n, MBR_n, \mathit{offset}_n \rangle\ \rangle$$

where $\boldsymbol{c}_i$, w_i, and r_i $(1 \leq i \leq n)$ are the same with those of the SS-tree, and MBR_i $(1 \leq i \leq n)$ denotes the minimum bounding rectangle of the ith child node. Thus, the difference between the SS-tree and the SR-tree is the addition of MBR_i. Each sub-region of the SR-tree is determined by the intersection of the bounding sphere (given by $\boldsymbol{c}_i$ and r_i) and the bounding rectangle (given by MBR_i). The tree structure of the SR-tree corresponds to the hierarchy of such regions (Figure 3). The experimental evaluation has proven that the incorporation of minimum bounding rectangles improves the performance of nearest neighbor search because minimum bounding rectangles reduce the region size of each node[**5**].

2.4. NN-Search Algorithms for the R-tree and its Variants. The NN-search algorithms for the R-tree and its variants are similar to those for the k-d tree. The difference resides in the way of computing the distance from the query point to each sub-region. Since the R-tree and its variants store bounding rectangles and/or bounding spheres of child regions in each internal node, the distance from the query point to sub-regions is computed by the distance to the bounding rectangles and/or the bounding spheres. Similarly to the k-d tree, the NN-search algorithms for the R-tree and its variants are classified into the depth-first search and the breadth-first search. The depth-first search proposed by Roussopoulos et al.[**12**] is the counterpart of the standard k-d tree search algorithm which is proposed by Friedman et al.[**13**], refined by Sproull[**14**], and by Arya and Mount[**15**]. The breadth-first search proposed by Hjaltason and Samet[**16**] is the counterpart of the priority search algorithm proposed by Arya and Mount[**15**].

Hjaltason et al.[**16**] and Berchtold et al.[**17**] showed that the breadth-first search visits only the minimum number of nodes, i.e., it achieves the optimal disk I/O. Berchtold et al.[**17**] presented the cost model of the breadth-first search with accounting for boundary effects and with using the L_2 metric, which is more practical for database applications than the cost models proposed for the k-d tree[**13, 18**].

2.5. Tree-Construction Algorithm of the SS-tree and the SR-tree. The tree-construction algorithm of the SS-tree and the SR-tree consists of the following three rules:

Rule 1: When a new point is to be inserted into a tree, the most suitable non-internal node to accommodate the new point is determined by the tree traversal from the root node to a non-internal node. At each internal node, the subtree whose centroid is the nearest to the point is chosen as the most suitable subtree to accommodate the new point.

Rule 2: When a node is full, a portion of its entries are orphaned and reinserted from the root node unless reinsertion has been made at the same node; otherwise it will be split into two nodes according to Rule 3. Entries which are farther from the centroid than the rest are chosen for the reinsertion.

Rule 3: When a node is to be split, the coordinate variance on each dimension is calculated and the dimension with the largest variance is chosen for the split dimension. After the entries are sorted along the dimension, the split position is located at the position where the sum of subtrees' variances is smallest.

The effectiveness of this algorithm is demonstrated through performance experiments [**2, 5**]. However, the rationale for its validity have not been clarified yet. Roughly speaking, this algorithm can be regarded as a clustering algorithm which tries to reduce the variances of regions based on local characteristics. Its effectiveness will be demonstrated in Section 3 by applying it to comprehensive and practical workloads.

2.6. Tree-Construction Algorithm of the VAMSplit R-tree. The VAMSplit R-tree is an R-tree built with a static construction algorithm called the VAMSplit[**3**]. The VAMSplit algorithm is very similar to the construction algorithm of the k-d tree. It splits the data space into disjoint regions as the k-d tree does. It splits the data space along such dimension whose variance is the largest. The split position is almost the median but it is slightly slid in order to generate such nodes that are fulfilled up to the maximum capacity. This is achieved by the number of points contained in a one-side region forced to be a multiple of the maximum capacity of a subtree. This sliding capability guarantees the VAMSplit R-tree to generate the minimum number of nodes and reduces disk I/O of NN-search operations. The name "VAMSplit" is named after the split orientation that is based on the *variance* and the split position that is *approximately* the *median*.

The VAMSplit consists of two parts: the choice of the split dimension and the choice of the split position. The major part is the choice of the split dimension, because the split position is determined by the node capacity regardless of data distribution. The dimension with the largest variance is chosen as the split dimension. This choice is identical to that of the SS-tree and the SR-tree. Similar to the SS-tree and the SR-tree, this algorithm can be regarded as a clustering algorithm which tries to reduce the variances of regions based on local characteristics.

3. Experimental Evaluation with Multimedia Applications

3.1. Similarity Retrieval of Images with NN-Search. We ran an experiment on the similarity retrieval of images in order to evaluate the performance of the SS-tree, the SR-tree, and the VAMSplit R-tree when they are used with practical multimedia application[1] (Figure 4). 40,745 images are collected from the photo and the video archives of NASA (Johnson Space Center[**19**], Keneddy Space Center[**20**], NASA Shuttle Web[**21**]). As for videos, scene changes are detected based on the transition of the color histogram and then representative images of each scene are extracted. The similarity of images is measured in terms of the color histogram. Munsell color system is used for the color space, which consists of hue, saturation, and intensity dimensions. It is divided into nine subspaces: black, gray, white, and six colors. For each image, histograms of four sub-regions, i.e., upper-left, upper-right, lower-left and lower-right, are calculated in order to take account of the composition of the image. Four histograms are concatenated to compose a 36-dimensional feature vector. Then, feature vectors are reduced to 20-dimensional vectors with the principal component analysis. Similarity of images

[1]The online demonstration of this experiment is available at our web site: http://research.nii.ac.jp/~katayama/homepage/research/srtree/demo/

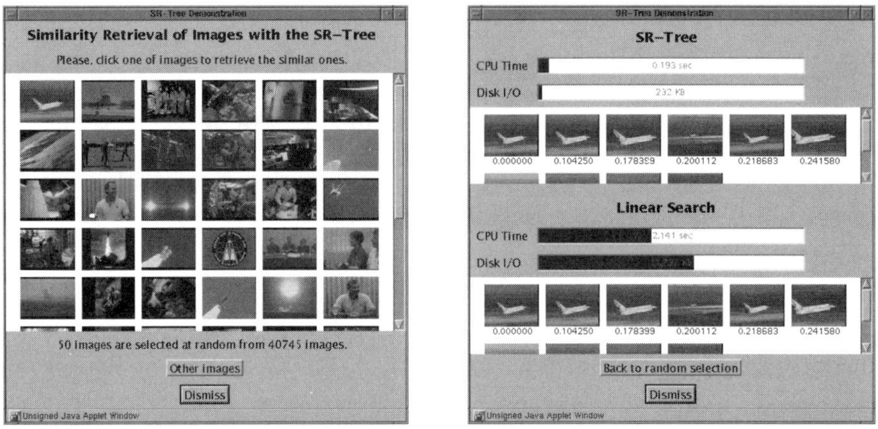

FIGURE 4. Online demonstration of the similarity retrieval of images.

TABLE 2. Characteristics of the data set.

Rank	Eigen Value (Variance)	Proportion (%)	Cumulative (%)	Minimum	Maximum	Spread
1	0.3121	24.40	24.40	-1.319	1.097	2.42
2	0.1858	14.53	38.92	-1.332	1.094	2.43
3	0.1590	12.43	51.35	-0.962	1.662	2.62
4	0.1590	12.43	63.78	-1.075	1.609	2.68
5	0.0828	6.48	70.26	-0.608	1.842	2.45
6	0.0590	4.61	74.87	-1.114	1.066	2.18
7	0.0364	2.85	77.71	-0.575	1.412	1.99
8	0.0355	2.78	80.49	-1.079	0.730	1.81
9	0.0300	2.34	82.83	-0.953	1.020	1.97
10	0.0269	2.10	84.93	-0.818	0.854	1.67
11	0.0185	1.44	86.38	-0.769	0.976	1.74
12	0.0176	1.37	87.75	-0.721	0.870	1.59
13	0.0171	1.34	89.09	-0.469	1.579	2.05
14	0.0161	1.26	90.34	-0.978	0.772	1.75
15	0.0135	1.05	91.40	-0.668	0.677	1.34
16	0.0120	0.94	92.33	-0.643	0.687	1.33
17	0.0099	0.77	93.10	-0.626	0.960	1.59
18	0.0099	0.77	93.87	-0.708	0.782	1.49
19	0.0085	0.66	94.53	-0.621	0.552	1.17
20	0.0069	0.54	95.07	-0.549	0.528	1.08

TABLE 3. Node capacity (dimension: 20, block size: 8,192, attribute size: 128).

	Internal Node	Non-Internal Node
R*-tree/VAMSplit R-tree	25	28
SS-tree	46	28
SR-tree	16	28

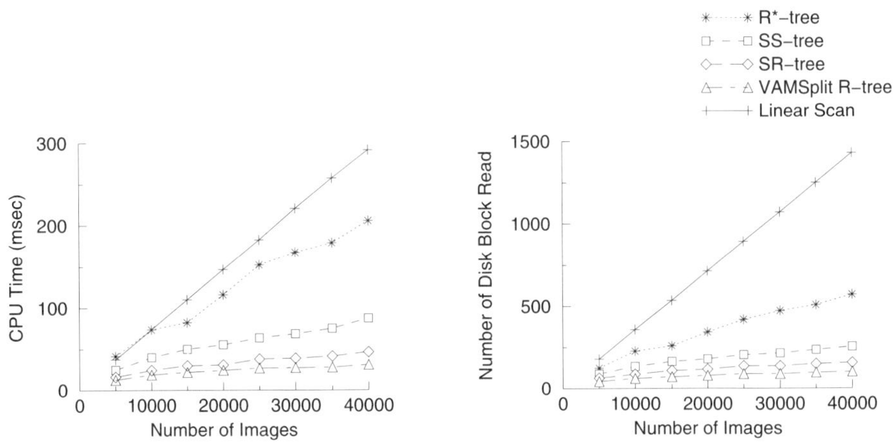

(a) Results of all data structures

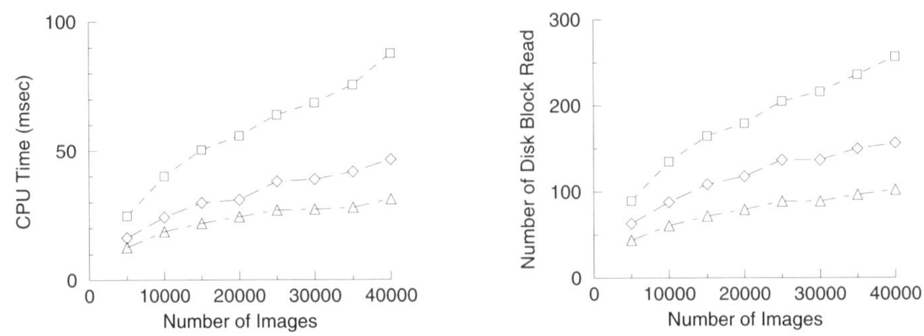

(b) Results of the SS-tree, the SR-tree, and the VAMSplit R-tree

FIGURE 5. Performance on the similarity retrieval of images.

is measured by Euclidean distance among these 20-dimensional vectors. Table 2 shows the characteristics of the data set.

All tests of this paper are conducted on a Sun Microsystems workstation, Ultra 60 (CPU: UltraSPARC-II 360MHz, main memory: 512Mbytes, OS: Solaris 2.6). All programs are implemented in C++. The size of disk blocks is set to 8,192 bytes. The size of an attribute associated to each point in a non-internal node is set to 128 bytes. This configuration determines the node capacity as shown in Table 3.

We composed multiple data sets, whose sizes varies from 5,000 to 40,000 by selecting subsets of images at random. For each data set, we measured the average performance of 1,000 random trials of finding 10 nearest neighbors. Query points are selected at random from the data set. Therefore, one of ten found neighbors is a query point itself. This workload is designed based on the "query by example" scheme of image database systems, i.e., a user picks up a query image from the contents of a database and the system returns several images similar to the query. The breadth-first search algorithm[**16**] that achieves the optimal disk I/O is used as the NN-search algorithm. Figure 5 shows the result of the experiment. The

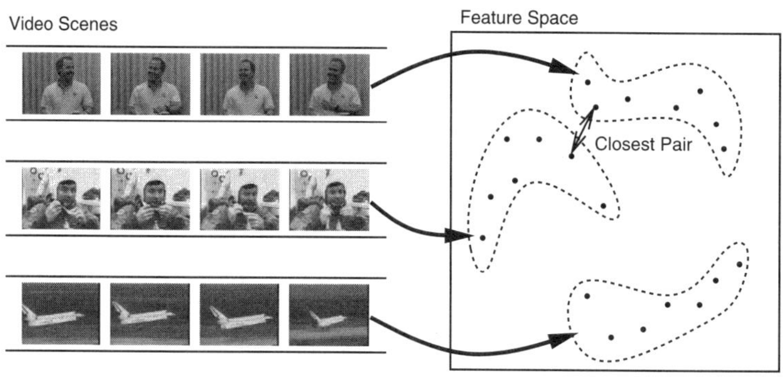

FIGURE 6. Similarity retrieval of video scenes.

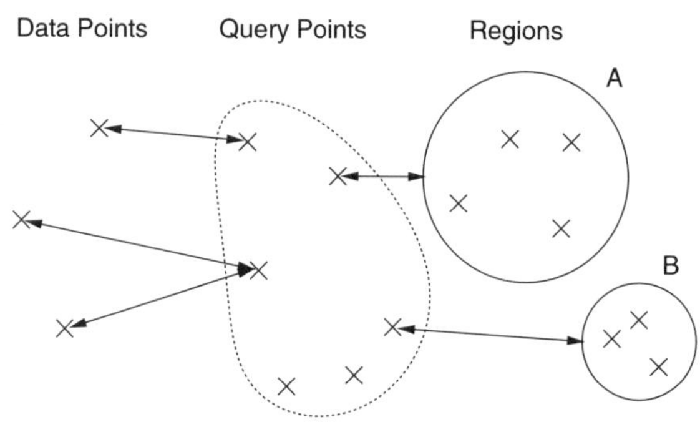

FIGURE 7. Distance from query points to data points and regions.

horizontal axis indicates the size of the data set, while the vertical axis indicates the CPU time and the number of disk block reads, i.e., the number of visited nodes. The upper half shows the results of all data structures, namely, the R*-tree, the SS-tree, the SR-tree, the VAMSplit R-tree, and the linear scan, while the lower half only shows the results of the SS-tree, the SR-tree, and the VAMSplit R-tree.

The VAMSplit R-tree achieves the best performance. When the data set size is 40,000, the CPU time of the VAMSplit R-tree is 11% of that of the linear scan and the number of disk block reads is 7.1%. The SR-tree reveals quite good performance even though it is built dynamically. Its performance is comparable to the VAMSplit R-tree. The increase of the CPU time is 48% and the increase of disk block reads is 53%. The SS-tree also achieves good performance but the increase of CPU time compared with the VAMSplit R-tree is 181% and the increase of disk block reads is 152%. These results verify the effectiveness of the data structures built by the variance-based construction algorithms.

3.2. Similarity Retrieval of Video Scenes with Colored NN-Search. In multimedia applications, an object to be indexed often generates more than one feature vectors. A typical example is the indexing of video scenes where a

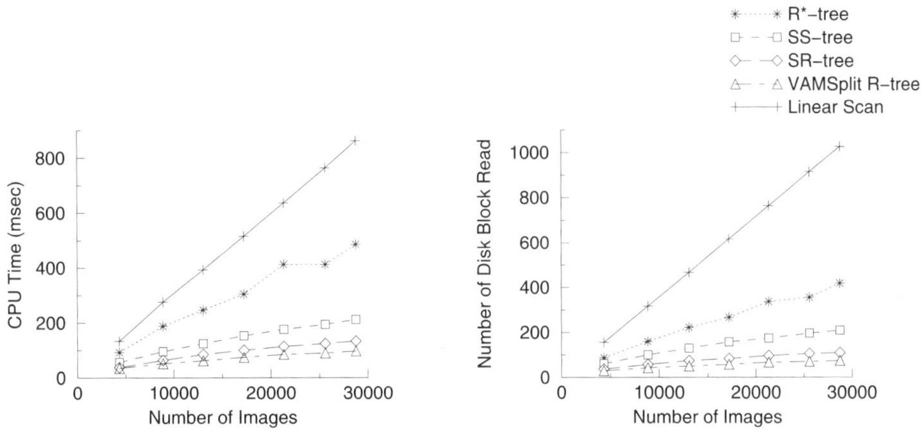

(a) Results of all data structures

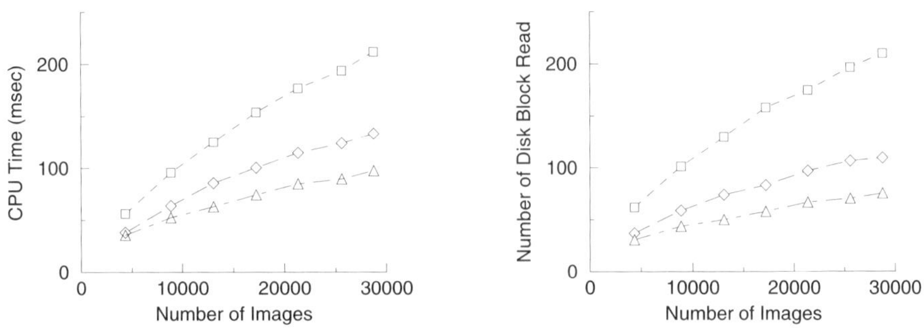

(b) Results of the SS-tree, the SR-tree, and the VAMSplit R-tree

FIGURE 8. Performance on the similarity retrieval of video scenes.

scene is characterized with feature vectors of one or more representative images (Figure 6). In this case, the similarity between two video scenes is measured by the distance between their closest-pair. This means that two video scenes are supposed to be similar if they share similar images. This type of metric is also used in the computer vision applications. For example, Nayar et al.[**22**] employs this metric in their appearance matching system which identifies objects according to their appearance.

This type of nearest neighbor search can be understood as colored nearest neighbor search. The goal of the search is to find the color which gives the most adjacent closest-pair. This search can be accomplished with the slight modification of the non-colored nearest neighbor search algorithm as follows. The modified algorithm shares distance computations and disk I/Os among a set of query points.

(1) A query is given as a set of points, instead of a single point.
(2) The result of a query is a color which provides the most adjacent closest-pair.

(3) During the search operation, the distance from the query points to a data point or a region is determined by a query point which is closest to the data point or the region (Figure 7). Then, similar to the non-colored NN-search, regions closer to query points are searched before the others. For example, the region A in Figure 7 will be searched before the region B.

We ran an experiment to evaluate the performance of the disk-based data structures for the colored NN-search. The data set is a subset of the one used in Section 3.1. While the original data set consists of images from photos and videos, only such images that are extracted from videos are selected for the new data set. Then, they are colored with the identifiers of videos. Since every video is very short and usually consists of only one scene, we can assume that each video corresponds to a single scene.

The data set contains 28,753 feature vectors of images which are extracted from 1,348 videos. Thus, each video is characterized by 21 feature vectors on average. We composed six subsets of the data set by sampling videos at random. The subsets contain 200 videos (4,348 vectors), 400 videos (8,876 vectors), 600 videos (13,060 vectors), 800 videos (17,235 vectors), 1,000 videos (21,368 vectors), and 1,200 videos (25,604 vectors), respectively. 2,242 feature vectors of 100 videos, which are not included in data points, are used for queries. The performance is measured with these 100 queries.

Figure 8 shows the results of the experiment. The horizontal axis indicates the size of the data set, i.e., the number of feature vectors, while the vertical axis indicates the CPU time and the number of disk block reads. The upper half shows the results of all data structures, namely, the R*-tree, the SS-tree, the SR-tree, the VAMSplit R-tree, and the linear scan, while the lower half only shows the results of the SS-tree, the SR-tree, and the VAMSplit R-tree.

The VAMSplit R-tree achieves the best performance. When the data set size is 28,753, the CPU time of the VAMSplit R-tree is 11% of that of the linear scan and the number of disk block reads is 7.4%. The SR-tree reveals quite good performance even though it is built dynamically. Its performance is comparable to the VAMSplit R-tree. The increase of the CPU time is 36% and the increase of disk block reads is 45%. The SS-tree also achieves good performance but the increase of CPU time compared with the VAMSplit R-tree is 117% and the increase of disk block reads is 178%. These results verify the applicability of the disk-based data structures to colored NN-search.

4. Comparing Disk-Based Data Structures with the k-d Tree

4.1. ANN: an Implementation of the k-d Tree. In order to clarify the merits and demerits of the disk-based data structures, we compared them with the well-known main-memory data structure, the k-d tree. We used an implementation of the k-d tree, called ANN, which is written by David M. Mount of the University of Maryland and Sunil Arya of the Hong Kong University of Science and Technology[2].

We compared the performance of the disk-based data structures with that of the k-d tree in terms of CPU time and disk I/O. It is natural to compare CPU time. However, disk I/O cannot be directly compared, because the k-d tree implementation is not intended to be used as a disk-based data structure. Therefore, we

[2]The ANN home page: http://www.cs.umd.edu/~mount/ANN

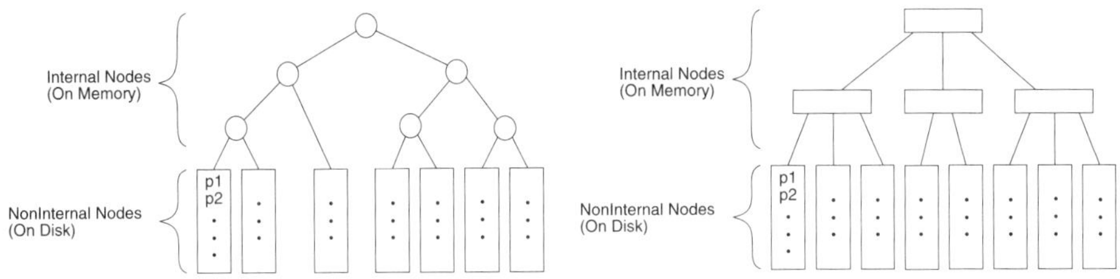

(a) k-d tree (b) disk-based data structures

FIGURE 9. Assumptions in comparing the disk-based data structure with the k-d tree.

employed the number of non-internal node visits as a measure of disk I/O basing on the following assumptions:

- The k-d tree is used as a disk-based data structure with internal nodes being located on primary memory and with non-internal nodes being located on secondary storage (Figure 9 (a)). Each non-internal node is stored in a disk block. The size of a disk block determines the bucket size of a non-internal node.
- Internal nodes of the disk-based data structures are also stored on primary memory; disk block read occurs only for non-internal nodes (Figure 9 (b)). This assumption is not impractical since internal nodes are likely to be cached on primary memory in practical cases.

Before comparing ANN with the disk-based data structures, we compared the construction algorithms of the k-d tree. We compared the following five algorithms. The first three algorithms come from the original implementation of ANN, while the remaining two algorithms are augmented by ourselves.

(1) standard split (ANN_KD_STD)
This algorithm splits the data space at the median along the axis having the maximum spread.
(2) midpoint split (ANN_KD_MIDPT)
This algorithm splits the data space at the midpoint along the axis having the maximum spread.
(3) sliding midpoint split (ANN_KD_SL_MIDPT)
This algorithm is a variant of the midpoint split. This prevents a trivial split which generates an empty node with sliding the split position to the upper or lower limit of the point location.
(4) maximum-variance median split (ANN_KD_MV_MEDIAN)
This algorithm splits the data space at the median along the axis having the maximum variance.
(5) maximum-variance approximate-median split (ANN_KD_MV_APPMED)
This algorithm is a variant of the maximum-variance median split. Similarly to the VAMSplit, this splits the data space at the approximate median along the axis having the maximum-variance. The split position is chosen where the number of points in a one-side region is the multiple of the bucket size. This fulfills non-internal nodes of the region and guarantees that the minimum number of nodes are generated. This algorithm

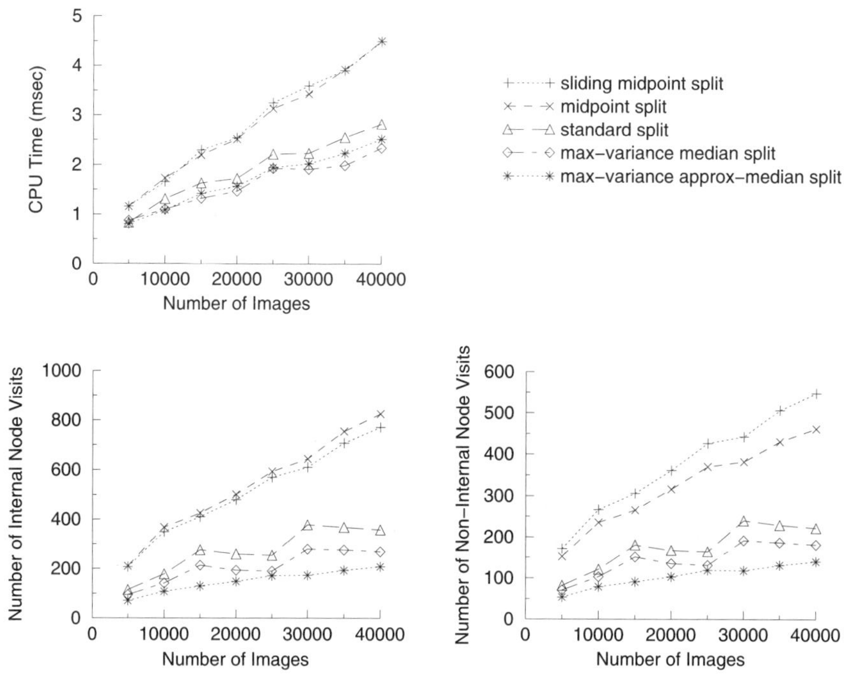

FIGURE 10. Performance of the k-d tree construction algorithms.

differs from the VAMSplit in that it packs only non-internal nodes into disk blocks, while the VAMSplit is designed to pack both internal and non-internal nodes into disk blocks.

The same experiment with Section 3.1 is conducted for the above construction algorithms. The bucket size of non-internal nodes is set to 28, which is equal to the non-internal node capacity of the disk-based data structures. The breadth-first search, i.e., the priority search algorithm, is employed as the NN-search algorithm, since it visits less nodes than the depth-first search.

Figure 10 shows the result. The maximum-variance median split outperforms other split algorithms. In terms of disk reads, the maximum-variance approximate-median split achieves the best performance. Its CPU time is slightly larger than that of the maximum-variance median split. However, the difference in CPU time is relatively smaller than the difference in disk block reads. According to these observations, we decided to use the maximum-variance approximate-median split for the split algorithm of the k-d tree.

4.2. Merits and Demerits of Disk-Based Data Structures. We compared the performance of the disk-based data structures with the performance of the k-d tree. Figure 11 shows the performance of the VAMSplit R-tree, the SR-tree, and the k-d tree. The left graph shows CPU time, while the right graph shows the number of non-internal node visits. The CPU time of the k-d tree is much smaller than that of the disk-based data structures. When the number of images is 40,000, the CPU time of the k-d tree is 8.0% of that of the VAMSplit R-tree and 5.4% of that of the SR-tree. On the other hand, the VAMSplit R-tree and the SR-tree

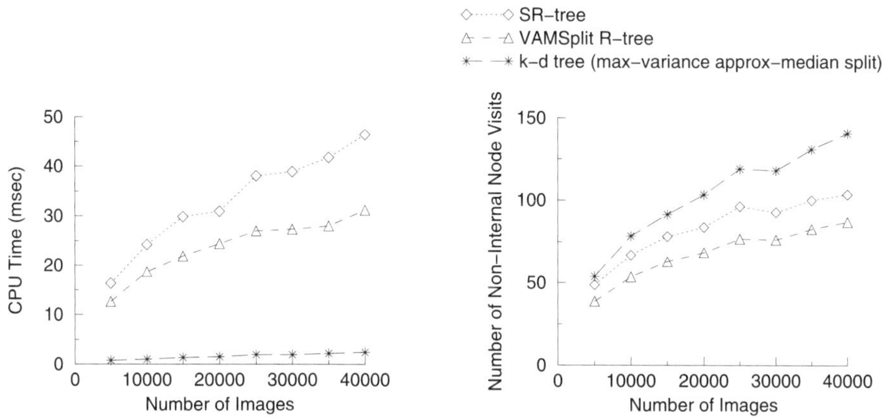

FIGURE 11. Performance of the VAMSplit R-tree, the SR-tree, and the k-d tree.

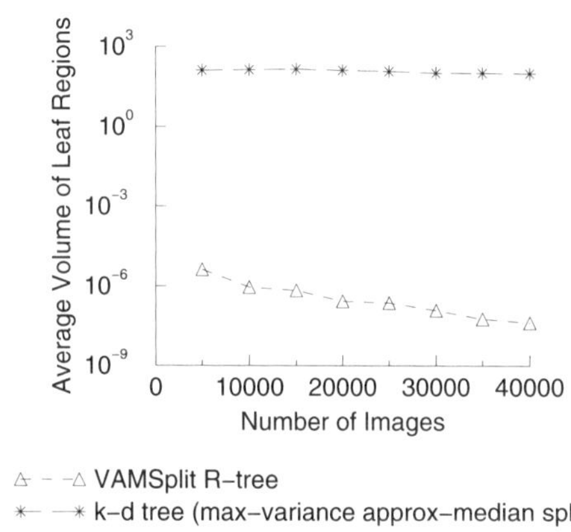

FIGURE 12. Average volume of non-internal node regions

visits less non-internal nodes than the k-d tree does. The number of non-internal node visits of the VAMSplit R-tree is 62% of that of the k-d tree, while the number of non-internal node visits of the SR-tree is 74% of that of the k-d tree. This result clearly indicates the merit and the demerit of the VAMSplit R-tree and the SR-tree: the merit is the reduction of disk I/O and the demerit is the increase of CPU time.

The reduction of disk I/O is achieved by the employment of minimum bounding rectangles. In this experiment, both the k-d tree and the VAMSplit R-tree employ the construction algorithm that splits the data space at the approximate median along the maximum variance axis. Therefore, the difference in disk I/O comes from the difference in the region management. While the k-d tree splits the data space into contiguous regions, the VAMSplit R-tree splits the data space into regions bounded by minimum bounding rectangles. The employment of the minimum bounding rectangle reduces the volume of regions. Figure 12 shows the average volume of non-internal node regions of the VAMSplit R-tree and the k-d tree. When the number of images is 40,000, the volume of the VAMSplit R-tree is 4.4×10^{-10}

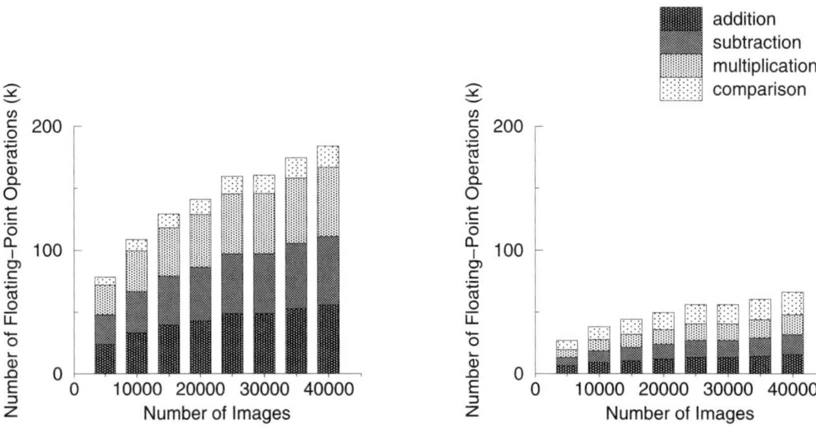

(a) VAMSplit R–tree

(b) k–d tree
(max–variance approx–median split)

FIGURE 13. Floating-point operations of the VAMSplit R-tree and the k-d tree.

of that of the k-d tree. Because the dimensionality is 20, this reduction in volume corresponds to 66% reduction in edge length ($1 - \sqrt[20]{4.4 \times 10^{-10}} = 0.66$). Thus, the employment of minimum bounding rectangles reduces disk I/O with decreasing the volume of non-internal node regions.

On the other hand, the employment of bounding rectangles increases CPU time as already shown in Figure 11. As for the increase of CPU time, we have to take it into account that the increase includes the overhead coming from the limitation of the implementation. Since the k-d tree implementation we used in the experiment is not intended to be used as a disk-based data structure, all information on the tree is stored on primary memory. Although the disk I/O of the k-d tree is estimated basing on the assumption that non-internal nodes are stored on disk, the actual implementation stores non-internal nodes on primary memory and causes no disk I/O at visiting non-internal nodes. In contrast, the VAMSplit R-tree and the SR-tree implementation store both internal and non-internal nodes on disk. Hence, every time internal or non-internal node is visited, CPU time is spent in reading a disk block and in extracting information from the disk block. Thus, the overhead of reading disk blocks is underestimated for the k-d tree and overestimated for the VAMSplit R-tree and the SR-tree.

Because CPU time reflects the limitation of the implementation, the comparison based on CPU time is not necessarily fair nor strict. Therefore, we measured the number of floating-point operations executed during NN-search. Figure 13 shows the result of the VAMSplit R-tree and the k-d tree. We used the "soft-float" option of the GNU C/C++ compiler in order to measure the number of floating-point operations. With this option, the compiler generates assembly codes containing library calls for floating-point operations. We made functions that work as a wrapper of a floating-point operation with counting the number of invocations. In this way, the obtained result is the exact number of floating-point operations that are executed during NN-search operations. As shown in Figure 13, the number of floating-point operations of the VAMSplit R-tree is much larger than that of the k-d tree. When the number of images is 40,000, the VAMSplit R-tree executes 2.79 times as many operations as the k-d tree does. Although the number of comparison operations of the VAMSplit R-tree is almost the same with that of the k-d tree, the number of addition, subtraction, and multiplication of the VAMSplit R-tree are 3.5 times as large as those of the k-d tree. This difference comes from the overhead of distance calculation. Because the k-d tree splits the data space into contiguous regions, the region of a child node inherits boundaries from the region of the parent node except for the split dimension. Therefore, on calculating the distance from a query point to a region, it is possible to save the common computation between the parent and the child. On the other hand, the VAMSplit R-tree splits the data space into regions bounded by minimum bounding rectangles. A child node does not always inherit the boundaries of the parent node. Hence, on calculating the distance from a query point to a region, it is necessary to compute the distance from the beginning.

5. Conclusion

As database systems are applied to multimedia applications, nearest neighbor search for large-scale databases are getting more and more important to database systems. This paper clarifies the properties of the disk-based data structures which employ the variance-based construction algorithms, namely the SS-tree, the SR-tree, and the VAMSplit R-tree. Firstly, the effectiveness of the disk-based data structures are examined by applying them to practical multimedia applications, namely similarity retrieval of images and video scenes. Secondly, the performance evaluation with multimedia applications has demonstrated the effectiveness of the data structures: the VAMSplit R-tree achieves the best performance and the SR-tree reveals quite good performance even though it is built dynamically. Finally, the merit and the demerit of the disk-based data structures have been clarified by the comparison with the k-d tree. The merit is the reduction of disk I/O and the demerit is the increase of CPU time. For large-scale persistent databases, disk I/O is the dominant cost compared with CPU time. Therefore, the reduction of disk I/O is the prominent advantage of the disk-based data structures over database systems.

References

[1] J. L. Bentley, "Multidimensional Binary Search Trees Used for Associative Searching," Comm. of the ACM, vol. 18, no. 9 (Sep. 1975) pp.509–517.

[2] D. A. White and R. Jain, "Similarity Indexing with the SS-tree," Proc. of the 12th Int. Conf. on Data Engineering, New Orleans, USA, pp.516–523, Feb. 1996.

[3] D. A. White and R. Jain, "Similarity Indexing: Algorithms and Performance," Proc. SPIE Vol.2670, San Diego, USA, pp.62–73, Jan. 1996.

[4] S. Berchtold, D. A. Keim, and H.-P. Kriegel, "The X-tree: An Index Structure for High-Dimensional Data," Proc. of the 22nd VLDB Conf., Bombay, India, pp.28–39, Sep. 1996.

[5] N. Katayama and S. Satoh, "The SR-tree: An Index Structure for High-Dimensional Nearest Neighbor Queries," Proc. of the 1997 ACM SIGMOD, Tucson, USA (May 1997) pp. 369–380.

[6] A. Henrich, "The LSD^h-tree: An Access Structure for Feature Vectors," Proc. of the 14th Int. Conf. on Data Engineering, Orlando, USA, pp.362–369, Feb. 1998.

[7] S. Berchtold, C. Bohm, and H.-P. Kriegel, "The Pyramid-Technique: Towards Breaking the Curse of Dimensionality," Proc. ACM SIGMOD, Seattle, USA, pp.142–153, Jun. 1998.

[8] R. Weber, H.-J. Schek, and S. Blott, "A Quantitative Analysis and Performance Study for Similarity-Search Methods in High-Dimensional Spaces," Proc. of the 24th VLDB Conf., New York City, USA, pp. 194–205, Aug. 1998.
[9] J. L. Bentley, "Multidimensional Binary Search Trees in Database Applications," IEEE Trans. Soft. Eng., vol. SE-5, no. 4 (Jul. 1979) pp.333–340.
[10] A. Guttman, "R-trees: a Dynamic Index Structure for Spatial Searching," Proc. ACM SIGMOD, Boston, USA, pp.47–57, Jun. 1984.
[11] N. Beckmann, H.-P. Kriegel, R. Schneider, and B. Seeger, "The R*-tree: an Efficient and Robust Access Method for Points and Rectangles," Proc. ACM SIGMOD, Atlantic City, USA, pp.322–331, May 1990.
[12] N. Roussopoulos, S. Kelley, and F. Vincent, "Nearest Neighbor Queries," Proc. ACM SIGMOD, San Jose, USA, pp.71–79, May 1995.
[13] J. H. Friedman, J. L. Bentley, and R. A. Finkel, "An Algorithm for Finding Best Matches in Logarithmic Expected Time," ACM Trans. Math. Soft., vol.3, no.3 (Sep. 1977) pp.209–226.
[14] R. Sproull, "Refinements to Nearest-Neighbor Searching in k-Dimensional Trees," Algorithmica, Vol.6, No.4, pp.579–589, 1991.
[15] S. Arya and D. M. Mount, "Algorithms for Fast Vector Quantization," Proc. of '93: Data Compression Conference, eds. J. A. Storer and M. Cohn, IEEE Press (1993) pp.381–390.
[16] G. Hjaltason and H. Samet, "Ranking in Spatial Databases," 4th Int. Symp. on Spatial Databases, SSD'95, Portland, USA, pp.83–95, Aug. 1995.
[17] S. Berchtold, C. Boehm, D. A. Keim, and H.-P. Kriegel, "A Cost Model For Nearest Neighbor Search in High-Dimensional Data Space," Proc. ACM PODS, Tucson, USA, pp.78–86, May 1997.
[18] S. Arya, D. M. Mount, and O. Narayan, "Accounting for Boundary Effects in Nearest Neighbor Searching," Proc. of the 11th Annual ACM Symp. on Computational Geometry, 1995, pp. 336–344.
[19] http://images.jsc.nasa.gov/iams/html/pao/shuttle.htm
[20] http://science.ksc.nasa.gov/shuttle/photos/
[21] http://shuttle.nasa.gov/archives.html
[22] S. A. Nene and S. K. Nayar, "A Simple Algorithm for Nearest Neighbor Search in High Dimensions," IEEE Trans. PAMI, vol. 19, no. 9, pp. 989–1003, Sep. 1997.

NACSIS (NATIONAL CENTER FOR SCIENCE INFORMATION SYSTEMS), TOKYO, JAPAN

Current address: National Institute of Informatics, 2-1-2 Hitotsubashi, Chiyoda-ku, Tokyo 101-8430, Japan

E-mail address: `katayama@nii.ac.jp`

NACSIS (NATIONAL CENTER FOR SCIENCE INFORMATION SYSTEMS), TOKYO, JAPAN

Current address: National Institute of Informatics, 2-1-2 Hitotsubashi, Chiyoda-ku, Tokyo 101-8430, Japan

E-mail address: `satoh@nii.ac.jp`

DIMACS Series in Discrete Mathematics
and Theoretical Computer Science
Volume **59**, 2002

Analysis of Approximate Nearest Neighbor Searching with Clustered Point Sets

Songrit Maneewongvatana and David M. Mount

ABSTRACT. Nearest neighbor searching is a fundamental computational problem. A set of n data points is given in real d-dimensional space, and the problem is to preprocess these points into a data structure, so that given a query point, the nearest data point to the query point can be reported efficiently. Because data sets can be quite large, we are primarily interested in data structures that use only $O(dn)$ storage.

A popular class of data structures for nearest neighbor searching is the kd-tree and variants based on hierarchically decomposing space into rectangular cells. An important question in the construction of such data structures is the choice of a *splitting method*, which determines the dimension and splitting plane to be used at each stage of the decomposition. This choice of splitting method can have a significant influence on the efficiency of the data structure. This is especially true when data and query points are clustered in low dimensional subspaces. This is because clustering can lead to subdivisions in which cells have very high aspect ratios.

We compare the well-known optimized kd-tree splitting method against two alternative splitting methods. The first, called the *sliding-midpoint* method, which attempts to balance the goals of producing subdivision cells of bounded aspect ratio, while not producing any empty cells. The second, called the *minimum-ambiguity* method is a query-based approach. In addition to the data points, it is also given a training set of query points for preprocessing. It employs a simple greedy algorithm to select the splitting plane that minimizes the average amount of ambiguity in the choice of the nearest neighbor for the training points. We provide an empirical analysis comparing these two methods against the optimized kd-tree construction for a number of synthetically generated data and query sets. We demonstrate that for clustered data and query sets, these algorithms can provide significant improvements over the standard kd-tree construction for approximate nearest neighbor searching.

1991 *Mathematics Subject Classification.* 68P10, 68W40.

Key words and phrases. Nearest neighbor searching, query-based preprocessing, kd-trees, splitting methods, empirical analysis.

The support of the National Science Foundation under grants CCR–9712379 and CCR–0098151 is gratefully acknowledged.

1. Introduction

Nearest neighbor searching is the following problem: we are given a set S of n *data points* in a metric space, X, and are asked to preprocess these points so that, given any *query point* $q \in X$, the data point nearest to q can be reported quickly. Nearest neighbor searching has applications in many areas, including knowledge discovery and data mining [**FPSSU96**], pattern recognition and classification [**CH67, DH73**], machine learning [**CS93**], data compression [**GG92**], multimedia databases [**FSN$^+$95**], document retrieval [**DDF$^+$90**], and statistics [**DW82**].

There are many possible choices of the metric space. Throughout we will assume that the space is R^d, real d-dimensional space, where distances are measured using any Minkowski L_m distance metric. For any integer $m \geq 1$, the L_m*-distance* between points $p = (p_1, p_2, \ldots, p_d)$ and $q = (q_1, q_2, \ldots, q_d)$ in R^d is defined to be the m-th root of $\sum_{1 \leq i \leq d} |p_i - q_i|^m$. The L_1, L_2, and L_∞ metrics are the well-known Manhattan, Euclidean and max metrics, respectively.

Our primary focus is on data structures that are stored in main memory. Since data sets can be large, we limit ourselves to consideration of data structures whose total space grows linearly with d and n. Among the most popular methods are those based on hierarchical decompositions of space. The seminal work in this area was by Friedman, Bentley, and Finkel [**FBF77**] who showed that $O(n)$ space and $O(\log n)$ query time are achievable for fixed dimensional spaces in the expected case for data distributions of bounded density through the use of kd-trees. There have been numerous variations on this theme. However, all known methods suffer from the fact that as dimension increases, either running time or space increase exponentially with dimension.

The difficulty of obtaining algorithms that are efficient in the worst case with respect to both space and query time suggests the alternative problem of finding *approximate* nearest neighbors. Consider a set S of data points in R^d and a query point $q \in R^d$. Given $\epsilon > 0$, we say that a point $p \in S$ is a $(1+\epsilon)$*-approximate nearest neighbor* of q if

$$dist(p, q) \leq (1+\epsilon)\, dist(p^*, q),$$

where p^* is the true nearest neighbor to q. In other words, p is within relative error ϵ of the true nearest neighbor. The approximate nearest neighbor problem has been heavily studied recently. Examples include algorithms by Bern [**Ber93**], Arya and Mount [**AM93b**], Arya, et al. [**AMN$^+$98**], Clarkson [**Cla94**], Chan [**Cha97**], Kleinberg [**Kle97**], Indyk and Motwani [**IM98**], and Kushilevitz, Ostrovsky and Rabani [**KOR98**].

In this study we restrict attention to data structures of size $O(dn)$ based on hierarchical spatial decompositions, and the kd-tree in particular. In large part this is because of the simplicity and widespread popularity of this data structure. A kd-tree is binary tree based on a hierarchical subdivision of space by splitting hyperplanes that are orthogonal to the coordinate axes [**FBF77**]. It is described further in the next section. A key issue in the design of the kd-tree is the choice of the splitting hyperplane. Friedman, Bentley, and Finkel proposed a splitting method based on selecting the plane orthogonal to the median coordinate along which the points have the greatest spread. They called the resulting tree an optimized kd-tree, and henceforth we call the resulting splitting method the *standard* *splitting method*. Another common alternative uses the shape of the cell, rather than the distribution of the data points. It splits each cell through its midpoint by a hyperplane orthogonal to its longest side. We call this the *midpoint split method*.

A number of other data structures for nearest neighbor searching based on hierarchical spatial decompositions have been proposed. Yianilos introduced the *vp-tree* [**Yia93**]. Rather than using an axis-aligned plane to split a node as in kd-tree, it uses a data point, called the vantage point, as the center of a hypersphere that partitions the space into two regions. There has also been quite a bit of interest from the field of databases. There are several data structures for database applications based on R-trees and their variants [**BKSS90, SRF87**]. For example, the *X-tree* [**BKK96**] improves the performance of the R*-tree by avoiding high overlap. Another example is the SR-tree [**KS97**]. The *TV-tree* [**LJF94**] uses a different approach to deal with high dimensional spaces. It reduces dimensionality by maintaining a number of active dimensions. When all data points in a node share the same coordinate of an active dimension, that dimension will be deactivated and the set of active dimensions shifts.

In this paper we study the performance of two other splitting methods, and compare them against the kd-tree splitting method. The first, called *sliding-midpoint*, is a splitting method that was introduced by Mount and Arya in the ANN library for approximate nearest neighbor searching [**MA97**]. This method was introduced into the library in order to better handle highly clustered data sets. We know of no analysis (empirical or theoretical) of this method. This method was designed as a simple technique for addressing one of the most serious flaws in the standard kd-tree splitting method. The flaw is that when the data points are highly clustered in low dimensional subspaces, then the standard kd-tree splitting method may produce highly elongated cells, and these can lead to slow query times. This splitting method starts with a simple midpoint split of the longest side of the cell, but if this split results in either subcell containing no data points, it translates (or "slides") the splitting plane in the direction of the points until hitting the first data point. In Section 3.1 we describe this splitting method and analyze some of its properties.

The second splitting method, called *minimum-ambiguity*, is a query-based technique. The tree is given not only the data points, but also a collection of sample query points, called the *training points*. The algorithm applies a greedy heuristic to build the tree in an attempt to minimize the expected query time on the training points. We model query processing as the problem of eliminating data points from consideration as the possible candidates for the nearest neighbor. Given a collection of query points, we can model any stage of the nearest neighbor algorithm as a bipartite graph, called the *candidate graph*, whose vertices correspond to the union of the data points and the query points, and in which each query point is adjacent to the subset of data points that might be its nearest neighbor. The minimum-ambiguity selects the splitting plane at each stage that eliminates the maximum number of remaining edges in the candidate graph. In Section 3.2 we describe this splitting method in greater detail.

We implemented these two splitting methods, along with the standard kd-tree splitting method. We compared them on a number of synthetically generated point distributions, which were designed to model low-dimensional clustering. We believe this type of clustering is not uncommon in many application data sets [**JD88**]. We used synthetic data sets, as opposed to standard benchmarks, so that we could adjust the strength and dimensionality of the clustering. Our results show that these new splitting methods can provide significant improvements over the standard kd-tree splitting method for data sets with low-dimensional clustering. The rest of the paper is organized as follows. In the next section we present background information on the kd-tree and how to perform nearest neighbor searches in this tree. In Section 3 we present the two new splitting methods. In Section 4 we describe our implementation and present our empirical results.

2. Background

In this section we describe how kd-trees are used for performing exact and approximate nearest neighbor searching. Bentley introduced the kd-tree as a generalization of the binary search tree in higher dimensions [**Ben75**]. Each node of the tree is implicitly associated with a d-dimensional rectangle, called its *cell*. The root node is associated with the bounding rectangle, which encloses all of the data points. Each node is also implicitly associated with the subset of data points that lie within this rectangle. (Data points lying on the boundary between two rectangles, may be associated with either.) If the number of points associated with a node falls below a given threshold, called the *bucket size*, then this node is a leaf, and these points are stored with the leaf. (In our experiments we used a bucket size of one.) Otherwise, the construction algorithm selects a splitting hyperplane, which is orthogonal to one of the coordinate axes and passes through the cell. There are a number of *splitting methods* that may be used for choosing this hyperplane. We will discuss these in greater detail below. The hyperplane subdivides the associated cell into two subrectangles, which are then associated with the children of this node, and the points are subdivided among these children according to which side of the hyperplane they lie. Each internal node of the tree is associated with its splitting hyperplane (which may be given as the index of the orthogonal axis and a cutting value along this axis).

Friedman, Bentley and Finkel [**FBF77**] present an algorithm to find the nearest neighbor using the kd-trees. They introduce the following splitting method, which we call the *standard splitting method*. For each internal node, the splitting hyperplane is chosen to be orthogonal to the axis along which the points have the greatest *spread* (difference of maximum and minimum). The splitting point is chosen at the median coordinate, so that the two subsets of data points have nearly equal sizes. The resulting tree has $O(n)$ size and $O(\log n)$ height. White and Jain [**WJ96**] proposed an alternative, called the *VAM-split*, with the same basic idea, but the splitting dimension is chosen to be the one with the maximum variance.

Queries are answered by a simple recursive algorithm. In the basis case, when the algorithm arrives at a leaf of the tree, it computes the distance from the query point to each of the data points associated with this node. The smallest such distance is saved. When arriving at an internal node, it first determines the side of the associated hyperplane on which the query point lies. The query point is necessarily closer to this child's cell. The search recursively visits this child. On returning from the search, it determines whether the cell associated with the other child is closer to the query point than the closest point seen so far. If so, then this child is also visited recursively. When the search returns from the root, the closest point seen is returned. An important observation is that for each query point, every leaf whose distance from the query point is less than the nearest neighbor will be visited by the algorithm.

It is an easy matter to generalize this search algorithm for answering *approximate* nearest neighbor queries. Let ϵ denote the allowed error bound. In the processing of an internal node, the further child is visited only if its distance from the query point is less than the distance to the closest point so far, divided by $(1+\epsilon)$. Arya et al. [**AMN$^+$98**] show the correctness of this procedure. They also show how to generalize the search algorithm for computing the k-closest neighbors, either exactly or approximately.

Arya and Mount [**AM93a**] proposed a number of improvements to this basic algorithm. The first is called *incremental distance calculation*. This technique can be applied for any Minkowski metric. In addition to storing the splitting hyperplane, each internal node of the tree also stores the extents of associated cell projected orthogonally onto its splitting axis. The algorithm does not maintain true distances, but instead (for the Euclidean metric) maintains squared distances. When the algorithm arrives at an internal node, it maintains the squared distance from the query point to the associated cell. They show that in constant time (independent of dimension) it is possible to use this information to compute the squared distance to each of the children's cell. They also presented a method called *priority search*, which uses a heap to visit the leaves of the tree in increasing order of distance from the query point, rather than in the recursive order dictated by the structure of the tree. Yet another improvement is a well-known technique from nearest neighbor searching, called *partial distance calculation* [**BG85, Spr91**]. When computing the distance between the query point and a data point, if the accumulated sum of squared components ever exceeds the squared distance to the nearest point so far, then the distance computation is terminated.

One of the important elements of approximate nearest neighbor searching, which was observed by Arya et al. [**AMN$^+$98**], is that there are two important properties of any data structure for approximate nearest neighbor searching based on spatial decomposition.

Balance:: The height of the tree should be $O(\log n)$, where n is the number of data points.

Bounded aspect ratio:: The leaf cells of the tree should have bounded aspect ratio, meaning that the ratio of the longest to shortest side of each leaf cell should be bounded above by a constant.

Given these two constraints, they show that approximate nearest neighbor searching (using priority search) can be performed in $O(\log n)$ time from a data structure of size $O(dn)$. The hidden constant factors in time grow as $O(d/\epsilon)^d$. Unfortunately, achieving both of these properties does not always seem to be possible for kd-trees. This is particularly true when the point distribution is highly clustered. Arya et al. present a somewhat more complex data structure called a *balanced box-decomposition tree*, which does satisfy these properties. The extra complexity seems to be necessary in order to prove their theoretical results, and they show empirically that it is important when data sets are highly clustered in low-dimensional subspaces. An interesting practical question is whether there exist methods that retain the essential simplicity of the kd-tree, while providing practical efficiency for clustered data distributions (at least in most instances, if not in the worst case).

Bounded aspect ratio is a sufficient condition for efficiency, but it is not necessary. The more precise condition in order for their results to apply is called the *packing constraint* [**AMN$^+$98**]. Define a *ball* of radius r to be the locus of points that are within distance r of some point in R^d according to the chosen metric. The packing constraint says that the number of large cells that intersect any such ball is bounded.

Packing Constraint:: The number of leaf cells of size at least s that intersect an open ball of radius $r > 0$ is bounded above by a function of r/s and d, but independent of n.

If a tree has cells of bounded aspect ratio, then it satisfies the packing constraint. Arya et al., show that priority search runs in time that is proportional to the depth of the tree times the number of cells of maximum side length $r\epsilon/d$ that intersect a ball of radius r. If the packing constraint holds, then this number of cells depends only on the dimension and ϵ. The main shortcoming of the standard splitting method is that it may result in cells of unbounded aspect ratio, and hence does not generally satisfy the packing constraint.

3. Splitting Methods

In this section we describe the splitting methods that are considered in our experiments. As mentioned in the introduction, we implemented two splitting methods, in addition to the standard kd-tree splitting method. We describe them further in each of the following sections.

3.1. Sliding-Midpoint. The sliding-midpoint splitting method was first introduced in the ANN library for approximate nearest neighbor searching [**MA97**]. This method was motivated to remedy the deficiencies of two other splitting methods, the standard kd-tree splitting method and the midpoint splitting method. To understand the problem, suppose that the data points are highly clustered along a few dimensions but vary greatly along some the others (see Fig. 1). The standard kd-tree splitting method will repeatedly split along the dimension in which the data points have the greatest spread, leading to many cells with high aspect ratio. A nearest neighbor query q near the center of the bounding square would visit a large number of these cells. In contrast, the midpoint splitting method bisects the cell along its longest side, irrespective of the point distribution. (If there are ties for the longest side, then the tie is broken in favor of the dimension along which the points have the highest spread.) This method produces cells of aspect ratio at most 2, but it may produce leaf cells that contain no data points. The size of the resulting tree may be very large when the data distribution is highly clustered data and the dimension is high.

The sliding-midpoint method works as follows. It first attempts to perform a midpoint split, by the same method described above. If data points lie on both sides of the splitting plane then the algorithm acts exactly as it would for the midpoint split. However, if a trivial split were to result (in which all the points lie to one side of the splitting plane), then it attempts to avoid this by "sliding" the splitting plane towards the points until it encounters the first data point (see Fig. 2). More formally, if the split is performed orthogonal to the ith coordinate, and all the data points have i-coordinates that are larger than that of the splitting plane, then the splitting plane is translated so that its ith coordinate equals the minimum ith

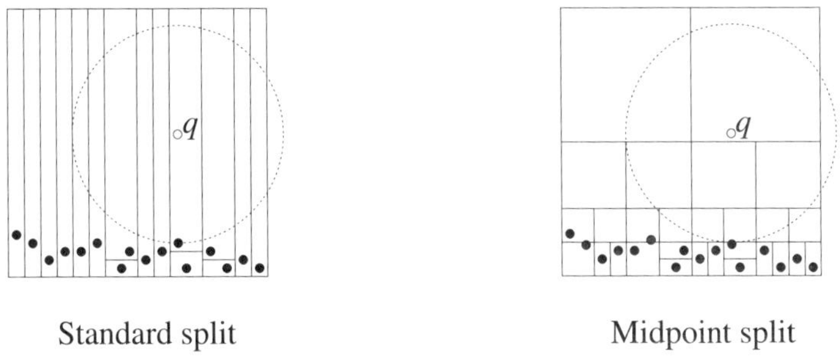

FIGURE 1. Standard and midpoint splitting methods with clustered point sets.

coordinate among all the data points. Let this point be p_1. Then the points are partitioned with p_1 in one part of the partition, and all the other data points in the other part. A symmetrical rule is applied if the points all have ith coordinates smaller than the splitting plane.

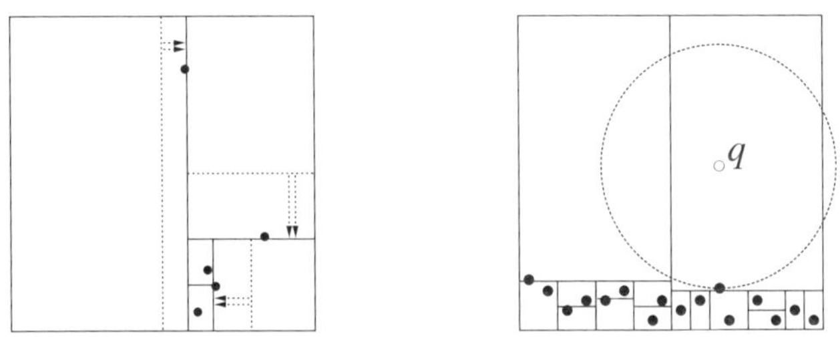

FIGURE 2. Sliding-midpoint splitting method.

This method cannot result in any trivial splits, implying that the resulting tree has size $O(n)$. Thus it avoids the problem of large trees, which the midpoint splitting method is susceptible to. Because there is no guarantee that the point partition is balanced, the depth of the resulting tree may exceed $O(\log n)$. However, based on our empirical observations, the height of this tree rarely exceeds the height of the standard kd-tree by more than a small constant factor.

Because of sliding, it is possible to generate a cell C of very high aspect ratio. Note that when this happens, the sibling C' of C is fat along the same dimension that C is skinny. Thus, it is not possible to generate a situation (as seen in the left of Fig. 1) where many skinny cells are stacked next to each other. Using this observation, we have shown that the sliding-midpoint rule satisfies the packing constraint [**MM99**].

The sliding-midpoint method can be implemented with little more effort than the standard kd-tree splitting method. But, because the depth of the tree is not necessarily $O(\log n)$, the $O(n \log n)$ construction time bound does not necessarily hold. There are more complex algorithms for constructing the tree that run in $O(n \log n)$ time [**AMN$^+$98**]. However, in spite of these shortcomings, we will see that the sliding-midpoint method, can perform quite well for highly clustered data sets.

3.2. Minimum-Ambiguity. All of the splitting methods described so far are based solely on the data points. This may be quite reasonable in applications where data points and query points come from the same distribution. However this is not always the case. (For example, a common use of nearest neighbor searching is in iterative clustering algorithms, such as the *k-means algorithm* [**For65, GG92, Mac67**]. Depending on the starting conditions of the algorithm, the data points and query points may be quite different from one another.) If the two distributions are different, then it is reasonable that preprocessing should be informed of the expected distribution of the query points, as well as the data points. One way to do this is to provide the preprocessing phase with the data points and a collection of sample query points, called *training points*. The goal is to compute a data structure which is efficient, assuming that the query distribution is well-represented by the training points. The idea of presenting a training set of query points is not new. For example, Clarkson [**Cla97**] described a nearest neighbor algorithm that uses this concept.

The *minimum-ambiguity splitting method* is given a set S of data points and a training set T of sample query points. For each query point $q \in T$, we compute the nearest neighbor of q in S as part of the preprocessing. For each such q, let $b(q)$ denote the *nearest neighbor ball*, that is, the maximum ball centered at q that contains no point of S in its interior. As observed earlier, the exact nearest neighbor search algorithm visits every leaf cell that overlaps $b(q)$.

Given any kd-tree, let $C(q)$ denote the set of leaf cells of the tree that overlap $b(q)$. This suggests the following optimization problem: given point sets S and T, determine a hierarchical subdivision of S of size $O(n)$ such that the *total overlap*, $\sum_{q \in T} |C(q)|$, is minimized. This is analogous to the packing constraint, but applied only to the nearest neighbor balls of the training set. This problem can be solved optimally through dynamic programming in polynomial time, but the running time would be unacceptably large given the number of data and training points that we are interested in. Instead, we devised a simple greedy heuristic, which is the basis of the minimum-ambiguity splitting method.

To motivate our method, we introduce a model for nearest neighbor searching in terms of a pruning process on a bipartite graph. Given a cell (i.e., a d-dimensional rectangle) C. Let S_C denote the subset of data points lying within this cell and let T_C denote the subset of training points whose such that the nearest neighbor balls intersects C. Define the *candidate graph* for C to be the bipartite graph on the vertex set $S \cup T$, whose edge set is $S_C \times T_C$. Intuitively, each edge (p, q) in this graph reflects the possibility that data point p is a candidate to be the nearest neighbor of training point q. Observe that if a cell C intersects $b(q)$ and contains k data points, then q has degree k in the candidate graph for C. Since it is our goal to minimize the number of leaf nodes that overlap C, and assuming that each leaf node contains at least one data point, then a reasonable heuristic for minimizing the number of overlapping leaf cells is to minimize the average degree of vertices in the candidate graph. This is equivalent to minimizing the total number of edges in the graph. (This method is similar to techniques used in the design of linear classifiers based on impurity functions [**BFOS84**]. The idea of using an ambiguity graph was suggested to us by Joe Mitchell [**Mit93**], who proposed it as a method for solving quite a different problem in pattern recognition.)

Here is how the minimum-ambiguity method selects the splitting hyperplane. If $|S_C| \leq 1$, then from our desire to generate a tree of size $O(n)$, we will not subdivide this cell any further. Otherwise, let H be some orthogonal hyperplane that cuts C into subcells C_1 and C_2. Let S_1 and S_2 be the resulting partition of data points into these respective subcells, and let T_1 and T_2 denote the subsets of training points whose nearest neighbor balls intersect C_1 and C_2, respectively. Notice that these subsets are not necessarily disjoint. We assign a *score* to each such hyperplane H, which is equal to the sum of the number of edges in the ambiguity graphs of C_1 and C_2. In particular,

$$\text{Score}(H) = |S_1| \cdot |T_1| + |S_2| \cdot |T_2|.$$

Intuitively a small score is good, because it means that the average ambiguity in the choice of nearest neighbors is small. The minimum-ambiguity splitting method selects the orthogonal hyperplane H that produces a nontrivial partition of the data points and has the smallest score. (For example, in Fig. 3 on the left, we show the score of 40 for the standard kd-tree splitting method. There are four points in each of the child cells. Two of the nearest neighbor balls intersect the left child and eight of the nearest neighbor balls intersect the right child, and hence the score is $4 \cdot 2 + 4 \cdot 8 = 40$. However, because of the higher concentration of training points on the right side of the cell, the splitting plane shown on the right actually has a lower score, and hence is preferred by the minimum-ambiguity method.) In this way the minimum-ambiguity method tailors the structure of the tree to the distribution of the training points.

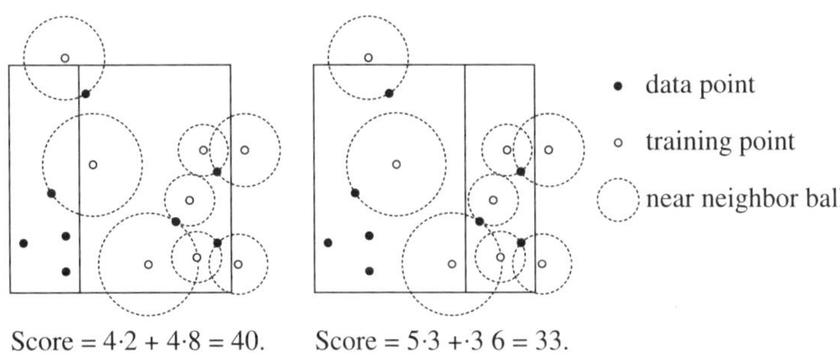

FIGURE 3. Minimum ambiguity splitting method.

The minimum-ambiguity split is computed as follows. First, the nearest neighbor for each of the training points is computed, and from these the nearest neighbor balls are computed. This may be done using any algorithm for computing nearest neighbors, e.g., by building a kd-tree using one of the other splitting methods. The algorithm then operates in a recursive manner, starting at the root of the new tree. At each stage it is given the current cell C (initially the bounding box for the data points) and the subsets S_C, T_C, and the nearest neighbor balls for the elements of T_C. For each coordinate axis, it projects the points of S_C and the extreme coordinates of the balls $b(q)$ for each $q \in T_C$ orthogonally onto this axis. It then sweeps through this set of projections, from the leftmost to the rightmost data point projection. The score can be updated in constant time as each point is swept. It selects the hyperplane with the minimum score over all the sweeps.

If there are ties for the smallest score, then some other criterion may be used, for example, selecting the split that most evenly partitions the data points.

To improve the efficiency of the sweep, for each axis, we presort the data point coordinates and the minimum and maximum coordinates of each nearest neighbor ball into d separate sorted lists. We store cross-reference links between these sorted lists, so that if a point is deleted from one sorted list it can be deleted from all the other lists in $O(d)$ time. With this preprocessing, we observe that each node of the new tree can be constructed in $O(d(|T_C| + |S_C|))$ time. This is done by sweeping through each of the sorted lists (which can be done in this time), then selecting the split with the lowest score and creating the new node (which takes constant time), and finally computing the sets $T_{C'}$ and $S_{C'}$ for each child C' of C. This can be done by first copying the d sorted lists, and then making a simple traversal through each copy, removing the elements that do not overlap the child's cell.

If we let $\mathfrak{C}$ denote the set of all of the cells associated with all of the nodes in the resulting minimum-ambiguity tree, the total running time for this procedure is on the order of

$$N(S,T) + dn \log n + d \sum_{C \in \mathfrak{C}} (|T_C| + |S_C|),$$

where $N(S,T)$ is the time to compute the nearest neighbors for each element of T in the data set S.

Since the running time of nearest neighbor searching $N(S,T)$ is a quantity that is reasonably well understood, the major unknown factor in the construction time is the final sum in the above equation. Observe that even if all the splitting planes were known in advance for the minimum-ambiguity tree, then the time needed to partition the points of S among the cells of the tree is on the order of $d \sum_{C \in \mathfrak{C}} |S_C|$. This is based on the fact that the time needed to partition the data points in each cell is proportional to d times the number of points in the cell (assuming presorting of points). Also observe that if we were to use the minimum-ambiguity tree to compute the nearest neighbor in S for each training point in T (using the standard recursive algorithm) then for each $q \in T$, we would visit each cell $C \in \mathfrak{C}$ that the nearest neighbor ball $b(q)$ intersects. Including an extra factor of d for computing distances, then running time is on the order of $d \sum_{C \in \mathfrak{C}} |T_C|$. Thus, in summary, the major factor in the construction time for the minimum-ambiguity tree is the time to partition the data points within the tree plus the time to compute nearest neighbors of the training points using this tree.

4. Empirical Results

We implemented a kd-tree in C++ using the three splitting methods: the standard method, sliding-midpoint, and minimum-ambiguity. For each splitting method we generated a number data point sets, query point sets, and (for minimum-ambiguity) training point sets. The tree structure was based on the same basic tree structure used in ANN [**MA97**]. The experiments were run on a Sparc Ultra, running Solaris 5.5, and the program was compiled by the g++ compiler. We measured a number of statistics for the tree, including its size, depth, and the average aspect ratio of its cells.

Queries were answered using priority search. For each group of queries we computed a number of statistics including CPU time, number of nodes visited in the tree, number of floating-point operations, number of distance calculations, and

ϵ	Avg. error	Std. dev.	Max. Error
1.0	0.03643	0.0340	0.248
2.0	0.06070	0.0541	0.500
3.0	0.08422	0.0712	0.687

FIGURE 4. Average error commited, the standard deviation of the error, and the maximum error versus the allowed error, ϵ. Values were averaged over all runs.

number of coordinate accesses. In our plots we show only the number of nodes in the tree visited during the search. We chose this parameter because it is a machine-independent quantity, and was closely correlated with CPU time. In most of our experiments, nearest neighbors were computed approximately.

For each experiment we fixed the number of data points, the dimension, the data-point distribution, and the error bound ϵ. In the case of the minimum-ambiguity method, the query distribution is also fixed, and some number of training points were generated. Then a kd-tree was generated by applying the appropriate splitting method. For the standard and sliding-midpoint methods the tree construction does not depend on ϵ, implying that the same tree may be used for different error bounds. For the minimum-ambiguity tree, the error bound was used in computing the tree. In particular, the nearest neighbors of each of the training points was computed only approximately. Furthermore, the nearest neighbor balls $b(q)$ for each training point q were shrunken in size by dividing their radius by the factor $1+\epsilon$. This is because this is the size of the ball that is used in the search algorithm.

For each tree generated, we generated some number of query points. The query-point distribution was not always the same as the data distribution, but it is always the same as the training point distribution. Then the nearest neighbor search was performed on these query points, and the results were averaged over all queries. Although we ran a wide variety of experiments, for the sake of conciseness we show only a few representative cases. For all of the experiments described here, we used 4000 data points in dimension 20 for each data set, and there were 12,000 queries run for each data set. For the minimum-ambiguity method, the number of training points was 36,000.

The value of ϵ was either 1, 2, or 3 in our experiments (allowing the reported point to be a factor of 2, 3, or 4 further away than the true nearest neighbor, respectively). Although these errors may seem exorbitantly large, we note that the observed errors were much smaller. We computed the exact nearest neighbors off-line to gauge the algorithm's actual performance. The actual error commited for each query was computed and then averaged over the runs (see Fig. 4). Note that average error committed was typically only about 1/30 of the allowable error. The maximum error was computed for each run of 12,000 query points, and then averaged over all runs. Even this maximum error was only around 1/4 of the allowed error. Some variation (on the order of a factor of 2) was observed depending on the choice of search tree and point distributions. For this reason, we feel that in applications where good average-case error performance is sufficient, running with such relatively high values of ϵ is not unreasonable.

4.1. Distributions Tested. The distributions that were used in our experiments are listed below. The clustered-gaussian distribution is designed to model point sets that are clustered, but in which each cluster is full-dimensional. The clustered-orthogonal-ellipsoid and clustered-ellipsoid distributions are both explicitly designed to model point distributions which are clustered, and the clusters themselves are flat in the sense that the points lie close to a lower dimensional subspace. In the first case the ellipsoids are aligned with the axes, and in the other case they are arbitrarily oriented.

Uniform:: Each coordinate was chosen uniformly from the interval $[-1, 1]$.

Clustered-gaussian:: The distribution is given a number of color classes c, and a standard deviation σ. We generated c points from the uniform distribution, which form cluster centers. Each point is generated from a gaussian distribution centered at a randomly chosen cluster center with standard deviation σ.

Clustered-orthogonal-ellipsoids:: The distribution can be viewed as a degenerate clustered-gaussian distribution where the standard deviation of each coordinate is chosen from one of two classes of distributions, one with a large standard deviation and the other with a small standard deviation. The distribution is specified by the number of color classes c and four additional parameters:

- d_{max} is the maximum number of fat dimensions.
- σ_{lo} and σ_{hi} are the minimum and maximum bounds on the large standard deviations, respectively (for the fat sides of the ellipsoid).
- σ_{thin} is the small standard deviation (for the thin sides of the ellipsoid).

Cluster centers are chosen as in the clustered-gaussian distribution. For each color class, a random number d' between 1 and d_{max} is generated, indicating the number of fat dimensions. Then d' dimensions are chosen at random to be fat dimensions of the ellipse. For each fat dimension the standard deviation for this coordinate is chosen uniformly from $[\sigma_{\text{lo}}, \sigma_{\text{hi}}]$, and for each thin dimension the standard deviation is set to σ_{thin}. The points are then generated by the same process as clustered-gaussian, but using these various standard deviations.

Clustered-ellipsoids:: This distribution is the result of applying d random rotation transformations to the points of each cluster about its center. Each cluster is rotated by a different set of rotations. Each rotation is through a uniformly distributed angle in the range $[0, \pi/2]$ with respect to two randomly chosen dimensions.

In our experiments involving both clustered-orthogonal-ellipsoids and clustered-ellipsoids, we set the number of clusters to 5, $d_{\text{max}} = 10$, $\sigma_{\text{lo}} = \sigma_{\text{hi}} = 0.3$, and σ_{thin} varied from 0.03 to 0.3. Thus, for low values of σ_{thin} the ellipsoids are relatively flat, and for high values this becomes equivalent to a clustered-gaussian distribution with standard deviation of 0.3.

4.2. Data and Query Points from the Same Distribution. For our first set of experiments, we considered data and query points from the same clustered distributions. We considered both clustered-orthogonal-ellipsoids and clustered-ellipsoid distributions in Figs. 5 and 6, respectively.

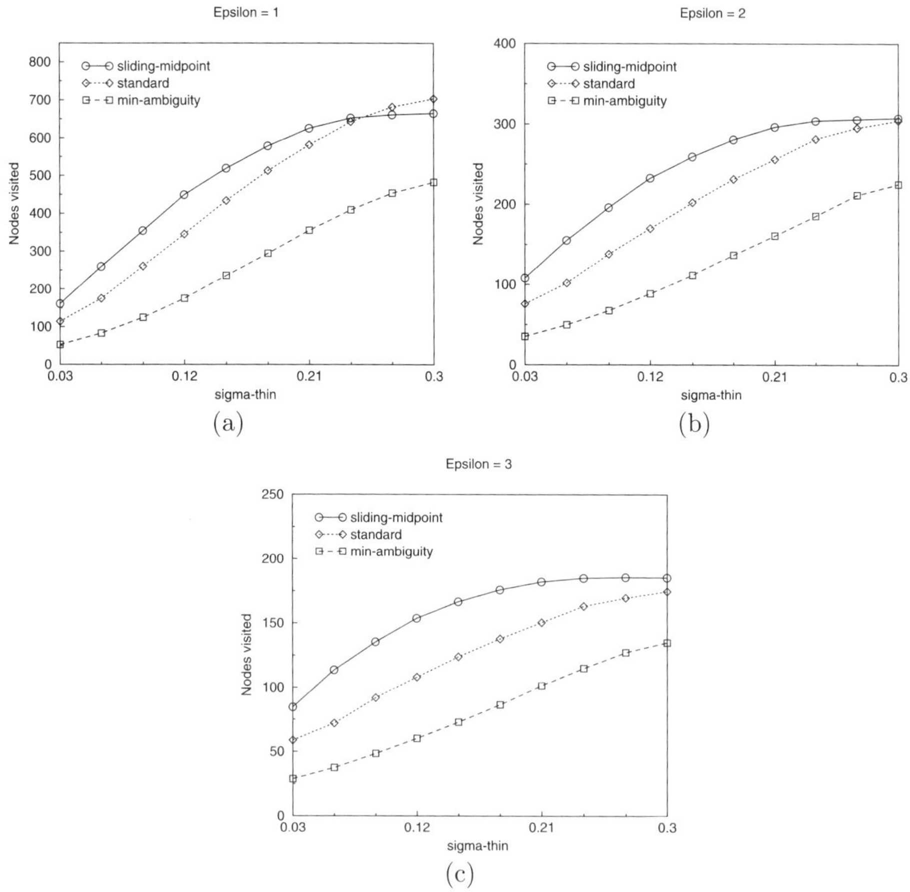

FIGURE 5. Number of nodes visited versus σ_{thin} for $\epsilon \in \{0, 1, 2\}$. Data and query points both sampled from the same clustered-orthogonal-ellipsoid distribution.

The three different graphs are for (a) $\epsilon = 1$, (b) $\epsilon = 2$, and (c) $\epsilon = 3$. In all three cases the same clusters centers were used. Note that the graphs do not share the same y-range, and in particular the search algorithm performs significantly faster as ϵ increases.

Observe that all of the splitting methods perform better when σ_{thin} is small, indicating that to some extent they exploit the fact that the data points are clustered in lower dimensional subspaces. The relative differences in running time were most noticeable for small values of σ_{thin}, and tended to diminish for larger values.

Although the minimum-ambiguity splitting method was designed for dealing with data and query points from different distributions, we were somewhat surprised that it actually performed the best of the three methods in these cases. For small values of σ_{thin} (when low-dimensional clustering is strongest) its average running time (measured as the number of noded visited in the tree) was typically from 30-50% lower than the standard splitting method, and over 50% lower than the sliding-midpoint method. The standard splitting method typically performed better than

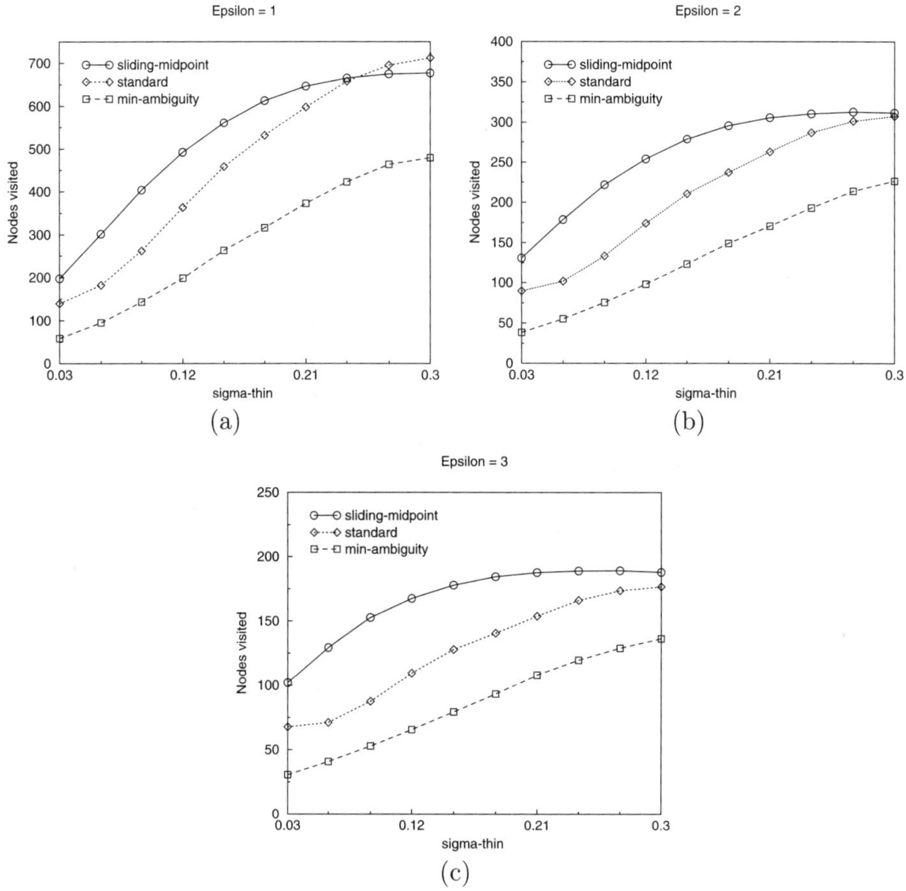

FIGURE 6. Number of nodes visited versus σ_{thin} for $\epsilon \in \{0, 1, 2\}$. Data and query points both sampled from the same clustered-ellipsoid distribution.

the sliding-midpoint method, but the difference decreased to being insignificant (and sometimes a bit worse) as σ_{thin} increased.

4.3. Data and Query Points from Different Distributions. For our second set of experiments, we considered data points from a clustered distribution and query points from a uniform distribution. This particular choice was motivated by the situation shown in Fig. 2, where the standard splitting method can produce cells with high aspect ratios.

For the data points we considered both the clustered-orthogonal-ellipsoids and clustered-ellipsoid distributions in Figs. 7 and 8, respectively. As before, the three different graphs are for (a) $\epsilon = 1$, (b) $\epsilon = 2$, and (c) $\epsilon = 3$. Again, note that the graphs do not share the same y-range.

Unlike the previous experiment, overall running times did not vary greatly with σ_{thin}. Sometimes running times increased moderately and other times they

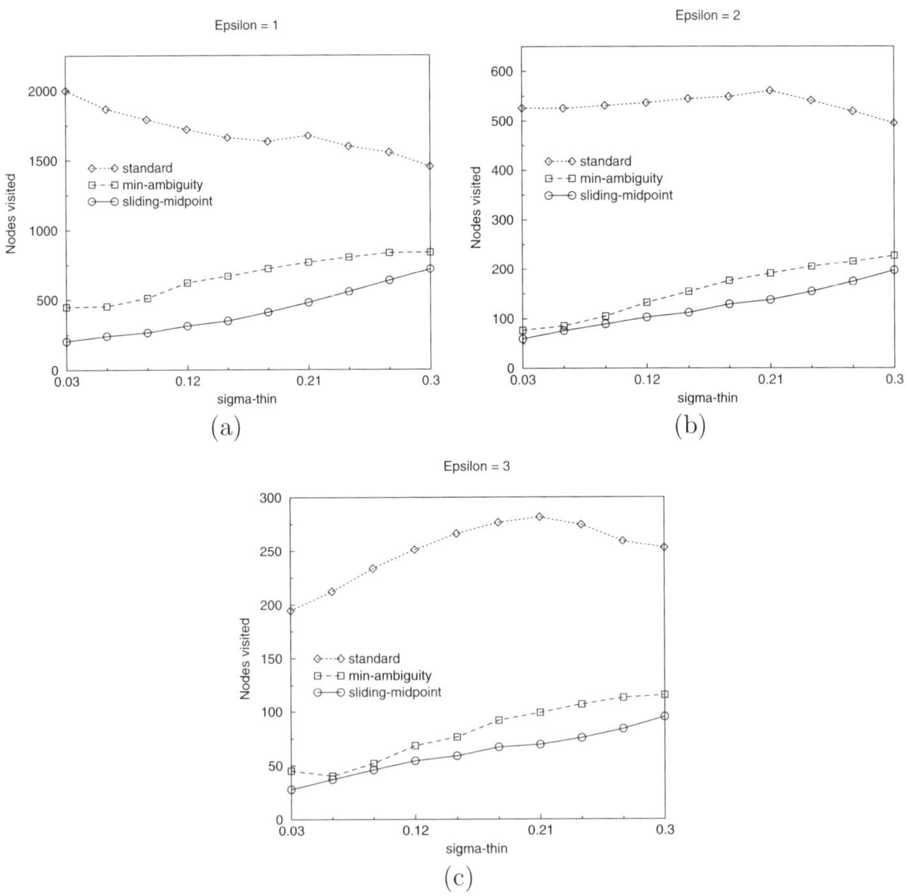

FIGURE 7. Number of nodes visited versus σ_{thin} for $\epsilon \in \{0, 1, 2\}$. Data sampled from the clustered-orthogonal-ellipsoid distribution and query points from the uniform distribution.

decreased moderately as a function of σ_{thin}. However, there were significant differences between the standard splitting method, which consistently performed much worse than the other two methods. For the smallest values of σ_{thin}, there was around a 5-to-1 difference in running time between then standard method and sliding-midpoint.

For larger values of ϵ (2 and 3) the performance of sliding-midpoint and minimum-ambiguity were very similar, with sliding-midpoint having the slight edge. It may seem somewhat surprising that minimum-ambiguity performed significantly worse (a factor of 2 to 3 times worse) than sliding-midpoint, since minimum-ambiguity was designed exactly for this the situation where there is a difference between data and query distributions. This may be due to limitations on the heuristic itself, or the limited size of the training set. However, it should be kept in mind that sliding-midpoint was specially designed to produce large empty cells in the uncluttered regions outside the clusters (recall Fig. 2).

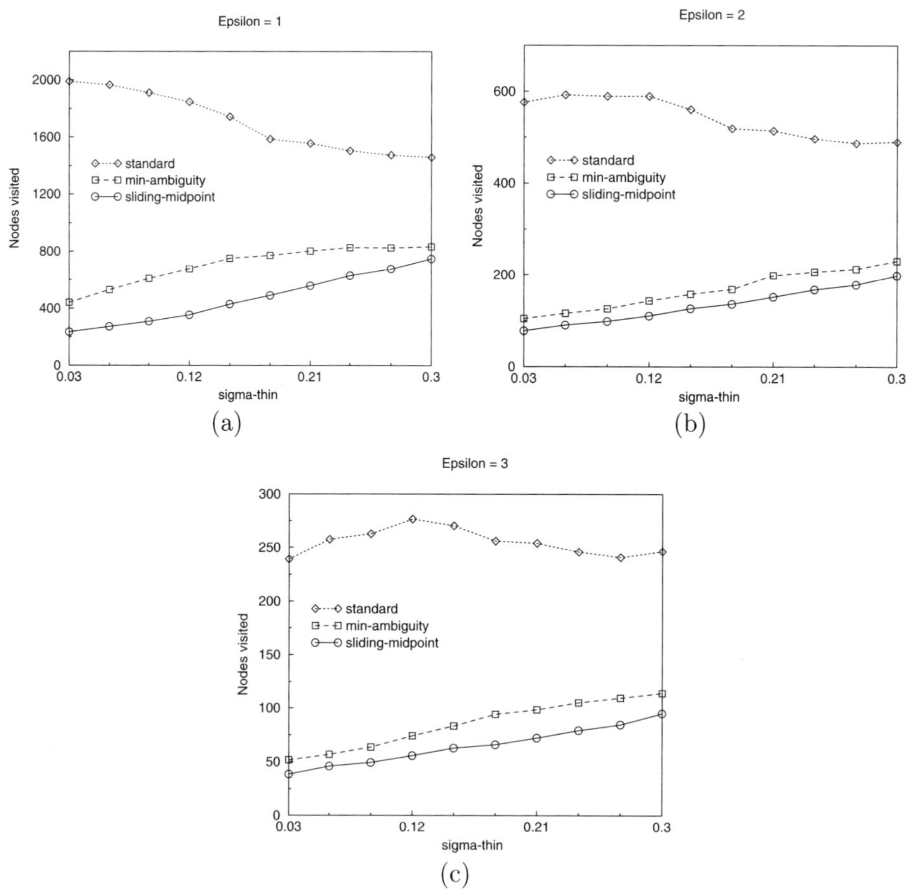

FIGURE 8. Number of nodes visited versus σ_{thin} for $\epsilon \in \{0, 1, 2\}$. Data sampled from the clustered-ellipsoid distribution and query points from the uniform distribution.

4.4. Construction Times. The results of the previous sections suggest that the minimum-ambiguity splitting produces trees that can answer queries efficiently for a variety of point and data distributions. Its main drawback is the amount of time that it takes to build the tree. Both the standard and sliding-midpoint methods can be built quite efficiently in time $O(nh)$, where n is the number of data points, and h is the height of the tree. The standard kd-tree has $O(\log n)$ height, and while the sliding-midpoint tree need not have $O(\log n)$ height, this seems to be true for many point distributions. For the 4000 point data sets in dimension 20, both of these trees could be constructed in under 10 CPU seconds.

However, the construction time for the minimum-ambiguity tree is quite a bit higher. As mentioned earlier, the time to construct the tree is roughly (within logarithmic factors) proportional to the time to compute the (approximate) nearest neighbors for all the training points. Since we used 9 times the number of data points as training points, it is easy to see that the minimum-ambiguity tree will take much longer to construct than the other two trees. Notice that when $\epsilon > 0$,

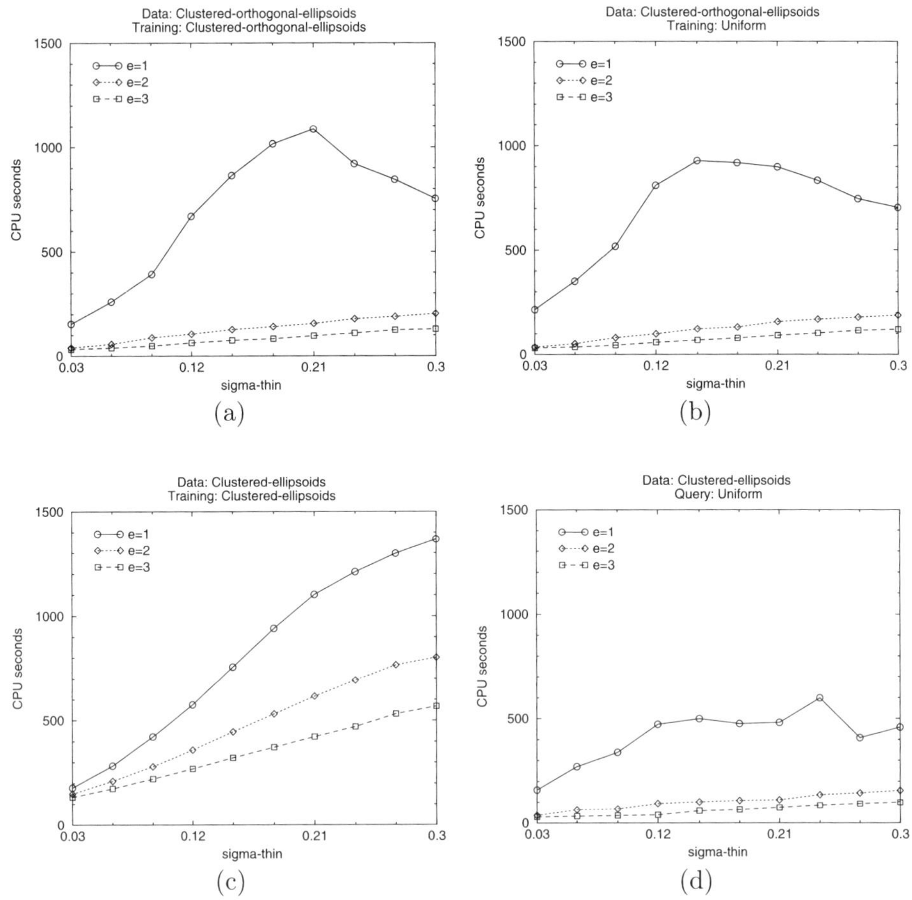

FIGURE 9. Time to construct minimum-ambiguity tree versus σ_{thin}.

we compute nearest neighbors approximately, and so this can offer an improvement in construction time. In Fig. 9 we present the construction time for the minimum-ambiguity tree for various combinations of data and training distributions. Observe that the construction times are considerably greater than those for the other two methods (which were under 10 CPU seconds), and that the construction time is significantly faster for higher values of ϵ.

5. Conclusions

In this paper we have presented an empirical analysis of two new splitting methods for kd-trees: sliding-midpoint and minimum-ambiguity. Both of these methods were designed to remedy some of the deficiencies of the standard kd-tree splitting method, with respect to data distributions that are highly clustered in low-dimensional subspaces. Both methods were shown to be considerably faster than the standard splitting method in answering queries when data points were drawn from a clustered distribution and query points were drawn from a uniform distribution. The minimum-ambiguity method performed better when both data and query points were drawn from a clustered distribution. But this method has a considerably higher construction time. The sliding-midpoint method, while easy to build, seems to perform sometimes better and sometimes worse than the standard kd-tree splitting method.

The enhanced performance of the minimum-ambiguity method suggests that even within the realm of kd-trees, there may be significant improvements to be made by fine-tuning the structure of the tree to the data and query distributions. However, because of its high construction cost, it would be nice to determine whether there are other heuristics that would lead to faster construction times. This suggest the intriguing possibility of search trees whose structure adapts dynamically to the structure of queries over time. The sliding-midpoint method raises hope that it may be possible to devise a simple and efficiently computable splitting method, that performs well across a wider variety of distributions than the standard splitting method.

6. Acknowledgements

We would like to thank Sunil Arya for helpful discussions on the performance of the sliding-midpoint method.

References

[AM93a] S. Arya and D. M. Mount, *Algorithms for fast vector quantization*, Proc. Data Compression Conference, IEEE Press, 1993, pp. 381–390.

[AM93b] S. Arya and D. M. Mount, *Approximate nearest neighbor queries in fixed dimensions*, Proc. 4th ACM-SIAM Sympos. Discrete Algorithms, 1993, pp. 271–280.

[AMN+98] S. Arya, D. M. Mount, N. S. Netanyahu, R. Silverman, and A. Wu, *An optimal algorithm for approximate nearest neighbor searching*, Journal of the ACM **45** (1998), 891–923.

[Ben75] J. L. Bentley, *Multidimensional binary search trees used for associative searching*, Communications of the ACM **18** (1975), no. 9, 509–517.

[Ber93] M. Bern, *Approximate closest-point queries in high dimensions*, Inform. Process. Lett. **45** (1993), 95–99.

[BFOS84] L. Breiman, J. H. Friedman, R. A. Olshen, and C. J. Stone, *Classification and regression trees*, Wadsworth, Belmont, California, 1984.

[BG85] C.-D. Bei and R. M. Gray, *An improvement of the minimum distortion encoding algorithm for vector quantization*, IEEE Transactions on Communications **33** (1985), no. 10, 1132–1133.

[BKK96] S. Berchtold, D. A. Keim, and H.-P. Kriegel, *The X-tree: An index structure for high-dimensional data*, Proc. 22nd VLDB Conference, 1996, pp. 28–39.

[BKSS90] N. Beckmann, H.-P. Kriegel, R. Schneider, and B. Seeger, *The R*-tree: An efficient and robust access method for points and rectangles*, Proc. ACM SIGMOD Conf. on Management of Data, 1990, pp. 322–331.

[CH67] T. M. Cover and P. E. Hart, *Nearest neighbor pattern classification*, IEEE Trans. Inform. Theory **13** (1967), 57–67.

[Cha97] T. Chan, *Approximate nearest neighbor queries revisited*, Proc. 13th Annu. ACM Sympos. Comput. Geom., 1997, pp. 352–358.

[Cla94] K. L. Clarkson, *An algorithm for approximate closest-point queries*, Proc. 10th Annu. ACM Sympos. Comput. Geom., 1994, pp. 160–164.

[Cla97] K. L. Clarkson, *Nearest neighbor queries in metric spaces*, Proc. 29th Annu. ACM Sympos. Theory Comput., 1997, pp. 609–617.

[CS93] S. Cost and S. Salzberg, *A weighted nearest neighbor algorithm for learning with symbolic features*, Machine Learning **10** (1993), 57–78.

[DDF+90] S. Deerwester, S. T. Dumals, G. W. Furnas, T. K. Landauer, and R. Harshman, *Indexing by latend semantic analysis*, J. Amer. Soc. Inform. Sci. **41** (1990), no. 6, 391–407.

[DH73] R. O. Duda and P. E. Hart, *Pattern classification and scene analysis*, John Wiley & Sons, NY, 1973.

[DW82] L. Devroye and T. J. Wagner, *Nearest neighbor methods in discrimination*, Handbook of Statistics (P. R. Krishnaiah and L. N. Kanal, eds.), vol. 2, North-Holland, 1982.

[FBF77] J. H. Friedman, J. L. Bentley, and R. A. Finkel, *An algorithm for finding best matches in logarithmic expected time*, ACM Trans. Math. Software **3** (1977), no. 3, 209–226.

[For65] E. Forgey, *Cluster analysis of multivariate data: Efficiency vs. interpretability of classification*, Biometrics **21** (1965), 768.

[FPSSU96] U. M. Fayyad, G. Piatetsky-Shapiro, P. Smyth, and R. Uthurusamy, *Advances in knowledge discovery and data mining*, AAAI Press/Mit Press, 1996.

[FSN+95] M. Flickner, H. Sawhney, W. Niblack, J. Ashley, Q. Huang, B. Dom, M. Gorkani, J. Hafner, D. Lee, D. Petkovic, D. Steele, and P. Yanker, *Query by image and video content: The QBIC system*, IEEE Computer **28** (1995), 23–32.

[GG92] A. Gersho and R. M. Gray, *Vector quantization and signal compression*, Kluwer Academic, Boston, 1992.

[IM98] P. Indyk and R. Motwani, *Approximate nearest neighbors: Towards removing the curse of dimensionality*, Proc. 30th Annu. ACM Sympos. Theory Comput., 1998.

[JD88] A. K. Jain and R. C. Dubes, *Algorithms for clustering data*, Prentice Hall, Englewood Cliffs, New Jersey, 1988.

[Kle97] J. M. Kleinberg, *Two algorithms for nearest-neighbor search in high dimension*, Proc. 29th Annu. ACM Sympos. Theory Comput., 1997, pp. 599–608.

[KOR98] E. Kushilevitz, R. Ostrovsky, and Y. Rabani, *Efficient search for approximate nearest neighbor in high dimemsional spaces*, Proc. 30th Annu. ACM Sympos. Theory Comput., 1998.

[KS97] N. Katayama and S. Satoh, *The SR-tree: An index structure for high-dimensional nearest neighbor queries*, Proc. ACM SIGMOD Conf. on Management of Data, 1997, pp. 369–380.

[LJF94] K. I. Lin, H. V. Jagdish, and C. Faloutsos, *The TV-tree: An index structure for high-dimensional data*, VLDB Journal **3** (1994), no. 4, 517–542.

[MA97] D. M. Mount and S. Arya, *Ann: A library for approximate nearest neighbor searching*, CGC 2nd Annual Fall Workship on Computational Geometry, URL: `http://www.cs.umd.edu/~mount/ANN.`, 1997.

[Mac67] J. MacQueen, *Some methods for classification and analysis of multivariate observations*, Proc. of the Fifth Berkeley Symposium on Math. Stat. and Prob., vol. 1, 1967, pp. 281–296.

[Mit93] J. S. B. Mitchell, 1993, Private communication.

[MM99] S. Maneewongvatana and D. Mount, *It's okay to be skinny, if your friends are fat*, Center for Geometric Computing 4th Annual Workshop on Computational Geometry, 1999.

[Spr91] R. F. Sproull, *Refinements to nearest-neighbor searching in k-dimensional trees*, Algorithmica **6** (1991), no. 4, 579–589.

[SRF87] T. Sellis, N. Roussopoulos, and C. Faloutsos, *The R^+-tree: A dynamic index for multi-dimensional objects*, Proc. 13th VLDB Conference, 1987, pp. 507–517.

[WJ96] D. A. White and R. Jain, *Algorithms and strategies for similarity retrieval*, Technical Report VCL-96-101, Visual Computing Lab., Univ. California, San Diego, CA, 1996.

[Yia93] P. N. Yianilos, *Data structures and algorithms for nearest neighbor search in general metric spaces*, Proc. 4th ACM-SIAM Sympos. Discrete Algorithms, 1993, pp. 311–321.

Department of Computer Science, University of Maryland, College Park, Maryland 20742

E-mail address: `songrit@cs.umd.edu`

Department of Computer Science and Institute for Advanced Computer Studies, University of Maryland, College Park, Maryland 20742

E-mail address: `mount@cs.umd.edu`

DIMACS Series in Discrete Mathematics
and Theoretical Computer Science
Volume **59**, 2002

Approximate Nearest Neighbor Search using the Extended General Space-filling Curves Heuristic

Juan-Carlos Perez-Cortes and Enrique Vidal

ABSTRACT. In this work, the *Extended General Space-filling Curves Heuristic (EGSH)* is used to obtain an approximate nearest neighbor search algorithm for vector spaces. Under this scheme, a mapping is established between a region of the space and an interval of the real line, and then the problem is solved in one dimension. The resulting data structure, a b-tree for instance, is suitable for main memory or disk storage. The experiments on artificial and real data sets show a clear speed advantage over other methods, mainly in high dimensionalities and for large size corpora.

1. Introduction

The search of the nearest neighbors of a given point in a set of prototypes is a task common to a large number of applications such as: the estimation of probability densities using the $k-$nearest neighbors rule [**FH90a**] [**FH90b**] [**CH67**] [**Fuk90**], some methods of multivariate function learning [**PC94**] [**PG90**] [**Omo90**], most clustering techniques in vector spaces, also known as vector quantization methods [**And73**], [**Har74**], etc. A large (and increasing) number of other problems can benefit from an accurate and efficient method of nearest neighbor retrieval.

In this work, a heuristic for fast approximate search of nearest neighbors in a vector space is proposed. It is a direct application of the *Extended General Space-filling Curves Heuristic (EGSH)*, with the general procedures instantiated to find an approximate solution to the nearest neighbor problem.

The EGSH is a general method that can be applied to combinatorial optimization problems dealing with multidimensional objects [**PC94**] [**PV98b**]. It is specially applicable if the problem involves distance or similarity computations among the objects. The EGSH is a direct extension of the General Space-filling Heuristic (GSH)[**BP88**]. The method starts by mapping each point into the real line, using a space-filling mapping, to obtain a simpler one-dimensional problem. Once this problem is solved, the solution is returned or extrapolated, if necessary, to the original space. The extension consists of applying the space-filling mapping

2000 *Mathematics Subject Classification.* 68T20.
Key words and phrases. Nearest Neighbor Search, Heuristics, Space-filling Curves.
Work partially supported by the Spanish CICYT under grant TIC2000-1703-CO3-01.

several times to transformed variations of the input points, in an intent to recover the loss of spatial information incurred with the n−D to 1−D mapping process.

In the particular case of nearest neighbor search in $\mathbb{R}^n$, the n−dimensional prototypes are mapped into the real interval $[0, 1]$ and stored in an efficiently searchable data structure. When a search has to be performed, the test point is also mapped several times into that interval, and its 1−D neighbors are retrieved. A pool of neighbors is formed with all of them, and an exhaustive search in that pool is conducted (using the original distance measure in the n−dimensional space) to finally obtain the approximate nearest neighbor.

The work is organized as follows: Section 2 is an introduction to the nearest neighbor problem and reviews some of the fast search algorithms that have been proposed in the literature; Section 3 presents in detail the EGSH; Section 4 deals with the application of the EGSH to approximate nearest neighbor search in $\mathbb{R}^n$; Section 5 shows the results of the experiments performed with synthetic as well as with real data, and, finally, in Section 6 some conclusions are presented.

2. The Nearest Neighbor Problem

The Nearest Neighbor Problem in $\mathbb{R}^n$ can be formally expressed as follows: Given a set of N points (prototypes or training observations) $S = \{x_1, x_2, \ldots x_N\}$ in a real vector space, $x_i \in \mathbb{R}^n$, $1 \le i \le N$, a distance measure D in that space and a point $p \in \mathbb{R}^n$ (test point), not necessarily belonging to S, find an element x_j from S which minimizes the distance measure D from it to p. Formally, find an integer j such that

$$k = \arg \min_{1 \le i \le N} \{D(p, x_i)\}.$$

We will say that x_j is a nearest neighbor of p in set S according to metric D.

The temporal cost of the trivial solution to this problem, an exhaustive search in S, is in $O(nN)$ if we suppose, as we will do from now on, that the temporal cost of D is proportional to the dimension of the space, n. The spatial cost is also in $O(nN)$, since this method does not require the construction of any special data structure.

Since the number of prototypes in S can be very large, exhaustive search is in many cases not feasible. When the problem to solve is classification (given a partition of S into equivalence classes, hypothesize the class of p based on its nearest neighbors in S), we find a number of techniques [**Har68**], [**Wil72**], [**DK80**] [**Koh88**], [**GS91**] intended to reduce the number of prototypes, keeping the classification ability of the resulting subset. To do this, either redundant elements are deleted or new artificial prototypes are created, each representing a number of the original points. These pre-processing techniques are generically called *condensing* procedures and have traditionally yielded good results. Their main drawbacks seem to come from the loss of potentially useful information that inevitably appears and the high pre-processing costs usually involved for very large prototype sets.

A number of algorithms able to perform a search in a set of prototypes more efficiently than the exhaustive approach have been proposed. The techniques applied to obtain lower temporal costs are diverse. In Figure 1, a taxonomy of these algorithms, according to their performance and working principles, is shown.

Most algorithms for vector spaces are directly based on the construction of a data structure known as kd−tree [**FBS75**], [**FBF77**], [**BWY80**], [**KP86**], [**YY85**].

Fast nearest neighbor search algorithms							
Exact search				Approximate search			
Metric spaces		Real vector spaces		Metric spaces		Real vector spaces	
Average case	Worst case	Average case	Worst case	Average case	Worst case	Average case	Worst case
[**FN75**]		[**FBS75**]	[**DL76**]			[**Ber93**](1)	[**Ber93**](2)
[**Set81**]		[**Yun76**]	[**YY85**]				This work
[**KM83**]		[**FBF77**]					
		[**BWY80**]					
		[**KP86**]					
		[**NG88**]					

FIGURE 1. A taxonomy of fast nearest neighbor search algorithms.

A $kd-$tree is a binary tree where each node represents a region in a $k-$dimensional space. Each internal node also contains a hyper-plane (a linear subspace of dimension $k-1$) dividing the region into two disjoint sub-regions, each of which is inherited by one of their sons. Most of the trees used in the context of our problem divide the regions according to the points that lay in them. This way, the hierarchical partition of the space can either be carried out to the last consequences to obtain, in the leaves, regions with a single point in them, or can be halted in a previous level so as each leaf node holds b points in its region. A detailed description of these structures appears on the renowned work of Bentley [**Ben75**]. The more recent study by Sproull [**Spr91**] presents a very illustrative general exposition of the methods based on $kd-$trees. In that work a number of refinements of these methods are presented along with a general setting that allows the reader to clearly identify the different existing variants and choose one (or a combination of them) according to the peculiarities of the problem.

In a $kd-$tree, the search of the nearest neighbor of a test point is performed starting from the root, which represents the whole space, and choosing at each node the sub-tree that represents the region of the space containing the test point. When a leaf is reached, an exhaustive search of the b prototypes residing in the associated region is performed. Unfortunately, the process is not complete at this point. In that case, the cost involved in the search would be logarithmic with the number of points and the technique would be definitive and extremely useful. However, as noted before, it is perfectly possible that among the regions defined by the initial partition, the one containing the test point be not the one containing its nearest prototype. It is easy to determine if this can happen in a given configuration, in which case the algorithm backtracks as many times as necessary until it is sure to have checked all the regions that can hold a prototype nearer to the test point than the nearest one in the original region. The resulting procedure can be seen as a Branch-and-Bound algorithm.

Other algorithms, as the one proposed by Fukunaga and Narendra [**FN75**] and the ones in [**KPK85**] and [**NG88**], based on the previous one, perform a hierarchical partition of the space resorting to concepts different to those used in the kd−trees. In [**FN75**], a tree is obtained by means of a hierarchical clustering of the data. In [**NG88**], the partition does not depend on the data and, at each level, it resembles the shape of an n−dimensional histogram. The search in the trees obtained by these methods is performed applying similar concepts to the ones discussed for the classical kd−trees. Other data structures intended to improve on the kd−trees are for example the VP-trees [**Yia93**] and the Geometric Near-neighbor Access Trees (Gnat) [**Bri95**].

The methods cited have been developed by researchers working in the fields of Algorithmics, Data Structures, Computational Geometry, Pattern Recognition, etc., and are oriented towards main memory storage of the data structure, but a large number of disk-oriented data structures have also been devised in the field of Spatial Databases, Geometric Queries in Databases, Image Search and Retrieval, etc., among them the K-D-B-Trees [**Rob81**], the R-trees [**Gut83**], the Buddy trees [**SK87**], the R^+-trees [**SRF87**], R^*-trees [**BKSS90**], RT-trees [**Xu90**], TV-trees [**LJF94**], X-trees [**BKK96**], SR-trees [**KS97**], etc. Unfortunately, methods coming from these somewhat distant fields have not been compared or combined often. Obviously, the sequential nature of disk accesses has an effect on the performance of many algorithms that assume random access to the data. This is not the case for our method, which could be used in both environments.

Another populated class of main memory oriented techniques is composed by those which take advantage of certain properties of the metrics, particularly the Triangle Inequality, to readily discard prototypes that cannot possibly be the nearest to the test point, therefore limiting the extension of the search. Many of these methods do not require that the objects be represented in a real vector space. Among them, we can cite the ones proposed in [**Set81**], [**KM83**] and [**SW90**]. In [**VRC85**] and [**Vid86**] an algorithm called AESA is presented. This method is especially efficient when the cost of the distance measurement is high. For example, in Speech Recognition tasks where the distance between utterances is measured using Dynamic Time-warping, that method has proved to be very useful. In [**MOV94**] and [**Vil96**], variants of the AESA are proposed to reduce the high spatial complexity and the overhead (time consumed by the algorithm, but not devoted to distance computations) of the original algorithm. In [**RP92**], a version for vector spaces, also with a smaller spatial cost, is presented.

Algorithms in another group use projections to sort the prototypes and be able to search efficiently using a table or another ordered data structure. In [**FBS75**], the projections of the prototypes onto each co-ordinate axis are used to estimate the nearest one, and then to scan them in order. Yunck [**Yun76**] improves this idea building a data structure with hypercubes that limit the extension of the search. This concept is improved again by Nene and Nayar [**NN97**] with a more sophisticated data structure and by limiting the nearest neighbor distance to a maximum value. Bentley, Weide and Yao [**BWY80**] define a spiral around the test point and subdivide the space using a partition along the path of the spiral. This method has an average cost independent on the number of prototypes if a certain distribution of the prototypes is assumed.

Finally, some algorithms cannot be classified in any of these groups and use methods based on different somewhat unrelated concepts. In [**MS90**], multidimensional Voronoi Diagrams are used to obtain a method with an astounding average temporal cost, asymptotically independent on the number of prototypes and on the dimension of the space, at the expense of exponential space and pre-processing costs. Similar considerations can be expressed about the method by Clarkson [**Cla97**], which uses a Randomized Post Office tree. In Table 1, a summary of the temporal and spatial asymptotic costs of most of the algorithms discussed is shown.

In many cases, an absolute guarantee of finding the real nearest neighbor of the test point is not necessary. In this sense, a number of algorithms of *approximate nearest neighbor search* have been proposed. Some of them appear with their associated costs in Table 2. These methods can also be regarded as sub-optimal algorithms for the original problem of exact nearest neighbor search.

In [**MD83**], direct search in a tree is proposed as an approximate nearest neighbor algorithm. In this case, unlike in the exact methods, backtracking is not allowed. This means that when a leaf is reached, the algorithm will not check if it is possible that the nearest neighbor is in another sub-region, but the nearest prototype of the ones lying in the accessed leaf node will be directly selected instead. The specific tree used in that work is the one proposed in [**FN75**], but the same idea can be applied to other kinds of trees. In [**MD83**], additional experiments are presented showing that the accuracy of a classifier based on the cited sub-optimal algorithm is practically indistinguishable of the exact nearest neighbor rule for low dimensionalities of the space. When the dimension grows larger, however, the results degrade seriously.

In [**Ber93**], a method also based in a tree is presented. In this case, the tree is built independently on the data. The method guarantees that the maximum distance from the test point to the prototype found (approximate nearest neighbor) is less than $12n^{1/2}$ times the distance to its true nearest neighbor. In a second method presented in the same work, lower temporal and spatial costs are obtained for sequences of consecutive search operations, at the expense of a slightly worse bound that guarantees that the maximum distance from the test point to the prototype found is less than $O(n^{3/2})$ times the distance to its true nearest neighbor. Table 2 shows the asymptotic costs of these algorithms.

The interpretation of the costs summarized in Tables 1 and 2 is not direct in terms of usefulness and real performance in a practical application. The average costs shown come in some cases from an analytic study in which a certain distribution (typically, a uniform or a normal distribution) of the points is assumed. In other cases, they come from an empirical evaluation based on synthetic and/or real data.

In most applications, it is reasonable to use the average cost as a reliable estimation to judge the potential usefulness of the method unless the application considered pose real-time demands on the response time. The risk that a search requires, in the worst case, scanning every prototype makes the use of some methods impractical for certain real-time applications such as process control, robotics, etc. In these cases, a reasonable worst case bound is essential.

On the other hand, in typical applications without time-critical requirements, the magnitude that usually defines the problem complexity is the size of the set of prototypes. The algorithms in [**BWY80**] and [**KP86**] have an expected search time independent on that size. This makes them specially suited for problems where it can grow immoderately. However, the dependence of the average cost of these algorithms on the dimension of the feature space is exponential. This severely

TABLE 1. Algorithms for exact nearest neighbor search in a set of N prototypes. The costs are computed for points in an n−dimensional space using Minkowsky metrics. The algorithms marked with an asterisk, can also work in general metric spaces.

Algorithm	**Worst / Avg. temporal costs**	**Spatial / Pre-processing costs**	**Comments**
Exhaustive search*	$O(nN)$ $O(nN)$	$O(nN)$ $O(1)$	
[**FN75**]* [**KPK85**]* [**NG88**]*	$O(nN)$ $O(nN)$	$O(nN)$ $O(nN \log N)$	Avg. num. of distance computations is much lower than N
[**FBS75**]	$O(nN)$ $O(nN^{1-1/n})$	$O(nN)$ $O(nN \log N)$	In [**PB80**], a variant is proposed in $O(nN^{1-\frac{1}{n}})$ worst case time for metric L
[**Yun76**]	$O(nN)$ $O(n+N)$	$O(nN)$ $O(nN \log N)$	Avg. num. of distance computations independent on N
[**DL76**]	$O(n \log N)$ -	$O(nN^{2n})$ -	See [**Ber93**]
[**FBF77**]	$O(nN)$ $O(2^n \log N)$	$O(nN)$ $O(nN \log N)$	
[**BWY80**]	- $O(3^n)$	$O(2^n N)$ -	Avg. temp. cost independent on N
[**Set81**]	$O(nN)$ $O(n+N)$	$O(N)$ $O(nN+N \log N)$	Propor. constants lower than for exhaustive search
[**KM83**]*	$O(nN)$ $O(k^n \log N)$	$O(nN)$ $O(nN \log N)$	
[**YY85**]	$O(nN^{1-\epsilon_n})$ -	$O(nN)$ -	ϵ_n shrinks when n grows [**Ber93**]
[**KP86**]	$O(nN)$ $O(k^n)$	$O(nN)$ $O(nN \log N)$	Avg. temp. cost independent on N. Uses a hash table
[**Vid86**]*	$O(nN+N^2)$ $O(n+N)$	$O(N^2)$ $O(nN^2)$	Avg. num. of distance computations independent on N
[**MS90**]	$O(nN)$ $O(1)$	$O(N^{n/2})$ $O(N^{(n+1)/2})$	The authors give slightly tighter spatial and preprocessing bounds
[**RP92**] [**MOV94**]*	$O(nN)$ $O(n+N)$	$O(N)$ $O(nN)$	Avg. num. of distance computations independent on N
[**NN97**]	$O(nN)$ $O(n \log n)$	$O(nN)$ $O(nN \log N)$	Restricts search to a hypercube around the test point

limits the kind of problems that can be solved using these methods. The dimension of many Pattern Recognition problems is often between ten and one hundred, or even more. In a recent work [**MS90**], Murphy and Selkow propose a method with a cost independent on the number of prototypes and on the space dimension as

TABLE 2. Algorithms for exact nearest neighbor search in a set of N prototypes. The costs are computed for points in an $n-$dimensional real vector space. The algorithms marked with an asterisk can also work in general metric spaces.

Algorithm (reference)	**Worst / Avg. temporal costs**	**Spatial / Pre-processing costs**	**Comments**
[**MD83**]	$O(n + \log N)$ -	$O(nN)$ $O(nN \log N)$	Performance degrades very fast with the dimensionality
[**Ber93**] (1)*	$O(n2^n \log N)$ -	$O(n2^n N)$ $O(n2^n N)$	
[**Ber93**] (2)*	- $O(n \log N \log m)$	$O(nN \log m)$ $O(nN \log m)$	For m consecutive searches
Proposed method	$O(n + \log N)$ -	$O(nN)$ $O(nN + N \log N$	For a constant number of sub-models r
Proposed method	$O(n^2 + n \log N)$ -	$O(nN)$ $O(n^2 N + nN \log N)$	For r proportional to the dimension, n

well. Unfortunately, this extremely interesting result is obtained at the expense of pre-processing and space complexities exponential on the dimension.

Similar remarks can be made about the algorithms presented in [**FBF77**] and [**KM83**]. Their dependence on the number of prototypes is logarithmic, providing very efficient manipulation of huge prototype sets, but they pose the same problem as the previous methods when the dimension of the space is considered. In [**FBS75**], on the other hand, the average cost is sub-linear, but it approaches asymptotically $O(nN)$ for large dimensionalities. The method in [**NN97**] shows a better scalability with the dimension, although requires specifying a suitable size for a hypercube around the test point, which is increasingly difficult for real tasks in high dimensions, since the expected diameter of a k-nearest neigborhood increases with the dimensionality for a given data-set size [**Fri97**].

Algorithms in another group [**FN75**], [**Set81**], [**Vid86**], [**SW90**], [**RP92**], [**MOV94**] are focused on limiting the expected number of distance computations in order to make it independent on the size of the set of prototypes. This feature is of great importance when the objects of the problem lay in a (pseudo)metric space where the computation of a distance (or dissimilarity) is expensive. In the particular context of nearest neighbor search in $\mathbb{R}^n$ using Minkowsky metrics, the cost of the distance is proportional to the dimension of the space, n. This means that these algorithms are only useful when n is comparable to the number of prototypes, which is not a common case.

All the algorithms discussed until now have *worst-case* asymptotic computational costs equal or larger than the exhaustive search. Nonetheless, there are also algorithms with better worst-case complexities in Tables 1 and 2. Among the exact search methods, only the one proposed in [**DL76**] shows this property, more precisely, its cost is logarithmic on the number of prototypes and linear on the dimension of the space. This extraordinary result is, again, unfortunately, of little practical significance, as the spatial cost involved is really exorbitant: an exponential with the number of prototypes as the basis and two times the dimension of the space as the exponent.

Among the algorithms for approximate search, the one in [**MD83**] has a worst-case time cost logarithmic on the number of points and linear on the dimension. The effectiveness of this method decreases very quickly when the dimensionality scales up. However, the author proposes an enhanced method that uses several trees, each with a different partition of the space. With that technique, the results are greatly improved for moderately high values of the dimension. If, following the proposal made in Section 3.3 for our own method, a number of trees proportional to the dimension of the space were employed, instead of a constant number as proposed in [**MD83**], it is possible that the decrease of accuracy for higher dimensionalities were reduced. This is the effect detected in our model when the number of sub-models, r, is proportional to the dimension of the space n (see Sections 5.3 and 5.4). If this variation was used, the asymptotic costs of the method proposed in [**MD83**], shown in Table 2, would be multiplied by n, thus coinciding with the cost of our method.

An important note respect to the average costs of the algorithms based on search trees (most of the ones analyzed here) appears in [**Spr91**]. According to that author, it is not correct to assume in many practical cases that these algorithms achieve logarithmic or lower average costs. That assumption is valid for a low dimensionality, but when n increases, the number of points necessary to keep the average cost in the same terms is often extremely big. An illustrative example is offered in that work: in a 16-D space, a search in a tree with $75,857$ uniformly distributed points requires computing the distance to $72,774$ of them. This number could be greatly reduced if most points lay near a linear subspace with a lower dimension. This would imply that the *intrinsic dimensionality* of the sample is lower than n. In a properly designed pattern recognition model, however, the input variables should not be linearly dependent, since the pre-processing of the observations should dismiss most redundancies and correlations among the measured variables. Therefore, the use of a method based on $kd-$trees in a task dealing with objects with a large number of components should be considered carefully.

In [**ZO96**], a thorough study of the cost of many $kd-$tree algorithms for different sample sizes, dimensionalities and values of b (number of points in a leaf node) is presented. In the recent work of [**MS97**], a search method based on performing different space-filling-like encodings of the data is presented. It has some similarities to the technique proposed here.

A problem closely related to the search in a set of prototypes of the nearest neighbor of a point is the search of a subset with the k nearest neighbors, for a given constant k. In classification applications, the k-Nearest Neighbors Rule is a classical method which offers consistently good results, ease of use and certain theoretical properties related to the expected error [**CH67**]. Many other applications exist which require the search of the k nearest neighbors. The extension of most of the referenced algorithms to this variation of the problem is simple, with a cost equivalent or lower than k times the cost of the original algorithm. The method proposed here can also be extended very easily at no additional asymptotic cost, as will be discussed in the next section.

3. The Extended General Space-filling Heuristic

Space-filling Curves, also known as Peano Curves, are a class of fractal curves originally described by G. Peano and D. Hilbert at the end of the eighteenth century [**Pea90**], [**Hil91**]. Simply stated, a Space-filling Curve is a recursive structure that completely fills a region S with positive content in R^n. This means that every point in S belongs to the curve.

The origin of these structures can be traced to the work of G. Cantor in the last quarter of the nineteenth century, on cardinality and other properties of certain infinite sets. These works caused a commotion in the scientific community. In 1878, Cantor proved that all smooth manifolds of any (finite) dimension have the same cardinality. Thus, a bijective map can be established between a segment of the real line and, for example, a region of $R^n, n > 1$ [**Can78**]. Although a year later, in 1879, E. Netto proved that this correspondence could not be continuous [**Net79**], an important advancement had been made towards the discovery of the Space-filling Curves.

In a very interesting paper [**Sag91**], Hans Sagan describes how the result of Cantor in 1883, where he presented the famous Cantor Set, prepared the discovery of the Space-filling Curves. In fact, the Cantor Set or the "set of the excluded middle thirds" allowed a simple (although not direct) definition of a continuous map between the interval $[0,1]$ and the square $[0,1]^2$. The development of this mapping could benefit from the result of Netto proving that it could not be bijective. Therefore, the elaboration of a continuous surjective mapping from $[0,1]$ onto $[0,1]^2$ was perfectly feasible at that moment.

It was not this construction, however, the one that Peano used in 1890 to define the first curve able to completely fill up a plane area. In his paper *"Sur une courbe qui remplit toute une aire plaine"* Peano carried out the construction of a continuous mapping from $[0,1]$ onto $[0,1]^2$ through a clever approach.

A continuous mapping from $[0,1]$ into $[0,1]^2$ was arithmetically defined by Peano as follows: let the prefix operator k be the complement in base 3. So, $k0 = 2$, $k1 = 1$ and $k2 = 0$. Let therefore k^n be the application of this operator n times. If the real number $t \in [0,1]$ is, represented in base 3,

$$t = 0_{\dot{3}} a_1 a_2 a_3 \cdots ,$$

its image in $[0,1]^2$ according to the mapping defined by Peano (also in base 3) is (t_x, t_y), where (angled brackets have been used to delimit digits)

$$t_x = 0_{\dot{3}} \langle a_1 \rangle \langle k^{a_2} a_3 \rangle \left\langle k^{a_2+a_4} a_5 \right\rangle \cdots \left\langle k^{a_2+a_4+\cdots+a_{2n-2}} a_{2n-1} \right\rangle \cdots$$

and

$$t_y = 0_{\dot{3}} \langle k^{a_1} a_2 \rangle \left\langle k^{a_1+a_3} a \right\rangle \cdots \left\langle k^{a_1+a_3+\cdots+a_{2n-1}} a_{2n} \right\rangle \cdots .$$

A proof that this mapping is continuous and surjective (every point in $[0,1]^2$ has an anti-image in $[0,1]$, so that the unit square is "filled-up") appears in the original work and also, with a more modern notation in [**Sag91**].

One year later, D. Hilbert developed a new formulation, in this case of a geometrical nature, which also showed the properties of a space-filling curve [**Hil91**]. In [**Sag91**], a brief description of that work is presented in English.

Peano and Hilbert state in their respective works that their constructions are continuous functions which lack a derivative in every point. Remarkably enough, none of them proves this assertion that, although true [**Moo00**] [**Sag91**], is neither trivial nor evident to prove. Another interesting property of some space-filling curves is *homogeneity.* A space-filling curve is said to be homogeneous if segments of equal length fill regions of equal area, which means that the curve fills the plane in an even way.

Other space-filling curves have appeared after these initial works, like Lebesgue's space-filling curve [**Sch38**], Sierpinski's curve (the one used here) [**Sie12**], etc. Recently, in [**OO91b**], [**OO91a**] and [**OO92**], a number of space-filling curves are obtained through a systematic survey of possible constructions using a geometrical generation model. Unfortunately, in these works all the curves considered are "plane-filling" and no mention is made of curves that completely fill regions of more than two dimensions.

3.1. Formal definition of a space-filling curve.

DEFINITION 3.1. [**Sag91**] The function $\psi : [0,1] \to R^n, n \geq 2$, represents a space-filling curve if it is continuous and the image of the interval $[0,1]$ is an $n-$dimensional region with positive content.

In this work, we have used the space-filling curve defined by Sierpinski in 1912 [**Sie12**]. The original definition, only for the plane, is as follows:

DEFINITION 3.2. [**Sie12**] Let t be a real value in the unit interval, $t \in [0,1]$. The function $\psi : [0,1] \to [0,1]^2$

$$\psi(t) = \left(f(t), f\left(t - \frac{1}{4}\right)\right)$$

defines a continuous curve, symmetric to both co-ordinate axis, and passing through every point in $[0,1]^2$.

The proofs of these facts appear in the work cited. Function f is defined as follows:

$$f = \frac{\theta(t)}{2} - \frac{\theta(t)\theta(\tau(t))}{2^2} + \frac{\theta(t)\theta(\tau(t))\theta(\tau^2(t))}{2^3} \cdots + (-1)^{n-1}\frac{\theta(t)\theta(\tau(t))\cdots\theta(\tau^{n-1}(t))}{2^n} \cdots$$

where

$$\theta(t) = \begin{cases} 1 & 0 \leq t < \frac{1}{4} \\ -1 & \frac{1}{4} \leq t < \frac{1}{2} \\ -1 & \frac{1}{2} \leq t < \frac{3}{4} \\ -1 & \frac{3}{4} \leq t < 1 \end{cases}$$

An interpretation of this curve by Sierpinski is that $\psi(t)$ is the limit of an infinite succession of closed polygonal curves. Some of the first terms of this succession are shown in Figure 2. The round shapes used in the picture are intended to emphasize the continuity of the curve. In fact, at a given level of detail, the function holds the same value in every point of each triangle.

In [**BP88**], a generalization of Sierpinski's curve to dimensionalities larger than 2 is proposed. The image $\psi(\rho)$ in a multidimensional space, of a real value $\rho \in [0,1]$, can be easily computed using the algorithm described in that work.

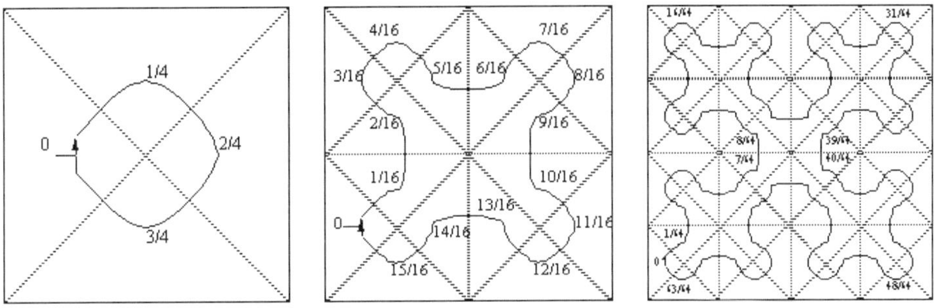

FIGURE 2. Three terms of the succession of curves defined by Sierpinski. This succession converges in the limit to Sierpinski's Space-filling Curve.

We can also easily compute a mapping ψ that can be considered an inverse of the previous one. In fact, ψ is a surjective mapping and, therefore, its inverse is not uniquely defined in general. In the plane, for example, the point $(0.5, 0.5)$, has four anti-images: $1/8, 3/8, 5/8$ and $7/8$, i.e. $\psi(1/8) = \psi(3/8) = \psi(5/8) = \psi(7/8) = (0.5, 0.5)$. We will call *space-filling curve mapping*, denoted by ψ^{-1}, to a certain function defined from $[0,1]^n$ into $[0,1]$, satisfying $\psi\left(\psi^{-1}(\rho)\right) = \rho$. It is not important the criterion used to decide which anti-image of ψ is used when more than one exists [**PB89**].

From an intuitive viewpoint, the value of $\psi^{-1}(x)$ can be obtained by computing the fraction of the course described by the curve from itsorigin to x, relative to the total length of the curve. This computation can be performed for some curves using extremely simple and efficient methods. In the case of Sierpinski's Curve, the spatial and temporal costs involved are in $O(kn)$, where n is the dimension of the original space and k is the number of binary digits of precision required per dimension. The result of this process is a value in the interval $[0,1]$ with kn binary digits of precision. We will study later in detail the actual computations involved.

The remarkable properties of the space-filling curves confer a high interest to this mapping. The most important of these properties is the preservation of a notion of proximity: any pair of points which are close in the original (multidimensional) space must be mapped into nearby points in the Real Line, and distant points in the space must be mapped into distant points in the Real Line. Although this does not seem possible in general, given the higher information content of most useful distance measures in high-dimensional spaces, mappings based in some continuous and homogeneous space-filling curves have a related property. It is formalized in Lemma 3.3 for the Curve of Sierpinski in the plane. It implies that, if the mapping ψ^{-1} is used, any pair of points which are close in $[0,1]$ are images of points close in $[0,1]^2$.

LEMMA 3.3. [**PB89**]

$$D\left(\psi(\rho), \psi(\rho')\right) \leq 2\sqrt{\Delta\left(\rho, \rho'\right)} \forall \rho, \rho' \in [0,1]$$

where D is the Euclidean Distance and Δ is the following cyclic metric in the unit interval: $\Delta[\rho, \rho'] = min\{|\rho - \rho'|, 1 - |\rho - \rho'|\}$. A proof of this lemma can be found in [**PB89**], along with other interesting properties of space-filling curves.

Although this property does not assure that the distances among points in the space are preserved by their images in the Real Line, at least one can be sure that a small distance between two points in the line guarantees a small distance between their anti-images in the high-dimensional space. Conversely, it is not true in general that long distances in the line correspond to long distances in the space. This fact precludes the *direct* use of space-filling curves in the nearest neighbor search and other applications that need a preservation of the relative distances among the points. We circumvent the problem by using more than one space-filling curve, as shown in Section 3.3.

In Algorithms 1 and 2, implementations in pseudo-code of ψ and ψ^{-1} are presented. Both are based on the one proposed in [**BP88**] [1] In Algorithm 3, efficient conversions from natural binary to binary reflected Gray code and vice-versa are given for convenience. Other Gray codes can be used. See Section 3.4.1.

Using this algorithm for function ψ^{-1}, the cost of the computation of the unidimensional value associated, via Sierpinski's Space-filling Curve Mapping, with an $n-$dimensional vector with k bits of precision per dimension is linear with n and with k (belongs to $O(kn)$) if the uniform cost criterion is adopted. This implies assuming that the costs of the basic operations are independent on the size (number of bits) of their arguments. It is only reasonable if the data involved can be represented with a fixed maximum number of bits, typically equal to the size of the numeric representation used.

The typical size of most modern floating point formats is between 16 and 128, values which can easily be lower than kn even for moderate values of k. Therefore, we have to take into account that the precision of the resulting real value, measured in terms of binary digits, depends linearly on the number of dimensions n, which makes necessary to apply the logarithmic cost criterion. According to this criterion, the number of steps S required for a basic operation is no longer constant, but depends linearly on the number of bits of its operands (logarithm of their absolute values). In our case, however (and exceptionally), the asymptotic cost does not change when we use this, more restrictive, criterion. Since the only quantities of variable size used in the algorithm of function ψ^{-1} are variables C, Q and S, which represent values in the unit interval derived from the $n-$dimensional input vector, the only additional cost is introduced in the lines where these variables appear. The increase in the cost of these lines, from constant to linear, does not change the total asymptotic cost of the algorithm, since this cost was already dominated by three loops with cost in $O(n)$, all of which only contain quantities with a precision independent on the dimension.

In [**Bia69**] [**But71**] and [**PB89**], efficient versions of algorithms for the generation of specific space-filling curves appear. In contrast with the generic algorithms shown here, these procedures make use of bit operations and are optimized at a low level. On the other hand, in [**Mas89**], the Iterated Functional Systems Theory is presented as the ideal framework for the geometric construction and description of

---

[1] The implementation of ψ^{-1} is directly based on the one proposed in [**BP88**], save a slight difference due to a typographical error in the original work. The algorithm for ψ has been derived to specifically perform the inverse of ψ^{-1}.

Algorithm 1 Function $\Psi(n, k, r)$

Problem: Given two positive integers k and n, and a real value $r \in [0, 1]$ with a precision of kn binary digits, compute the vector $x = \psi(r) \in [0, 1]^n$, with a precision of k binary digits for each component of x.

Input: $n, k \in \mathbb{N}$; $r \in \mathbb{R}$

Output: $\Psi \in \mathbb{R}^n$ {Ψ_i will denote the ith binary digit of Ψ}

Variables: $i, j \in \mathbb{N}$; $t, g \in \mathbb{R}^n$; $C, Q, S \in \mathbb{R}$

Auxiliary Functions:

Function Int: $\mathbb{R} \to \mathbb{Z}$ {Int(y) computes the greater integer less or equal to y (e.g. Int(-1.3)=-2)}

Function Fract: $\mathbb{R} \to [0, 1)$ {Fract(y) computes the fractional part of y. Fract(y)= y−Int(y) (e.g. Fract(-1.3)=0.7)}

Function GrayToDec: $\{0, 1\}^n \to \mathbb{N}$ {Converts a Gray-coded binary number into a decimal integer.}

Function DecToGray: $\mathbb{N} \to \{0, 1\}^n$ {Converts a decimal integer into a Gray-coded binary number.}

Method:

```
C ← GrayToDec(11...1) {Value with n ones in the chosen Gray code}
if k = 0 or r = 0.5 then
  for i = 1 to n do
    Ψ_i ← 1
  end for
else
  Q ← Int(2^n r + C) mod 2^n
  S ← Fract(2^n r − Q + C)
  j ← 1
  for i = 1 to n do
    if x_i ≥ 0.5 then
      j ← 1 − j
    end if
  end for
  if j = 0 then
    S ← 1 − S
  end if
  t ← Ψ(n, k − 1, S)
  g ← DecToGray(Q)
  for i = 1 to n do
    if g_i = 1 then
      Ψ_i ← t_i/2 + 0.5
    else
      Ψ_i ← 0.5 − t_i/2
    end if
  end for
end if
```

Algorithm 2 Function $\Psi^{-1}(n, k, x)$

Problem: Given two positive integers k and n, and a vector $x \in [0,1]^n$, compute a real value $r \in [0,1]$, with a precision of kn binary digits, such that $\psi(r) = x$.
Input: $n, k \in \mathbb{N}$; $x \in \mathbb{R}^n$
Output: $\Psi^{-1} \in \mathbb{R}$
Variables: $i, j \in \mathbb{N}$; $t, y \in \mathbb{R}^n$; $C, Q, S \in \mathbb{R}$
Auxiliary Functions: See Algorithm 1
Method:

```
C ← GrayToDec(11...1) {Value with n ones in the chosen Gray code}
if k = 0 or (x_i = 1 ∀i, 1 ≤ i ≤ n) then
  Ψ^{-1} ← C
else
  for i = 1 to n do
    t_i ← min(Int(2x_i), 1)
  end for
  Q ← GrayToDec(t)
  for i = 1 to n do
    y_i ← 2|x_i − 0.5|
  end for
  S ← Ψ^{-1}(n, k − 1, y)
  j ← 1
  for i = 1 to n do
    if x_i ≥ 0.5 then
      j ← 1 − j
    end if
  end for
  if j = 0 then
    S ← 1 − S
  end if
  Ψ^{-1} ← Fract((Q+S−C)/2^n)
end if
```

space-filling curves. More specifically, it is shown there that a space-filling curve is an attractor of an iterated function system.

3.2. Applications of space-filling curves. A number of practical applications can be found in the literature, mainly in the fields of Mathematical Programming, Information Theory and Combinatorial Optimization, among others.

In the later 60's, Patrick *et al.* tackled the problem of computer screen representation of multivariate functions [**PAB68**]. The proposed method consisted of a simple scan of the multidimensional space using continuous curves. Among the curves studied appears a space-filling curve designated by the authors as the "Column Mapping" curve.

One year later, Butz proposed an application of space-filling curves to the solution of difficult problems in Mathematical Programming and Numerical Analysis, such as the resolution of equation and inequation systems, and the search of values lower than a given threshold in functions of several variables [**But69**]. The

Algorithm 3 Auxiliary functions

Function GrayToDec(b)**:** Converts a Binary-Reflected Gray-coded number into a decimal integer.
Input: $b \in \{0,1\}^n$
Output: GrayToDec $\in \mathbb{N}$
Variables: $i \in \mathbb{N}$; $bnat \in \{0,1\}^n$
Method:

```
bnat_n ← b_n {Sub-indices represent binary digits}
for i = n − 1 to 1 with step -1 do
  if b_i ≠ bnat_{i+1} then
    bnat_i ← 1
  else
    bnat_i ← 0
  end if
end for
GrayToDec ← Decimal(bnat)
```

Function DecToGray(r)**:** Converts a decimal integer into a Binary-Reflected Gray-coded number.
Input: $r \in \mathbb{R}$
Output: DecToGray $\in \{0,1\}^n$
Variables: $i \in \mathbb{N}$; $rnat, rgray \in \{0,1\}^n$
Method:

```
rnat ← Binary(r)
rgray_n ← rnat_n {Sub-indices represent binary digits}
for i = n − 1 to 1 with step -1 do
  if rnat_i ≠ rnat_{i+1} then
    rgray_i ← 1
  else
    rgray_i ← 0
  end if
end for
DecToGray ← rgray
```

interesting method proposed by Butz can be described as an "implicitly exhaustive search", given that *every point* in the domain is taken into account, without performing explicit computations in all of them. More specifically, assuming a certain smoothness property in the function, the procedure gives values to a variable r_i in the unit interval, computing at each step the value of the function in the associated point of the multidimensional space. This method guarantees that a point that meets the target condition is never bypassed. To achieve this, each step from $r_i - 1$ to r_i moves the scanning point in the real line as much as possible, depending on the value of the function on the previous point, making sure that a convergence point is not surpassed. The examples reported show a very good scanning speed in problems with at least one solution and also in cases where the condition cannot be met. The curve used in that work is Hilbert's space-filling curve, which is shown to have a number of advantages over Peano's and Lebesgue's curves for that application.

Also in the year 1969, Bially proposed the use of a space-filling curve for reducing the bandwidth in telecommunications [**Bia69**]. In this case, the idea consisted of grouping n consecutive values in a waveform to form an $n-$dimensional vector. The waveform is then converted into a sequence of vectors and each of them is mapped into a real value, reducing the required bandwidth by a factor of n. The advantage of using a mapping based on a space-filling curve is that small distortions on the transmitted values produce small changes in the decoded waveform. This is a direct consequence of the continuity of these curves in the $n-$dimensional space. In the cited work, an interesting method for the generation of space-filling curves is proposed, based on a special type of state diagrams.

Chauny et al. [**CHW87**] used a 3$-$dimensional space-filling curve in a problem of drill operations sequencing in an industrial environment. The procedure is based on a scheme that encodes two spatial dimensions of a metal sheet to be drilled plus one dimension related to the kind of tool used. The operations are sorted according to a path that is a solution of the Traveling Salesman Problem in that space. The solution proposed is inspired by the method presented in [**BP83**]: the drilling points are mapped into one dimension through the space-filling curve and these values are then sorted to obtain the sequence of operations to follow.

Bartholdi and Platzman [**BP83**], [**BP88**], [**PB89**] apply space-filling curves to approximately solve the Planar Traveling Salesman Problem and the Planar Matching Problem. They also suggest the way to apply space-filling curves to other path-finding, combinatorial optimization and clustering problems. Moreover, they generalize the resolution method to obtain a general heuristic that will be analyzed in the next section. An extension originally proposed in [**PC94**] that greatly expands its range of applications is also presented in the next section [**PV98b**], [**PV98a**].

3.3. An extension to the General Space-filling Heuristic. In [**BP88**], the General Space-filling Heuristic (GSH) is presented as a generic procedure, useful in many combinatorial optimization problems where the data-set is composed by points in a multidimensional space, and the solution involves the preservation of some notion of proximity among them. The method consists of mapping each point into the real line (using a space-filling mapping such as ψ^{-1}) to get an easier or more efficiently tractable problem in one dimension. Once the reduced problem is solved, the points, along with the solution found, are returned to the original space.

The General Space-filling Heuristic is not really a heuristic, but a complete family, a methodology. This is the reason for the adjective *"general"*. Its application to a specific problem requires an instantiation of the idea and the particular details involved. Perhaps the examples that follow can help to clarify the technique.

The first instantiation of this general heuristic is proposed by its authors [**BP83**], and has been cited in the previous section. It deals with finding an approximate solution to the Traveling Salesman Problem in the plane, and its asymptotic cost is in $O(n \log(n))$ where n is the number of points to visit. According to the general heuristic, each data point is in first place mapped into the real line. The resulting set on n values can be sorted with a cost in $O(n \log(n))$ using a classical sort algorithm such as *merge-sort* or *heap-sort*. Taking the one-dimensional values in ascending order, the corresponding points on the plane will arrange a path with a length close to the minimum. As proved in [**PB89**], the worst ratio between the length of the approximate solution and the minimum length is in $O(\log(n))$. In that work, it is conjectured that the bound is not tight and that the ratio is probably in $O(1)$. However, in [**BG89**] a counterexample is presented which proves that Platzman and Bartholdi's bound is tight. Finally, in [Steele,89] a more detailed bound is proposed which is valid in spaces with more than two dimensions. In [**Ima86**] a more efficient variation of the cited algorithm is presented, and the behavior of both versions in the worst case is studied.

These approximate solutions to the Planar Traveling Salesman Problem are used in [**BP83**] and [**Ima86**] to obtain an (also approximate) solution to the Minimum-Weight Matching Problem on the plane, defining the pairs of matching points as the consecutive pairs of points in the Traveling Salesman Path. In the cited references, some bounds are proposed on the quality ratio between the approximate and the optimal solution, which has an asymptotic worst case cost in $O(n^3)$.

In [**BP88**], another interesting application of the GSH is presented: clustering on the plane. As in previous cases, a real value is obtained using the space-filling curve for every point of the problem and a clustering procedure is applied in one dimension. In that work, the use of the $k-$means algorithm is suggested. That setting seems to be of little value, as the $k-$means algorithm can be directly used on the plane and, in general, in $\mathbb{R}^n, n > 0$. In [**San93**], we proposed the use of a clustering algorithm based on Dynamic Programming, which is globally optimal but only applicable to values in the real line. The results did not appear to be useful in practice.

The GSH is simple and extremely fast in general but, as a consequence of the fact that ψ^{-1} cannot map consistently any connected region of the space into a (connected) interval of the Real Line, it often gives rise to intolerable discontinuities in the resultant mapping. These discontinuities are especially remarkable in certain areas that we will call *conflictive regions*. The following example in the plane can be clarifying: among the points near $(0.5, 0.5)$, those that belong to different quadrants lay in very distant positions of the curve (see Figure 3) and are therefore mapped into very distant values in the Real Line.

It should be noticed that these conflictive regions are not restricted to a finite number of areas localized in the hypercube. Instead, they are widespread in it, and its number is only bounded by the accuracy in the computation of the mapping. In other words, every region in the hypercube is, in a sense, conflictive, since it introduces discontinuities at a given level of precision. This can be easily understood if the recursive nature of space-filling curves is recalled. Its recursive definition implies a reproductive property that guarantees that at any level of detail, we can find small sub-curves identical to the whole curve.

Nonetheless, not every region holds discontinuities of the same significance. A *degree of conflictivity* can thus be established for a region. The central area in Figure 3 has the highest degree of conflictivity, since it gives rise to the highest possible dispersion in the Real Line of the values resulting from the mapping to one dimension of some points in that bi-dimensional region.

As a solution to the discontinuity problem, we have developed an extension to Platzman and Bartholdi's heuristic. The ***Extended*** *General Space-filling Heuristic* consists, in essence, of applying the space-filling mapping r times, where r is a

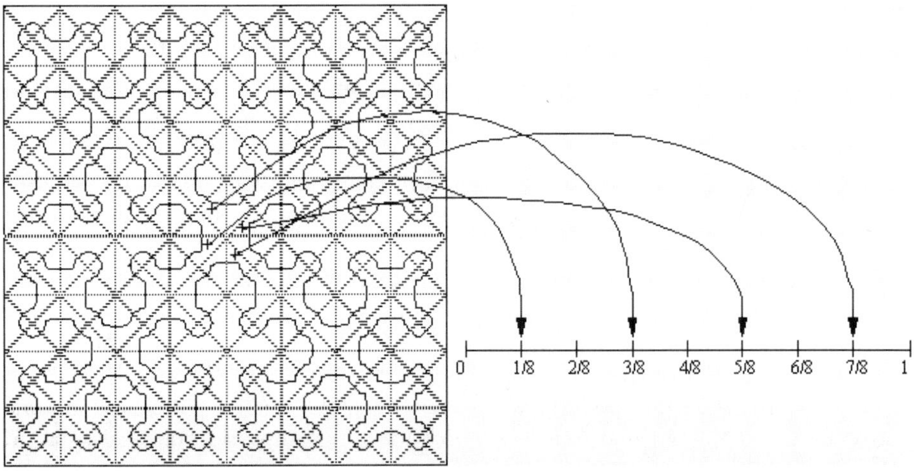

FIGURE 3. An example in the plane. Four points near $(0.5, 0.5)$ and their mapping into the Real Line using Sierpinski's Space-filling curve. This example illustrates the fact that nearby points in the Real Line *always* come from nearby points in the multidimensional space, but *it is not true that nearby points in the space be always mapped into nearby points on the line.*

constant to be defined later. Of course, if the mapping was applied repeatedly to the same data, the outcome would be always the same. Instead, each application of the mapping works on the original data affected by a distinct transformation. Therefore, the areas introducing major distortions will correspond to points in different regions of the original representation space. Each tandem transformation-mapping will constitute a distinct uni-dimensional sub-model of the problem. All these sub-models, adequately combined, will configure the final model.

The sequence of operations of this first solution is:

(1) Normalize the set of points to fit into the unit Hypercube $[0, 1]^n$
(2) For each sub-model i :
   - Apply a transformation to all the $n-$dimensional points of the problem,
   - Map each transformed point into $[0, 1]$ by applying a space-filling mapping (for instance, ψ^{-1})
   - Solve the uni-dimensional problem.
(3) Combine the solutions of the different sub-models to obtain a global solution. In some cases, this combination can include a weight factor for each partial solution, according to a measure of its local quality.

The number of models r can be as high as necessary to obtain a satisfactory solution to the problem. It seems reasonable that this parameter be proportionally related to the dimension of the input space, n. Using, for instance, $r = n$ sub-models, n real values are obtained (one per sub-model) from input vectors with n

components, which suggests a certain degree of conservation of the original information[2]. Values of $r = 2n$ or $r = 3n$ are also typical in cases where better results are needed and, values of $r = n/2$, $r = n/3$, etc. can be used if lower costs are more important (see Section 5.4).

3.4. The transformations. The simplest choice for the required set of transformations is probably a set of translations. Since the transformed data must lay in the unit hypercube, a "re-normalizing" procedure has to be used. A simple option consists of restoring the points that have been taken out from the unit hypercube (by the translation) again into it, simply by taking the fractional part of the "overflowed" components. More formally, to obtain a model with r sub-models, the following r transformations, $\mathcal{T}_i : \mathbb{R}^n \to \mathbb{R}^n, 1 \leq i \leq r$, can be defined:

$$\mathcal{T}_i(x) = \mathcal{T}_i \begin{pmatrix} x_1 \\ x_2 \\ \vdots \\ x_n \end{pmatrix} = \begin{pmatrix} \text{fract}(O_{i,1} + x_1) \\ \text{fract}(O_{i,2} + x_2) \\ \vdots \\ \text{fract}(O_{i,n} + x_n) \end{pmatrix}, \quad 0 \leq O_{i,j} \leq 1, \quad \begin{matrix} 1 \leq i \leq r \\ 1 \leq j \leq n \end{matrix}$$

where fract(y) returns the fractional part of y and $O_i \in \mathbb{R}^n, 1 \leq i \leq r$, are the parameter vectors of the translations. An adequate choice of these vectors is essential (see Section 3.5).

A problem inherent in these transformations is the discontinuity they produce in the points near the new axes, causing some nearby points in the original set to be very distant after the transformation. This is not a very important problem, since it concerns only a reduced set of points *different for every transformation.* A more serious problem is created by the discontinuity present near the axes of the original hypercube, which makes possible that very distant points (in the original space) become neighbors in *many or even all the transformations.* In Figure 4, an example of this phenomenon is depicted.

As a solution to this problem, a new set of transformations $\mathcal{T}'_i : \mathbb{R}^n \to \mathbb{R}^n, 1 \leq i \leq r$, can be defined as follows:

$$\mathcal{T}'_i(x) = \mathcal{T}'_i \begin{pmatrix} x_1 \\ x_2 \\ \vdots \\ x_n \end{pmatrix} = \begin{pmatrix} \begin{cases} O_{i,1} + x_1 & \text{if} \quad O_{i,1} + x_1 \leq 1 \\ 1 - \text{fract}(O_{i,1} + x_1) & \text{if} \quad O_{i,1} + x_1 > 1 \end{cases} \\ \begin{cases} O_{i,2} + x_2 & \text{if} \quad O_{i,2} + x_2 \leq 1 \\ 1 - \text{fract}(O_{i,2} + x_2) & \text{if} \quad O_{i,2} + x_2 > 1 \end{cases} \\ \vdots \\ \begin{cases} O_{i,n} + x_n & \text{if} \quad O_{i,n} + x_n \leq 1 \\ 1 - \text{fract}(O_{i,n} + x_n) & \text{if} \quad O_{i,n} + x_n > 1 \end{cases} \end{pmatrix}$$

$$0 \leq O_{i,j} \leq 1, \quad \begin{matrix} 1 \leq i \leq r \\ 1 \leq j \leq n \end{matrix}$$

[2]In fact, if a precision of kn bits is held in the result, being k the number of bits of precision of the original variables, the information of the whole vector is kept by each unidimensional value (the original vector can be exactly recovered using function ψ). However, an intuitive notion of structural or topological information is meant in this context, representing the potential to recover the scheme of relative proximities of the original space.

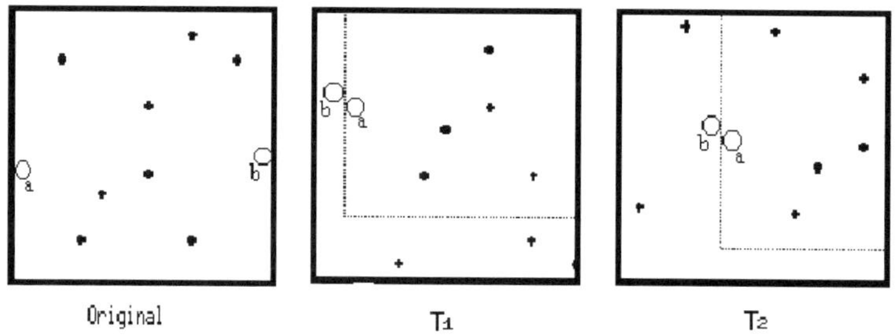

FIGURE 4. Points a and b, distant in the original set, are very near in all the transformed spaces. This can generate a serious problem since it could distort subsequent estimations, typically based on neighborhood concepts.

These new transformations do not present the problem just discussed, since their effect on the points that are "taken out" of the hypercube is *symmetrically opposed to the previous one.* The discontinuity introduced is similar, but in this case it affects the points in a different way for each transformed set. The generation of the parameter vectors of the translations will be discussed in a subsequent section, but it is interesting to note now that we will typically use parameter vectors uniformly distributed in the unit hypercube.

The experiments carried out, however (see Section 5.2), suggest that $\mathcal{T}$ is a better option than $\mathcal{T}'$ in the nearest neighbor search problem. Additionally, as we will see in Section 3.4.2, all these transformations will be preceded in the final model by different rotation operations that will cancel out the effects mentioned.

3.4.1. *The curse of dimensionality.* The proposed method, as stated, poses a serious problem when it is applied to high-dimensional spaces. When the space-filling mapping is applied, the course of the curve causes that the image of some axes, when mapped into the real line, at a given precision, become composed of connected intervals longer than those of other axes (see Figure 5). This means that the potential neighborhood of two given points, due to close values in a very "fragmented" axis are respected to a lesser extent than a neighborhood emanated from close values of a component with an axis offering a more "connected" set of image intervals in the real line. This is derived from the use of the simple Binary Reflected Gray code in the computation of the mapping (see auxiliary functions in Algorithm 3). Other Gray Codes exist which do not show this behavior.

The interpretation of this fact in more than three dimensions is possible if we consider the direct relation between the fragmentation present in the image of the $i-$th axis, via Sierpinski's space-filling curve computed with a given precision level, and the number of consecutive *ones* (or *zeroes*) of the $i-$th bit in the succession of integers expressed in a Gray code. This codification is the one used to number the vertices of the unit hypercube in such a way that any two consecutive vertices are always adjacent. With this setting, it is easy to see that the most significant bits change less often than the least significant bits, as shown in 5.

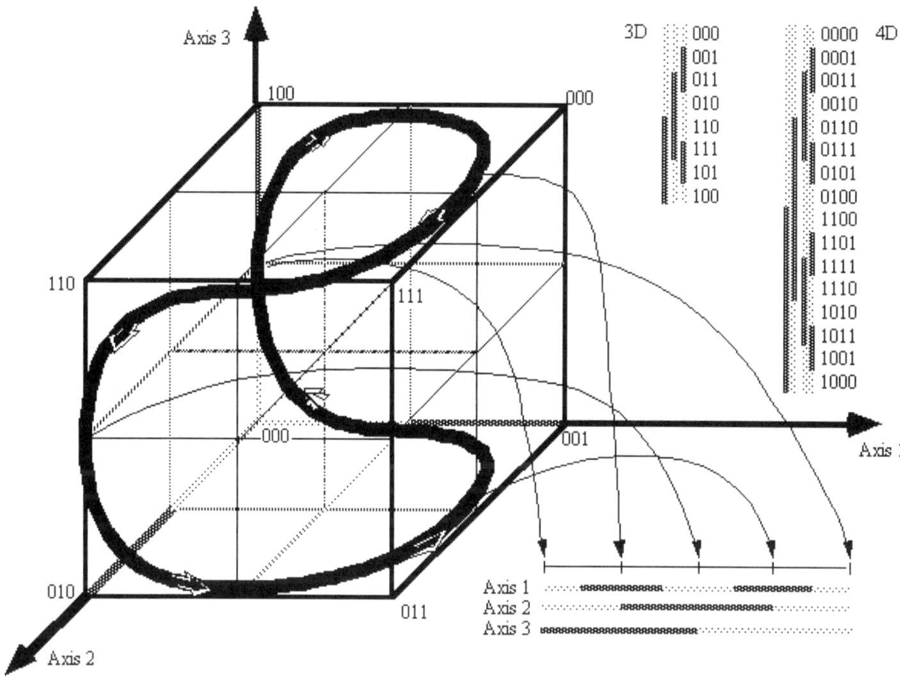

FIGURE 5. Effect of the "fragmentation" of the image of certain components of the input vectors when mapped into the real line. The representation corresponds to Sierpinski's curve in three dimensions with a precision of 1 bit per dimension. Consequently, each axis has been divided into two parts and the image of each of these parts in the real line has been drawn with the same pattern. In the upper-right area of the figure, the relation of these images with the number of the octant traversed by the curve, expressed in Binary Reflected Gray code, has been depicted. This allows an easy extension of the visualization of this phenomenon into more than three dimensions.

A solution for this important problem can be devised by introducing a new component in the transformations, to obtain not only a translation but, for each transformed component, a linear combination of the original input components. If the contribution of each original component to each transformed component varies (randomly or in some appropriate way) with the index of the transformation, the preponderance of the last (or whatever) components will vanish.

The formulation used will be based on *preceding* the transformation already discussed with a rotation of the space with center in the origin. Obviously, the normalization before the translation is still necessary and has to be applied *after* the rotation to keep the points inside the unit hypercube.

Other, possibly complementary, solutions to this problem, based on using Balanced Gray codes instead of the usual Binary Reflected Gray code to compute the

TABLE 3. Binary Reflected Gray Code and Cyclic Approximately Balanced Gray Codes for 4 and 5 bit words

4-bit Binary Reflected Gray Code	4-bit Balanced Gray Code	5-bit Binary Reflected Gray Code		5-bit Balanced Gray Code	
0000	0000	00000	10000	00000	10111
0001	1000	00001	10001	10000	10101
0011	1100	00011	10011	11000	10001
0010	1101	00010	10010	11100	11001
0110	1111	00110	10110	11110	11101
0111	1110	00111	10111	11111	01101
0101	1010	00101	10101	01111	01100
0100	0010	00100	10100	01110	01000
1100	0110	01100	11100	00110	01010
1101	0100	01101	11101	00010	11010
1111	0101	01111	11111	00011	11011
1110	0111	01110	11110	01011	10011
1010	0011	01010	11010	01001	10010
1011	1011	01011	11011	00001	10110
1001	1001	01001	11001	00101	10100
1000	0001	01000	11000	00111	00100

space-filling mapping, are being studied. Balanced Gray Codes are exhaustive listings of $n-$bit strings in which successive strings differ in exactly one bit position (Gray codes) and which have an (approximately) equal number of transitions, 0 to 1 or 1 to 0, in each of the n components. In Table 3, examples of cyclic Balanced Gray codes for two values of n are shown. In [**BS96**], the fact that approximately balanced cyclic Gray Codes exist for all n is proved. In our case, the use of such a code in Algorithm 3 would probably improve significantly the quality of the mapping, although we have yet not been able to conduct experiments to confirm it. Even in that case, the rotations should be an important part of the process for the other reasons exposed: they improve the shuffling of the data and allow for a representation of all the input components even if limited numerical accuracy is used for the mapping computation.

Each rotation $\mathcal{R}_i$ can be described, as in the previous cases, by a parameter vector O'_i. Since a rotation is a linear transformation of the set of points using an orthonormal basis different to the canonical, vector O'_i can be used to define one of the axes of the new base. The remaining axes must be orthogonal. This leads to the following expression:

$$\mathcal{R}_i(x) = \mathcal{R}_i \begin{pmatrix} x_1 \\ x_2 \\ \vdots \\ x_n \end{pmatrix} = \begin{pmatrix} b_{i_{1,1}}x_1 + b_{i_{1,2}}x_2 + \cdots + b_{i_{1,n}}x_n \\ b_{i_{2,1}}x_1 + b_{i_{2,2}}x_2 + \cdots + b_{i_{2,n}}x_n \\ \vdots \\ b_{i_{n,1}}x_1 + b_{i_{n,2}}x_2 + \cdots + b_{i_{n,n}}x_n \end{pmatrix}$$

A similar notation to the previous description of the transformations has been adopted. The computation of the coefficients $b_{i_{j,k}}$ from the set of parameter vectors $O'_i, 1 \le i \le r$, distributed in the unit hypercube, is not direct.

In this case the parameter vectors are $(n-1)-$dimensional. Therefore, we define a parameter vector $O'_i \in \mathbb{R}^{n-1}$ for each rotation $\mathcal{R}_i$, with $0 \leq O_{i,j} \leq 1$ for $1 \leq i \leq r$ and $1 \leq j \leq n-1$. The method requires taking each of this $(n-1)-$dimensional vectors, expressed in spherical co-ordinates (assuming module= 1 and multiplying by 2π each component beforehand), as the first vector of the new basis of each sub-model. Therefore, the coefficients for the projection on the first axis are, obviously, the components of this first vector and are computed as follows:

$$\begin{array}{lcll}
b_{i,1,1} & = & \sin(2\pi O'_{i,n-1})\sin(2\pi O'_{i,n-2})\ldots\sin(2\pi O'_{i,2})\sin(2\pi O'_{i,1}) & 1 \leq i \leq r \\
b_{i,1,2} & = & \sin(2\pi O'_{i,n-1})\sin(2\pi O'_{i,n-2})\ldots\sin(2\pi O'_{i,2})\cos(2\pi O'_{i,1}) & 1 \leq i \leq r \\
b_{i,1,3} & = & \sin(2\pi O'_{i,n-1})\sin(2\pi O'_{i,n-2})\ldots\cos(2\pi O'_{i,2}) & 1 \leq i \leq r \\
\vdots & & & \\
b_{i,1,n-1} & = & \sin(2\pi O'_{i,n-1})\cos(2\pi O'_{i,n-2}) & 1 \leq i \leq r \\
b_{i,1,n} & = & \cos(2\pi O'_{i,n-1}) & 1 \leq i \leq r
\end{array}$$

The use of spherical co-ordinates is related to the convenience of using the same methods employed in the transformations for the generation of the parameter vectors $O_{i,j}$, to generate in this case the parameter vectors $O'_{i,j}$. For instance, a uniform distribution of these vectors in the unit hypercube gives rise, according to the proposed method, to basis vectors with orientations also uniformly distributed across the unit hyper-sphere. This is not true if, making use of a simpler procedure, rectangular co-ordinates are employed. Since all the points in the unit hypercube lying in a given straight line which passes through the origin would generate the same basis vector, giving rise to an uneven distribution favoring, for example, the major diagonals. (A generation of parameter vectors in the unit diameter hyper-sphere instead of in the unit hypercube would however have been perfect for the simpler method).

The remaining vectors that will form the new basis have to be orthogonal to the first one and also unitary. To achieve this, the Gram-Schmidt orthonormalization method (see e.g. [**Apo57**]) can be used. Using $\{b_{i,1}, (0,1,0,0,...0), (0,0,1,0,...0)\ldots(0,0,0,0,...,1)\}$ as the seed vectors, the orthonormal basis obtained is:

$$b_{i,j} = \frac{b'_{i,j}}{\|b'_{i,j}\|},\ 1 \leq i \leq r,\ 2 \leq j \leq n$$

where

$$b'_{i,j} = \begin{cases} -\sum_{k=1}^{j-1} b_{i,k,j} b_{i,k,l} & l \neq j \\ 1 - \sum_{k=1}^{j-1} b^2_{i,k,j} & l = j \end{cases}$$

The normalization step that follows the rotation makes the whole process independent on the center of rotation. This means that choosing a point different to the origin as the rotation center would not change the result. This is an important feature, since it guarantees that the method is not dependent on the absolute position of the set of points in the space.

3.4.2. *The complete transformation process.* In summary, the complete procedure that must be applied to the data before each application of the space-filling mapping (in each sub-model i) is composed of: a rotation $\mathcal{R}_i$, a normalization to locate the points in the unit hypercube, and finally a transformation $\mathcal{T}_i$. Therefore, the final complete sequence of steps is:

(1) For each sub-model i:
- For each $n-$dimensional point, apply rotation $\mathcal{R}_i$
- Normalize the resulting set of points into the unit hypercube $[0, 1]^n$
- For each rotated and normalized point, apply transformation $\mathcal{T}_i$
- For each rotated, normalized and transformed point, obtain the associated real value in $[0, 1]$, applying a space-filling mapping (for instance, ψ^{-1})
- Solve the resultant one-dimensional problem

(2) Combine the solutions of the different sub-models to obtain a global solution. This combination can be optionally weighed according to a measure of the quality of the partial solutions.

It could be argued that the transformations $\mathcal{T}_i$ are not necessary, since the rotations can provide for the required "shuffle" effect adequately enough. Actually, it is true that the rotations $\mathcal{R}_i$ can be used as transformations since they relocate the points in a pseudo-random way similarly to the transformations. However, an important problem arises in that case when there are points located near the center of the hypercube, since their position can be virtually the same after any of the rotations. The circumstance that the space-filling mapping used in this work shows its major critical region in the central part of the unit hypercube makes this problem even more serious. The effect is clearly visible in the experiments (see Section 5.2). The composition *rotation-normalization-transformation* solves this problem in a very satisfactory way.

The fact that, in each sub-model, the components of the transformed data are different linear combinations of the original variables allows a simplification of the computation of the space-filling mapping that has been revealed very important for its practical application. It consists on limiting the number of dimensions in the computation of this mapping. Since each transformed axis represents (receives some influence from) all the original ones, and since the relative influences vary for the different sub-models, the elimination of a number of components in the computation of each sub-model does not imply the exclusion or loss of significance of *any of the original variables in the construction of any sub-model.*

The idea of a limitation on the maximum dimension in the space-filling mapping computation comes from the convenience of taking advantage of the arithmetic routines present in the computation system adopted, typically floating point with a given number of bits. If this is the case, in a high dimensionality space, the precision kept per component can be too small and give rise to poor results. Also, in each sub-model, the fragmentation of the images of some components implies that their spatial relations do not appear in the real line, meaning that the contribution of these "fragmented" axes can become negligible, as shown in the previous section.

The results of the experiments presented in Section 5 were obtained using a floating point implementation of real arithmetic with 64 bits (mantissa+exponent) and a limitation to 16 dimensions for the computation of the space-filling curve mapping. The excellent results achieved with dimensionalities up to 100 support the reasons exposed.

3.5. Selection of the parameters of the transformations. We will now analyze some methods for the generation of a set of r vectors that adequately characterize the rotations and transformations associated to the r sub-models that compose any procedure based on the Extended General Space-filling Heuristic. These r vectors, according to the definition of the transformations proposed in this work, must be distributed in the unit hypercube. It is worthwhile to recall that our main goal is that the transformations scatter the critical regions of the space-filling curve so as the points affected by such a region in one sub-model can be favorably located in other sub-models.

3.5.1. *Unsupervised parameter vectors selection.* Probably, the simplest reasonable method for the generation of the translation and rotation parameter vectors is to follow a uniform random distribution in the unit hypercube. However, since the number of sub-models, r is typically low, we cannot hope (in the statistical sense) that a small random sample of a uniform distribution contains necessarily points homogeneously spread throughout the selected domain.

An easy way to obtain such a set of points consists on generating a large number of candidates using a uniform distribution and selecting an "homogeneously dispersed" subset among them. This can be easily done by means of a greedy procedure based on successively generating sets of random points and selecting at each step the one which maximizes, for example, the Euclidean Distance to the nearest of the previously selected points. This procedure will be referred to as "greedy random method".

The experiments carried out (Section 5.2) show a perceptible improvement on the results for this method over the plain uniform random generation of the parameters.

3.5.2. *Supervised parameter vectors selection.* The experiments also show that a supervised parameter vectors selection provides much better results than a "blind" method where no information present in the data is used. The main idea consists on generating a set of random vectors larger than necessary, building with them complete sub-models, testing them with a validation set, and sequentially choosing those with a smaller *accumulated error.*

Each application will have a natural error measure. In the nearest neighbor problem, for instance, the ratio between a) the distance from the test point to the approximate nearest neighbor to b) the distance from the test point to the real nearest neighbor, is a reasonable error measure. Other error measures are proposed and used in Section 5.

The term *accumulated error* means, in this context, that the first sub-model to choose will be the one with the smallest error, the second sub-model will be the one that *when combined with the first* (i.e. when a complete model is formed with the initial sub-model plus this one) gives rise to a smaller total error, etc. In this sense, it is not adequate at all to choose in a single step the sub-models with smaller individual errors, since some (or most) of them can be based on nearby parameter vectors and, consequently, give rise to a bad combination, probably yielding an error only slightly better than the one obtained by each sub-model separately.

3.6. Solution to the uni-dimensional problem. As a consequence of the previous steps, each sub-model holds now N real numbers obtained from the N $n-$dimensional vectors that configure the original data-set. This fact can constitute a clear difference, since a set of real values holds a number of important properties, which a set of multidimensional vectors does not observe. Some of these useful properties are summarized here:

- Easy and meaningful ordering of the data according to the trivial order relation ("$>$"). This allows the use of a number of powerful and efficient algorithmic techniques, like Dynamic Programming, dichotomic search, sequential access in neighborhood operations, etc.
- Direct formation of a linear graph related to a potentially more general graph representative of the original problem where the arcs are defined between nearby points. This implies that, in some combinatorial problems, there can be defined paths in the n-dimensional space (Salesman Traveling Problem, for instance), special arrangements on the points (Clustering Problems, Planar Matching Problem), etc.

Of course, new uses and applications of this heuristic are possible in fields as Pattern Recognition, Machine Learning, Database Design, etc.

3.7. Combination of the uni-dimensional solutions. Once the problem has been solved in the real line using a number of transformed data sets, the task of combining these solutions to obtain a more exact global solution is often relatively simple. The alternatives range from computing means (possibly weighted proportionally to the error of each sub-model) to choosing in each particular case one of the solutions according to a certain criterion of local performance of the sub-model. Since it is possible to keep a pointer to each point in the original space for each value in the real line, we can also check the accuracy of each sub-solution in the space and choose the best there.

Obviously, the exact nature of the combination depends heavily of the problem. The procedures used in the applications presented in [**PV99**] can serve as models. For new applications, more sophisticated methods may be necessary.

4. An application of the EGSH: Approximate Nearest Neighbor Search in $\mathbb{R}^n$

The algorithm proposed is a direct application of the EGSH, presented in Section 3. The instantiation of the general scheme is as follows:

- The vectors received by the first stage of the EGSH (rotations, normalization and transformations) are directly the prototypes of the reference set S.
- The uni-dimensional values that correspond to each sub-model of the extended heuristic will be sorted and stored into a vector, inserted into a b-tree or inserted into an indexed table.
- In the operating phase (when a test point p is presented to the system), the usual method of mapping the point onto the Real Line is employed, with a different transformation for each of the r sub-models.

The b nearest neighbors of the uni-dimensional value *in the Real Line,* for each sub-model, can be readily found using a dichotomic search in the vector, a conventional search in the b-tree, in $O(\log N + b)$, or even a direct access operation to a table indexed by those values, in $O(b)$. The union of the r sets of b neighbors obtained from the r sub-models produces a set (of size $\leq rb$, typically much lower than that upper bound) which will be exhaustively searched to find the nearest neighbor of p in the original multidimensional space. Comparing this method with the ones based on $kd-$trees, the constant b can be considered loosely related (and, intentionally homonymous here) to the number of prototypes that is assigned to each leaf node in the models where the tree does not partition the space completely.

More formally, given a set of N prototypes $x_i \in \mathbb{R}^n$, $1 \leq i \leq N$, the pre-processing is as follows:

(1) Defined a number of sub-models, r, compute for each one the N transformed and normalized vectors:

$$x'_{i,j} = \mathcal{S}(x_i),\ \ 1 \leq i \leq N,\ \ 1 \leq j \leq r$$

where $\mathcal{S}()$ represents the sequence of operations *rotation-normalization-transformation* defined in Section 3.3.

(2) Compute the uni-dimensional values associated to those vectors, via a Space-filling Mapping (see Section 3.1):

$$p'_{i,j} = \psi^{-1}(x'_{i,j}),\ \ 1 \leq i \leq N,\ \ 1 \leq j \leq r$$

(3) For j from 1 to r, sort each set of real values $\{p_{1,j}, p_{2,j} \dots p_{N,j}\}$ in ascending order (or insert them in a b-tree or other suitable data structure).

Given a test vector $x \in \mathbb{R}^n$, which nearest neighbor is to be found, the operating phase consists on the following steps:

(1) Normalize and transform x for each sub-model:

$$x'_j = \mathcal{S}(x),\ \ 1 \leq j \leq r$$

(2) Compute the corresponding uni-dimensional values using the chosen space-filling curve:

$$p'_j = \psi^{-1}(x'_j),\ \ 1 \leq j \leq r$$

(3) For j from 1 to r, locate via a dichotomic search (or a search in a b-tree or another data structure) the b nearest neighbors of p_j in $\{p_{1,j}, p_{2,j} \dots p_{N,j}\}$. The distance in the line is defined as a cyclic metric: $\Delta(p, p') = min\{|p - p'|, 1 - |p - p'|\}$. Actualize the set B, initially empty, with the union of the b points found for each sub-model j.

(4) Compute the "real" distance in the multidimensional space between p and each element in B and select the nearest neighbor.

Obviously, the extension of the method to the search of the k nearest neighbors is trivial. It is only necessary to modify the last step of the operating phase to find the k nearest prototypes instead of the nearest one.

4.1. Asymptotic costs. In the study of costs, the limitation imposed to the computation of the Space-filling Curve (see Section 3.4.2) has been considered. In the experiments carried out, the maximum dimensionality allowed for this computation (regardless of the dimension of the original space) has been 16. This allows us to use a uniform cost criterion, since the accuracy with which the real values obtained through the space-filling mapping are stored does not depend on the dimensionality of the data. For this same reason, the computation of the space-filling mapping has also a constant asymptotic cost, independent on the dimension. It must be recalled (see Section 3.4.2) that, when $n > 16$, the use of a different rotation in each sub-model allows that every dimension of the space be adequately represented.

The pre-processing cost is in $O(nN + NlogN)$ per sub-model, where the first term corresponds to the normalization and the transformations, and the second one is the cost of the space-filling mapping and the sort of the values in the Real Line. As is suggested in Section 3.3, the number of sub-models r was set to a value proportional to the dimension, n. Therefore, the total pre-processing cost is in $O(n^2N + nN \log N)$. The asymptotic spatial cost is r times the necessary to store the original points, namely in $O(rnN)$, or in $O(n^2N)$, for r proportional to n.

The search of the nearest neighbor of a previously unknown point (operating phase) involves a cost per sub-model:

(1) in $O(n)$ for the normalization and transformation of the point.
(2) in $O(1)$ for the computation of the space-filling mapping (given the limitation to a constant in the maximum dimension of the computation).
(3) in $O(\log N)$ for the binary search.
(4) in $O(nb)$ for the computation of the distances from the point to the b nearest neighbors in the Real Line, and the selection of the nearest one.

The temporal cost is therefore, considering a number of sub-models r proportional to n and a constant b, in $O(n^2 + n \log N)$.

5. Experiments

A study of the behavior of the proposed method was carried out, involving a number of experiments on synthetic and real data. The design of these experiments is intended to reflect the conditions present in many tasks where the search of the nearest neighbor(s) is required. Tests dealing with uniform and normal distributions of prototypes have been performed, as well as experiments with data belonging to OCR and image recognition tasks. In all cases, the tests have spanned a range of dimensionalities of the space. The magnitudes measured reflect the accuracy of the method in the determination of the true nearest neighbor, and the potential loss of precision of classifiers based on the $k-$nearest neighbors rule.

In the first set of experiments, a set of $N = 25000$ prototypes and a test set of $N' = 1000$ points are used, if not stated otherwise. In each test, the nearest prototype(s) to each point in the test set have been determined using an exhaustive search and an approximate search with the proposed method.

For each test point, a sequence of prototypes ordered from smaller to larger distance to the point has been constructed (using an exhaustive search method) and the sequence number of the point selected as the nearest neighbor by the approximate method has been determined. (For instance, if the prototype selected as the approximate nearest neighbor is actually the nearest neighbor, this number is 1, if it is not the nearest but the second nearest, it is 2, etc.) If repeated values existed in the sequence, the number chosen would be, obviously, the smallest. We will call this number *rank number* of the approximate point. The *average rank number,* as well as the *worst rank number,* for the N' test points, have been calculated in each experiment.

Another important measure of the quality of the results is the ratio of the distance from the point to a real nearest neighbor and the distance to the approximate nearest neighbor. The actual expression used is:

$$D_{\text{rel}} = 100 \frac{D_{\text{aprox}}}{D_{\text{real}}}$$

where D_{rel} is the measure defined, as a percentage, D_{aprox} is the distance from the test point to the approximate nearest neighbor and D_{real} is the distance to a real nearest neighbor. An average for all the searches is computed in each experiment. This relative measure is often used to express the quality of sub-optimal solutions in optimization problems (see for example [**MC79**]).

The number of sub-models has been set equal to the dimension of the space in every experiment: $r = n$. Using higher multiples of n gives rise to better results at the expense of higher computational cost. For the number of neighbors kept in one dimension, b, a slight variant of the original method has been used. Instead of keeping the b nearest values, the $b/2$ nearest on each side have been retrieved [3]. The actual value used in all the experiments (but one) was $b = 16$. The exception was made in one experiment where the value was decreased ($b = 4$) to get a sufficient number of errors, in order to improve the legibility of the results. Each point plotted in the first set of experimental results corresponds to the average of 4 experiments with different random values for the parameters of the transformations and rotations.

In a second set of experiments, the desired accuracy of the method is fixed (in terms of average rank number or of relative distance), and the values of the parameters needed to keep that accuracy for a range of data-set sizes and dimensionalities are measured. Some experiments dealing with classification on real data-sets have also been performed. The voting k-Nearest Neighbors Rule [**Fuk90**] has been used for several values of k, and the percentage of successful classifications obtained with an exhaustive search of the k nearest neighbors has been measured along with the percentage of successful classifications of the proposed approximate search algorithm.

5.1. Data-sets used. Two different kinds of multivariate distributions have been used to generate the data sets: uniform and normal bimodal. In both cases, every point has been labelled with a class identifier in order to conduct classification experiments with the data sets (in addition to the experiments that measure the accuracy of the nearest neighbors search, which do not require any class labels).

The point sets uniformly distributed in the unit hypercube have been generated using a pseudo-random number generation algorithm. More specifically, the combined linear congruent multiplicative algorithm for 32 bit machines proposed in [**L'E88**] has been used. The seeds employed in the prototype sets were $s_1 = 1001$ and $s_2 = 500$. In the test sets, we used $s_1 = 2002$ and $s_2 = 1001$. The vectors have been filled from the first to the last component, completely filling each vector before starting with the next one.

The synthetic data sets with a normal bimodal distribution have been generated using the combined linear congruent multiplicative algorithm cited before. That algorithm produces uniformly distributed numbers in $[0, 1]$. The Box-Muller

[3] This leads to a slightly simpler and faster code. Some comparetive experiments were conducted, showing no significant differences between both approaches

transformation[**Knu81**] was then used to obtain a typified normal distribution. The required multivariate normal distribution is obtained in this case through a simple linear combination of some of these uni-variate ones. The seeds employed were the same as in the previous case.

The Gaussian distributions defined are an extension of the well-known Kohonen's "easy problem" [**Koh88**]. This problem is defined in two dimensions as follows: the first Gaussian (class 1) has a mean $\mu_1 = (0,0)$ and a diagonal covariance matrix with components $\sigma^2_{1,1} = \sigma^2_{2,2} = 1$. The second one (class 2) with a mean $\mu_2 = (2.32, 0)$ and a diagonal covariance matrix with components $\sigma^2_{1,1} = \sigma^2_{2,2} = 4$. The extension to more than two dimensions keeps the covariances unchanged and the mean of the first Gaussian in the origin. The mean of the second Gaussian is shifted 2.32 units along the co-ordinate axis number $\lfloor n/2 \rfloor + 1$, where n is the dimension of the space. Formally:

$$\mu_{1,i} = 0, \quad 1 \leq i \leq n,$$
$$\mu_{2,i} = 0, \quad 1 \leq i \leq n, \quad i \neq \lfloor n/2 \rfloor + 1,$$
$$\mu_{2,\lfloor n/2 \rfloor + 1} = 2.32,$$

$$\sigma^2_{1,i,i} = 1, \quad 1 \leq i \leq n,$$
$$\sigma^2_{1,i,j} = 0, \quad 1 \leq i,j \leq n, \quad i \neq j,$$
$$\sigma^2_{2,i,i} = 4, \quad 1 \leq i \leq n,$$
$$\sigma^2_{2,i,j} = 0, \quad 1 \leq i,j \leq n, \quad i \neq j.$$

The associated classification task (each Gaussian defines a class) shows an important overlapping. This kind of distribution seems to make more difficult finding the nearest neighbors, since the points densely populate the areas near the center of each Gaussian.

5.2. Experiments with different initializations and transformations. The first experiments try to reveal the influence of the *type of transformation* applied to the data before it is presented to each sub-model on the accuracy of the search (see Section 3.4). In the graphs, transformation $\mathcal{T}$ is referred to as *warped translation* and $\mathcal{T}'$ as *specularly warped translation.*

In Figures 6, 7 & 8, the three magnitudes cited in Section 5: average rank number, worst rank number and relative distance, are represented as averages of the results of four experiments. The maximum and minimum values found in the four experiments performed are shown as small segments. In order to obtain easily distinguishable results, the data set used came from a uniform distribution in 64 dimensions. This high dimensionality gives rise to an extremely difficult problem with high error values.

The superiority of the combination "rotation + translation" is thus confirmed, as introduced in Section 3.4.2. To study the influence of the method used to generate the parameters of the transformations on the results, a similar set of experiments has been performed. In Figures 9, 10 & 11, the same three values presented before (average neighbor number, worst neighbor number, and relative distance) are shown averaged over four experiments. The considerations expressed in Section 3.5.1 are also confirmed by these results.

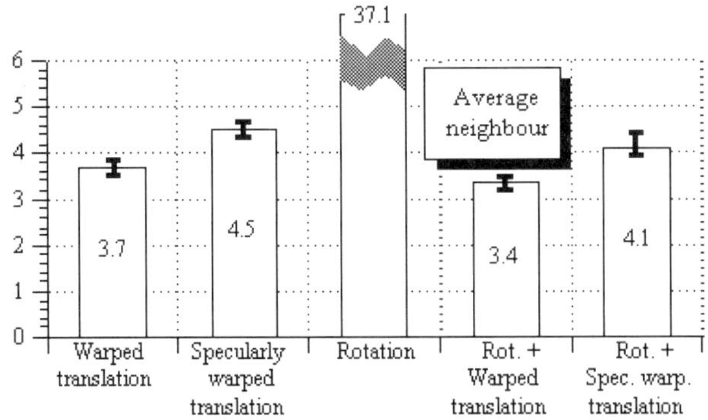

FIGURE 6. Average rank number of the approximate nearest neighbor found with the proposed method (a value of 1 means finding the nearest neighbor, 2 means finding the second, etc.) in a uniform random distribution in 64 dimensions, $r = 64$ and $b = 16$. The average values are shown, along with the maximum and minimum among four experiments performed with different random parameters for the transformations and the rotations. Each bar represents a transformation method.

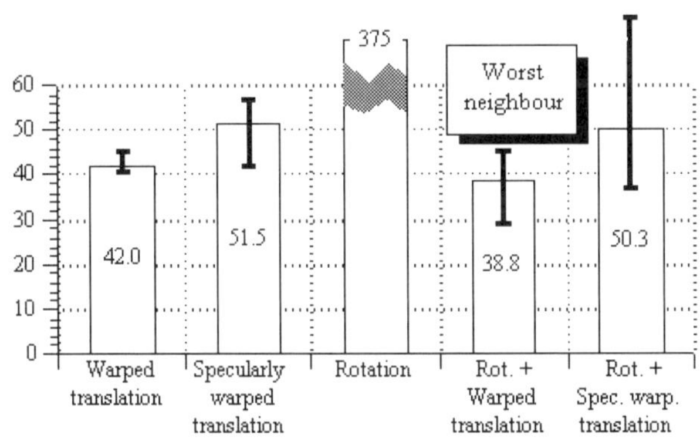

FIGURE 7. Rank number of the approximate nearest neighbor found with the proposed method in a uniform random distribution in 64 dimensions, $r = 64$ and $b = 16$. The worst values are shown, along with the maximum and minimum among four experiments performed with different random parameters for the transformations and the rotations. Each bar represents a transformation method.

5.3. Experiments varying the number of prototypes. To establish the influence of the number of prototypes on the results, a number of experiments have been performed increasing the number of prototypes N while keeping the other conditions constant. A set of points drawn from a uniform random distribution in two dimensions has been used, with values for N from $8,000$ to $700,000$. The

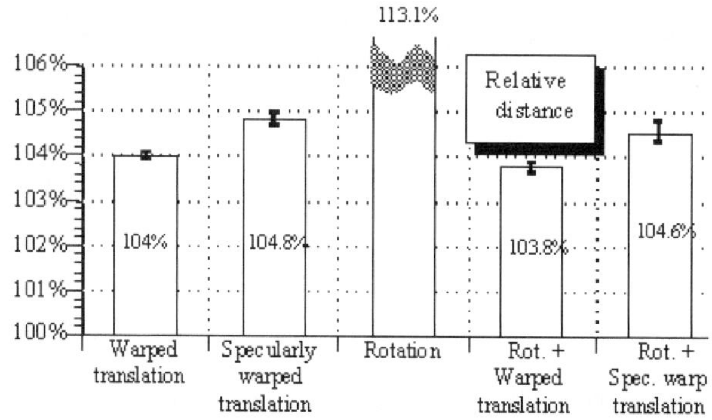

FIGURE 8. $D_{\rm rel}$ ratio found with the proposed method in a uniform random distribution in 64 dimensions, $r = 64$ and $b = 16$. The average values are shown, along with the maximum and minimum among four experiments performed with different random parameters for the transformations and the rotations. Each bar represents a transformation method.

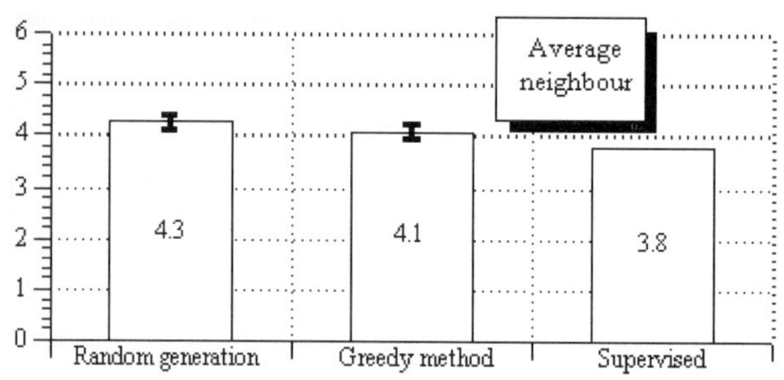

FIGURE 9. Average rank number of the approximated nearest neighbor found with the proposed method (a value of 1 means finding the nearest neighbor, 2 means finding the second, etc.) in a uniform random distribution in 64 dimensions, $r = 64$ and $b = 16$. The average values are shown, along with the maximum and minimum among four experiments. Each bar represents a different method of parameter generation.

results are shown in Figures 12 & 13. No accuracy decrease due to the size of the set of prototypes is evidenced.

In this experiment, the value assigned to b is 4 in order to make the error rates larger, since with such a low dimension, the errors obtained using larger values of b are too low to be useful when represented in the graphs. In the rest of experiments, $b = 16$. The transformation used is rotation + $\mathcal{T}$, and the generation of the parameters was performed using the greedy random method (see Section 3.5.1).

To check if this excellent behavior is retained in spaces of higher dimensionality, the previous experiments have been repeated in an 8-dimensional space. The values of N used reach in this case only $128,000$, due to the higher memory requirements for the simulations. The value used for b is in this case the general for all the

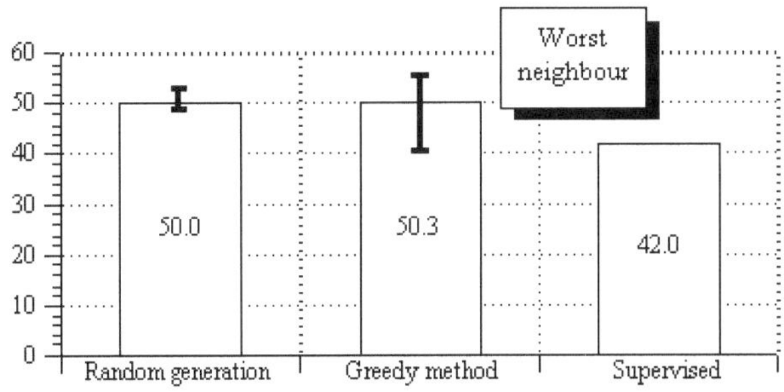

FIGURE 10. Rank number of the approximated nearest neighbor found with the proposed method (a value of 1 means finding the nearest neighbor, 2 means finding the second, etc.) in a uniform random distribution in 64 dimensions, $r = 64$ and $b = 16$. The worst values are shown, along with the maximum and minimum among four experiments. Each bar represents a different method of parameter generation.

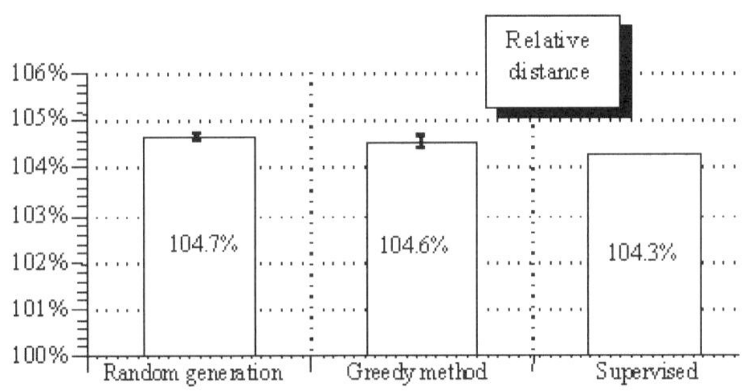

FIGURE 11. $D_{\rm rel}$ ratio found with the proposed method in a uniform random distribution in 64 dimensions, $r = 64$ and $b = 16$. The average values are shown, along with the maximum and minimum among four experiments performed. Each bar represents a different method of parameter generation.

experiments, i.e. $b = 16$. The results obtained are shown in Figures 14 & 15. The average and worst sequence numbers, and the relative distance increase *very slightly* (note the high resolution of the ordinate axis and the logarithmic scale on the number of prototypes) as the number of prototypes grows.

5.4. Experiments varying the number of dimensions. A key factor in the cost of many fast nearest neighbor search algorithms is the dimensionality n of the space where the elements are defined. It has been shown in Section 2 that the average cost of most of them climbs up steeply with n. It has been also noted that the accuracy of the approximate search algorithms drops very quickly as n gets larger. To evaluate the effect of the dimensionality on our method, a number of experiments have been performed.

The number of prototypes used in the experiments was $N = 25000$. The test set was composed of 1000 elements. As in the previous cases, the transformation

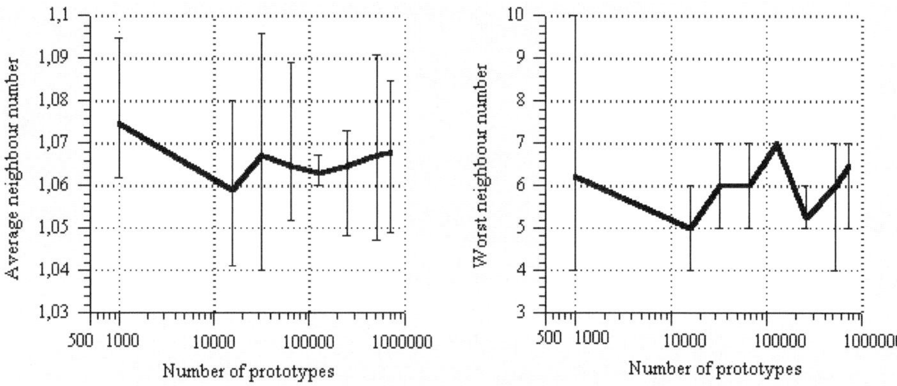

FIGURE 12. Average and worst rank numbers of the approximate nearest neighbor found with the proposed method against the size of the set of prototypes, in a uniform random distribution in $n = 2$ dimensions, with $r = 2$ and $b = 4$.

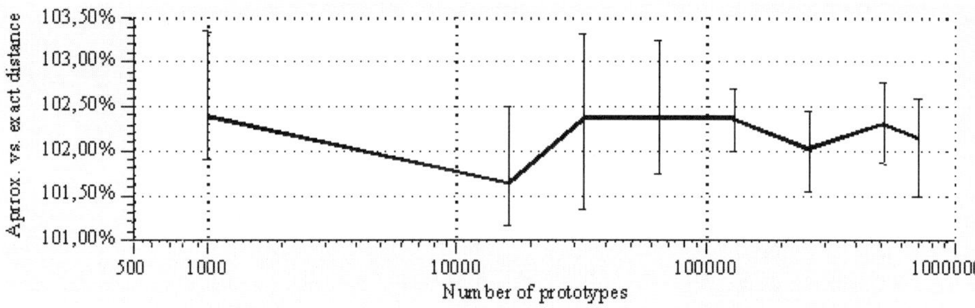

FIGURE 13. D_{rel} obtained for increasing values of the number of prototypes N in a uniform random distribution in $n = 2$ dimensions, with $r = 2$ and $b = 4$.

chosen was rotation + $\mathcal{T}$ and the parameters have been generated using the greedy random method Section 3.5.1).

The results of the first experiment with increasing dimensionality, where the points are drawn from a uniform random distribution, are shown in Figures 16 & 17.

In Figure 16, a least squares fit of the results is shown (since the controlled variable is represented in a logarithmic scale, a linear fit appears as an exponential function). The lines obtained are defined by the expressions $\text{Neighb}_{\text{avg}}(n) = 0.94 + 0.042n$, for the average neighbor, and $\text{Neighb}_{\text{worst}}(n) = 4.16 + 0.53n$, for the worst neighbor. These equations show very small slopes, which means that the dimension of the space has only a moderate influence on the quality of the results.

A magnitude which is probably more significant than the previous ones is the relative distance (see Section 5), shown in Figure 17. The results can be fitted to a logarithmic function through a least squares approximation, namely $D_{\text{rel}}(n) = -0.25 + 0.98 \ln(n)$ Obviously, a logarithmic increase of this magnitude with the dimension is an excellent result.

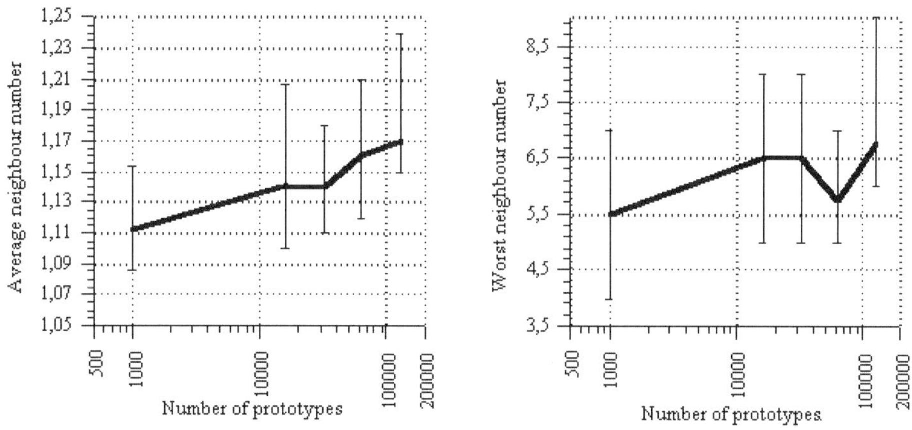

FIGURE 14. Average and worst rank number of the approximated nearest neighbor found with the proposed method against the size of the set of prototypes, in a uniform random distribution in $n = 8$ dimensions, with $r = 8$ and $b = 16$.

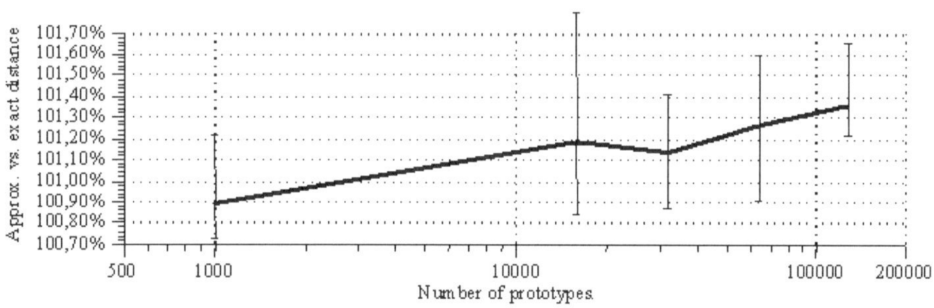

FIGURE 15. D_{rel} obtained for increasing values of the number of prototypes N in a uniform random distribution in $n = 8$ dimensions, with $r = 8$ and $b = 16$.

An interesting possibility is to choose a value for the number of neighbors retained along the real line, b, dependent (linearly) on the dimension n. In that case, the cost of the search is increased from $O(n^2 + n \log N)$ to $O(n^3 + n \log N)$ (see Section 3.4.2). Results taking $b = n$, and keeping the same conditions as in the previous experiments are shown in Figures 18 & 19.

In this case, the growth of the magnitudes representing the mean and worse rank numbers is no longer linear, but logarithmic: $\text{Neigh}_{\text{avg}}(n) = 0.94 + 0.135 \ln(n)$ and $\text{Neigh}_{\text{worst}}(n) = 4.25 + 1.13 \ln(n)$.

The value of D_{rel}, does not seem to grow at all in this case, (it rather appears to decrease, although, of course, not significantly).

The synthetic data sets traditionally used to test the performance of approximate nearest neighbors search methods are composed of multidimensional uniform distributions of random points. We have performed also some tests with a normal bimodal random distribution (see Section 5.1). Normally distributed data-sets are

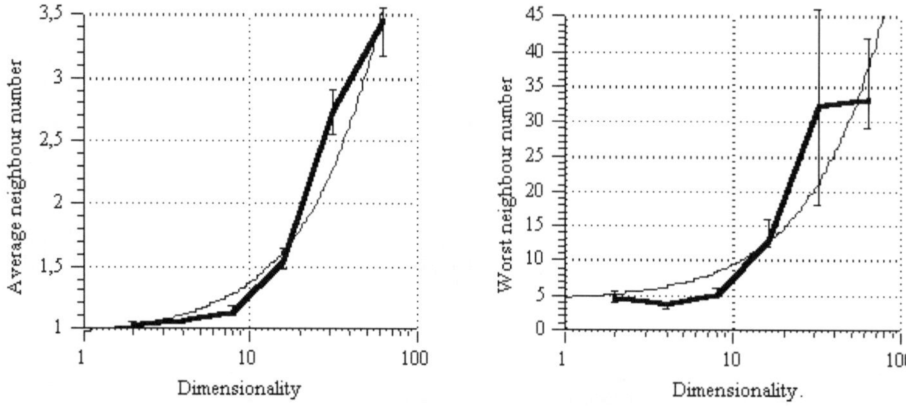

FIGURE 16. Average and worst rank number of the approximated nearest neighbor found with the proposed method against the number of dimensions n, in a uniform random distribution with $r = n$ and $b = 16$. The thin line corresponds to a linear least squares fit of the data.

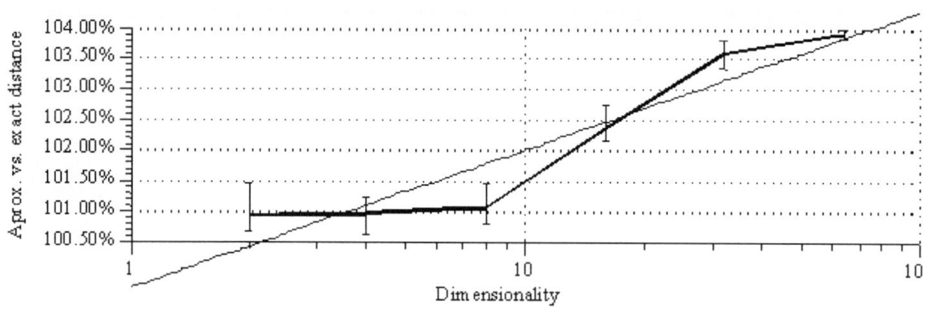

FIGURE 17. D_{rel} obtained for increasing values of the dimension n in a uniform random distribution with $r = n$ and $b = 16$. The thin line represents a logarithmic function fitted to the data using least squares.

often regarded as more difficult, since they include densely populated areas, which can be harder to deal with. The results obtained are shown in Figures 20 & 21.

The expressions obtained for the linear least squares fits shown in Figure 20 are $\mathrm{Neigh}_{\mathrm{avg}}(n) = 0.084 + 0.18n$ and $\mathrm{Neigh}_{\mathrm{worst}}(n) = -8.8 + 2.87n$. The slopes are in this case clearly larger than in the previous experiment with a uniform distribution (around 4 and 5 times larger, respectively). The higher difficulty of this problem is thus confirmed, although only by a multiplicative constant.

In Figure 21, the evolution of D_{rel} (see Section 5) is shown with respect to the space dimensionality n. A logarithmic least squares fit yields the equation $D_{\mathrm{rel}}(n) = 0.15 + 0.97 \ln(n)$. It is surprising that the linear term multiplying the logarithm (analogous to the slope in a linear least-squares fit) is almost equal to the one obtained for a uniform distribution (in fact, marginally lower). We could not

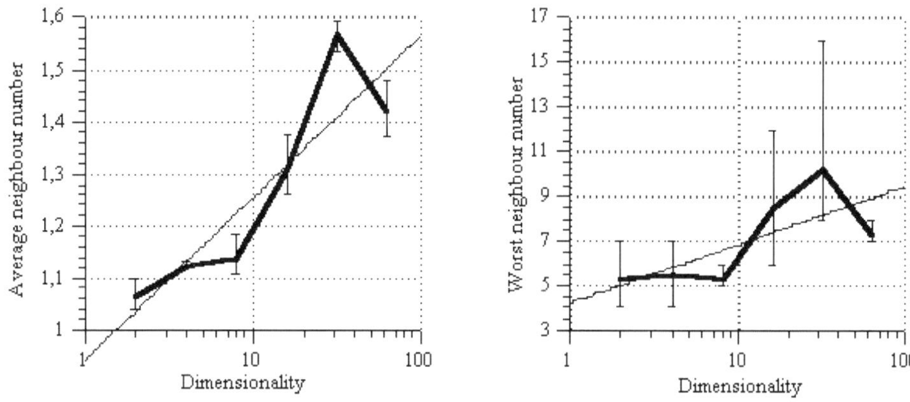

FIGURE 18. Average and worst rank number of the approximated nearest neighbor found with the proposed method against the number of dimensions n, in a uniform random distribution with $r = n$ and $b = n$. The thin line corresponds to a *logarithmic* least squares fit of the data.

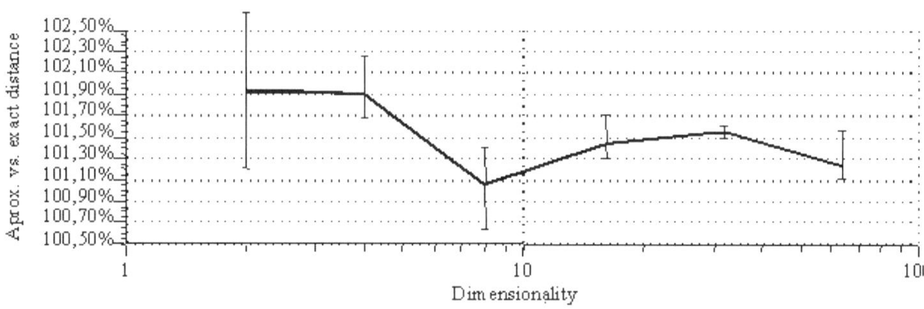

FIGURE 19. D_{rel} obtained for increasing values of the dimension n in a uniform random distribution with $r = n$ and $b = n$.

find a simple interpretation of this fact, although it somewhat confirms that this measure is more relative, and perhaps more significant, than the previous ones.

5.5. Constant precision experiments. In this section, we will present a number of experiments trying to find out the increase of resources (number of submodels, r, and number of neighbors on the real line, b, being thus br the total number of distances to compute) needed to keep the quality of the results fixed as the number of prototypes or the space dimensionality is increased. The quality of the results has been measured, as in the previous sections, in terms of the average rank number of the approximate nearest neighbor found, and of its distance relative to an exact nearest neighbor. These values have been fixed to three different levels for each experiment, and the parameters r and b needed to keep the result as near to those levels as possible have been plotted.

In Figure 22, the number of neighbors on the real line, b, required to keep average rank numbers under 1.2 and 2, are plotted for space dimensionalities ranging from 4 to 100. Several curves are presented in each plot, for several numbers of

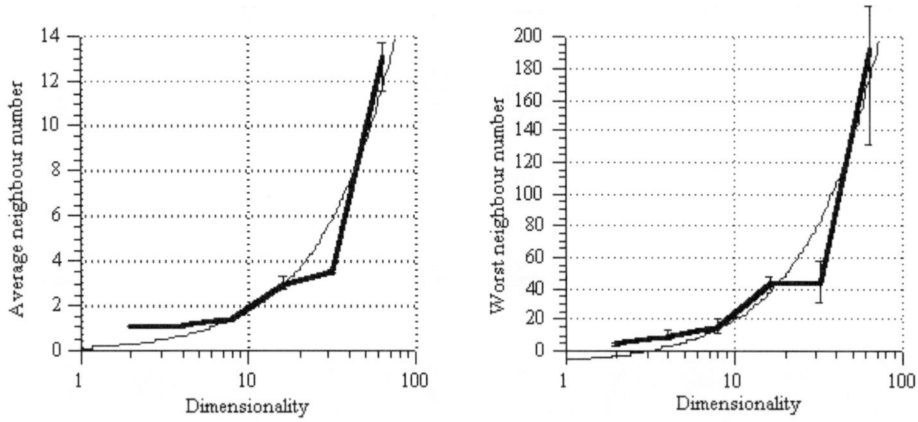

FIGURE 20. Average and worst rank number of the approximated nearest neighbor found with the proposed method against the number of dimensions n, in a normal bimodal random distribution with $r = n$ and $b = 16$. The thin line corresponds to a linear least squares fit of the data.

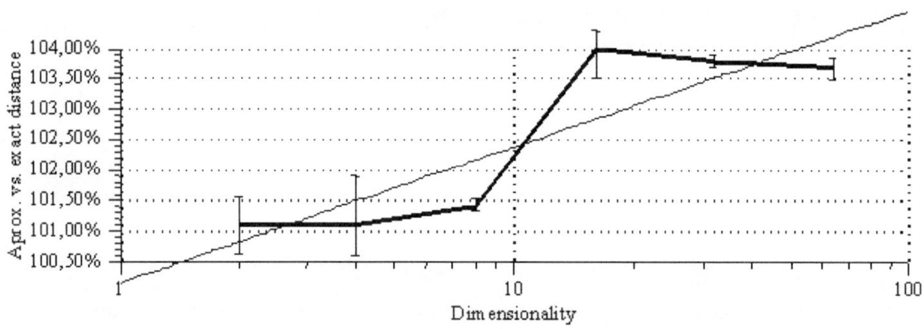

FIGURE 21. D_{rel} obtained for increasing values of the dimension n in a normal bimodal random distribution with $r = n$ and $b = 16$. The thin line represents a logarithmic function fitted to the data using least squares.

sub-models, r, chosen as small multiples of the space dimensionality, n. In Figure 23 the same curves are plotted, but the product of b and r (number of distances computed) is represented in ordinates, instead of just the value of b.

In Figure 24, the number of sub-models, r, required to keep the average rank numbers of 1.2 and 2, are plotted for space dimensionalities ranging from 4 to 100. In this case, the curves presented in each plot correspond to different values of the number of neighbors on the real line, b, also selected as small multiples of the space dimensionality, n. In Figure 25, as before, the same curves are plotted with the product of b and r in ordinates.

In Figure 26, as before, the number of neighbors on the real line, b is plotted, but in this case it is required to keep the approximate distance below 101% and

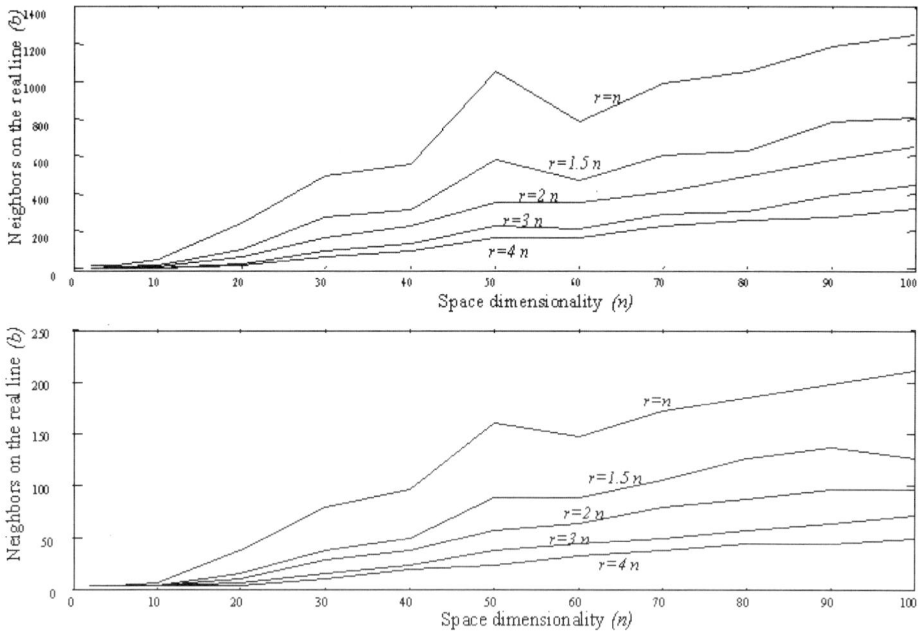

FIGURE 22. Values of neighbors on the real line, b, required to keep the average rank number under 1.2 and 2.0, respectively, with numbers of sub-models, r, multiples of the dimensionality, n.

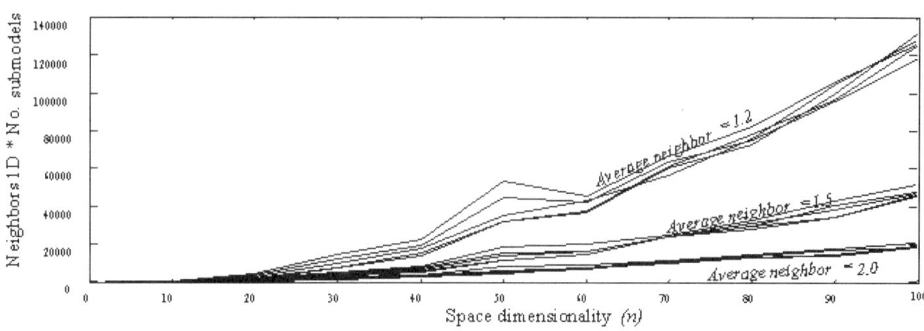

FIGURE 23. Number of distances computed, (br), required to keep the average rank number under 1.2, 1.5 and 2.0 with numbers of sub-models, r, multiples of the dimensionality, n.

105% of the exact one. In Figure 27, as before, the same curves are plotted with the product of b and r in ordinates.

In Figure 28, the number of sub-models, r, required to keep approximate distance below 101% and 105% of the exact one, are plotted with curves representing different values of the number of neighbors on the real line, b, as small multiples of the space dimensionality, n. In Figure 29, as before, the same curves are plotted with the product of b and r in ordinates.

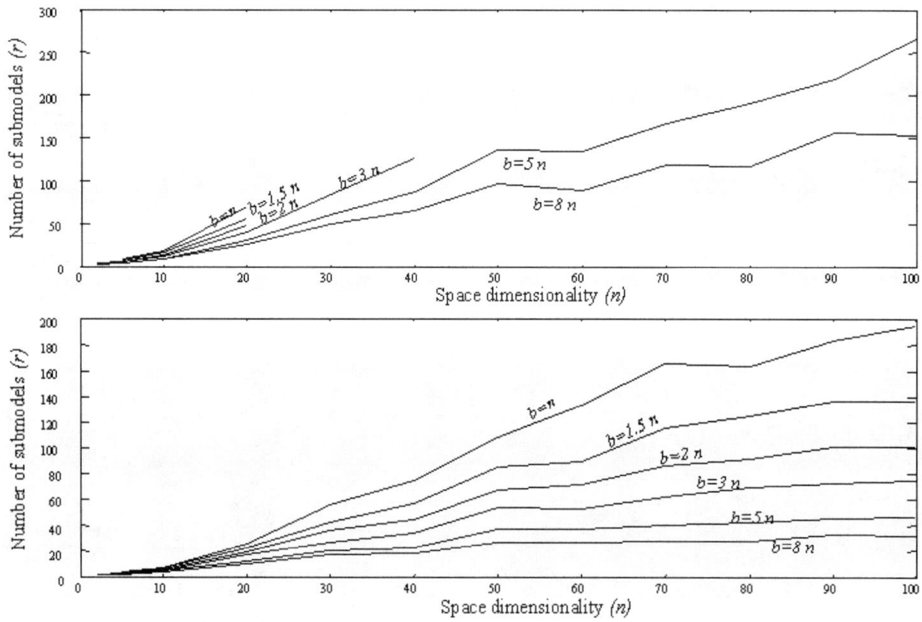

FIGURE 24. Number of sub-models, r, required to keep the average rank number under 1.2 and 2, respectively, with numbers of neighbors on the real line, b, multiples of the dimensionality, n.

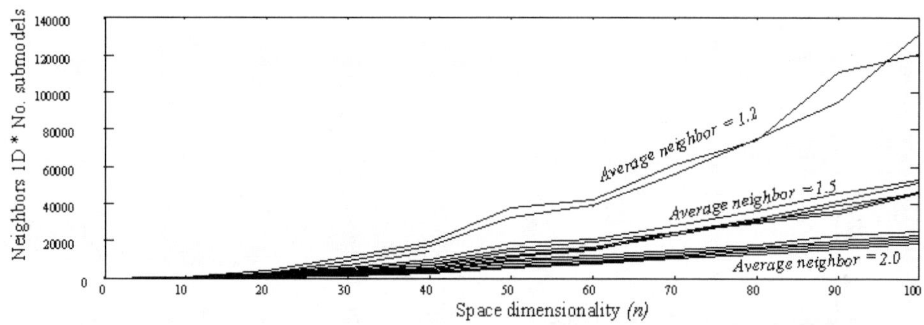

FIGURE 25. Number of distances computed, (br), required to keep the average rank number under 1.2, 1.5 and 2.0, with numbers of neighbors on the real line, b, multiples of the dimensionality, n.

Finally, in Figure 30, the number of prototypes in the data set is increased, and the increment of the neighbors on the real line, b, needed to keep a fixed precision is measured. It seems that b reaches a certain saturation for large date set sizes.

5.6. Real data sets experiments. In this section, an experiment on a real data set is performed. The data is composed of 200000 training and 23124 test handwritten characters, each of them being a 30−dimensional vector obtained through Principal Component Analysis from scaled and normalized bitmaps of the images of the NIST Database 3 [**Gar92**]. The nearest neighbor classification rule has been used to classify the test images with the results and times shown in Figures 31

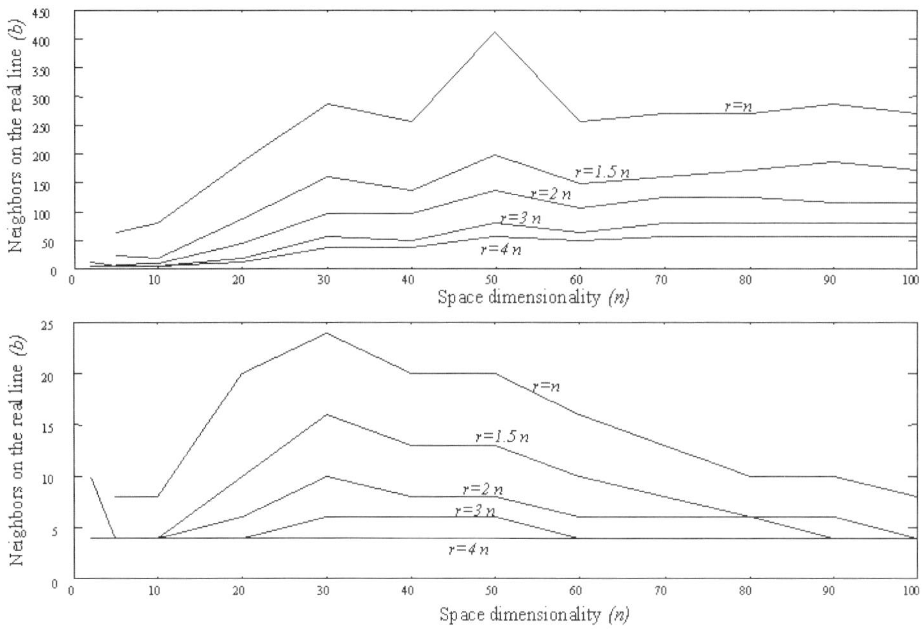

FIGURE 26. Values of neighbors on the real line, b, required to keep the approximate distance under 101% and 105%, respectively of the exact one, with numbers of sub-models, r, multiples of the dimensionality, n.

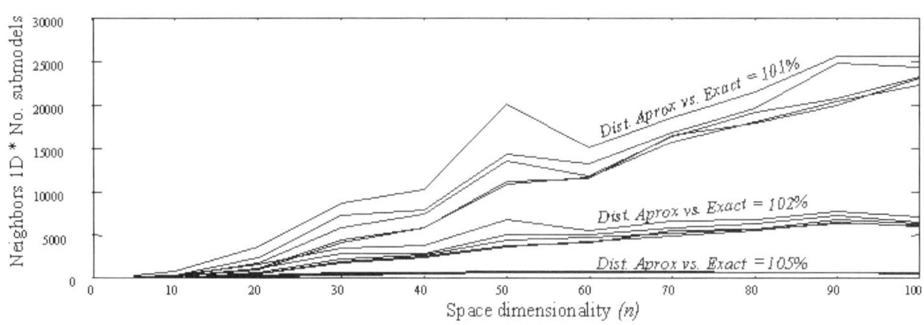

FIGURE 27. Number of distances computed, (br), required to keep the approximate distance under 101%, 102%, and 105% of the exact one, with numbers of sub-models, r, multiples of the dimensionality, n.

& 32 , which suggest that an exact nearest neighbor search is not always necessary to achieve a good classification error. Other experiments suggest that, when the $k-$nearest neighbor rule is used with k larger than one, this fact is even more evident.

5.7. Comparative experiments. In this section, we compare the results of the proposed method with those of other algorithms. The first test is against a

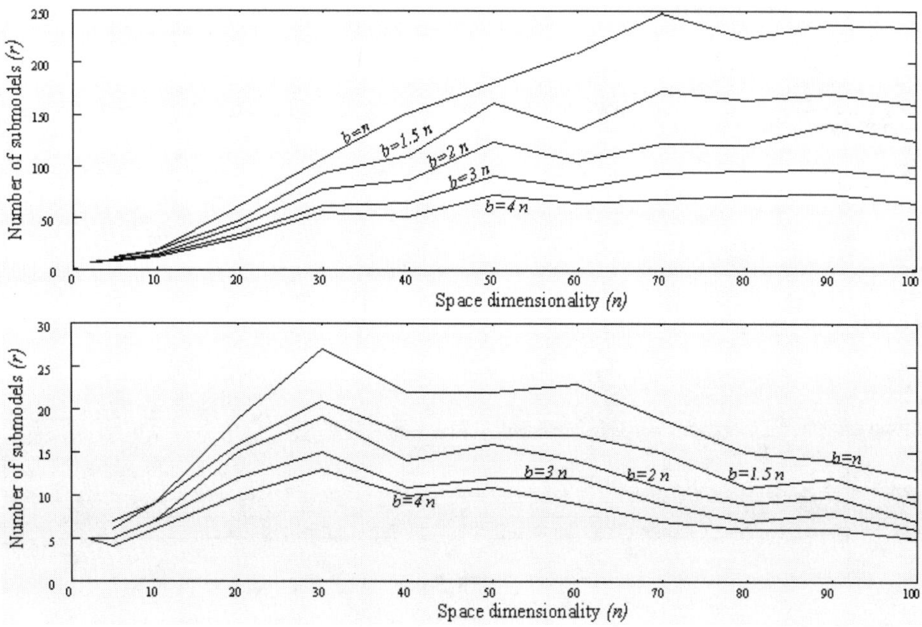

FIGURE 28. Number of sub-models, r, required to keep the approximate distance under 101% and 105%, respectively, of the exact one, with numbers of neighbors on the real line, b, multiples of the dimensionality, n.

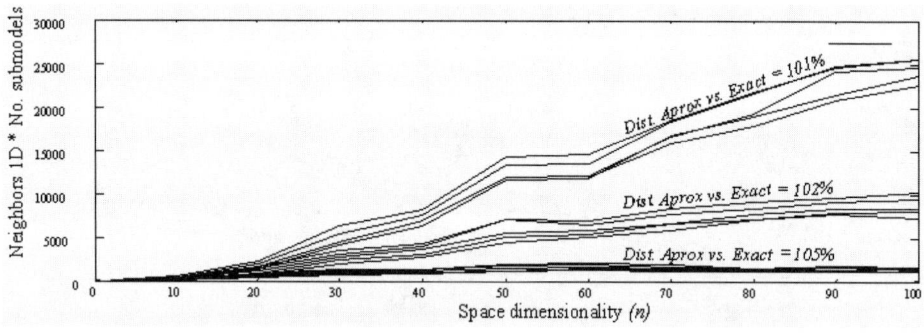

FIGURE 29. Number of distances computed, (br) required to keep the approximate distance under 101%, 102%, and 105% of the exact one, with numbers of neighbors on the real line, b, multiples of the dimensionality, n.

simple method that projects the points on the coordinated axes and indexes the real values obtained. In fact, it is the same algorithm proposed, but using linear projections instead of the space-filling mapping. Of course, this is only intended to check the relevance of the space-filling mapping in the whole method.

In Figure 33 the poor results obtained using linear projections appear clearly.

The second comparison has been established between our model and one of the most popular and successful main-memory-based fast nearest neighbors search data

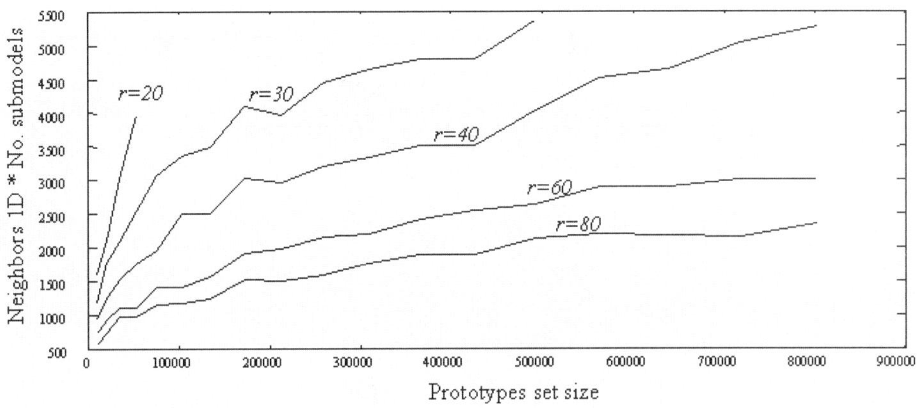

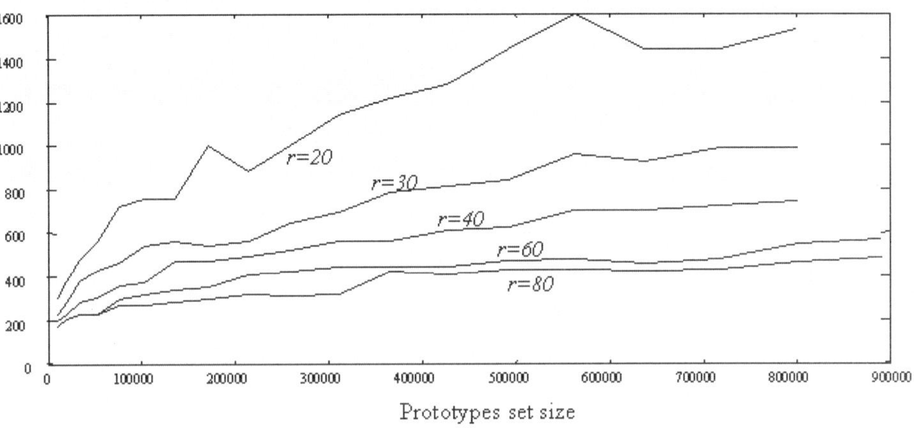

FIGURE 30. Number of distance computations, (br), needed to keep the average rank number under 1.2 and 2.0, respectively, for an increasing number of prototypes in 20−dimensional space ($n = 20$). The results for different numbers of sub-models are shown.

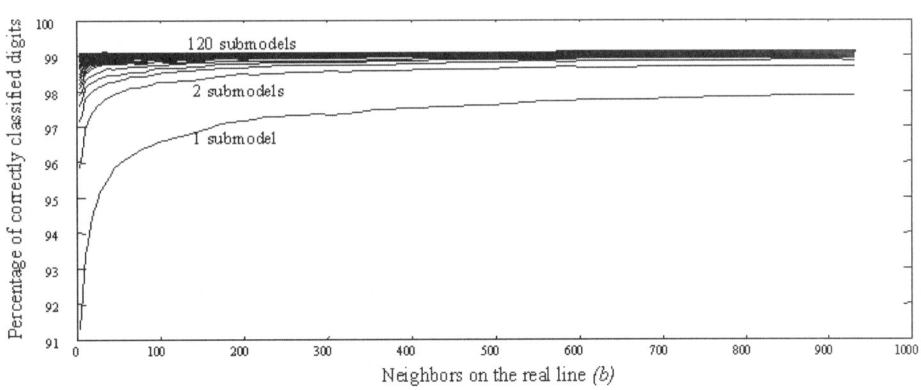

FIGURE 31. Results of exact and approximate 1-NN classifiers on the NIST database 3.

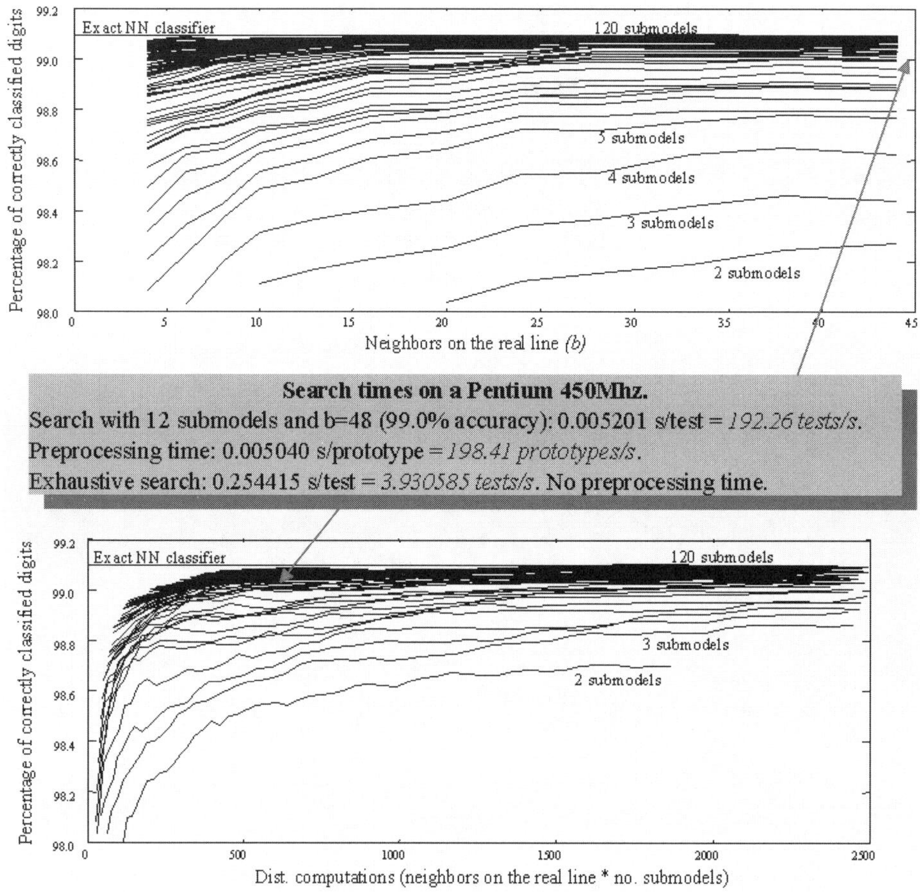

FIGURE 32. Detail on the results of exact and approximate 1-NN classifiers on the NIST database 3, and computation times (real time, not CPU time) measured for that task.

structures, the *kd*−tree, which will be used as a benchmark for performance. The implementation used has been ANN, a library written in C++ to support exact and approximate nearest neighbor searching in Euclidean spaces of various dimensions, implemented by David M. Mount and Sunil Arya (`http://www.cs.umd.edu/~mount/ANN`). The splitting rule used was the one denoted ANN_KD_STD, as the standard, and uniform random distributions were used in 10D, 30D and 60D spaces. Additional experiments with clustered distributions will be conducted in the future.

The CPU times needed in a Pentium III – 450 Mhz class machine to search the 10 approximate nearest neighbors with a constant performance in increasingly large sets of prototypes have been represented in Figures 33, 34 & 35, the results show faster search times for the *kd*-tree in dimension 10, but not in higher dimensions, where the space-filling method gives lower times with a slower increase with the data set size.

One of the reasons for this behaviour is perhaps that a very slight or null decrease of ϵ (the parameter that controls when to stop traversing the tree) is

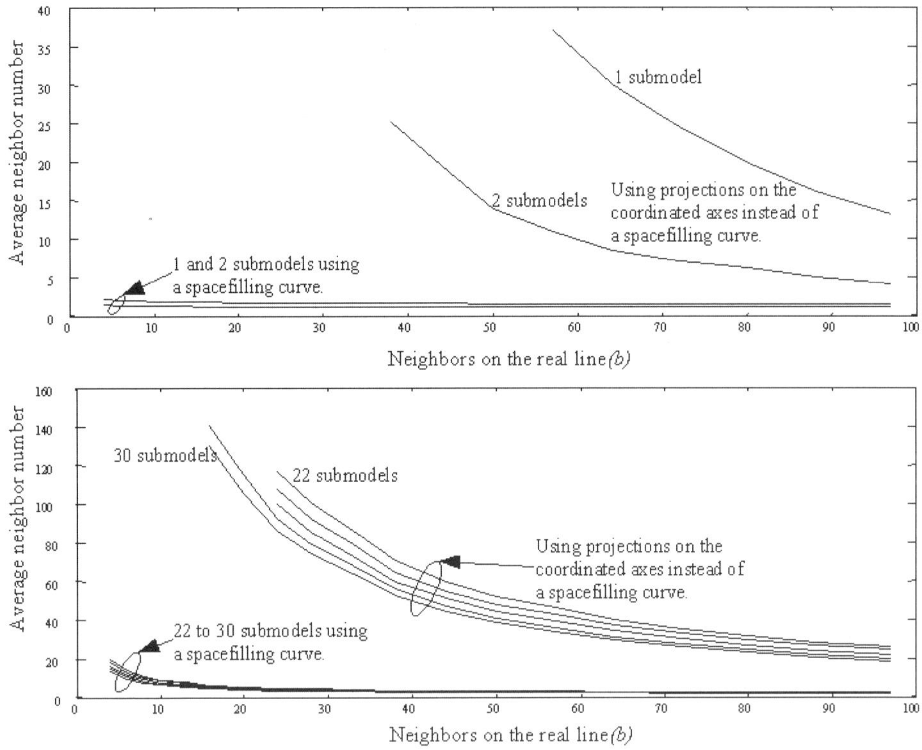

FIGURE 33. Comparison between the average rank numbers obtained in 2 and 30 dimensions for several numbers of neighbors on the real line, b, and sub-models, r, using projections of the points onto the coordinated axes, and using the proposed model.

needed to keep the approximate neighbour under a fixed limit for larger and larger data sets in the 10 dimensional space. In 30 and 60 dimensions, however, decreasing values of ϵ are needed to keep the precision fixed. The same is applicable to our method: increasing values of b and r have to be used when the data set grows, but in the higher dimensional spaces, the growth of the resulting CPU time seems to be lower than that of the *kd*-trees. Other elements of comparison are the memory occupation, which is fixed for the *kd*-trees and grows in our model linearly with r, and the preprocessing time, which also scales with r. In the spacefilling based method, however, new points can be added to or removed from the set without the need to reprocess the whole set, and the number of disk accesses, if the data has to be stored on disk, is logarithmic with the data set size.

6. Conclusions

Fast approximate search of the nearest neighbours of a point in a set of prototypes in a vector space is a key problem in many disciplines, due to its theoretical appeal and its practical applications. The results presented here are very promising, and tests on the performance of the proposed method on real applications are being carried out, showing a real practical value. These applications include optical

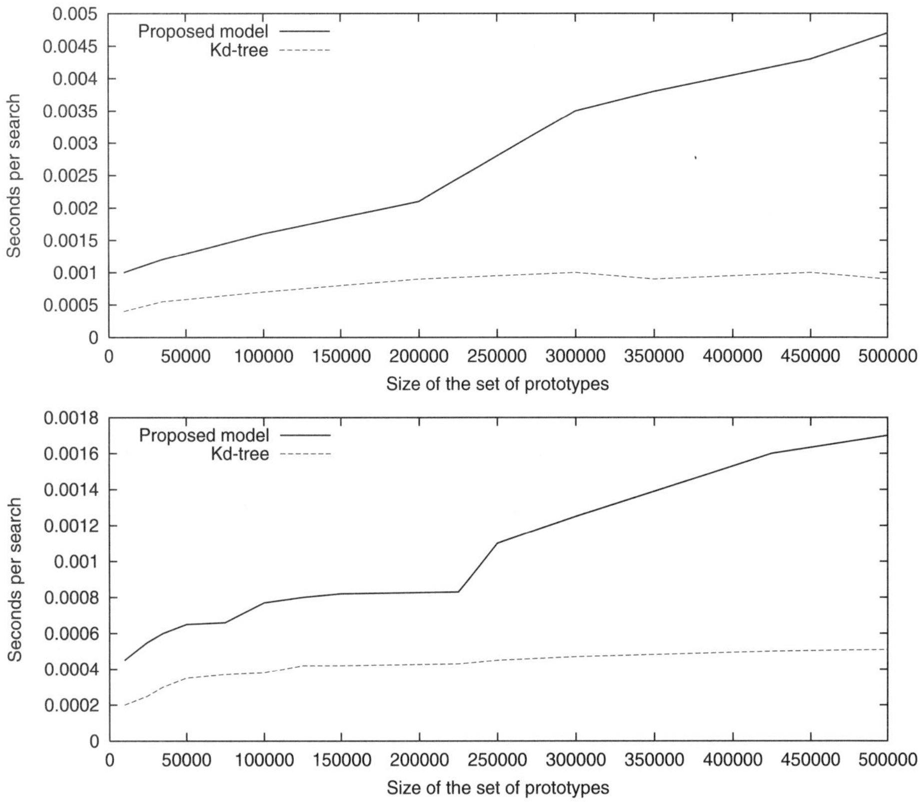

FIGURE 34. Search times, in seconds, of a *kd*-tree and the proposed model in a 10-dimensional space, with increasingly large data sets and keeping the average rank number under 1.2 (first graph) and 2.0 (second graph).

character recognition, and identification using fingerprints in a large database. In every case, a huge reduction of the actual search time has been achieved at the expense of a small loss of precision.

The tests comparing the classification errors incurred using the exhaustive $k-$nearest neighbours rule and the approximate search algorithm do not show significant differences for a surprisingly wide range of parameter settings. This is in agreement with the recent results of [**SK96**], where a single spacefilling mapping is used in several simple low-dimensionality $k-$nearest neighbour classification tasks, with error rates similar to the exhaustive search method.

The method proposed is easy to adapt to the demands of most tasks, whether disk-based or memory resident, with a fixed data-set or with a need of frequent insertions and deletions, and a specially good behaviour is being observed in classification applications where very large sets of prototypes are involved. In those cases, the time savings are especially important and the size of the manageable data-sets is enlarged many orders of magnitude.

A larger and more detailed set of experiments can be found in [**PV99**].

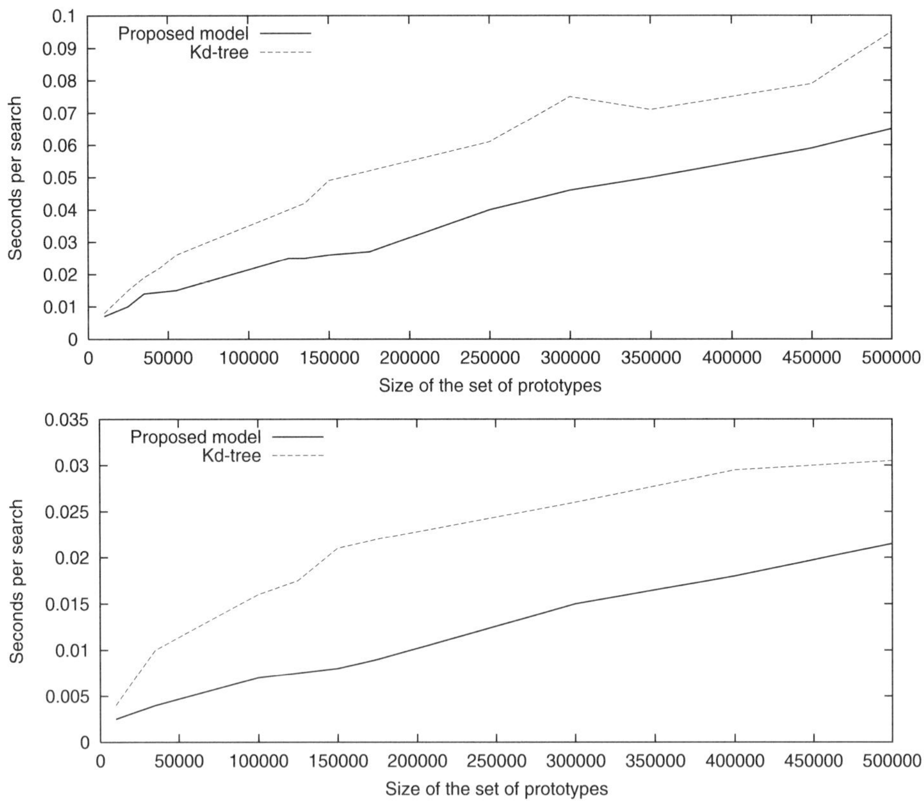

FIGURE 35. Search times, in seconds, of a *kd*-tree and the proposed model in a 30-dimensional space, with increasingly large data sets and keeping the average rank number under 1.2 (first graph) and 2.0 (second graph).

References

[And73] M.R. Anderberg, *Cluster analysis for applications*, Academic Press Inc., New York, 1973.

[Apo57] Tom M. Apostol, *Mathematical analysis: A modern approach to advanced calculus*, Addison-Wesley, Reading, MA, USA, 1957.

[Ben75] J.L. Bentley, *Multidimensional binary search trees used for associative searching*, Communications of the ACM **18** (1975), no. 9, 509–517.

[Ber93] M. Bern, *Approximate closest-point queries in high dimensions*, Pattern Recognition **45** (1993), 95–99.

[BG89] D. Bertsimas and M. Grigni, *Worst-case examples for the spacefilling curve heuristic for the euclidean traveling salesman problem*, Operation Research Letters **8** (1989), 241–244.

[Bia69] T. Bially, *Space-filling curves: Their generations and their application to bandwith reduction*, IEEE Transactions on Information Theory **15** (1969), no. 6, 658–664.

[BKK96] S. Berchtold, D.A. Keim, and H.P. Kriegel, *The x-tree: An index structure for high-dimensional data*, Proc. 22nd Very Large Database Conference, Bombay, India, 1996, pp. 28–39.

[BKSS90] N. Beckmann, H.-P. Kriegel, R. Schneider, and B. Seeger, *The r*-tree: An efficient and robust access method for points and rectangles*, ACM SIGMOD Conf. on the Management of Data 90, Atlantic City., May 1990.

[BP83] J.J. Bartholdi and L.K. Platzman, *A fast heuristic based on spacefilling curves for minimum-weight matching in the plane*, Information Processing Letters, **17** (1983), 177–180.

[BP88] ———, *Heuristics based on spacefilling curves for combinatorial problems in euclidean space*, Management Science **34** (1988), 291–305.

[Bri95] S. Brin, *Near neighbor search in large metric spaces*, Proc. 21st Inter. Conf. on Very Large Data Bases, 1995, pp. 574–584.

[BS96] G.S. Bhat and C.D. Savage, *Balanced gray codes*, Electronic Journal of Combinatorics **3** (1996), no. R25.

[But69] A.R. Butz, *Convergence with hilbert's space filling curve*, Journal of Computer and System Sciences **3** (1969), 128–146.

[But71] ———, *Alternative algorithm for hilbert's space filling curve*, IEEE Transactions on Computers (1971), 424–426.

[BWY80] J.L. Bentley, B.W. Weide, and A.C. Yao, *Optimal expected time algorithms for closest point problems*, ACM Trans. on Math. Software **6** (1980), 563–580.

[Can78] G. Cantor, *Ein beitrag zur mannigfaltigkeislehre*, Crelle J. **84** (1878), 242–258.

[CH67] T.M Cover and P.E. Hart, *Nearest neighbor pattern classification*, IEEE Transactions on Information Theory, **13** (1967), no. 1, 21–27.

[CHW87] F. Chauny, A. Haurie, and E. Wagneur, *Sequencing punch operation in an fms: A three-dimensional spacefilling curve approach*, INFOR **25** (1987), no. 1, 26–45.

[Cla97] K. L. Clarkson, *Nearest neighbor queries in metric spaces*, Proc. 29th Symp. Theory Comput., 1997.

[DK80] P. A. Devijver and J. Kittler, *On the edited nearest neighbour rule*, Proceedings of the 5th International Conference on Pattern Recognition, IEEE Computer Society Press, Los Alamitos, CA, 1980, pp. 72–80.

[DL76] D.P. Dobkin and R. Lipton, *Multidimensional search problems*, SIAM Journal Comput. **5** (1976), 181–186.

[FBF77] J. H. Friedman, J. L. Bentley, and R. A. Finkel, *An algorithm finding best matches in logarithmic expected time*, ACM Trans. Math. Software **3** (1977), 209–226.

[FBS75] J.H. Friedman, F. Baskett, and L.J. Shustek, *An algorithm for finding nearest neighbor*, TC **24** (1975), 1000–1006.

[FH90a] E. Fix and J.L. Hodges, *Discriminatory analysis– nonparametric discrimination: Consistency properties*, Nearest Neighbor (NN) Norms: NN Pattern Classification Techniques (B.V. Dasarathy, ed.), IEEE Computer Society Press, Los Alamitos, CA, 1990, pp. 261–279.

[FH90b] ———, *Discriminatory analysis– nonparametric discrimination: Small sample performance*, Nearest Neighbor (NN) Norms: NN Pattern Classification Techniques (B.V. Dasarathy, ed.), IEEE Computer Society Press, Los Alamitos, CA, 1990, pp. 280–322.

[FN75] K. Fukunaga and P. M. Narendra, *A branch and bound algorithm for computing k-nearest neighbors*, IEC **24** (1975), 750–753.

[Fri97] J.H. Friedman, *On bias, variance, 0/1 - loss, and the curse-of-dimensionality*, Data Mining and Knowledge Discovery **1** (1997), 55–77.

[Fuk90] K. Fukunaga, *Introduction to statistical pattern recognition*, Academic Press, San Diego, CA., 1990.

[Gar92] M. Garris, *Design and collection of a handwriting sample image database*, Social Science Computing Journal **10** (1992), 196–214.

[GS91] S. Geva and J. Sitte, *Adaptive nearest neighbor pattern classification*, IEEE Trans on Neural Networks **2** (1991), no. 2, 318–322.

[Gut83] A. Guttman, *R-trees: A dynamic index structure for spatial searching*, UCB, Elec.Res.Lab, Res.R. No.M83-64, with Stonebraker,M., 1983.

[Har68] P.E. Hart, *The condensed nearest neighbor rule*, IEEE Trans. on Information Theory **125** (1968), 515–516.

[Har74] J.A. Hartigan, *Clustering algorithms*, Wiley, New York, 1974.

[Hil91] D. Hilbert, *Ueber die steitge abbildung einer linie auf ein flaechenstueck*, Math. Ann. **38** (1891), 459–460.

[Ima86] H. Imai, *Worst-case analysis for planar matching and tour heuristics with bucketing techniques and spacefilling curves*, Journal of the Operations Research Society of Japan **29** (1986), no. 1, 43–67.

[KM83] I. Kalantari and G. McDonald, *A data structure and an algorithm for the nearest point problem*, IEEE Trans. on Software Engineering **9** (1983), 631–634.

[Knu81] D.E. Knuth, *The art of computer programming*, Addison Wesley, 1981.

[Koh88] T. Kohonen, *Self organization and associative memory*, Springer-Verlag., 1988.

[KP86] B. S. Kim and S. B. Park, *A fast k nearest neighbor finding algorithm based on the ordered partition*, IEEE Trans. on PAMI **8** (1986), 761–766.

[KPK85] B. Kamgar-Parsi and L. N. Kanal, *An improved branch and bound algorithm for computing k-nearest neighbours*, Pattern Recognition Letters **3** (1985), 7–12.

[KS97] N. Katayama and S. Satoh, *The sr-tree: an indexing structure for highdimensional nearest neighbor queries*, Proc. ACM SIGMOD Int. Conf. on Management of Data (Tucson, Arizona), 1997, pp. 369–380.

[L'E88] P. L'Ecuyer, *Efficient and portable combined random number generators*, Communications of the ACM **31** (1988), no. 6.

[LJF94] K.I. Lin, H.V. Jagadish, and C. Faloutsos, *The tv-tree: An index structure for high-dimensional data*, Very Large Databases Journal **3** (1994), 517–542.

[Mas89] P.R. Massopust, *Fractal peano curves*, Journal of Geometry **34** (1989), 127–138.

[MC79] J.M. Mulvey and H.P. Crowder, *Cluster analysis: an application of lagrangian relaxation*, Management Science **25** (1979), no. 4, 329–340.

[MD83] L. Miclet and M. Dabouz, *Approximative fast nearest neighbor recognition*, Pattern Recognition Letters **1** (1983), 277–285.

[Moo00] E.H. Moore, *On certain crinkly curves*, Transactions of the American Mathematical Society **1** (1900), 72–90.

[MOV94] M.L. Mico, J. Oncina, and E. Vidal, *A new version of the nearest-neighbor aproximating and eliminating search algorithm (aesa) with linear preprocessing time and memory requirements*, Pattern Recognition Letters **15** (1994), 9–17.

[MS90] O.J. Murphy and S.M. Selkow, *Finding nearest neighbors with voronoi tessellations*, Information Processing Letters **34** (1990), 37–41.

[MS97] N. Megiddo and U. Shaft, *Efficient nearest neighbor indexing based on a collection of space filling curves*, Tech. report, IBM Almaden Research Center, 1997.

[Net79] E. Netto, *Beitrag sur mannigfaltigkeitslehre*, 1879, pp. 263–268.

[NG88] H. Niemann and G. Goppert, *An efficient branch-and-bound nearest neighbour classifier*, Pattern Recognition Letters **7** (1988), 67–72.

[NN97] Nene and Nayar, *A simple algorithm for nearest neighbor search in high dimensions*, IEEETPAMI: IEEE Transactions on Pattern Analysis and Machine Intelligence **19** (1997).

[Omo90] S.M. Omohundro, *Geometric learning algorithms*, Physica D **42** (1990), 307–321.

[OO91a] Y. Ohno and K. Ohyama, *A catalog of non-symmetric self-similar space-filling curves*, Journal of Recreational Mathematics **23** (1991), no. 4, 247–254.

[OO91b] ———, *A catalog of symmetric self-similar space-filling curves*, Journal of Recreational Mathematics **23** (1991), no. 3, 161–174.

[OO92] ———, *Self-similar space-filling curves consisting on non-identical segments*, Journal of Recreational Mathematics **24** (1992), no. 1, 38–43.

[PAB68] E.A. Patrick, D.R. Anderson, and F.K. Bechtel, *Mapping multidimensional space to one dimension for computer output display*, IEEE Transactions on Computers **17** (1968), no. 10, 949–953.

[PB80] Christos H. Papadimitriou and Jon Louis Bentley, *A worst-case analysis of nearest neighbor searching by projection*, Automata, Languages and Programming, 1980, pp. 470–482.

[PB89] L.K. Platzman and J.J. Bartholdi, *Spacefilling curves and the planar travelling salesman problem*, Journal of the ACM **36** (1989), no. 4, 719–737.

[PC94] J.C. Perez-Cortes, *Algoritmos de aprendizaje automatico en reconocimiento geometrico de formas*, Ph.D. thesis, E. Vidal (adv.) Dept. Sistemas Informaticos y Computacion, Univ. Politecnica de Valencia, Valencia, Spain., 1994.

[Pea90] G. Peano, *Sur une courbe qui remplit toute une aire plane*, Math. Ann. **36** (1890), 157–160.

[PG90] T. Poggio and F. Girosi, *Networks for approximation and learning*, Proceedings of the IEEE **78** (1990), no. 9, 1481–1497.

[PV98a] J.C. Perez and E. Vidal, *An approximate nearest neighbours search algorithm based on the extended general spacefilling curves heuristic*, Workshop on Statistical Pattern Recognition SPR-98, Sydney, Australia., 1998.

[PV98b] J.C. Perez and E. Vidal, *The extended general spacefilling curves heuristic*, Intl. Conf. on Pattern Recognition ICPR-98, Brisbane, Australia., 1998.

[PV99] J.C. Perez and E. Vidal, *The extended general spacefilling curves heuristic*, Tech. report, Univ. Politecnica de Valencia, Valencia, Spain, `http://plutarco.disca.upv.es/~jcperez/Documentos/The\_Extended\_SFC\_He%uristic.ps.gz`, 1999.

[Rob81] J.T. Robinson, *K-d-b-tree: A search structure for large multidimensional dynamic indices*, Proceedings of the ACM SIGMOD, Ann Arbor, ACM, New York, 1981, pp. 10–18.

[RP92] V. Ramasubramanian and K.K. Paliwal, *An efficient approximation-elimination algorithm for fast nearest-neighbour search based on a spherical distance coordinate formulation*, Pattern Recognition Letters **13** (1992), 471–480.

[Sag91] H. Sagan, *Some reflections on the emergence of space-filling curves: The way it could have happened and should have happened, but did not happen*, Journal of The Franklin Institute, **32** (1991), no. 4, 419–431.

[San93] J. Sanlorenzo, *Reduccion de la dimensionalidad para aplicacion de "clustering" optimo a conjuntos de datos vectoriales*, Master's thesis, Facultad de Informatica, Universidad Politecnica de Valencia. J.C. Perez-Cortes (adv.), 1993.

[Sch38] E.H. Schoenberg, *On the peano curve of lebesgue*, Bulletin of the American Mathematical Society, **1** (1938), 519.

[Set81] I.K. Sethi, *A fast algorithm for recognizing nearest neighbors*, IEEE Transactions on Systems, Man and Cybernetics, **11** (1981), no. 3, 245–248.

[Sie12] M.W. Sierpinski, *Sur une nouvelle courbe continue qui remplit toute une aire plane*, Bull. Acad. Sci. de Cracovie, (1912), 462–478.

[SK87] B. Seeger and H.P. Kriegel, *The buddy tree: An efficient and robust access method for spatial database systems*, Proc. 16th International Conference on Very Large Databases,, Morgan Kauffman Publishers, Los Altos, Calif., 1987, pp. 590–601.

[SK96] E. Skubalska and A. Krzyzak, *Fast k-nn classification rule using metric on space-filling curves*, Proceedings of ICPR-96, 1996, pp. 121–125.

[Spr91] R.F. Sproull, *Refinements to nearest-neighbor searching in k-dimensional trees*, Algorithmica **6** (1991), 579–589.

[SRF87] T. Sellis, N. Roussopoulos, and C. Faloutsos, *The r+-tree: A dynamic index for multi-dimensional objects*, Proceedings of the Conference on Very Large Databases, Morgan Kaufman pubs. (Los Altos CA), Brighton, UK., no. 13, September 1987.

[SW90] D. Shasha and T. Wang, *New techniques for best-match retrieval*, ACM Transactions on Information Systems, **8** (1990), no. 2, 140–158.

[Vid86] E. Vidal, *An algorithm for finding nearest neighbours in (approximately) constant average time*, Pattern Recognition Letters **4** (1986), 145–158.

[Vil96] J.M Vilar, *Reducing the overhead of the aesa metric-space nearest neighbour searching algorithm*, Information Processing Letters (1996).

[VRC85] E. Vidal, H. Rulot, and F. Casacuberta, *Is the dtw "distance" really a metric? an algorithm reducing the number of dtw comparisons in isolated word recognition*, Speech Communications, (1985), 333–344.

[Wil72] D.L. Wilson, *Asymptotic properties of nearest neighbor rules using edited data*, IEEE Trans. on Systems, Man and Cybernetics **2** (1972), 408–420.

[Xu90] X. et al. Xu, *Rt-tree: an improved r-tree index structure for spatio-temporal databases*, Proceedings of the 4rd International Symposium on Spatial Data Handling, 1990.

[Yia93] P. Yianilos, *Data structures and algorithms for nearest neighbor search in general metric spaces*, 4th ACM Symp. on Discrete Algorithms, 1993, pp. 311–321.

[Yun76] T.P. Yunck, *A technique to identify nearest neighbors*, SMC **6** (1976), no. 10, 678–683.

[YY85] A.C. Yao and F.F. Yao, *A general approach to $d-$dimensional geometric queries*, Proceedings of the 17th Annual ACM Symposium on the Theory of Computing, 1985, pp. 163–168.

[ZO96] P. Zakarauskas and J.M. Ozard, *Complexity analysis for partitioning nearest-neighbor searching algorithms*, IEEE Trans. on PAMI **18** (1996), no. 6, 663–668.

JUAN-CARLOS PEREZ-CORTES, DEPARTMENT OF COMPUTER ENGINEERING, POLYTECHNIC UNIVERSITY OF VALENCIA, 46071 VALENCIA (SPAIN)

Current address: Department of Computer Engineering, Polytechnic University of Valencia, 46071 Valencia (Spain)

E-mail address: `jcperez@disca.upv.es`

ENRIQUE VIDAL, INSTITUTO TECNOLGICO DE INFORMTICA, POLYTECHNIC UNIVERSITY OF VALENCIA, 46071 VALENCIA (SPAIN)

Current address: Instituto Tecnolgico de Informtica, Polytechnic University of Valencia, 46071 Valencia (Spain)

E-mail address: `evidal@iti.upv.es`

DIMACS Series in Discrete Mathematics
and Theoretical Computer Science
Volume **59**, 2002

Locally Lifting the Curse of Dimensionality for Nearest Neighbor Search

Peter N. Yianilos

ABSTRACT. Our work gives a positive result for nearest neighbor search in high dimensions. It establishes that radius-limited search is, under particular circumstances, free of the *curse of dimensionality*. It further illuminates the nature of the curse, and may therefore someday contribute to improved general purpose algorithms for high dimensions and for general metric spaces.

We consider the problem of nearest neighbor search in the Euclidean hypercube $[-1, +1]^d$ with uniform distributions, and the additional natural assumption that the nearest neighbor is located within a constant fraction R of the maximum interpoint distance in this space, i.e. within distance $2R\sqrt{d}$ of the query.

We introduce the idea of *aggressive pruning* and give a family of practical algorithms, an idealized analysis, and describe experiments. Our main result is that search complexity measured in terms of d-dimensional inner product operations, is i) strongly sublinear with respect to the data set size n for moderate R, ii) asymptotically, and as a practical matter, independent of dimension.

Given a random data set, a random query within distance $2R\sqrt{d}$ of some database element, and a randomly constructed data structure, the search succeeds with a specified probability, which is a parameter of the search algorithm. On average a search performs $\approx n^\gamma$ distance computations where n is the number of points in the database, and $\gamma < 1$ is calculated in our analysis. Linear and near-linear space structures are described, and our algorithms and analysis are free of large hidden constants, i.e. the algorithms perform far less work than exhaustive search – both in theory and practice.

1. Introduction

Finding nearest neighbors in Euclidean spaces of very low dimension is theoretically fast, and practical, using the notion of a Voronoi diagram [**Aur91**]. In moderate dimension, or in general metric spaces with *intrinsically* moderate dimension, recursive projection-decomposition techniques such as kd-trees [**FBS75, FBF77, BF79, Ben80**] and vantage-point techniques [**Uhl91b, Uhl91a, RP92, Yia93**] for general metric spaces of intrinsically low dimension, are effective.

1991 *Mathematics Subject Classification.* 68W01, 68W05, 68W40, 68P10.
Key words and phrases. Nearest neighbor search, kd-tree, curse of dimensionality.
Completed during 1999 while visiting the Princeton University computer science department. A preliminary version appeared as [**Yia00**].

As dimension d grows large, these tree techniques perform significantly better than brute-force search only if the number of dataset points n grows exponentially in d. Or, in the case of Voronoi diagrams, if space increases exponentially.

The motivation for this work is the observation that, in practice, one is usually interested in nearest neighbors only if they are somewhat close to the query. The main contribution of this paper is the algorithmic idea of *aggressive pruning* and its analysis for the uniformly distributed hypercube. In this setting, with a natural definition of *somewhat close*, we show that the expected time complexity of finding nearest neighbors is invariant with respect to dimension[1] — and the space cost[2] is independent of d, and linear in n.

In a Euclidean hypercube the maximum distance between two points grows with $\sqrt{d}$. By *somewhat close* we mean within a neighborhood whose radius is a constant fraction R of this distance. A parameter $0 < p < 1$ controls the probability that a search will locate the nearest neighbor within this search domain. For each choice of R and p we calculate an exponent $\gamma < 1$ such that the search will perform on average $\approx n^\gamma$ distance computations, and this dominates the work performed. Notice that γ is independent of d.

The practical significance of our work is that search time is strongly sublinear given moderately large values for R and acceptable success probabilities. For example, searching $1,000,000$ points uniformly distributed in $[-1,+1]^{1000}$ with our experimental software, given $R = 0.1$, requires on average $\approx 30,000$ distance computations, and succeeds with probability 0.9988. In this example $\gamma \approx 0.78$ from our analysis. Arbitrarily high success probabilities can be obtained at the expense of distance computations.

We remark that this work was motivated by the author's recent work of [**Yia99**], where the objective is to build a data structure that provides worst-case sublinear-time radius-limited nearest neighbor search (independent of query) for a given dataset. With uniform distributions in Euclidean space, the resulting structures support search neighborhood of only $O(1)$ size, in contrast with those of this paper that scale linearly with the maximum interpoint distance.

Early work in nearest neighbor search is surveyed in [**Das91**]. There is a large literature on the search problem, much of it elaborating on a single fact: that certain projections from a metric space to $\mathbb{R}$ have the property that projected distances are dominated by those in the original space.

The two most important such projections are i) inner product with a unit vector in Euclidean space, and ii) distance from a chosen *vantage point.*[3] These ideas were recognized early on in work including [**BK73, Fuk75, Fuk90, FS82, Sha77**].

Taking the inner product with a canonical basis element in Euclidean space leads to the well-known *kd-tree* of Friedman and Bentley [**FBS75, FBF77, BF79, Ben80**]. They recursively divide a pointset in $\mathbb{R}^d$ by projecting each element onto a distinguished coordinate. Improvements, distribution adaptation, and incremental searches, are described in [**EW82**], [**KP86**], and [**Bro90**] respectively.

---

[1]Measured as d-dimensional inner product operations

[2]In addition to the space required to store the dataset itself

[3]The first of these may be viewed as the second *in the limit* as a vantage point moves toward infinity along the direction of the unit vector.

The search tree we build has essentially the same structure as a kd-tree built given randomly pretransformed data[4], and constrained to use the same cut coordinate for all nodes at a given tree level. Our criterion for pruning branches during search, and its analysis, are the primary contributions of this paper and distinguish our methods from kd-tree search.

More recently, the field of computational geometry has yielded many interesting results such as those of [**Vai89, Cla88, Cla87, FMT92**] and earlier [**DL76**].

Very recently a number of papers have appeared striving for more efficient algorithms with worst-case time bounds for the *approximate* nearest neighbor problem [**AMN$^+$94, Kle97, KOR98, IM98**]. These exploit properties of random projections beyond the simple *projection distance dominance* fact mentioned above, and additional ideas to establish worst case bounds. Our work may be viewed as exploiting the fact that random projections of uniformly random data in a hypercube, and of neighborhood balls of radius proportional to $\sqrt{d}$, both have constant variance with respect to d. See also [**Cla97**] for very recent work on search in general metric spaces.

Several of the papers mentioned above include interesting theoretical constructions that trade polynomial space, and in some cases expensive preprocessing, for fast performance in the worst case. We remark that to be useful in practice, a nearest neighbor algorithm must require very nearly linear space — a stringent requirement. As datasets grow, even low-degree polynomial space becomes rapidly unacceptable.

For completeness, early work dealing with two special cases should be mentioned. Retrieval of similar binary keys is considered by Rivest in [**Riv74**] and the L_∞ setting is the focus of [**Yun76**]. Also see [**BM80**] for worst case data structures for the *range search* problem. Finally, recent works [**BOR99**] and [**CCGL99**] establish nontrivial lower bounds for nearest neighbor search.

In the following section we give construction and search algorithms specialized for our uniform setting. Section 3 gives a *concrete* analysis of these algorithms that include calculations of the applicable search time complexity exponent, and failure probability. Experiments are presented in section 4, which confirm in practice the dimensional invariance established by analysis. Finally, some directions for further work are mentioned in section 5.

2. Algorithms

2.1. Construction: A search tree is built with the set of data points as its leaves. It has essentially the same structure as a kd-tree built on data that has first been transformed to a random coordinate system. Construction time is easily seen to be $O(n \log n)$ and space is linear.

Construction proceeds recursively. Each interior node has as input a list of points. The root's list is the entire set. Associated with each interior node is a randomly selected unit vector u_i, where i denotes level (distance from the root). The number of such vectors is then equal to the depth of tree minus one (because there is no vector associated with a leaf). This set is constructed so as to be

[4]That is, where the dataset is first transformed to the coordinate system induced by a random basis. When the kd-tree *cuts* space using a single coordinate in this transformed setting, is then the same as cutting based the inner product of a data element with a particular basis vector.

orthonormal. First, random vectors are drawn, then they are orthonormalized in the usual way (Gram-Schmidt).

Construction of a node consists of reading its input list, computing the inner product of each element with the node's associated u_i, and adding the element to a *left* or *right* output list depending on its sign. In general the dividing point is chosen more intelligently, e.g. by computing the median of the inner product values. But in our uniform $[-1,+1]^d$ setting we just use zero for simplicity. Left and right children are then generated recursively. If a node's input list consists of a single element, then that node becomes a leaf and stores the element within it.

2.2. Search: The search is parameterized by a query q, a value $R \in (0,1)$ giving the proportional size of the search domain, and a probability $0 < p < 1$ that is related to the success rate we expect.

The inner product of q and each u_i is first computed. Next the positive threshold distance $\ell = \Phi^{-1}_{4R^2}(p)$ is computed, where Φ denotes the cumulative distribution function for a normal density with the variance indicated by subscript.

Search proceeds recursively from the root. For a node at level i the value $< q, u_i >$ is examined. If it is less than ℓ then the left child is recursively explored. If it exceeds $-\ell$ then the right child is explored. Notice that when $< q, u_i > \in (-\ell, +\ell)$ both children are explored. When a leaf is encountered, the distance is computed between the element it contains and q.

This decision rule is centered at zero because of our particular uniform $[-1,+1]^d$ setting, but is easily translated to an arbitrary cut point, e.g. the median of the projected values.

After each distance computation $d(q,x)$ is performed the proportion $d(q,x)/2\sqrt{d}$ is computed. If smaller than R, then R is reduced and ℓ recomputed.

This concludes the description of our search algorithm and we now briefly discuss related issues and extensions.

An important idea in kd-tree search involves the computation of the minimum distance from the query to the subspace corresponding to a node to be explored. If this distance grows beyond the radius of interest, the node is pruned. We do not, however, include it in our analysis or experimental implementation because in our high dimensional setting, in the absence of exponentially many data elements, this idea has vanishingly little effect. Intuitively, this is because the search tree is not nearly deep enough for the minimum distance to grow larger than the search radius.

The analogue of this kd-tree idea in our setting is an alternative version of our algorithm above that slightly reduces ℓ while descending through interior nodes to reflect the fact that the distribution of data elements within a ball about the query is no longer uniform. But, again, this is a second order effect.

Finally we remark that the ℓ-cutoff approach taken above might be replaced with an entirely probabilistic pruning scheme that passes probabilities from our analysis down to each child during search. The probabilities upward to the root are then multiplied and search continues downward until the result falls below a specified threshold.

3. Analysis

We assume both data points and queries are uniformly distributed within the hypercube $[-1,+1]^d$. The Euclidean distance metric applies and the maximum distance between two points in this space is $2\sqrt{d}$. We consider the problem of finding the nearest neighbor of a query q within some distance δ that is a constant proportion of the maximum interpoint distance, i.e. $\delta = 2R\sqrt{d}$ with $0 < R < 1$.

Any unit vector u gives rise to a projection π_u mapping $x \in \mathbb{R}^d$ into $\mathbb{R}$ defined by $< x, u >$. It is immediate that distances in the range of this projection are dominated by distances in the domain. It is this fact that kd-trees exploit to prune branches during branch-and-bound search.

If τ represents the distance to the nearest neighbor encountered so far during a search, then this fact implies that every member of the ball of radius τ centered at the query q maps under any π_u into the interval $[\pi_u(q) - \tau, \pi_u(q) + \tau]$. So kd-tree search may confidently disregard any data points that project outside of this interval. Unlike the kd-tree, which finds nearest neighbors with certainty, we will consider randomized constructions that succeed with some specified probability.

Since δ scales up linearly with $\sqrt{d}$, the interval grows $[\pi_u(q) - \delta, \pi_u(q) + \delta]$ too, and soon the kd-tree can *confidently* prune almost nothing, and performs a nearly exhaustive search.

But in our uniformly random setting we will show that the δ ball about q projects to a distribution about $\pi(q)$ having constant variance. This is why it is possible to continue to *probabilistically* prune just as effectively even as $d \to \infty$. Since dimension does not affect our ability to prune, we have lifted the curse of dimensionality in our setting.

We now proceed with the description and idealized analysis of our algorithm with the following proposition, which establishes two elementary but key dimensional invariants

PROPOSITION 3.1. *i) Let u be a random unit vector, and let X denote a random dataset in our setting, then the one dimensional set of values $\pi_u(X)$ has mean zero and variance $1/3$ – independent of dimension – where both u and X are random variables. ii) Consider any $q \in \mathbb{R}^d$ and let r denote a random vector located on the surface of a ball centered at q of radius $2R\sqrt{d}$. Then for any unit vector u, the distribution of values $\pi_u(r)$ has mean $\pi_u(q)$ and variance $4R^2$ – independent of dimension.*

PROOF. The variance of each component of u is $1/d$ since $< u, u >= 1$ by definition and the components are i.i.d. Consider a random element $x \in [-1, +1]^d$. Here a simple integration establishes that the variance of each component is $1/3$. So the variance of each term of $< u, x >$ is $1/3d$, and that of the entire inner product is then $1/3$ as required. Now each component of u and x has mean zero so that $< u, x >$ has mean zero — and part i) is established.

$\pi_u(r)$ is centered at $\pi_u(q)$ by linearity of inner product. So we may assume without loss of generality that $q = 0$. Now the inner product of two random unit vectors is easily seen to have variance $1/d$. Scaling one of them by a factor of $2R\sqrt{d}$ increases the variance by a factor of $4R^2d$, so that it becomes $4R^2$ as required by part ii). □

Now fix some unit vector u and consider the query's projection $\pi_u(q)$. Then by Proposition 3.1, and ignoring hypercube *corner effects*, the projection of the data points within the domain of search are distributed about $\pi_u(q)$ with variance no greater than $4R^2$.

Because distances between projected points are dominated by their original distance it is clear that $|\pi_u(x) - \pi_u(q)| < 2R\sqrt{d}$ for any x in the search domain.

So any data points with projections farther than $2R\sqrt{d}$ from $\pi_u(q)$ can be confidently ruled out during search. It is this *hard* pruning that kd-trees (and many related structures) exploit to avoid considering every point during nearest neighbor search.

But notice that this pruning *cutoff* distance $2R\sqrt{d} \to \infty$ with d while the projection variance remains constant. As a result hard pruning is asymptotically ineffective, and this gives rise to the *curse of dimensionality* for nearest neighbor search using kd-trees in our setting.

Next observe that as a consequence of the central limit theorem the distributions of Proposition 3.1 are asymptotically normal — and we remark that as a practical matter this is a good approximation; even for moderate dimension. So from this point on in our analysis we will simply assume normality, i.e. that d is sufficiently large so that its deviation from normality is negligible.

We then arrive at one of the main observations of this paper: that the nearest neighbor's projection is within constant distance of $\pi_u(q)$ with arbitrarily high and easily calculated probability p depending only on this constant, and not on d.

Recall that the tree we build recursively bisects the set of data points using a randomly selected u by separating its projection into left and right branches at a cut point c near the median. Given a query q we prune one of these branches if $\pi_u(q)$ is at least some cutoff distance ℓ from c. We refer to this idea as *aggressive pruning*.

PROPOSITION 3.2. *Using cutoff distance $\ell = \Phi^{-1}_{4R^2}(p)$ to prune branches will exclude the nearest neighbor (assuming one exists within distance $2R\sqrt{d}$ of the query) with probability $1-p$ at each node; where $\Phi_{\sigma^2}(x)$ denotes the cumulative distribution function for the zero mean normal density with variance σ^2.*

PROOF. Equating the target failure rate $1-p$ with the mass of the distribution's positive tail gives $1-\Phi_{4R^2}(\ell) = 1-p$, so $\ell = \Phi^{-1}_{4R^2}(p)$. □

Again, note that this cutoff distance ℓ is constant despite the fact that the absolute size of our search domain is expanding with $\sqrt{d}$ as $d \to \infty$. We can now establish a single tree's expected search complexity and success probability.

PROPOSITION 3.3. *Given n data points, R, p, and ℓ from proposition 3.2, and assuming $d = \Omega(\log n)$, then i) our search will visit $\approx n^\gamma$ leaf nodes where $\gamma = \log_2 2\Phi_{1/3}(\ell)$, and compute a d-dimensional Euclidean distance at at each; and ii) the search will succeed with probability no smaller than $\approx p^{\log_2 n}$.*

PROOF. Recall that we expect that at each node of the tree the projection of the remaining database elements will have mean/median close to zero and variance of approximately 1/3. We fix our attention on one such node with corresponding unit vector u and assume the cut point is exactly zero and variance is exactly 1/3. Since we have assumed that the queries are also uniformly distributed, their projection is identical. So we can easily calculate the probability b that a query q lies within distance ℓ of the zero. In this event both left and right branches must be explored. Otherwise, with probability $1-b$ we can prune one so that only one is explored.

The mass of one tail (beyond ℓ) is $1-\Phi_{1/3}(\ell)$ from which it follows that $1-b$ is twice this value. So $b = 2\Phi_{1/3}(\ell) - 1$. Then the expected number F of branches visited is $2 \cdot b + 1 \cdot (1-b) = 2\Phi_{1/3}(\ell)$

Since $d = \Omega(\log n)$ it is possible to choose unit vectors from root to leaf that are independent (e.g. the canonical basis), random vectors will be nearly so, and our random orthonormalization process will certainly succeed. So except for corner effects, which we disregard, it is reasonable to assume that query projections and failure probabilities are independent along each root-leaf path.

Since the tree's depth is $\log_2 n$ (we'll assume perfect balance) the search will visit $F^{\log_2 n}$ nodes. That is $2^{\log_2 F \log_2 n}$ or $n^{\log_2 F}$, establishing i).

Now the nearest neighbor is located somewhere as a leaf of the tree. To succeed, the search must not prune it at any of the $\log_2 n$ nodes along a path up to the root. This happens with probability $p^{\log_2 n}$ establishing ii) — where independence follows from the orthogonality of the set of projectors and the assumption of a uniform distribution.[5] □

Notice that the exponent of n in proposition 3.3 is within $[0, 1)$. Also, the requirement that $d = \Omega(\log n)$ is not very restrictive since otherwise the number of data points is exponential in d and earlier techniques can be used to efficiently locate nearest neighbors.

The probability estimate of Proposition 3.3 is extremely conservative. The actual failure probabilities are much smaller because: i) our analysis has implicitly assumed that the query always projects to a point exactly ℓ from the cut point. This is the worst case. If the distance is smaller, then nothing is pruned and no error can be made; and if the distance is larger, the effective cutoff distance is effectively increased; and ii) we have assumed that the nearest neighbor is always just within the domain of search. In reality queries will be distributed with this domain.

Even without considering these factors our calculations suggest that efficient search is possible for moderately large values of R.

Table 3 gives exponent values for selected values of R and p. For example, if $R = 0.05$ and $p = 1 - 10^{-4} = 0.9999$ then the exponent is ≈ 0.566. Given $n = 10,000,000$ data points our results state that no more than $n^{0.566} \approx 9,162$ inner product operations will be performed, and that the nearest neighbor will be located with probability $0.9999^{log_2 n} \approx 0.9977$. Choosing $p = 1 - 10^{-6}$ corresponds to $48,194$ inner products with the probability of success increasing to 0.999977. All of these calculations are asymptotically independent of dimension.

We continue this example to illustrate the use of forests to improve performance in some settings. Later we will give a theoretical consequence of this idea. Consider two independent trees with $p = 1 - 10^{-4}$. That is, the choice of random unit vectors is independent. Both trees are searched for each query. We then expect a failure rate of $\approx (1 - 0.9977)^2 = .00000529$, and $2 \cdot 9,162 = 18,324$ inner products are performed.[6] Now this failure rate is considerably better than the $1 - 0.999977 = 0.000023$ resulting from a single tree using $p = 1 - 10^{-6}$, and far fewer inner products are computed, but space consumption is doubled. This example illustrates the space-time design tradeoff that arises when applying our ideas in practice.

The natural generalization of this idea leads to a forest of independent trees. Recall that a failure rate of a single tree grows, albeit slowly, with n. By using

[5]Negligible dependence results from the hypercube's corners, but for simplicity we ignore this effect.

[6]We must have d large enough to allow independent unit vectors to be drawn, and will say more about this later.

R	$1-p$					
	10^{-2}	10^{-4}	10^{-6}	10^{-8}	10^{-10}	10^{-12}
0.01	0.090	0.141	0.177	0.207	0.232	0.254
0.02	0.174	0.267	0.331	0.381	0.423	0.458
0.03	0.252	0.379	0.463	0.526	0.577	0.618
0.04	0.325	0.479	0.575	0.645	0.698	0.740
0.05	0.393	0.566	0.669	0.739	0.790	0.829
0.06	0.456	0.642	0.746	0.813	0.859	0.892
0.07	0.513	0.707	0.808	0.869	0.908	0.935
0.08	0.566	0.763	0.858	0.911	0.943	0.963
0.09	0.615	0.810	0.897	0.941	0.965	0.979
0.10	0.660	0.850	0.926	0.962	0.980	0.989
0.11	0.700	0.882	0.949	0.976	0.989	0.995
0.12	0.737	0.909	0.965	0.986	0.994	0.998
0.13	0.770	0.931	0.977	0.992	0.997	0.999
0.14	0.800	0.948	0.985	0.995	0.999	1.000
0.15	0.826	0.961	0.990	0.997	0.999	1.000
0.16	0.850	0.971	0.994	0.999	1.000	1.000
0.17	0.871	0.979	0.996	0.999	1.000	1.000
0.18	0.890	0.985	0.998	1.000	1.000	1.000
0.19	0.906	0.990	0.999	1.000	1.000	1.000
0.20	0.921	0.993	0.999	1.000	1.000	1.000

TABLE 1. Searches in our setting with a single tree require $\approx n^\gamma$ inner product operations and linear space. This table gives γ values for various choices of R and p from our analysis.

enough trees one can force the forest's failure rate to zero as n increases while preserving sublinear search times; at the expense of polynomial space to pay for the additional trees. To analyze this let x denote the tree's depth and observe that $(1-p^x)^y$ gives the probability of failure for a forest of y distinct random trees. It can be shown that if $y = p^{-(1+\epsilon)x}$ for any $\epsilon > 0$, then this probability tends to zero as x (and therefore n) increases[7]. Since $x = \log_2 n$ the number of trees $y = n^{-(1+\epsilon)\log_2 p}$ in terms of n. Search time (the number of inner product operations) also increases by a factor of y. Space increases from linear to $O(yn)$. Finally, to maintain independence we must increase the lower bound on d to $\Omega(y \log n)$.

It is apparent from table 3 that this idea works for many values of R and p. For example, if $R = 0.05$ and $p = 1 - 10^{-6}$ then the original exponent 0.566 increases by only $\approx 1.44 \times 10^{-6}$ – far less than the table's precision. But it does not work for arbitrary R and p. For large values of R the exponent is so close to 1 that the added complexity makes the total superlinear.

Note that $O(nd)$ space is required to store the data elements themselves, but only $O(n)$ space is needed for the interior tree nodes, which point to data elements. So, in practice, we can afford $O(d)$ trees while remaining linear space. In practice this means that in high dimension one can easily afford many trees without materially affecting space consumption. In theory it means that if d is assumed to grow

[7]However it may increase somewhat before eventually decreasing.

as an appropriate small power of n as $n \to \infty$, then the entire forest occupies linear space.

Returning to our choice of the $[-1,+1]^d$ hypercube, we observe that i) All of our arguments apply immediately to $[0,1]^d$ after compensating for the shifted mean, and ii) that our arguments apply as well to the d-dimensional hypersphere. To see this note that the dot product of a random unit vector and a random database element has variance $1/d$, and the maximum interpoint distance is constant, so the projection of a proportional neighborhood balls also falls with $1/d$.

Finally we remark that as an alternative to forests, one can build a single tree in which each level is *overlapped*, i.e. items near the center are stored in both the left and right branches. This effectively reduces ℓ and with it search time – at the expense of polynomial space (given a constant fraction of overlap at each level).

4. Experiments

To confirm our analysis we wrote an ANSI-C program to build and search trees. It accepts d, n, R, p as arguments, in addition to the number of random queries to test, and a random seed.

The data points are distributed uniformly in $[-1,+1]^d$. Queries are generated by choosing a data point x at random, then a random unit vector u, and forming the sum $x+(1-\epsilon)2R\sqrt{D}u$ – so that the query lies just inside of the search domain. We use $\epsilon = .0001$. This ensures that a nearest neighbor exists within the domain.

An indexed set of projection vectors is generated by starting with random vectors and orthonormalizing them in the standard way. Each level in the tree uses the corresponding vector in this set as its projector. So the size of the set is $O(\log n)$, and in practice is $\approx 2\log_2 n$ because the resulting trees are not perfectly balanced. For simplicity zero is always used as the cut point during tree construction.

In order to allow us to simultaneously explore large n and d without exceeding available RAM, we represent the data points to be searched using a pseudorandom generator seed that suffices to construct them. As a result we can easily study $n = 1,000,000$ and higher in almost arbitrarily high dimension.

Figure 1 illustrates that search complexity measured in the number of inner product operations performed is very nearly dimension-invariant — confirming our analysis. So total work scales up only linearly with dimension with the complexity of an inner product operation.

Note that for simplicity we regard an inner product operation and a Euclidean distance computation as having identical complexity. Also, the table's results exclude the roughly $2\log_2 n$ inner products required to compute the query's projection at each level of the tree.

Recall that our analysis of failure rate was quite conservative and experiments confirm this. Actual failure rates for every case in Figure 1 were somewhat lower than those from analysis. For example, in the $R = 0.20$ case, analysis predicts that the search will succeed with probability ≈ 0.85, and the actual value is ≈ 0.97. Note that one reason for using the moderate value $p = 0.99$ in our study is that we have confirmed that values far closer to zero result in no observable experimental error given the limited number of queries we have time to perform.

We compare performance in our setting with kd-tree search [**FBS75, FBF77, BF79, Ben80**]. We are interested in neighbors within a specified distance of the query. To reproduce this setting, kd-tree search is initialized as though an element at the specified distance has already been encountered.

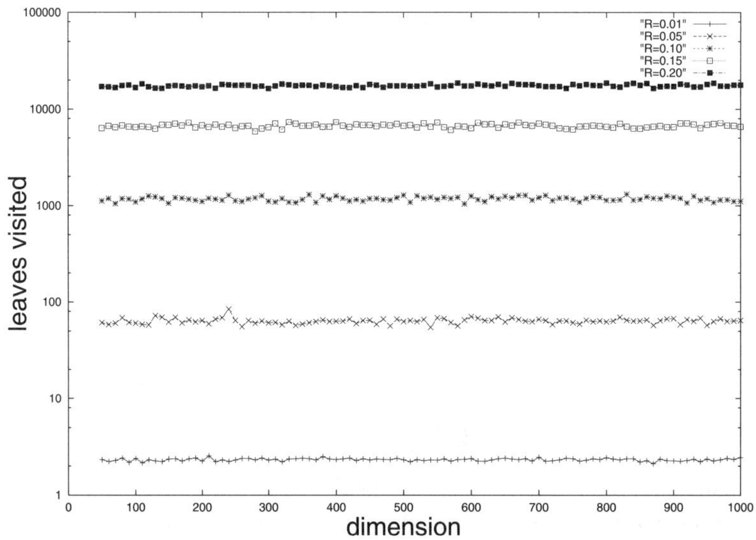

FIGURE 1. Proportional radius search complexity is constant with respect to dimension — confirming our analysis. We measure the number of leaves visited. Each visit corresponds to a Euclidean distance computation. In this experiment the number of uniformly distributed data points $n = 100,000$, and the p from our analysis is 0.99. Each query is generated so as to be slightly less than distance $2R\sqrt{d}$ from some database element, so that our radius-limited search always succeeds. The results of $1,000$ such random queries are averaged to produce each data point. Our analysis predicts constant values of approximately 3, 92, 1987, $13,553$, and $40,114$ corresponding to R values of $0.01, 0.05, 0.10, 0.15$, and 0.20 respectively. The experimental values compare well with these estimates, and in general are dominated by them by a factor of approximately two.

A recent kd-tree implementation [**MA99**] is modified for our experiments. Its core routines are altered to support radius-limited search as described above, and the distribution's sample program is adapted to report the average number of distance computations performed in response to each query. As in our earlier experiments, queries are generated by starting at a database element, and moving the specified distance away in a random direction. So every query in our experiment locates a nearest neighbor within the radius of interest. As a self-check the sample program is further modified to verify this condition. After these modifications, a direct comparison is possible between our method and kd-tree search.

From our analysis it is clear that kd-tree search will not exhibit the same dimensional invariance, and figure 2 confirms this. Moreover, search time grows so rapidly for the $R \geq 0.10$ cases that the tree is essentially ineffective by dimension 100. By contrast (figure 1) our method remains effective for arbitrarily high dimension. Recall, however, that kd-tree search is guaranteed to find the nearest neighbor within in the domain, while our method will fail with some small probability.

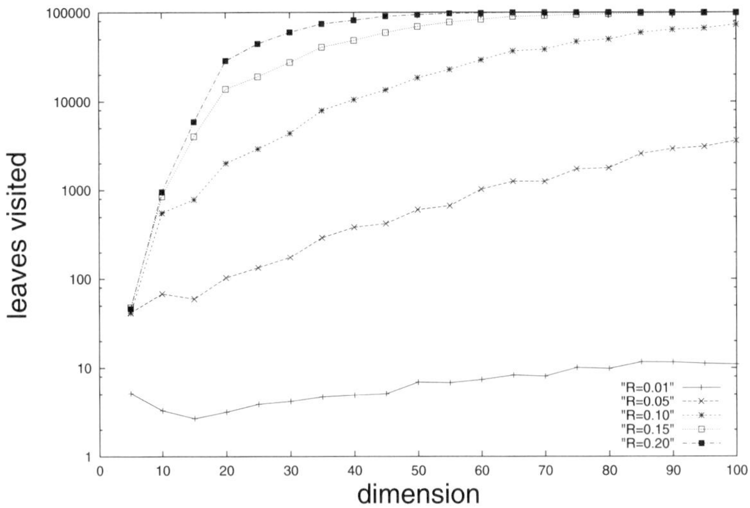

FIGURE 2. Proportional radius kd-tree search complexity is *not* constant with respect to dimension, and increases rapidly for $R \geq 0.10$ so that by dimension 100 the search is nearly exhaustive. Each node visit corresponds to a Euclidean distance computation. The number of uniformly distributed data points $n = 100,000$, and the results of 100 random queries generated as in figure 1 are averaged to produce each data point.

A primary motivation for this paper was our discovery in [**Yia99**] that kd-trees, and a related general structure called a *vantage point forest*, do exhibit search complexity that is invariant with respect to dimension for a domain of *constant radius* — and substantial savings over exhaustive search are realized only for disappointingly small radii. The experiment reported in figure 3 confirms this, and illustrates the fundamentally different asymptotic behavior (with respect to d) of kd-tree search and our aggressive pruning approach. The flat graphs of figure 1 are in the presence of a search radius that *grows* with $\sqrt{d}$, where those of 3 assume a search radius that is *constant* with respect to d. For example, by dimension 32 a domain of unity radius generates a nearly exhaustive search. By contrast figure 1 shows that for $R = 0.1$ and $d = 1000$ (corresponding to a radius of $2R\sqrt{d} \approx 6.33$), our search visits only roughly 1% of the leaf nodes.

We conclude our discussion of experiments by describing a single example of our method in greater detail that pushes n upward to $1,000,000$, p up to 0.999, and the number of queries up to $20,000$. The dimension is $1,000$. Here, analysis predicts success probability 0.9803 and we observe 0.9988. The tree's depth is 39 and $27,899$ leaves are visited on average during a search. The predicted value is $47,020$. The experiment required $2,801$ seconds on a 400Mhz Pentium II processor.

5. Concluding Remarks

We hopes this work takes us closer to practical and useful nearest neighbor search in high dimension. In addition to sharpening our analysis for the uniform

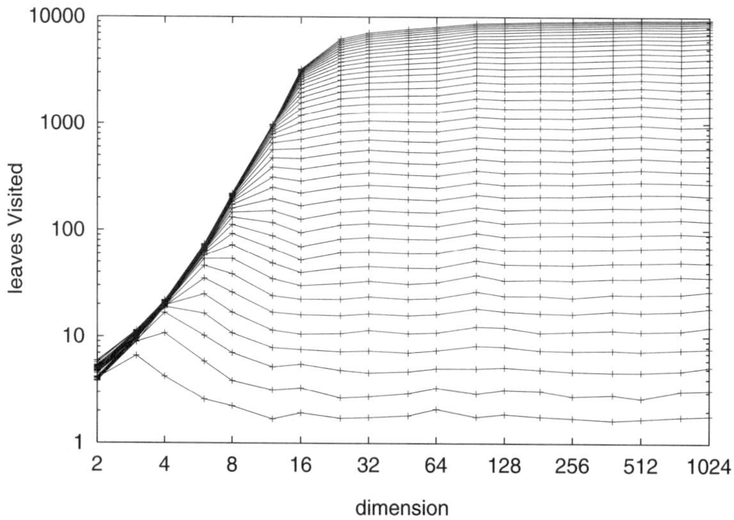

FIGURE 3. The average complexity of *fixed-radius* kd-tree search *is* invariant with respect to dimension. Here $n = 10,000$ and the graphs from bottom to top correspond to radii from 0.025 to 1.0 in increments of 0.025.

case, future theoretical work might target distribution-independent bounds for approximate nearest neighbor search within an R-domain. While generalizing we expect that the definition of an R-domain will have to change, and that it may be necessary to move to the approximate nearest neighbor framework where the objective is to find neighbors within a $(1+\epsilon)$ factor of the closest.

Also, the work of this paper motivates us to consider techniques for general metric spaces and arbitrary distributions that *learn* the projection distributions and ℓ from examples — adapting to the problem domain.

Ultimately we envision a high-level procedure that like the `qsort()` function from the standard Unix library, views its underlying database through a layer of abstraction. In the case of sorting, a comparison function is provided. For nearest neighbor search projection and distance computation must be supported.

Sorting is, however, a much simpler problem in as much as practical algorithms exist with acceptable worst case time and space complexity — independent of the dataset. For nearest neighbor search we suggest that a general tool must be flexible and ideally support:

- User supplied distance functions and projectors.

  If the projectors are known to be independent (as in orthogonal Euclidean projections) then search should exploit this. Most generally a system might try to learn patterns of independence from examples.

  Special support for discrete-valued distance functions is also desirable.
- A user specified target success probability, perhaps requiring the user to provide a function to generate *random* queries for the problem domain.
- A user specified approximation factor ϵ, where success is then defined as locating an element within a factor of $1+\epsilon$ of the nearest.

- A simple bound on the work performed during search, after which it is simply truncated.
- Control over the time invested in construction to optimize the resulting data structure.
- Control over the time-space tradeoff. That is, the ability to invest additional space to improve search performance.
- Dynamic operation, i.e. the addition and deletion of points from the data structure during use (not discussed in this paper — but clearly possible).

We hope that the ideas and results of this paper brings us closer to the development of such a tool.

Acknowledgments

The author thanks Joe Kilian and Warren Smith for helpful discussions.

References

[AMN+94] S. Arya, D. Mount, N. Netanyahu, R. Silverman, and A. Wu, *An optimal algorithm for approximate nearest neighbor searching in fixed dimension*, Proc. 5th ACM-SIAM SODA, 1994, pp. 573–583.

[Aur91] Franz Aurenhammer, *Voronoi diagrams – a survey of a fundemental geometric data structure*, ACM Computing Surveys **23** (1991), no. 3.

[Ben80] Jon Louis Bentley, *Multidimensional divide-and-conquer*, Communications of the ACM **23** (1980), no. 4.

[BF79] Jon Louis Bentley and Jerome H. Friedman, *Data structures for range searching*, Computing Surveys (1979).

[BK73] W. A. Burkhard and R. M. Keller, *Some approaches to best-match file searching*, Communications of the ACM **16** (1973), no. 4.

[BM80] J. L. Bentley and H. A. Maurer, *Efficient worstcase data structures for range searching*, Acta Informatica **13** (1980), no. 2, 155–168.

[BOR99] Allan Borodin, Rafail Ostrovsky, and Yuval Rabani, *Lower bounds for high dimensional nearest neighbor search and related problems*, Proc. 31st ACM STOC, 1999, pp. 312–321.

[Bro90] Alan J. Broder, *Strategies for efficient incremental nearest neighbor search*, Pattern Recognition **23** (1990), no. 1/2.

[CCGL99] Amit Chakrabarti, Bernard Chazelle, Benjamin Gum, and Alexy Lvov, *A lower bound on the complexity of approximate nearest neighbor searching on the hamming cube*, Proc. 31st ACM STOC, 1999, pp. 305–311.

[Cla87] Kenneth L. Clarkson, *New applications of random sampling in computational geometry*, Discrete & Computational Geometry **2** (1987), 195–222.

[Cla88] Kenneth L. Clarkson, *A randomized algorithm for closest-point queries*, SIAM Journal on Computing **17** (1988), no. 4.

[Cla97] Kenneth L. Clarkson, *Nearest neighbor queries in metric spaces*, Proc. 29th ACM STOC, 1997, pp. 609–617.

[Das91] Belur V. Dasarathy (ed.), *Nearest neighbor pattern classification techniques*, IEEE Computer Society Press, 1991.

[DL76] David Dobkin and Richard J. Lipton, *Multidimensional searching problems*, SIAM Journal on Computing **5** (1976), no. 2.

[EW82] C. M. Eastman and S. F. Weiss, *Tree structures for high dimensionality nearest neighbor searching*, Information Systems **7** (1982), no. 2.

[FBF77] Jerome H. Friedman, Jon Louis Bentley, and Raphael Ari Finkel, *An algorithm for finding best matches in logarithmic expected time*, ACM Transactions on Mathematical Software **3** (1977), no. 3.

[FBS75] Jerome H. Friedman, Forest Baskett, and Leonard J. Shustek, *An algorithm for finding nearest neighbors*, IEEE Transactions on Computers (1975).

[FMT92] Alan M. Frieze, Gary L. Miller, and Shang-Hua Teng, *Separator based parallel divide and conquer in computational geometry*, SPAA 92 (1992).

[FS82] Charles D. Feustel and Linda G. Shapiro, *The nearest neighbor problem in an abstract metric space*, Pattern Recognition Letters (1982).

[Fuk75] Keinosuke Fukunaga, *A branch and bound algorithm for computing k-nearest neighbors*, IEEE Transactions on Computers (1975).

[Fuk90] Keinosuke Fukunaga, *Introduction to statistical pattern recognition*, second ed., Academic Press, Inc., 1990.

[IM98] Piotr Indyk and Rajeev Motwani, *Approximate nearest neighbors: Towards removing the curse of dimensionality*, Proc. 30th ACM STOC, 1998, pp. 604–613.

[Kle97] Jon M. Kleinberg, *Two algorithms for nearest-neighbor search in high dimensions*, Proc. 29th ACM STOC, 1997, pp. 599–608.

[KOR98] Eyal Kushilevitz, Rafail Ostrovsky, and Yuval Rabani, *Efficient search for approximate nearest neighbors in high dimensional spaces*, Proc. 30th ACM STOC, 1998, pp. 614–623.

[KP86] Baek S. Kim and Song B. Park, *A fast nearest neighbor finding algorithm based on the ordered partition*, IEEE Transactions on Pattern Analysis and Machine Intelligence **8** (1986), no. 6.

[MA99] David Mount and Sunil Arya, *Ann: Library for approximate nearest neighbor searching*, http://www.cs.umd.edu/~mount/ANN/, 1999, Version 0.2 (Beta release).

[Riv74] Ronald L. Rivest, *On the optimality of Elias's algorithm for performing best-match searches*, Information Processing 74 (1974).

[RP92] V. Ramasubramanian and K. K. Paliwal, *An efficient approximation-elimination algorithm for fast nearest-neighbor search based on a spherical distance coordinate formulation*, Pattern Recognition Letters **13** (1992), 471–480.

[Sha77] Marvin Shapiro, *The choice of reference points in best match file searching*, Communications of the ACM **20** (1977), no. 5.

[Uhl91a] Jeffrey K. Uhlmann, *Metric trees*, Applied Mathematics Letters **4** (1991), no. 5.

[Uhl91b] Jeffrey K. Uhlmann, *Satisfying general proximity/similarity queries with metric trees*, Information Processing Letters (1991).

[Vai89] Pravin M. Vaidya, *An O*(n *log* n) *algorithm for the all-nearest-neighbor problem*, Discrete & Computational Geometry **4** (1989), no. 2, 101–115.

[Yia93] Peter N. Yianilos, *Data structures and algorithms for nearest neighbor search in general metric spaces*, Proceedings of the Fifth Annual ACM-SIAM Symposium on Discrete Algorithms (SODA), 1993.

[Yia99] Peter N. Yianilos, *Excluded middle vantage point forests for nearest neighbor search*, Tech. report, NEC Research Institute, 1999, Presented at the Sixth DIMACS Implementation Challenge: Near Neighbor Searches workshop, January 15, 1999.

[Yia00] Peter N. Yianilos, *Locally lifting the curse of dimensionality for nearest neighbor search*, Proceedings of the Eleventh Annual ACM-SIAM Symposium on Discrete Algorithms (SODA), 2000, pp. 361–370.

[Yun76] Thomas P. Yunck, *A technique to identify nearest neighbors*, IEEE Transactions on Systems, Man, and Cybernetics (1976).

NETRICS INC., 707 STATE ROAD #212, PRINCETON, NJ 08540
E-mail address: `pny@cs.princeton.edu`

DIMACS Series in Discrete Mathematics
and Theoretical Computer Science
Volume **59**, 2002

The role of experiment in the theory of algorithms

Richard J. Anderson

ABSTRACT. In this note, I discuss the difference between analytical and empirical study of algorithms. The main point is that the two methods of study can be reinforce each other, leading to a deeper understanding of algorithms. However, experimental work is not easy, and there are many pitfalls to avoid. One particular problem I discuss is performing experiments which are doomed in advance and have no chance of producing interesting results.

1. Study of Algorithms.

There are two complementary approaches to the study of algorithms. I will refer to these as the *Analytic Approach* and the *Empirical Approach*. The analytic approach is to "prove theorems about algorithms" based upon a mathematical model of computation. In contrast, the empirical approach is to draw conclusions about algorithms by looking at actual implementations. (I'm using the term *empirical* since the work is generally "look and see what happens" as opposed to setting up an experiment with a falsifiable hypothesis, as the *experimental method* requires.)

In this note, I will present a few ideas on how empirical and analytic work can be mutually beneficial, and I will also attempt to make a distinction between good and bad empirical work.

The goal of algorithmic research is to understand how problems can be solved. There is a very strong emphasis on determining the "best" algorithm for specific problems (where there are many different interpretations of "best," including both run time and quality of solution), so that algorithms which are inferior are of less interest. For the analytic approach, almost all of the work is asymptotic, so results apply in the limit. There are many very good reasons for considering asymptotic behavior including the importance of understanding performance for large problems, and the fact that the mathematical treatment of algorithms is much easier in the asymptotic regime. Very often the complexity measure of interest is worst case performance, so the goal is to find an upperbound on the run time or on the quality of solution. Empirical work is to measure the performance of algorithms on specific inputs, so it is neither worst case nor asymptotic. Empirical studies cannot make fine grained in-the-limit distinctions. There are many asymptotic

1991 *Mathematics Subject Classification.* Primary 68W40; Secondary 68W25, 90C59.
Key words and phrases. experimental analysis, algorithms, methodology.

distinctions which are too narrow to discern by observation. Since the worst case input distribution for many problems is very sparse, in general it is not possible to determine what the worst case result is by sampling inputs. The domain of empirical work is "in practice", whatever that means – it is a distinct domain from what is addressed by the analytic approach. The positive view on how these two approaches of study relate is that they are addressing the same general question, but from different directions - one is in the sky, looking down, the other, on the ground, looking up.

2. Combining Approaches.

Since the domains of analytic and empirical algorithmic study are different, how should they relate? Although they could be completely different disciplines, in the best case, they can be complementary, with empirical work strengthening analytic work, and vice versa. Empirical work can motivate theoretical work by raising additional questions and also by giving relevance to analytic results. Analytic work can provide the raw material for experiments, and can also make sense of experimental results. Here is a collection of ways that the two approaches can benefit each other.

- Experiments can strengthen the impact of an analytic result by showing that it is also a practical advance. A worst-case, asymptotic result can rarely answer the "is it useful" question because of the constant factors involved, and because the worst-case analysis may be pessimistic with respect to "practical" inputs. Various results on Linear Programming are particularly strong examples of this.
- Empirical work introduces a new evaluation criteria for algorithms, motivating additional algorithmic research. Even though asymptotically optimal algorithms for certain problems may be known, the question of "best in practice" remains open. As an extreme example, the fact the the AKS network is optimal depth, does not mean the the parallel sorting problem has been solved.
- Understanding experimental results can require interesting and deep analytic results. This both motivates new analytic work as well as strengthening the experimental results (since this allows results to be proved true, while experiments only suggest the result). To promote one of my favorite, understudied problems, I would love to see progress made on understanding the average run time of network flow algorithms on structure families of random graphs. This could give some insight into why network flow algorithms run so much faster in practice than their worst case bounds suggest.
- Analytic results raise many questions which can be addressed empirically. Evaluating new algorithms and understanding crossover points is the most obvious. There are also may questions raised in analytic work which can't immediately be answered with a theorem, where an experiment can provide the answer (but not the proof!).

3. What is Good Empirical Work?

What distinguishes good empirical work from bad? This is a key question for us to address. There are two important tests that good experimental work must pass:

it must be both "convincing" and "interesting". The easier of the two to address is what it means for experimental work to be convincing. Experiments should aim at general algorithmic results, as opposed to results about a specific implementation on a specific piece of hardware. This means that distinctions in performance must be large enough that they are not likely to be artifacts of the experimental set up, but indicative of the intrinsic performance of the algorithms. There have been a number of very good discussions of experimental methodology published elsewhere, so I will not go into the topic in detail. It is harder to define "interestingness". A partial definition (which pushes the undefined concepts one level out) is: An experimental result is interesting if it provides non-trivial insight into the "in-practice" behavior of algorithms for important problems. Of course, the next question is what makes a problem important - a very weak definition is that it has arisen elsewhere in a time-critical application. In the theory of algorithms, many problems have been studied, to which no one will ever be interested in having an implemented solution. This is entirely appropriate - since these studies give insight into wider algorithmic questions. However, experimental study of these problems is harder to justify. Work is enhanced if it is building upon published work in the same area, ideally giving new results which are comparable with previous ones. It is important the results are not obvious – for example, a careful implementation showing that a quadratic algorithm is slower than a linear algorithm on sufficiently large inputs is not going to be of much interest. Work should go beyond just computation time to show what is going on in the computation. If there is a wide variation of run times on different inputs, it can be significant to identify what properties of the inputs lead to the differences. Experimental work is often more interesting if it gives results different from what is given by a worst case analysis.

It is the nature of experimental work that the interestingness of the result depends on how it comes out. This is just one of the risks of experimentation - there can be a possibility of a positive result which is easily publishable, but a negative result which is less publishable. Experimental research requires this risk (and also a research strategy that is adaptive to this risk). Negative results are not inherently bad. A common negative result is a theoretically better algorithm which fails to outperform its theoretically less good cousin. This can be made into an interesting result with the appropriate spin. Inconclusive results are worse, and unfortunately often published in a papers of the style "here are some tables of results ...".

4. An Example: Network Flow.

An area where experimental work has presented strong results is the study of network flow algorithms. A series of studies have shown that the best implementations of preflow push algorithms are generally superior to the best implementations of augmenting path algorithms. These studies make a solid case by showing a substantial difference in performance across a wide range of inputs and implementations. The experiments established something that could not have been proved analytically: the algorithms under study had roughly the same asymptotic complexity, so that the worse case separation was not large. The asymptotically fastest algorithms also employed sophisticated data structures, and *a priori* it was not clear whether these data structures were necessary or would be useful in practice.

The preflow push algorithms turned out to be superior only if an additional heuristic was incorporated in the algorithm – a heuristic which *did not* give asymptotic benefit. On almost all inputs, the preflow push algorithms ran much faster than the worst case analysis predicted, and the situation which motivated the inclusion of sophisticated data structures was not observed in practice. The key result from the network flow studies was that the preflow-push algorithms are the fastest "in-practice" algorithm for the problem. This is a result outside of the scope of analytic evaluation.

5. Bad Empirical Work.

What is bad experimental work? There are many mistakes which can be made when doing algorithmic experiments, including invalid comparisons, insufficient input selection, poor choice of distributions, and bad implementations. It is necessary to guard against these pitfalls, but even if work is done with proper methodology, it can fail to be good work.

The *worst* kind of experimental work, is work which shouldn't have been performed in the first place. Although this may sound strong (and violate the spirit of free academic enquiry), I believe there are plenty of cases where it could have been determined in advance that an experiment was not worth performing. Since careful implementations of algorithms are a lot of work, it makes sense to only make the investment when there is some hope of payoff. Here are three classes of *doomed* experiments, where the researcher should have foresight to avoid the experiment (as opposed to hindsight[1]).

(1) Experiments which could be avoided by a much simpler experiment. It is often possible to use a simple experiment to get the same result that a complicated experiment would give. A simple experiment may be used to test the feasibility of the larger one - so a negative result on the first experiment would rule out a positive result on the full experiment. An important example of this occurs in studying the implementation of parallel algorithms. It is quite common for a parallel algorithm to exhibit very poor speedup over a sequential algorithm because the algorithm just does not have enough inherent parallelism. The potential parallelism of an algorithm can often be determined by instrumenting a sequential implementation instead of building a parallel implementation. If this indicates that there is very little parallel work, there is little benefit in the parallel implementation, but if there is the potential for parallel speedup, then the full experiment can investigate how much of the potential can be realized.

(2) Experiments which are dominated by *obvious* architectural features. The experimenter should understand the basic hardware that is being used, and discovering a result about the hardware does not qualify as a good result. For example, an algorithmic study which reaches the conclusion "the machine has a cache" is not making much of a contribution. (Of course, there is lots of interesting work to do in understanding how algorithm performance relates to machine characteristics). Machine characteristics which are likely to have a significant impact on the experiment

[1]Needless to say, these observations are based upon hindsight – not on foresight!

(e.g., memory limitations, time sharing) should be explicitly dealt with in the study, as opposed to dominating the conclusions.

(3) Experiments which could have been replaced by a simple back-of-the-envelope calculation. There are many interesting algorithmic phenomena which occur only for input sizes beyond the feasible range. Quite often, a simple calculation can show that a crossover point will occur at such a large value of n that there is no point in running an experiment. For example, if the input size n must satisfy $\log \log n \geq 12$ inorder to show the interesting behavior, the experiment is not going to be possible. A related case is if the "bad case" inputs are unlikely to occur, so that the data structures needed to defeat the bad case are not going to give a speed up. A little thought in advance (and maybe a hand simulation of the algorithm on paper), may yield the same result as a full implementation – and perhaps guide the experimenter to perform tests which may give non-trivial conclusions.

6. Summary.

Empirical algorithmic work has the potential to complement the analytic work, and create a deeper understanding of the field of algorithms. However, it is non-trivial to do good experimental algorithms work. Good empirical algorithmic work must have a result and be convincing, as opposed to just measuring a set of run times or reporting solutions. One major pitfall in experimental work is going ahead and doing an experiment when the experiment shouldn't have been performed in the first place, because its outcome could have been predicted by an easier means.

Department of Computer Science and Engineering, University of Washington
E-mail address: `anderson@cs.washington.edu`

DIMACS Series in Discrete Mathematics
and Theoretical Computer Science
Volume **59**, 2002

Towards a Discipline of Experimental Algorithmics

Bernard M.E. Moret

Abstract. The last 30 years have seen enormous progress in the design of algorithms, but comparatively little of it has been put into practice, even within academic laboratories. Indeed, the gap between theory and practice has continuously widened over these years. Moreover, many of the recently developed algorithms are very hard to characterize theoretically and, as initially described, often suffer from large running-time coefficients. Thus the algorithms and data structures community needs to return to implementation as one of its principal standards of value; we call such an approach *Experimental Algorithmics*.

Experimental Algorithmics studies algorithms and data structures by joining experimental studies with the traditional theoretical analyses. Experimentation with algorithms and data structures is proving indispensable in the assessment of heuristics for hard problems, in the characterization of asymptotic behavior of complex algorithms, in the comparison of competing designs for tractable problems, in the formulation of new conjectures, and in the evaluation of optimization criteria in a multitude of applications. Experimentation is also the key to the transfer of research results from paper to production code, providing as it does a base of well-tested implementations.

We present our views on what is a suitable problem to investigate with this approach, what is a suitable experimental setup, what lessons can be learned from the empirical sciences, and what pitfalls await the experimentalist who fails to heed these lessons. We illustrate our points with examples drawn from our research on solutions for NP-hard problems and on comparisons of algorithms for tractable problems, as well as from our experience as reviewer and editor.

1. Introduction

Implementation, although perhaps not rigorous experimentation, was characteristic of early work in algorithms and data structures. Donald Knuth insisted on implementing every algorithm he designed and on conducting a rigorous analysis of the resulting code (in the famous MIX assembly language) [**26**], while other pioneers such as Floyd are remembered as much for practical "tricks" (e.g., the four-point method to eliminate most points in an initial pass in the computation of a convex hull, see, e.g. [**37**]) as for more theoretical contributions. Throughout

The author is grateful for past support by the Office of Naval Research under grants N00014-92-C-2144, N00014-95-1-1010, and N00014-97-1-0244, and for current support by the National Science Foundation under grants ACI 00-81404, EIA 01-21377, EIA 01-13095, and DEB 01-20709.

the last 20 years, Jon Bentley has demonstrated the value of implementation and testing of algorithms, beginning with his text on writing efficient programs [**3**] and continuing with his invaluable *Programming Pearls* columns in *Communications of the ACM*, now collected in a new volume [**6**], and his *Software Explorations* columns in the *UNIX Review*. Over 10 years ago, David Johnson, in whose work on optimization for NP-hard problems experimentation took pride of place, started the annual ACM/SIAM Symposium on Discrete Algorithms (SODA), which has sought, and every year featured a few, experimental studies. It is only in the last few years, however, that the algorithms community has shown signs of returning to implementation and testing as an integral part of algorithm development. Other than SODA, publication outlets remained rare until the late nineties: the *ORSA J. Computing* and *Math. Programming* have published several strong papers in the area, but the standard journals in the algorithm community, such as the *J. Algorithms*, *J. ACM*, *SIAM J. Computing*, and *Algorithmica*, as well as the more specialized journals in computational geometry and other areas, have been slow to publish experimental studies. (It should be noted that many strong experimental studies dedicated to a particular application have appeared in publication outlets associated with the application area; however, many of these studies ran tests to understand the data or the model rather than to understand the algorithm.) The online *ACM J. Experimental Algorithmics* is dedicated to this area and is starting to publish a respectable number of studies. The two workshops targeted at experimental work in algorithms, the *Workshop on Algorithm Engineering* (WAE), held every late summer in Europe,[1] and the *Workshop on Algorithm Engineering and Experiments* (ALENEX), held every January in the United States, are also attracting growing numbers of submissions. Support for an experimental component in algorithms research is growing among funding agencies as well. We may thus be poised for a revival of experimentation as a research methodology in the development of algorithms and data structures, a most welcome prospect, but also one that should prompt some reflection.

As we contemplate approaches based on (or at least making extensive use of) experimentation, we may want to reflect on the meanings of the two adjectives used to denote such approaches. According to the *Collegiate Webster*, these adjectives are defined as follows.

- **experimental**: 1. relating to or based on experience; 2. founded upon experiments; 3. serving the ends of experimentation; 4. tentative.
- **empirical**: 1. relying on experience or observation alone; 2. based on experience or observation; 3. capable of being verified or disproved through experience or observation.

Part (2) of the definition of "experimental" and parts (2) and (3) of the definition of 'empirical" capture much of what most of us would agree is essential in the use of experiments. Unfortunately, both words have problematic connotations, namely the "tentative" meaning of "experimental" and the exclusion of theory in the first definition of "empirical." A completely empirical approach may be perfectly suitable for a natural science, where the final arbiter is nature as revealed to us through experiments and measurements and where the "laws of nature" can at best be approximated through models, but it is incomplete in the artificial and mathematically precise world of computing, where the behavior of most algorithms

[1]and now merged with the *European Symposium on Algorithms* (ESA)

or data structures can, at least in principle, be characterized analytically. Natural scientists run experiments because they have no other way of learning from nature. In contrast, algorithm designers run experiments mostly because a precise analytical characterization is too hard to achieve in practice. Compared to computational scientists, who also run large-scale computational experiments, but use them to obtain model values to predict the behavior of a physical system, algorithm designers run experiments to obtain actual values—for computational scientists, the computation is a model that needs to be compared to reality, whereas for algorithm designers the computation *is* the reality.

Why this epistemological digression? Because it points to the necessity of both learning from the natural sciences, where experimentation has been used for centuries and where the methodology known as "the scientific method" has been developed to optimize the use of experiments, and of staying aware of the fundamental difference between the natural sciences and computer science, since the goal of experimentation in algorithmic work differs in important ways from that in the natural sciences.

2. Background and Motivation

For over thirty years, the standard mode of theoretical analysis, and thus also the main tool used to guide new designs, has been the asymptotic analysis ("big Oh" and "big Theta") of worst-case behavior (running time or quality of solution). The asymptotic mode eliminates potentially confusing behavior on small instances due to start-up costs and clearly shows the growth rate of the running time. The worst-case (per operation or amortized) mode gives us clear bounds and also simplifies the analysis by removing the need for any assumptions about the data. The resulting presentation is easy to communicate and reasonably well understood, as well as machine-independent. However, we pay a heavy price for these gains:

- The range of values in which the asymptotic behavior is clearly exhibited ("asymptopia," as it has been named by many authors) may include only instance sizes that are well beyond any application. A typical example is the algorithm of Fredman and Tarjan for minimum spanning trees. Its asymptotic worst-case running time is $O(|E|\beta(|E|,|V|))$—where $\beta(m,n)$ is given by $\min\{i \mid \log^{(i)} n \leq m/n\}$, so that, in particular, $\beta(n,n)$ is just $\log^* n$. This bound is much better for dense graphs than that of Prim's algorithm, which is $O(|E|\log|V|)$, but experimentation [**39**] verifies that the crossover point occurs for dense graphs with well over a billion edges—beyond the size of most reasonable data sets.
- In another facet of the same problem, the constants hidden in the asymptotic analysis may prevent any practical implementation from running to completion, even if the growth rate is quite reasonable. An extreme example of this problem is provided by the theory of graph minors: Robertson and Seymour (see [**44**]) gave a cubic-time algorithm to determine whether a given graph is a minor of another, but the proportionality constants are gigantic—on the order of 10^{150}—and have not been substantially lowered yet, making the algorithm entirely impractical.
- The worst-case behavior may be restricted to a very small subset of instances and thus not be at all characteristic of instances encountered in practice. A classic example here is the running time of the simplex method

for linear programming; for over thirty years, it has been known that the worst-case behavior of this method is exponential, but also that its practical running time is typically bounded by a low-degree polynomial [**1**]. Approximation algorithms with performance guarantees often present the same pattern: the approximations they return are often much better than the bounds indicate, even when these bounds are known to be tight.

- Even in the absence of any of these problems, deriving tight asymptotic bounds may be very difficult. All optimization metaheuristics for NP-hard problems (such as simulated annealing or genetic algorithms) suffer from this drawback: by considering a large number of parameters and many values computed by the program over the last few iterations, they create a complex state space which is very hard to analyze with existing methods, whether to bound the running time or to estimate the quality of the returned solution. Another classic example is the deceptively simple Union-Find data structure (see, e.g., [**37**], Section 3.2): the combination of Union by rank (or size) and path compression was known to yield very efficient behavior, yet its exact characterization eluded researchers for many years, until Tarjan proved tight bounds [**49**]. (Of course, in this particular case, experimentation would have proved futile, since no amount of experimentation, on any conceivable dataset, could show supralinear growth in the running time.)

These are the most obvious drawbacks. A more insidious drawback, yet one that could prove much more damaging in the long term, is that worst-case asymptotic analysis tends to promote the development of "paper-and-pencil" algorithms, that is, algorithms that never get implemented. This problem compounds itself quickly, as further developments rely on earlier ones, with the result that many of the most interesting algorithms published over the last few years rely on several layers of complex, unimplemented algorithms and data structures. In order to implement one of these recent algorithms, a programmer would face the daunting prospect of developing implementations for all successive layers. Moreover, the "paper-and-pencil" algorithms often ignore issues critical in making implementations efficient: low-level algorithmic issues (from elementary ideas such as the use of sentinels to more elaborate ones such as the use of "sacks" in sophisticated priority queues [**39**]) and architecture-dependent issues (particularly caching issues); the implementer will have to resolve these issues "on the fly," possibly with very poor results. Transforming paper-and-pencil algorithms into efficient and useful implementations is today referred to as *algorithm engineering*. We recently found that the use of algorithm engineering techniques, all of which are based on experimentation, improved the running time of code by three to five orders of magnitude [**36, 40**]. Algorithm engineering has also yielded robust libraries of data structures with minimal overhead, as exemplified by the LEDA library [**34, 35**]. Algorithm engineering is reviving many of the approaches used by computing pioneers such as Floyd and Knuth, who combined theoretical insights with practical ideas and even machine-dependent "tricks" to derive efficient algorithms that performed well in both theory and practice.

There is no reason to abandon asymptotic worst-case analysis: it has served the community very well for over thirty years and led to major algorithmic advances. But there is a definite need to supplement it with experimentation, which implies that most algorithms should be implemented, not just designed. Many algorithms are in fact quite difficult to implement well—because of their intricate nature and also because the designers described them at a very high level. Many examples of such can be found in computational geometry: Chazelle's linear-time simplicity testing [**9**], Chazelle's convex decomposition algorithm [**8**], and Chang and Yap's "potato-peeling" algorithm [**7**] all are very intricate and remain—to our knowledge—unimplemented. But the practitioner is not the only one who stands to benefit from implementation: often an implementation forces the theoretician to face issues glossed over in the high-level design phase. Resolving these issues may bring about a deeper understanding of the algorithm and a resulting simplification or more modestly may lead the theoretician to new conjectures. Major theoretical breakthroughs, such as Chazelle's linear-time simplicity test or Robertson and Seymour's polynomial-time minor test, are their own justification, but incremental results should be judged on more practical grounds: do they lead to better, faster, more robust implementations? Finally, experimentation should also test the usefulness of a problem formulation: not only is it too easy to devise cute puzzles of dubious interest, but even in problems motivated by real applications we need to find out what criteria to optimize and what parameters to take into account. Validating a model or a particular criterion requires large-scale experimentation; in a recent study, we used over 20 years of CPU time (on modern workstations) to obtain data on the quality of phylogeny reconstructions produced by quartet-based algorithms [**47**].

3. Modes of Empirical Assessment

We can classify modes of empirical assessment into a number of non-exclusive categories:

- Checking for accuracy or correctness in extreme cases (e.g., standardized test suites for numerical computing).
- Assessing the quality of heuristics for the approximate solution of NP-hard problems.
- Measuring the running time of (exact or approximate) algorithms on real-world instances of NP-hard problems.
- Comparing the actual performance of competing algorithms for tractable problems and characterizing the effects of algorithm engineering.
- Discovering the speed-up achieved by parallel algorithms on real machines.
- Investigating and refining models and optimization criteria—what should be optimized? and what parameters matter?
- Testing the quality and robustness of simulations, of optimization strategies for complex systems, etc.

The first category has reached a high level of maturity in numerical computing, where standard test suites are used to assess the quality of new numerical codes. Similarly, the operations research community has developed a number of test cases for linear program solvers. We have no comparable emphasis to date in combinatorial and geometric computing. The last category is the target of large efforts within the Department of Defense, whose increasing reliance on modeling and simulation has placed it at the forefront of a movement to develop validation and verification tools; the algorithm community can help by providing certification levels for the various data structures and optimization algorithms embedded within large simulation systems. Studying speed-ups in parallel algorithms remains for now a rather specialized endeavor, in part because of the dedicated nature of software (which typically cannot be run on another machine without major performance losses) and because of our attending lack of a good model of parallel computation. Investigation and refinement of models and optimization criteria is of major concern today, particularly in application areas such as computational biology and computational chemistry. While many studies are published, most demonstrate a certain lack of sophistication in the conduct of the computational studies—suffering as they do from various sources of errors. We eschew a lengthy discussion of this important area and instead present sound principles and illustrate pitfalls in the context of the two categories that have seen the bulk of research to date in the algorithms community. Most of these principles and pitfalls can be related directly to the testing and validation of discrete optimization models in the natural sciences.

3.1. Assessment of Competing Algorithms and Data Structures for Tractable Problems. The goal here is to measure the actual performance of competing algorithms for well-solved problems. This is fairly common work in Operations Research, but relatively new in combinatorial algorithms and data structures—although early (1960s) work in data structures typically included code and examples, it did not include systematic studies. The 1970s were a dry time in the area, until Sedgewick's work on quicksort [**46**]. More recent and comprehensive work began with Bentley's many contributions in his *Programming Pearls* (starting in 1983 [**4**]), then with Jones' comparison of data structures for priority queues [**25**], Dandamudi and Sorenson's empirical comparison of k-d tree implementations [**14**], and Stasko and Vitter's combination of analytical and experimental work in the study of pairing heaps [**48**]. Among the first experimental studies on a large scale were those of Moret and Shapiro on sorting algorithms [**37**] (Chapter 8) and on algorithms for constructing minimum spanning trees [**37, 39**]. In 1991, Johnson and others initiated the very successful DIMACS Computational Challenges, the first of which [**23**] focused on network flow and shortest path algorithms, indirectly giving rise to several modern, thorough studies, by Cherkassky *et al.* on shortest paths [**11**], by Cherkassky *et al.* on the implementation of the push-relabel method for matching and network flows [**12, 13**], and by Goldberg and Tsioutsiouliklis on cut trees [**19**]. The DIMACS Computational Challenges (the fifth, in 1996, focused on another tractable problem, priority queues and point location data structures) have served to highlight work in the area, to establish common data formats (particularly formats for graphs and networks), and to set up the first tailored test suites for a host of problems.

Recent conferences (such as the *Workshop on Algorithm Engineering* and the *Workshop on Algorithm Engineering and Experiments*[2]) have emphasized the need to develop libraries of robust, well-tested implementations of the basic discrete and combinatorial algorithms, a task that only the LEDA project [**34, 35**] has successfully undertaken to date.

Much interest has focused over the last 3–4 years on the question of tailoring algorithms and implementations to the cache structure and policies of the architecture. Pioneering studies by Ladner and his coworkers [**28, 29, 30**] established

[2]See the front page of the *ACM J. Experimental Algorithmics* at `www.jea.acm.org` for links to these conferences.

that such optimization was feasible, algorithmically interesting, and worthwhile, even for such old friends as sorting algorithms [**2, 30, 42, 51**] and priority queues [**29, 45**]; indeed, even matrix multiplication, which has been optimized in numerical libraries for over 30 years, is amenable to such techniques [**16**]. We found that even *ad hoc* reduction in memory usage and improvement in patterns of memory addressing gained us speedups of as much as a factor of 10 [**36**]. The related, and much better studied, model of out-of-core computing, as pioneered by Vitter and his coworkers [**50**], has inspired new work in cache-aware and cache-independent algorithm design. (Out-of-core computing is also a modern revival of what was an active field of research some 40 years ago—for instance, Knuth gives a detailed treatment of out-of-core sorting in his Volume III [**27**]. The modern approach is both more general and more detailed, with explicit tradeoffs.)

3.2. Assessment of Heuristics. Here the goal is to measure the performance of heuristics on real and artificial instances and to improve the theoretical understanding of the problem, presumably with the aim of producing yet better heuristics or proving that current heuristics are optimal. By performance are implied both the running time of the code and the quality of the solution produced.

Since the behavior of heuristics is very difficult to characterize analytically, experimental studies have been the rule. The Operations Research community, which has a long tradition of application studies, has slowly developed some guidelines for experimentation with integer programming problems (see [**1**], Chapter 18). Some of the first large-scale combinatorial studies to include both real-world and generated instances include the classic and exemplary studies of simulated annealing by David Johnson's group [**21, 22**] and our work on the minimum test set problem [**38**]. The Second DIMACS Computational Challenge [**24**] was devoted to satisfiability, graph coloring, and clique problems and thus saw a large collection of results in this area. The ACM/SIAM Symposium on Discrete Algorithms (SODA) has included a few such studies in each of its dozen events to date, such as the study of cut algorithms by Chekuri *et al.* [**10**]. The Traveling Salesperson problem has seen large numbers of experimental studies (including the well publicized study of Jon Bentley [**5**]), made possible in part by the development of a library of test cases [**43**]. Graph coloring, whether in its NP-hard version of chromatic number determination or in its much easier (yet still challenging) version of planar graph coloring, has seen much work as well; the second study of simulated annealing conducted by Johnson's group [**21**] discussed many facets of the problem, while Morgenstern and Shapiro [**41**] provided a detailed study of algorithms to color planar graphs.

Challenges in this area include the generation of meaningful test instances and the derivation of strong lower bounds that enable us to assess the quality of the heuristic solutions.

4. Worthwhile Problems

In view of the preceding, what should researchers in the area be working on? We propose below a partial list and briefly discuss the reasons for our choices.

4.1. Testing and improving algorithms for hard problems. Understanding how a heuristic works to cut down on computational time is generally too difficult to achieve through formal derivations; much the same often goes for bounding the quality of approximations obtained with many heuristics.[3] Yet both aspects are crucial in evaluating performance and in helping us design better heuristics.

In the same vein, understanding when an exact algorithm runs quickly is often too difficult for formal methods. It is much easier to characterize the worst-case running time of an algorithm than to develop a classification of input data in terms of a few parameters that suffice to predict the actual running time in most cases. Experimentation can help us assess the performance of an algorithm on real-world instances (a crucial point) and develop at least *ad hoc* boundaries between instances where the algorithm runs fast and instances where it exhibits its exponential worst-case behavior.

4.2. Comparing existing algorithms and data structures for tractable problems. Our task is somewhat easier with algorithms for tractable problems than with heuristics for intractable problems, yet characterizing the behavior of either on real-world instances is generally very hard simply because we lack the crucial instance parameters with which to correlate running times. Experimentation can quickly pinpoint good and bad implementations and whether theoretical advantages are retained in practice. In the process, newer insights may be gleaned that might enable a refinement or simplification of the algorithm. Experimentation can also enable us to determine the actual constants in the running time analysis; determining such constants beforehand is quite difficult (see [**17**] for a possible methodology), but a simple regression analysis from the data can give us quite accurate values. Experimental studies naturally include caching effects, whereas adding those into the analysis in a formal manner is very challenging.

4.3. Algorithm engineering. Many of the goals described under the previous two rubrics also fall under this heading. More specifically, however, algorithm engineering seeks to produce the most efficient, as well as most usable, implementation possible. A cycle of testing and refinement, supported by profilers and other measurement tools, is the key to removing bottlenecks in running time and to obtaining a good balance among the various routines. Reducing the use of memory, changing the addressing patterns to make the implementation more cache-friendly (which may imply some data structure changes as well), unrolling loops to keep variables in registers or first-level cache, and taking a good look at what information is really needed and how it is used at each stage in the algorithm, are all measures that can lead to significant improvements in running time: in a recent effort, we used all of these techniques to obtain a speed-up by three to five orders of magnitude [**36, 40**].

4.4. Supporting and refining conjectures. Any theoretician knows the pangs of committing to a research question without being too sure of the outcome and the frustration of attempting to prove a statement that might not even be true. Having a means of testing a conjecture over a range of instances might, in the best case, set one's mind at rest and, in the worst case, avoid a lot of wasted work. More importantly, good experiments are a rich source of new conjectures and theorems.

---

[3]Of course, we have many elegant results bounding the worst-case performance of approximation algorithms, but many of these bounds, even when attainable, are overly pessimistic for real data.

4.5. Developing tools. Anyone contemplating the coding of a library module for some data structure or basic algorithm must take reasonable precautions to ensure that their implementation will be as efficient as possible and to document conditions under which it will perform well or poorly. Testing the implementation on a range of machines with various compilers and environments will increase confidence in the characterizations. For instance, extensive testing of the LEDA modules by their developers and many others led to a 2- to 3-fold reduction in their running-time overhead [**33**].

At a more basic level, we need flexible tools to collect data (how do we measure cache behavior, for instance?) and analyze it. We should not underestimate the value of experimentation with algorithms as a discovery tool; in order to make such experimentation even more valuable, statistical tools with good graphical and animation capabilities are urgently needed.

4.6. Conducting experiments to assess the relevance of optimization criteria. The pure theoretician often has only one answer when asked why (s)he worked on a problem: because it was intriguing. But it is fatally easy to generate volumes of intriguing, unsolved optimization problems; before committing scarce resources to their solution, it behooves us to evaluate their importance and relevance as well as we can. Applications provide sufficient justification to study problems; but the model used by the algorithm designer, which is necessarily a simplification of the real problem, must be validated through large-scale experimentation, preferably using a mix of real data and simulations.

5. Experimental Setup

How should an experimental study be conducted, once a topic has been identified? Surely the most important criterion to keep in mind is that an experiment is run either as a discovery tool or as a means to answer specific questions. Experiments as explorations are common to all endeavors, in computing, in the sciences, and indeed in any human activity; the setup is essentially arbitrary—in particular it should not be allowed to limit one's creativity. So we shall focus instead on experiments as means to answer specific questions—the essence of the scientific method used in all physical sciences. In this methodology, we begin by formulating a hypothesis or a question, then set about gathering data to test or answer it, while ensuring reproducibility and significance. In terms of experiments with algorithms, these characteristics give rise to the following procedural rules—but the reader should keep in mind that most researchers would mix the two activities for quite a while before running their "final" set of experiments:

- Begin the work with a clear set of objectives: which questions will you be asking, which statements will you be testing?
- Once the experimental design is complete, simply gather data. (No alterations are to be made until all data have been gathered, so as to avoid bias or drift.)
- Analyze the data to answer only the original objectives. (Later, consider how a new cycle of experiments can improve your understanding.)

At all stages, we should beware of a number of potential pitfalls, including various biases due to:

- The choice of machine (caching, addressing, data movement), of language (register manipulation, built-in types), or of compiler (quality of optimization and code generation).
- The quality of the coding (consistency and sophistication of programmers).
- The selection or generation of instances (we must use sufficient size and variety to ensure significance).
- The method of analysis (many steps can be taken to improve the significance of the results as well as to bring out trends).

Caching, in particular, may have very strong effects when comparing efficient algorithms. For instance, in our study of MST algorithms, we observed 3:1 ratios of running time depending on the order in which the adjacency lists were stored. Pioneering studies by Ladner and his students [**28, 29, 30**] have quantified many aspects of caching and offer suggestions on how to work around (or take advantage of) caching effects.

Other typical pitfalls that arise in experimental work with algorithms include

- Uninteresting work: comparing programming languages or specific platforms, in particular unusual ones; comparing algorithms with widely different behavior (linear and quadratic, say); etc.
- Bad setup: testing up to some fixed running time or space without verifying whether the asymptotic behavior has manifested; testing too few instances; using rough code without any attempt at optimization and measuring running times; using "found code" without any documentation (a temptation these days on the net); ignoring existing test suites; ignoring existing and widely used libraries; etc.
- Bad analysis or presentation: discarding data that do not fit without any explanation or even warning; presenting all of the data without analysis; using comparisons to undefined "standards" (e.g., to the system sort routine).

Johnson [**20**] offers a much more detailed list of the various problems he has observed in experimental studies, particularly those dealing with heuristics for hard optimization problems.

Most of these pitfalls can be avoided with the type of routine care used by experimentalists in any of the natural sciences. However, we should point out that confounding factors can assume rather subtle forms. Knuth long ago pointed out curious effects of apparently robust pseudorandom number generators (see [**26**], Vol. II); the creation of unexpected patterns as an artifact of a hidden routine (or, in the case of timing studies, as an artifact of interactions between the memory hierarchy and the code) could easily lead the experimenter to hypothesize nonexistent relationships in the data. The problem is compounded in complex model spaces, since obtaining a fair sampling of such a space is always problematic. Thus it pays to go over the design of an experimental study a few times just to assess its sensitivity to potential confounding factors—and then to examine the results with the same jaundiced eye.

6. What to Measure?

One of the key elements of an experiment is the metrology. What do we measure, how do we measure it, and how do we ensure that measurements do not interfere with the experiments? If there is one universal piece of advice in this area, it is *always look beyond the obvious measures!* Obvious measures may include the value of the solution (for heuristics and approximation algorithms), the running time (for almost every study), the running space, etc. These measures are indeed useful, but a good understanding of the algorithm is unlikely to emerge from such global quantities. We also need structural measures of various types (number of iterations; number of calls to a crucial subroutine; etc.), if only to serve as a scale for determining such things as convergence rates. Knuth [**27**] has advocated the use of *mems*, or memory references, as a structural alternate (or adjunct) to running time. Other authors have used the number of comparisons, the number of data moves (both classical measures for sorting algorithms), the number of assignments, etc. Most programming environments offer some type of profiler, a support system that samples code execution at fixed intervals and sets up a profile of where the execution time was spent (which routines used what percentage of the CPU time) as well as of how much memory was used; with suitable hardware support, profilers can also report caching statistics. Profiling is invaluable in algorithm engineering—multiple cycles of profiling and revising the most time-consuming routines can easily yield gains of one to two orders of magnitude in running time.

In our own experience, we have found that there is no substitute, when evaluating competing algorithms for tractable problems, for measuring the actual running time; indeed, time and mems measurements, to take one example, may lead one to entirely different conclusions. However, the obvious measures are often the hardest to interpret as well as the hardest to measure accurately and reproducibly. Running time, for instance, is influenced by caching, which in turn is affected by any other running processes and thus effectively not reproducible exactly. In the case of competing algorithms for tractable problems, the running time is often extremely low (we can obtain a minimum spanning tree for a sparse graph of a million vertices in much less than a second on a typical desktop machine), so that the granularity of the system clock may create problems—this is a case where it pays to repeat the entire algorithm many times over on the same data, in order to obtain running times with at least two digits of precision. Memory accesses are equally difficult to measure, in part because we cannot make accurate predictions of the number of memory transfers based on high-level language statements—we would need to look at the assembly language program produced by the compiler to do that—and in part because even an accurate count is misleading, since contiguous memory accesses (likely to result in cache hits) are very much faster than noncontiguous ones (likely to result in cache faults). Measuring the quality of a solution can also be quite difficult, due to the fact that the optimal solution can be very closely approached on instances of small to medium size or due to the fact that the solution is essentially a zero-one decision (as in determining the chromatic index of a graph or the primality of a number), where the appropriate measure is statistical in nature (how often is the correct answer returned?) and thus requires a very large number of test instances.

7. How to Present and Analyze the Data

Perhaps the first requirement in data presentation is to ensure reproducibility by other researchers: we need to describe in detail what instances were used (how they were generated or collected), what measurements were collected and how, and, preferably, where the reader can find all of this material on-line. The second requirement is rather obvious, but often ignored for all that: we cannot just discard what appear to be anomalies, at least not unless we can explain their presence; an anomaly without an explanation is not an error, but an indicator that something unusual (and possibly interesting) is going on. We have already mentioned several times that every effort should be made to minimize the influence of the environment (platform, coding, compiling, paging, caching, etc.) through cross-checking across multiple platforms and environments, through the use of normalization routines, and through environmental precautions (such as running on otherwise quiescent machines).

The data should then be analyzed with suitable statistical methods. Since attaining levels of statistical significance may be quite difficult in the large state spaces we commonly use, various techniques to make the best use of available experiments should be applied (see McGeoch's excellent survey [**31**] for a discussion of several such methods). Cross-checking the measurements with any available theoretical results, especially those that attempt to predict the actual running time (such as the "equivalent code fragments" approach of [**17**]), is crucial; any serious discrepancy needs to be investigated.

Finally, the data need to be presented to the readers in a form that humans can easily process—not in tabular form, not as raw plots with multiple crossing curves, but with suitable scaling and normalization and with the use of good graphics, colors, etc. Normalization and scaling are a particularly important part of both analysis and presentation: not only can they bring out trends not otherwise evident, but they can help in filtering out noise and thus increase the significance of the results. Animations can convey enormous amounts of information very succinctly, so consider providing such if the work needed to produce them is not excessive.

8. Illustration: Algorithms for Constructing a Minimum Spanning Tree

We shall not repeat here the results given in [**39**], but rather highlight the problems encountered during the study and some of the solutions we found to be effective. We studied MST algorithms because of their practical importance, because instances encountered in practice can be very large, and because the implementer faces a very large number of algorithmic choices, each with its own choice of supporting data structures. In 1989, when we started the study, we had at least the following choice of algorithms: Kruskal's (with a priority queue, with prior sorting, or with sorting on demand), Prim's (with any of a large number of priority queues, from binary heaps to rank- and run-relaxed heaps), Cheriton and Tarjan's (with and without the lazy variation) Fredman and Tarjan's, Gabow *et al.*'s, and the entirely different algorithm of Fredman and Willard; to this list we could now add newer and asymptotically faster algorithms by Klein and Tarjan, by Karger, by Chazelle, and by Pettie and Ramachandran. Prim's algorithm, the most commonly used (for good reason, as our study demonstrated), could in turn be implemented with any of a dozen or more priority queue designs, each with its own implementation choices. Very few of these choices had been implemented at that time.

We ran an experimental study using three different platforms (two CISC machines and one RISC machine) and multiple languages and compilers, but with one programmer writing all of the code, so as to keep the level of coding consistent throughout. We explored low-level decisions (pointers vs. array indices, data moves vs. indirection, etc.) before committing to specific implementations. We used five different graph families in the tests and also constructed specific worst-case families with adversaries; all of our families included very large graphs (up to a million vertices and over a million edges). We ran independent series of experiments, in which each series consisted of at least 20 instances at each size; we then checked the independent series for consistency of results. Finally, we took precautions from the start to minimize the effects of paging (easy) and of caching (hard).

Our data collection and analysis had four goals: (i) to minimize any residual effects of caching and any other machine dependencies; (ii) to normalize running times across machines; (iii) to gauge the influence of lower-order terms and to verify the asymptotic behavior; and (iv) to visualize quickly the relative efficiency of each algorithm for each type and size of graph. We realized all four goals at once by the simple strategy of normalizing, independently on each platform, the running times measured for the various MST algorithms by the running times of a simple, linear-time procedure with roughly similar memory reference patterns—in our case a procedure that counted the number of edges of the graph by traversing the adjacency lists. The similar memory addressing patterns canceled out most of the caching effects; the similar work in dereferencing pointers canceled out most of the CISC machines peculiarities; and the direct comparison to the (then unattainable) lower bound of a linear-time procedure immediately showed the asymptotic behavior and highlighted the relative efficiency of each algorithm. (This type of normalization has since been used to equally good effect in other studies, such as that of Goldberg's on shortest path algorithms [**18**].)

Early in the implementation phase, we realized that Fibonacci heaps and relaxed heaps were not competitive. We followed a suggestion made by Driscoll *et al.* [**15**] about relaxed heaps: to group nodes into larger units so that changes in key value would most often be resolved within a unit and not require restructuring the heap; we implemented this idea, which we called *sacks*, for other types of heaps. This was a crucial decision for Fibonacci heaps, which became much more competitive with the addition of sacks—a new result that could only have come about through implementation.

At the conclusion of our work, we had comforting findings for the practitioner: the fastest algorithm by far was also the simplest, Prim's, implemented with pairing heaps or simple binary heaps. The more sophisticated implementations could not pay off for reasonable graph sizes, nor could the more sophisticated algorithms. But we also had a sobering report: our last implementations of Prim's algorithm with Fibonacci heaps were nearly ten times faster than our first! Thus even experienced programmers who understand the details of their data structures and algorithms can refine implementations to the point of evolving entirely new conclusions—a key aspect of algorithm engineering.

This study, along with an earlier study on sorting algorithms, enables us to draw some conclusions regarding experimental studies of algorithms for well-solved problems:

- Multi-machine, multi-compiler trials are needed. The preference of one architecture for data moves over indirection, for instance, could easily mask other effects, as could the highly variable details of the caching system. The first DIMACS challenge used the simple strategy of running a collection of benchmarks on each platform to enable comparison of results, but more sophisticated approaches are required, particularly with respect to cache-awareness. One attractive possibility is normalization by the running time of a known routine with well understood characteristics, but even this strategy is limited to relatively simple programs.

- A very large range of sizes is indispensable. Since the algorithms compared are all efficient and since sophisticated algorithms tend to demonstrate their asymptotic behavior for larger sizes than simpler algorithms, we should run our tests up to the largest sizes that can be accommodated on our platforms, even if these sizes may exceed any likely to be encountered in practice. A large range of sizes will also help visualizing the asymptotic behavior and may uncover unexpected problems attributable to the memory hierarchy.
- Extreme care must be used when generating instances. This problem is particularly acute when instances are defined by multiple parameters, as in graphs and networks: large numbers of different families can be defined, with potentially very different behaviors. We should ensure that realistic instances are being generated, that large instances generated with pseudo-random number generators do not present artificial patterns caused by problems with the generator, and also that, whenever possible, some worst-case families are included in the study.[4]
- Real datasets should always be used. Few data generators can accurately reproduce the structure of real data. Researchers have long known that real instances of hard optimization problems can be surprisingly easy to solve (as well as, more rarely, surprisingly hard), but much the same can be said of instances of tractable problems.
- Normalization by a suitable baseline routine is very successful in smoothing out variations in architecture and caching, as well as in highlighting the asymptotic behavior and relative efficiency of the competing algorithms. Whenever our competing algorithms are closely tied, data presentation is of crucial importance.

9. Conclusions

Experimentation should become once again the "gold standard" in algorithm design, for several compelling reasons:

- Experimentation can lead to the establishment of well tested and well documented libraries of routines and instances.
- Experimentation can bridge the gap between practitioner and theoretician.
- Experimentation can help theoreticians develop new conjectures and new algorithms, as well as lead to a deeper understanding (and thus perhaps a simpler version) of existing algorithms.

[4]We observed one curious and totally unexpected behavior with generated data for the MST problem. One of our families of datasets consists of worst-case instances for Prim's algorithm run with binary heaps—the data are created by running the algorithm and picking values that maximize the number of elementary heap manipulations. These data, when fed to the version of Kruskal's algorithm that uses quicksort (implemented with a median-of-three strategy for choosing the partitioning element) uniformly caused quicksort to exhibit quadratic behavior!

- Experimentation can point out areas where additional research is most needed.

However, experimentation in algorithm design needs some methodological development. While it can and, to a large extent, should seek inspiration from the natural sciences, its different setting (a purely artificial one in which the experimental procedure and the subject under test are unavoidably mixed) requires at least extra precautions. Fortunately, a number of authors have blazed what appears to be a good trail to follow; hallmarks of good experiments include:

- clearly defined goals;
- large-scale testing, both in terms of a range of instance sizes and in terms of the number of instances used at each size;
- a mix of real-world instances and generated instances, including any significant test suites in existence;
- clearly articulated parameters, including those defining artificial instances, those governing the collection of data, and those establishing the test environment (machines, compilers, etc.);
- statistical analyses of the results and attempts at relating them to the nature of the algorithms and test instances; and
- public availability of instances and instance generators to allow other researchers to run their algorithms on the same instances and, preferably, public availability of the code for the algorithms themselves.

References

[1] Ahuja, R.K., Magnanti, T.L., and Orlin, J.B. *Network Flows*. Prentice Hall, NJ, 1993.

[2] Arge, L., Chase, J., Vitter, J.S., and Wickremesinghe, R., "Efficient sorting using registers and caches," *Proc. 4th Workshop on Algorithm Eng. WAE 2000*, to appear in LNCS series, Springer Verlag (2000).

[3] Bentley, J.L. *Writing Efficient Programs*. Prentice-Hall, Englewood Cliffs, NJ, 1982.

[4] Bentley, J.L., "Programming pearls: cracking the oyster," *Commun. ACM* **26**, 8 (1983), 549–552.

[5] Bentley, J.L. Experiments on geometric traveling salesman heuristics. AT&T Bell Laboratories, CS TR 151, 1990.

[6] Bentley, J.L. *Programming Pearls*. 2nd ed., ACM Press, 1999.

[7] Chang, S., and Yap, C.K., "A polynomial solution for potato-peeling and other polygon inclusion and enclosure problems," *Discrete & Comput. Geom.* **1** (1986), 155–182.

[8] Chazelle, B., "Convex decompositions of polyhedra, a lower bound and worst-case optimal algorithm," *SIAM J. Comput.* **13** (1984), 488–507.

[9] Chazelle, B., "Triangulating a simple polygon in linear time," *Discrete & Comput. Geom.* **6** (1991), 485–524.

[10] Chekuri, C.S., Goldberg, A.V., Karger, D.R., Levine, M.S., and Stein, C., "Experimental study of minimum cut algorithms," *Proc. 8th ACM/SIAM Symp. on Discrete Algs. SODA97*, SIAM Press (1997), 324–333.

[11] Cherkassky, B.V., Goldberg, A.V., and Radzik, T., "Shortest paths algorithms: theory and experimental evaluation," *Math. Progr.* **73** (1996), 129–174.

[12] Cherkassky, B.V., and Goldberg, A.V., "On implementing the push-relabel method for the maximum flow problem," *Algorithmica* **19** (1997), 390–410.

[13] Cherkassky, B.V., Goldberg, A.V., Martin, P, Setubal, J.C., and Stolfi, J., "Augment or push: a computational study of bipartite matching and unit-capacity flow algorithms," *ACM J. Exp. Algorithmics* **3**, 8 (1998), `www.jea.acm.org/1998/CherkasskyAugment/`.

[14] Dandamudi, S.P., and Sorenson, P.G., "An empirical performance comparison of some variations of the k-d tree and bd tree," *Int'l J. Computer and Inf. Sciences* **14**, 3 (1985), 134–158.

[15] Driscoll, J.R., Gabow, H.N., Shrairman, R., and Tarjan, R.E., "Relaxed heaps: an alternative to Fibonacci heaps with applications to parallel computation," *Commun. ACM* **11** (1988), 1343–1354.
[16] Eiron, N., Rodeh, M., and Stewarts, I., "Matrix multiplication: a case study of enhanced data cache utilization," *ACM J. Exp. Algorithmics* **4**, 3 (1999), `www.jea.acm.org/1999/EironMatrix/`.
[17] Finkler, U., and Mehlhorn, K., "Runtime prediction of real programs on real machines," *Proc. 8th ACM/SIAM Symp. on Discrete Algs. SODA97*, SIAM Press (1997), 380–389.
[18] Goldberg, A.V., "A simple shortest path algorithm with linear average time," *Proc. 9th European Symp. Algs. ESA'01*, in *LNCS* **2161**, Springer Verlag (2001), 230–241.
[19] Goldberg, A.V., and Tsioutsiouliklis, K., "Cut tree algorthms: an experimental study," *J. Algs.* **38**, 1 (2001), 51–83.
[20] Johnson, D.S., "A theoretician's guide to the experimental analysis of algorithms," this volume.
[21] Johnson, D.S., Aragon, C.R., McGeoch, L.A., and Schevon, C., "Optimization by simulated annealing: an experimental evaluation. 1. Graph partitioning," *Operations Research* **37** (1989), 865–892.
[22] Johnson, D.S., Aragon, C.R., McGeoch, L.A., and Schevon, C., "Optimization by simulated annealing: an experimental evaluation. 2. Graph coloring and number partitioning," *Operations Research* **39** (1991), 378–406.
[23] Johnson, D.S., and McGeoch, C.C., eds. *Network Flows and Matching: First DIMACS Implementation Challenge, DIMACS Series in Discrete Mathematics and Theoretical Computer Science* **12**, 1993.
[24] Johnson, D.S., and Trick, M., eds. *Cliques, Coloring, and Satisfiability: Second DIMACS Implementation Challenge, DIMACS Series in Discrete Mathematics and Theoretical Computer Science* **26**, to appear.
[25] Jones, D.W., "An empirical comparison of priority queues and event-set implementations," *Commun. ACM* **29** (1986), 300–311.
[26] Knuth, D.E. *The Art of Computer Programming*, Volumes I (3rd ed.), II (3rd ed.), and III (2nd ed.). Addison-Wesley, Mass., 1997, 1997, and 1998.
[27] Knuth, D.E. *The Stanford GraphBase: A Platform for Combinatorial Computing.* Addison-Wesley, Reading Mass., 1993 (p. 460).
[28] Ladner, R., Fix, J.D., and LaMarca, A., "The cache performance of traversals and random accesses," *Proc. 10th ACM/SIAM Symp. on Discrete Algs. SODA99*, SIAM Press (1999), 613–622.
[29] LaMarca, A., and Ladner, R., "The influence of caches on the performance of heaps," *ACM J. Exp. Algorithmics* **1**, 4 (1996), `www.jea.acm.org/1996/LaMarcaInfluence`.
[30] LaMarca, A., and Ladner, R., "The influence of caches on the performance of sorting," *Proc. 8th ACM/SIAM Symp. on Discrete Algs. SODA97*, SIAM Press (1997), 370–379.
[31] McGeoch, C.C., "Analysis of algorithms by simulation: variance reduction techniques and simulation speedups," *ACM Comput. Surveys* **24** (1992), 195–212.
[32] McGeoch, C.C., "A bibliography of algorithm experimentation," this volume.
[33] Mehlhorn, K., private communication (1998).
[34] Mehlhorn, K., and Näher, S., "LEDA, a platform for combinatorial and geometric computing," *Commun. ACM* **38** (1995), 96–102.
[35] Melhorn, K., and Näher, S. *The LEDA Platform of Combinatorial and Geometric Computing.* Cambridge U. Press, 1999.
[36] Moret, B.M.E., Bader, D.A., Warnow, T., Wyman, S.K., and Yan, M., "A detailed study of breakpoint analysis," *Proc. 6th Pacific Symp. Biocomputing PSB 2001*, Hawaii, World Scientific Pub. (2001), 583–594.
[37] Moret, B.M.E., and H.D. Shapiro. *Algorithms from P to NP, Volume I: Design and Efficiency.* Benjamin-Cummings Publishing Co., Menlo Park, CA, 1991.
[38] Moret, B.M.E., and Shapiro, H.D., "On minimizing a set of tests," *SIAM J. Scientific & Statistical Comput.* **6** (1985), 983–1003.
[39] Moret, B.M.E., and Shapiro, H.D., "An empirical assessment of algorithms for constructing a minimal spanning tree," in *Computational Support for Discrete Mathematics*, N. Dean and G. Shannon, eds., *DIMACS Series in Discrete Mathematics and Theoretical Computer Science* **15** (1994), 99–117.

[40] Moret, B.M.E., Tang, J., Wang, L.-S., and Warnow, T., "Steps toward accurate reconstruction of phylogenies from gene-order data," *J. Comput. Syst. Sci.*, special issue on Computational Biology, to appear, 2002.

[41] Morgenstern, C., and Shapiro, H.D., "Heuristics for rapidly four-coloring large planar graphs," *Algorithmica* **6** (1991), 869–891.

[42] Rahman, N., and Raman, R., "Analysing cache effects in distribution sorting," *Proc. 3rd Workshop on Algorithm Eng. WAE99*, in LNCS **1668**, Springer Verlag (1999), 183–197.

[43] Reinelt, G. *The Traveling Salesman: Computational Solutions for TSP Applications. Lecture Notes in Computer Science* **840** (1994), Springer Verlag, Berlin.

[44] Robertson, N., and Seymour, P., "Graph minors—a survey," in *Surveys in Combinatorics*, J. Anderson, ed., Cambridge U. Press, Cambridge, UK (1985), 153–171.

[45] Sanders, P., "Fast priority queues for cached memory," *ACM J. Exp. Algorithmics* **5**, 7 (2000), `www.jea.acm.org/2000/SandersPriority/`.

[46] Sedgewick, R., "Implementing Quicksort programs," *Comm. ACM* **21**, 10 (1978), 847-857.

[47] St. John, K., Warnow, T., Moret, B.M.E., and Vawter, L., "Performance study of phylogenetic methods: (unweighted) quartet methods and neighbor-joining," *Proc. 12th Ann. Symp. Discrete Algs. SODA 01*, SIAM Press (2001), 196–205.

[48] Stasko, J.T., and Vitter, J.S., "Pairing heaps: experiments and analysis," *Commun. ACM* **30** (1987), 234–249.

[49] Tarjan, R.E., "Efficiency of a good but not linear set union algorithm," *J. ACM* **22**, 2 (1975), 215–225.

[50] Vitter, J.S., "External memory algorithms and data structures: dealing with massive data," *ACM Comput. Surveys* **33**, 2 (2001), 209–271.

[51] Xiao, L., Zhang, X., and Kubricht, S., "Improving memory performance of sorting algorithms," *ACM J. Exp. Algorithmics* **5**, 3 (2000), `www.jea.acm.org/2000/XiaoMemory/`.

Department of Computer Science, University of New Mexico, Albuquerque, NM 87131-1836

E-mail address: `moret@cs.unm.edu`

DIMACS Series in Discrete Mathematics
and Theoretical Computer Science
Volume **59**, 2002

A Theoretician's Guide to the Experimental Analysis of Algorithms

David S. Johnson

ABSTRACT. It is based on lessons learned by the author over the course of more than a decade of experimentation, survey paper writing, refereeing, and lively discussions with other experimentalists. Although written from the perspective of a theoretical computer scientist, it is intended to be of use to researchers from all fields who want to study algorithms experimentally. It has two goals: first, to provide a useful guide to new experimentalists about how such work can best be performed and written up, and second, to challenge current researchers to think about whether their own work might be improved from a scientific point of view. With the latter purpose in mind, the author hopes that at least a few of his recommendations will be considered controversial.

Introduction

It is common these days to distinguish between three different approaches to analyzing algorithms: worst-case analysis, average-case analysis, and experimental analysis. The above ordering of the approaches is the one that most theoretical computer scientists would choose, with experimental analysis treated almost as an afterthought. Indeed, until recently experimental analysis of algorithms has been almost invisible in the theoretical computer science literature, although experimental work dominates algorithmic research in most other areas of computer science and related fields such as operations research.

The past emphasis among theoreticians on the more rigorous and theoretical modes of analysis is of course to be expected. Moreover, it has strong justifications. To this day it is difficult to draw useful extrapolations from experimental studies. Indeed, it was the lack of scientific rigor in early experimental work that led Knuth and other researchers in the 1960's to emphasize worst- and average-case analysis and the more general conclusions they could provide, especially with respect to asymptotic behavior. The benefits of this more mathematical approach have been many, not only in added understanding of old algorithms but in the invention of new algorithms and data structures, ones that have served us well as faster machines and larger memories have allowed us to attack larger problem instances.

1991 *Mathematics Subject Classification.* Primary 68W40; Secondary 68W25, 90C59.
Key words and phrases. experimental analysis, algorithms, methodology.

Recently, however, there has been an upswing in interest in experimental work in the theoretical computer science community. This is not because theorists have suddenly discovered a love of programming (although some have) or because they are necessarily good at it (although some are), but because of a growing recognition that theoretical results cannot tell the full story about real-world algorithmic performance. Encouragement for experimentation has come both from those like myself who are already actively experimenting and from funding agencies who view experimentation as providing a pathway from theory into practice. As a result, we now have several relatively new forums that include both experimental and theoretical work or highlight hybrids of the two. These include the ACM Journal on Experimental Algorithmics, the ACM-SIAM Symposium on Discrete Algorithms (SODA), the European Symposium on Algorithms (ESA), the Workshop on Algorithm Engineering (WAE), and the Workshop on Algorithm Engineering and Experimentation (ALENEX).

These are in addition to traditional forums for experimental work such as those in the Operations Research, Mathematical Programming, Artificial Intelligence, and Scientific Computing communities. What, if any, is the value added by involving theoretical computer scientists with experimentation? One very real possibility is that experience with real-world computing may in turn reinvigorate our theoretical research agenda by suggesting new questions to study and establishing connections to applications. In this paper, however, I am interested in influences that go in the other direction. How can a background in theoretical analysis of algorithms help in doing experimentation? My hope, strongly supported by work of such researchers as Bentley, Goldberg, and others [**Ben92, CGR94, FJMO95**] is that the theoretician's concern for asymptotics, generality, and understanding can help drive a more scientific approach to experimentation. It is this scientific bias that I will be stressing in this paper, while also providing more general advice for would-be experimentalists.

Unfortunately, as many researchers have already discovered, the field of experimental analysis is fraught with pitfalls. In many ways, the implementation of an algorithm is the easy part. The hard part is successfully using that implementation to produce meaningful and valuable (and publishable!) research results. For the purposes of argument, there are perhaps four basic reasons why it might be worthwhile to implement an algorithm, each giving rise to a different type of paper (although many papers end up being hybrids of more than one type).

- To use the code in a particular application. This typically gives rise to an *application paper*, whose purpose is to describe the impact of the algorithm in that context. (This includes much of what is called *experimental mathematics*, where the "application" is the generation and proof of mathematical conjectures and we are primarily interested in the output of the algorithm, not its efficiency.)
- To provide evidence of the superiority of your algorithmic ideas. This often gives rise to what I will call a *horse race paper*, where results are published for standard benchmark instances to illustrate the desirability of this algorithm in comparison to previous competitors.
- To better understand the strengths, weaknesses, and operation of interesting algorithmic ideas in practice. This is the motivation behind what I will call an *experimental analysis paper*.

- To generate conjectures about the average-case behavior of algorithms under specific instance distributions where direct probabilistic analysis is too hard. This leads to what I will call an *experimental average-case paper.*

Although much of what I have to say will be applicable to all four types of paper, in what follows I will concentrate mainly on the third type, which is in a sense the most general and is also a type with which I have much experience, both as an author and as a reader, referee, editor, and scholar (i.e., survey paper writer). In these latter roles I have had the opportunity to read widely in the experimental literature, with special emphasis on papers about the Traveling Salesman Problem (TSP), which I surveyed in [**JM97**]. I have unfortunately seen many more papers that are seriously defective than ones that set good examples. Even fairly good papers typically receive referee's reports suggesting significant revisions, often involving substantial additional experiments. In this note I shall attempt to draw on my experience by articulating a set of general principles applicable to experimental papers and explaining how and how not to satisfy them. The presentation will be organized in terms of ten basic (and overlapping) principles that I believe should govern the writing of experimental papers:

(1) Perform newsworthy experiments.
(2) Tie your paper to the literature.
(3) Use instance testbeds that can support general conclusions.
(4) Use efficient and effective experimental designs.
(5) Use reasonably efficient implementations.
(6) Ensure reproducibility.
(7) Ensure comparability.
(8) Report the full story.
(9) Draw well-justified conclusions and look for explanations.
(10) Present your data in informative ways.

The remainder of this paper will discuss each of these principles in turn, explaining what I mean by them and elaborating on their implications. Along the way I will highlight "Pitfalls" (temptations and practices that can lead experimenters into substantial wastes of time) and my personal "Pet Peeves" (literally, "favorite annoyances" – common experimental and paper-writing practices that seem to me to be particularly misguided). Some of these practices may seem so obviously bad as to be not worth mentioning, but I have seen each of them more than once, and so they still seem worth an explicit discussion. Others of the practices I list as Pet Peeves are in such common use that my labeling them as "misguided" may come as a surprise, although I will argue that they violate one or more of the above principles. In some cases I will also highlight "Suggestions" for avoiding a a given Pitfall or Pet Peeve, and cite papers where the suggested practices are exploited/explained. Specific citations of bad behavior will for the most part be omitted to spare the guilty, myself included. My view of these issues has evolved over the years. Even now it may be well-nigh impossible to write a paper that avoids all the Pet Peeves. An Appendix will collect all the Pitfalls, Pet Peeves, and Suggestions into separate lists for ease of reference.

Most of this paper concentrates on the study of algorithms for problems in the standard format where both instances and outputs are finite objects, and the key metrics are resource usage (typically time and memory) and (in the case of approximation algorithms) quality of the output solution. Many key computational problems do not fit this model, and in a short section at the end of the paper I will mention some of them and challenge the reader to think about how the ideas presented here might be adapted/extended to these other domains, as well as what other issues arise in them. I conclude with a final collection of warnings that I was unable to fit conveniently into the main body of the text.

As I have said, several of the principles enunciated in this paper may be somewhat controversial, at least as I elaborate them. Indeed, although there is much common agreement on what makes good experimental analysis of algorithms, certain aspects have been the subject of debate, such as the relevance of running time comparisons. For other points of view, see such recent papers as [**BGK$^+$95, CS00, Hoo93, McG96, MM99, RU01**]. This particular paper was constructed using my earlier short draft [**Joh96**] as a template and adding in material I have developed in the process of giving talks expanding on that draft. The points of view expressed in this paper are my own, although they have been refined (and augmented) over the years in stimulating discussions with other researchers, including Richard Anderson, David Applegate, Jon Bentley, Andrew Goldberg, Cathy and Lyle McGeoch, Kurt Mehlhorn, Bernard Moret, Panos Pardalos, Mauricio Resende, and Gerhard Woeginger.

Section 1. Discussions of the Principles

In this, the main section of the paper, I discuss and illustrate each of the ten principles outlined in the introduction. Because these principles are so interlinked, the discussion of each will unavoidable refer to several of the others, but I have tried to avoid repetition as much as possible (although some of the points made are worth repeating).

Principle 1. Perform Newsworthy Experiments

This principle applies to all scientific papers: the results should be new and of interest and/or use to some reasonably-sized collection of readers. However, the standards for "interest" are more stringent for experimental algorithms papers.

For instance, it is much harder to justify experimental work on problems with no direct applications than it is to justify theoretical work on such problems. In theoretical work, researchers often chooses to work on problems because of their amenability to analysis (and in the hope that they are representative enough that the lessons learned or proof techniques developed may be more widely applicable). In contrast, most problems are amenable to experimental analysis of some sort, and lessons learned from experimental analysis are typically highly problem- and instance-specific. Moreover, problems without applications do not have real-world instances, so the experimenter is left to invent (and justify) test data in a vacuum. And referees may well question the testing of code for algorithms that will never be used in practice.

A second dimension of "newsworthiness" has to do with the algorithms studied. A key question about any algorithm is whether it might be a useful alternative in practice. Since theoretical analysis (especially worst-case analysis) often cannot be relied on for an answer, one can justify studying a wide variety of algorithms, at least to the point where the question of practicality is answered (assuming there was at least some plausible argument in favor of practicality in the first place). When the answer is a definitive *No*, however, the value of writing papers about the algorithm is limited, although it is not necessarily eliminated. Consider for example the case of the *dominated* algorithm, i.e., one that is always slower than some already well-studied competitor (and, in the case of approximation algorithms, never produces better solutions).

PITFALL 1. *Dealing with dominated algorithms.*

Suppose you spend much time implementing and testing an algorithm that turns out to be dominated. All may not be lost. Indeed, much of the experimental literature is devoted to dominated algorithms. In many cases, however, the fact that the algorithm was dominated was not known at the time the paper about it was written (or at least was not known to the author or referees...)

PET PEEVE 1. *Authors and referees who don't do their homework.*

Particularly annoying are those authors who do cite the relevant references but clearly haven't read the parts of them that are relevant to their experiments.

What do you do if you *know* (or discover) that your algorithm is dominated? If the algorithm is newly invented and has not yet been written about, you are pretty much out of luck. Few people are likely to be interested in the fact that a previously unknown algorithm is bad. If it is a known algorithm, and assuming it has not been adequately studied before, there are several possible situations:

- The algorithm is already in widespread use or the algorithms that dominate it are so complicated that they are not soon likely to enter into widespread use. A detailed study of the algorithm's performance and how much it gives up over the more sophisticated approaches might well be of interest.
- The algorithm in question embodies a general approach applicable to many problem domains or provides a mechanism for studying the performance of data structures or other algorithmic constructs, so that studying how best to adapt the underlying approach to the current domain may have more general consequences. This argument can for example be viewed as a possible justification for some of the many papers that have been published about dominated metaheuristic algorithms for the TSP (see [**JM97**]).
- The algorithm is known but already expected to behave poorly, although this had not been verified (and the previous options do not apply). In this case you are again out of luck, although the negative result might be worth including in a more general paper that talked about undominated algorithms as well.
- The algorithm is of sufficient independent interest (either because of promising theoretical results or widespread publicity) that the fact that it *is* dominated is unexpected. This might be worth a note on its own, although again it would be better as part of a more comprehensive study.

In this last situation, the fact that the algorithm is dominated is itself newsworthy. Note, however, that domination is not always easy to establish conclusively, given that running times can depend strongly on implementations or machine/operating system interactions. In many cases simply getting within a factor of two of another algorithm's running time may be enough to claim competitiveness. Moreover, you are facing the difficult task of proving a negative experimentally: Even if you demonstrate great differences in performance, you still must convince the readers that you have not missed some important instance class for which the supposedly-dominated algorithm outperforms its competitors. You also must convince readers that you have not simply mis-implemented the algorithm. For example, several early papers on simulated annealing claimed that it was dominated by other approaches within the domains in question. The implementations described in these papers, however, used parameter settings that severely limited the computation time, whereas subsequent experiments showed that allowing the annealing process to take a (very) long time enabled it to perform very well in these domains, even when compared to other long-running algorithms. Thus the original papers did not show that simulated annealing was dominated, just that their particular (bad) implementations of it were. For a more precisely defined algorithm than simulated annealing, convincing readers that you have an efficient and correct implementation may be easier, but still is an added burden, requiring extra measurements to identify unavoidable bottlenecks in the algorithm's operation.

A third dimension of newsworthiness has to do with the generality, relevance, and credibility of the results obtained and the conclusions derivable from them. One is of necessity limited to a finite number of tests, but for a paper to be interesting, the results should yield broader insights, either in terms of asymptotics or presumptions of robustness, a point on which we shall elaborate when discussing Principle 3 below. (This is one way in which an experimental paper aspires to higher goals than a horse race paper, which can settle for the simple conclusion that the tested algorithm produces the stated results on the set of benchmark instances.) Also, the conclusion that algorithm A outperforms algorithm B becomes more interesting (and more believable) when supported by measurements (operation counts, subroutine profiling, etc.) that show in detail *why* this happens.

Given the above, let us talk a little about strategies for getting newsworthy results from your experiments, and the pitfalls along the way.

PITFALL 2. *Devoting too much computation to the wrong questions.*

With computational cycles becoming so cheap these days, it is tempting not to worry too much about wasted computation time. However, "computation time" includes your own time spent setting up, running, and evaluating the experiments, not just the "user time" reported by the operating system. If you want your paper production process to be as efficient as your algorithms it pays to be more systematic. Examples of potential wastes of time include

- Excessive study of results for just one or two instances. This is a natural temptation when one has a parameterized algorithm that needs tuning. Typically, however, your computing time will be better spent testing a variety of instances in a systematic way.
- Running full experimental suites before you finish figuring out how to make your implementation efficient. You'll no doubt have to rerun the experiments with the new code anyway, and the later runs will probably take less time.

- Running full experimental suites before you've decided what data to collect (and hence before you've instrumented the code to report that data). Again, you'll probably have to rerun the experiments.

SUGGESTION 1. *Think before you compute.*

Some of the issues that need to be resolved before you begin a major data generation project include the following. What algorithmic phenomena do you want to study, and what are the questions you want your experiments to address? Will anyone besides yourself care about the answers, given the current state of the literature in the area? Have you implemented the algorithm correctly, incorporating all the features/variants you want to study and providing for the production of all the output data you'll need? What is an adequate set of test instances and runs to yield convincing answers to the questions being asked? Given current computer speeds and memory capacity, which instances are either too small to yield meaningful distinctions or too large to yield feasible running times?

Of course, some of this thinking presupposes that you have already done at least a little computation. In order to resolve issues like those mentioned, one often will have to perform exploratory experiments.

SUGGESTION 2. *Use exploratory experimentation to find good questions.*

By "exploratory experimentation" I mean the testing one does before beginning the formal data collection process for a computational study. This includes experiments performed while debugging and optimizing the code as well as pilot studies of various sorts. In addition to trying to confirm that the algorithm is competitive with previous approaches, one can be examining how performance varies with instance type and size, and profiling the code to determine where the computational bottlenecks are and what sorts of tradeoffs are involved in various program design and data structure choices. Of special interest are unexpected anomalies in performance, which if reproducible may merit further study. Assuming that this further study does not simply reveal that there were bugs in your code, it may suggest surprising insights into the way the algorithm performs. In my own research, I tend to take an iterative approach:

(1) Spend the first half of your proposed experimentation time generating lots of data and looking for patterns and anomalies.
(2) Based on the above, finalize the algorithm implementation, decide what the interesting questions are, and design and perform comprehensive experiments to investigate these.
(3) Analyze the resulting data. If it fails to answer the questions or raises new ones, go back to Step 2.

This tends to lead to newsworthy results, although it has its own dangers:

PITFALL 3. *Getting into an endless loop in your experimentation.*

Although most experimental papers could be improved by more extensive experimentation, at some point you have to draw the line and leave the remaining questions for the infamous "future research" section of the paper. (In this, you must be prepared to resist not only your own temptation to keep going, but also requests from referees for additional but non-essential experiments.) A newsworthy paper that never gets finished does not provide much news.

At this point, having discussed the dangers of working on the wrong questions and described techniques for finding the right questions, let me say a bit about what some of those good questions might be and which sorts of answers to them might be newsworthy, given that the problems and algorithms studied pass the newsworthiness test. The following list is by no means exhaustive, but will at least cover a range of possibilities. A typical paper might address several such questions. In the following list, I for simplicity follow common practice and use "algorithm" as a shorthand for "your implementation of the algorithm." Most descriptions of algorithms in technical papers and texts omit technical details that an implementer must fill in, and these can affect performance. Thus our experiments typically give us direct information only about the implementations used. With extensive study we may be able to deduce something about the implementation-independent properties of an algorithm or the specific implementation details that need to be included in the description of an algorithm if we are to promote its best performance. Hence our first question:

(1) How do implementation details, parameter settings, heuristics, and data structure choices affect the running time of the algorithm?
(2) How does the running time of the algorithm scale with instance size and how does this depend on instance structure?
(3) What algorithmic operation counts best help to explain running time?
(4) What in practice are the computational bottlenecks of the algorithm, and how does this depend on instance size and structure? How does this differ from the predictions of worst-case analysis?
(5) How is running time (and the running time growth rate) affected by machine architecture, and are there operation counts that help explain this?
(6) Given that one is running on the same or similar instances and on a fixed machine, how predictable are running times/operation counts? (If there is wide variability, this might affect the usability of the algorithm.)
(7) How does the algorithm's running time compare to those of its top competitors, how are these comparisons affected by instance size and structure or by machine architecture, and can the differences be explained in terms of operation counts?
(8) What are the answers to the above questions when "running time" is replaced by "memory usage" or the usage of some other computational resource, assuming the algorithm is such that this usage isn't easily predictable from theory?
(9) What are the answers to questions 1,2,6,7 when one deals with approximation algorithms and "running time" is replaced by "solution quality"? (Standards of comparison that can be used to measure solution quality will be covered in the discussion of Principle 6.)
(10) Given a substantially new class of instances that you have identified, does it cause significant changes in the algorithmic behavior for previously-studied algorithms?

Let me conclude the discussion of newsworthiness by mentioning one other temptation that can lead an experimentalist astray.

PITFALL 4. *Start by using randomly generated instances to evaluate the behavior of algorithms, but end up using algorithms to investigate the properties of randomly-generated instances.*

One example of this kind of behavior is the recent flurry of activity around random instances of 3SAT. Early experimenters looking for hard instances to test discovered that if one randomly generates m clauses on n variables, one obtains a transition when $m \sim 4.24n$: Instances with fewer clauses are highly likely to be satisfiable, instances with more clauses are most probably unsatisfiable, and instances with just about that many clauses tend to be difficult for all known algorithms to solve. This observation was useful to algorithm evaluators, as it gave a nice (if unrealistic) class of challenging test examples. It also suggested interesting mathematical questions about the precise nature of the "phase transition" and its asymptotic properties. Unfortunately, it has also had the effect of hijacking much of the experimental research on SATISFIABILITY algorithms to examining just this class of instances and their variants, even though it is not at all clear that such experiments will tell us anything about performance on the much more structured instances that tend to occur in real-world applications.

A second, perhaps more benign example is the experimental work of [**JMR96, PM96**] devoted to estimating the expected optima for random Euclidean instances of the TSP. For the TSP, random geometric instances like these do seem to provide a barometer for performance in practice. Tight bounds on expected optima may thus give us a useful metric for evaluating the quality of the solutions produced by approximation algorithms, at least for instances so large that good instance-specific bounds are not easy to obtain.

Of course, performing experiments in order to deduce properties of random instances can be justified on straight mathematical grounds, and may be of more intrinsic interest than the performance of yet another heuristic. However, this is "experimental mathematics" rather than "experimental analysis of algorithms," and so in that sense represents a diversion from the task with which we are concerned here.

Principle 2. Tie Your Paper to the Literature

One key component in establishing the newsworthiness of a paper is placing it in proper context with respect to the literature on the problem being studied. Indeed, before undertaking any experimental project, you should do your best to discover and thoroughly study the prior literature if it exists. This should go without saying, but surprisingly many papers have failed because of lack of diligence on this point. Moreover, knowing what has been done can not only save you from performing "uninteresting" experiments, it can also suggest what the interesting questions should be. What behavior needs explaining? What algorithms seem open to further improvement? What types of test instances have not yet been adequately studied?

When your problem does have a literature, there are obligations as well as opportunities, however. Assuming an earlier paper studied instances that are large enough to be considered interesting today, you should provide comparisons between your results and those in the earlier paper. Here is another case where the experimenter's job may be more difficult than the theoretician's. The potential difficulty is that direct comparisons may be problematic. Although the earlier paper may have dealt with the same algorithm and similar test instances, it may not have dealt with precisely the same test instances or with the same implementation of the algorithm, and it most likely did not provide running times on the same machine/operating system combination you are using today.

Ideally, if your goal is to provide comparisons to a previously-studied algorithm, you should obtain the code for the implementation of the algorithm that was used in the previous experiments, and report results for that code on your own machine (while verifying that those results are consistent with those reported for the code previously). If that is not possible, the next best option is to develop a comparable implementation of the previous algorithm which you can run on your own machine and which, based on comparisons with the previously-reported results, seems to be of comparable effectiveness. (This would have the added benefit of helping to confirm the algorithmic claims of the earlier paper.) In the unfortunate event that the two implementations do not appear to be of comparable effectiveness, for example when one appears to run in quadratic time and the other in linear time, this point should be noted and explanations provided if possible (and your implementation should be the linear time one; see Principle 5).

The least desirable option, but one to which one must occasionally resort when attempting to provide comparisons to a hard-to-implement or incompletely-specified algorithm from the literature, is simply to compare your results on your own machine and test instances to those reported in the previous paper. In some cases, where the previous experiments were performed on some unfamiliar architecture, this may be impossible. Typically, however, you can provide significantly accurate ballpark bounds on relative machine speeds to at least answer the question of whether running times are possibly competitive or whether one implementation is clearly faster than the other. Even such rough comparisons are better than nothing. Readers need to see how your paper fits into the literature, even if the fit is at best only approximate.

Principle 3. Use Instance Testbeds that Can Support General Conclusions

There are basically two types of test instances available to experimenters: particular instances from real-world applications (or pseudo-applications) and randomly generated instances. The former are typically found in standard repositories, such as `TSPLIB` [**Rei81**], but might come from private sources proprietary to the author. The latter are provided by instance generators that, given a seed and a list of instance parameters, such as size and perhaps other details of instance structure, produce a random instance consistent with those parameters. Note that random instances need not be structureless (like random graphs and random distance matrices), and indeed should preferably be structured in ways that reflect some aspects of real-world instances.

A key property for random instance generators is that they be able to generate instances of arbitrarily large size. This allows you to get a partial handle on the types of asymptotic questions typically addressed by theoretical analysis, although machine dependent effects such as cache limitations will typically make precise asymptotics impossible. What you *can* determine, however, is the biggest instance you can reasonably run on your machine, and some idea about how much larger the runnable instances could be on a next-generation machine with greater speed, memory, etc. (These can be key questions in practice.) This gives random instances an advantage in experimental studies, although one that can be substantially dissipated if there is no evidence that the random instance class says anything about what will happen for real-world instances.

PET PEEVE 2. *Concentration on unstructured random instances.*

Not only may unstructured random instances tell us little about real-world performance, they may actively mislead us as to the difficulty of the problem. For example, many papers on optimization algorithms for the asymmetric TSP concentrate on asymmetric distance matrices with entries chosen independently and randomly from small ranges such as $\{1, 2, \ldots, N\}$, where N is the number of cities. These instances are particularly easy since as N increases the optimal tour length is likely to equal the easily computed "Assignment Problem" lower bound. Thus there are authors who proudly proclaim the ability of their codes to find optimal solutions for instances of this sort with many thousands of cities, while the same codes have great difficulty with structured instances from `TSPLIB` containing 53 cities or less.

One can also get in trouble by concentrating solely on real-world instances, especially out-dated ones:

PET PEEVE 3. *The millisecond testbed.*

Computer speeds have grown at such a rate that in many problem areas modern running times for old testbeds have shrunk to negligibility. I have seen more than one paper in which the maximum running time reported for any of the algorithms tested on any of the instances studied is a second or less. Despite this fact, the papers devote much effort to determining which algorithm is fastest. I would maintain that in most applications, if an algorithm takes a second or less, running time is probably irrelevant, and an algorithm that takes 0.01 seconds on your machine doesn't provide a significant advantage over one that takes the 0.1, even though it is 10 times faster. The exception might be real-time computing applications (usually not relevant to the applications in question) or the need to solve thousands of instances quickly (also usually not relevant). One might also argue that that factor of 10 *would* make a difference for larger instances, but in that case one should test such larger instances to confirm that the advantage persists as instance size grows.

PET PEEVE 4. *The already-solved testbed.*

This is a related, perhaps more philosophical objection. When you are evaluating approximation algorithms, you need some standard against which to measure the solutions found, and the most desirable standard is of course the optimal solution value. Thus a natural temptation is to restrict your testing to instances for which the optimal value is known. However, one of the major reasons for resorting to approximation algorithms is to handle cases where it is too hard to find the optimal values, so restricting your tests to instances for which optima are known essentially ignores the domain for which the algorithms were intended. One might argue that the approximation algorithm is much faster than the optimization algorithm, and hence you are examining the trade-off between running time and solution quality. However, most papers that restrict attention to instances for which optima are known simply take the optimum values from the literature and do not seriously address the question of relative running times. Moreover, typically the only non-trivial instances for which optimum solutions are known are relatively small. Thus, as with the previous Pet Peeve, restricting to such instances doesn't allow you to address questions about how well an algorithm's performance scales with instance size. An alternative that is occasionally tried is to construct large artificial instances in such a way that the optimum solution value is known in advance. Unfortunately, restricting your tests solely to such instances is likely to yield unconvincing results because of the narrow and artificial nature of the instances. As to how you can evaluate instance quality for instances with unknown optima, we will discuss this in detail when we get to the Principle 6.

Returning to our general discussion about real-world test beds, note that even when such a test bed contains a reasonable range of instance sizes, papers that study only instances from the testbed can still have a hard task in drawing general conclusions about how algorithms operate and why they do so, as one can't design experiments that isolate instance properties and test how they affect performance. If the set of real-world instances is broad and varied enough, one may however at least be able to draw conclusions about the robustness of various performance measures across instance types.

Nevertheless, a hybrid approach is clearly to be recommended. The idea is to study one or more structured random instance classes, combined with results for real-world instances that enable the reader to evaluate the predictive quality of the random results. Especially useful are parameterized random instance generators such as the `washington` network generator of R. Anderson (available from DIMACS at `ftp://dimacs.rutgers.edu/pub/netflow/generators/`), which allow you to investigate the effect of structure as well as size on performance.

Principle 4. Use Efficient and Effective Experimental Designs

I earlier warned about the danger of spending too much computation time on the wrong questions, but even when you have identified the right questions, or at least the ones you want to answer, there are still computational savings to be had. In particular, there exist important techniques that will not only help you reduce the amount of computation you need to perform but also allow you to get broader and more accurate answers. Let me mention just a few specific ones.

SUGGESTION 3. *Use variance reduction techniques.*

When one is dealing with randomized algorithms (or randomly generated instances), the variability between runs of the algorithms (and between instances) may obscure your results and make it hard to draw conclusions. Thus one may have to perform large numbers of runs or test large numbers of instances to obtain reliable estimates of average performance. Variance reduction techniques help reduce these numbers. For an introduction to and broad-ranging survey of such techniques, see [**McG92**]. Here I will mention one that I have found useful for reducing the effects of instance variability.

Suppose you are attempting to compare average performance for several approximation algorithms over a class of randomly generated instances. Rather than independently estimate the average performance of each algorithm over the instance class and then comparing the estimates, use the *same* set of randomly generated instances for all your tests. Since each algorithm sees the same instances, the variability between instances will be factored out of the comparison. Thus, even though one may not have tight enough confidence intervals on the average solution qualities for the two algorithms to distinguish them statistically, the estimate of the average *difference* between solution values may be statistically significant and allow one to claim that one is better than the other.

I have used a variant of this technique in studying algorithms for the TSP, where I evaluate solution quality (tour length) in terms of its excess over the Held-Karp bound for the given instance. For the popular model in which cities correspond to points uniformly distributed in the unit square and distances are Euclidean, one can obtain very good estimates of what the expected value of that bound is for any number of cities N [**JMR96**], and so could compare algorithmic results to these estimates. However, one gets a more precise performance metric (with fewer samples) if one focuses on the difference between the algorithm's tour length and the Held-Karp bound for each instance.

SUGGESTION 4. *Use bootstrapping to evaluate multiple-run heuristics.*

For randomized approximation algorithms, one in practice may want to exploit the variability of the results by performing multiple runs and taking the best solution found. The naive way to estimate the expected behavior of the algorithm "Perform k runs of algorithm A and take the best" would be to run that algorithm itself some number m times, and compute the average of the m "best of k"s. This requires mk total runs of A, but those runs can be better spent using the technique known as "bootstrapping" First sort the mk results in order of solution value. It is now a relatively simply matter to compute the expected best value of a random sample of k of these results, chosen independently (with replacement), and this estimate makes better use of all the data than simply taking the average of the m bests. Moreover, using the same data set, one can also estimate the expected "best of k'" results for values of k' other than k.

Note that if we are going to take this approach, special attention must be paid to obtaining correct estimations of running time, especially for those "best of k" algorithms that only need to read the instance and perform any preprocessing steps once, thus amortizing these operations over all k runs. Since we may have performed these steps just once for all our km runs, we must be sure to measure the time for them separately in order to account for it properly in our final running time figures. This however is only a minor addition to the total work involved. It also leads to my final suggestion on experimental design.

SUGGESTION 5. *Use self-documenting programs.*

This suggestion is designed to reduce the experimenter's own time, rather than that needed for computation. When you generate large quantities of data, you must deal with the problem of organizing and accessing that data. And note that the accesses may take place years in the future, for example in response to a referee's report or your own desire to do a follow-up study. Thus it is dangerous to rely simply on personal memory. Saving data in files and directories with descriptive names can help, as can constructing `README` files providing directory road maps and other information. However, data that cannot be accurately interpreted after the fact is useless data. Thus it is desirable to have output files that contain (or are linked to) all the information one would want to know about the experiment that generated them. This includes not only performance metrics such as running time and solution quality, but also the name (and version) of the algorithm used, the machine on which it was run (and date, to help in case that machine gets upgraded), the name of the instance to which it was applied, the settings of all adjustable parameters, and any subsidiary measurements (operation times, counts, intermediate solution values) that you think may be of interest later. Moreover, to minimize the possibility of later misinterpretation, one should not rely on the syntax of the output file to tell you which data item is which, but should include the name of the item ("algorithm version," etc.) along with each item.

Principle 5. Use Reasonably Efficient Implementations

This is surprisingly a somewhat controversial principle. Although it would at first glance seem obvious that we should want to use efficient implementations (especially in a field like algorithm design where efficiency is one of our main goals), efficiency does come at a cost in programming effort and there are several situations in which researchers have argued that they should be allowed to settle for less.

For example, in some problem domains (the Traveling Salesman Problem is again an example) the best algorithms gain much of their speed from sophisticated data structures and speed-up tricks. This places a fairly high barrier to entry for researchers with new algorithmic ideas they want to promote: in order to get competitive codes that incorporate the new ideas, one may have to implement all those complicated speed-up mechanisms as well. Thus, many researchers have attempted to argue that it's permissible to forgo the speed-ups and still get meaningful results.

PET PEEVE 5. *Claiming inadequate programming time/ability as an excuse.*

In some cases, researchers simply assert that their implementations would likely be competitive with those of previous algorithms had they only had the time or skill to use the same speed-up mechanisms. A slightly more sophisticated variant on this involves comparing the results for a speed-up-free implementation of your algorithm to an implementation of its competitor with the speed-up mechanisms disabled. Here the implicit claim is that running time comparisons made for the speed-up-free case would translate directly to the situation in which both codes included the speed-up mechanisms.

This is a highly suspect argument. First of all, it is hard to quantify how much of a speed-up one would have obtained by implementing the additional mechanisms unless one actually does implement and test them. Second, there is no guarantee that a given speed-up mechanism will be equally effective for different algorithmic approaches. And third, with the slower implementations one cannot perform as many tests or handle as large instances, and so crucial comparative data will be missed.

A second reason why one might argue for saving programming time at the expense of additional computation time, and one that I myself have been guilty of using, arises in the case where one is primarily studying some other metric, such as the quality of solutions produced by an approximation algorithm, and the speed-up mechanisms would affect only the running time, not the solutions. If your machine is sufficiently fast to enable your inefficient implementation to generate all the data you need, this would seem to be acceptable (at least until the referees start asking for more data on larger instances).

In general, however, the advantages of efficiency are many:

(1) Efficient implementations make it easier for you to support claims of practicality and competitiveness.
(2) Results for implementations significantly slower than those one would want to use in practice may yield distorted pictures.
(3) Faster implementations allow one to perform experiments on more and/or larger instances, or to finish the study more quickly.

Note that this principle does not imply you need go overboard on efficiency issues and fine tune your code mercilessly to save the last 10% in running time. Nor does it mean you must implement all the theoretical refinements that yield only small improvements in worst-case running time, especially if there is no indication that such tweaking will have a major practical impact. This is why the current principle refers only to *reasonable* efficiency. Unless your specific experimental goal is to evaluate the impact on running time of such theoretical refinements and speed-up tricks, you are advised to avoid the following pitfall.

PITFALL 5. *Too much code tuning.*

You should certainly make efficient use of data structures when this is called for and when real-world implementers would be likely to do so, e.g., $\Theta(N^2)$ sorting algorithms should typically be avoided. However, this is another situation where advance thinking and experimental exploration can save you effort. By understanding where the computational bottlenecks in the algorithm lie, and by profiling early implementations, you can determine where code optimizations and more sophisticated data structures are likely to have a major effect, and thus concentrate your programming effort where it will do the most good. Ideally the efficiency of the code you test should be (at least to within a constant factor in practice) as good as that of a code you would expect people to use in the real world.

Principle 6. Ensure Reproducibility

As with all scientific studies, a key part of an experimental paper is the reproducibility of the results. But what does "reproducibility" mean in the context of the experimental analysis of algorithms? In the strictest sense it means that if you ran the same code on the same instances on the same machine/compiler/operating system/system load combination you would get the same running time, operation counts, solution quality (or the same averages, in the case of a randomized algorithm).

This, however, would not be very informative, nor does it correspond to what is meant by "reproducibility" in classical scientific studies. In reproducing such a study, a scientist must use the same basic methods, but will typically use different apparatus, similar but distinct materials, and possibly different measuring techniques. He will be said to have reproduced the original results if the data he obtains is consistent with that of the original experiments and supports the same conclusions. In this way he helps confirm that the results of the original experiment (and the conclusions drawn from them) are independent of the precise details of the experiment itself.

It is this broader notion of reproducibility that I consider to be the most important. To ensure it, a paper must describe the algorithms, test instances, computing environment, results, etc. in enough detail so that a reader could at least in principle perform similar experiments that would lead to the same basic conclusions. It is not typically necessary, however, to provide the precise instances that were tested, except perhaps those with unique properties that would be difficult to reproduce. If the results of the original experiment are reproducible in the broader sense, then we should be able to obtain similar results for similar but distinct instances. By the same token, if the original conclusions were claimed to hold for an algorithm rather than a particular implementation of one, then the broader notion of reproducibility would require that we test an independent implementation of the algorithm described in the paper, rather than the original author's code, even if the latter is available. Not only does this enhance our confidence in the conclusions, but it avoids a significant danger.

PET PEEVE 6. *Supplied code that doesn't match a paper's description of it.*

All too often I have found that the code an author supplies does not precisely implement the algorithm described in the corresponding paper. Differences can range from incorrect input specifications to more serious issues such as missing or added steps. Typically this is an honest mistake, due to poor record keeping on the author's part, but it is no less frustrating.

Of course, if the conclusions of the original paper refer to the performance of a specific code rather than the algorithm it implements, then reproducibility does require that the author provide access to his code. This might happen for instance in the evaluation of software packages, where papers often do not provide complete description of the details of the algorithms involved. Similarly, if we are dealing with a "horse race" paper where the main conclusion is that algorithm/implementation A beats algorithm/implementation B on a given testbed of instances, reproducibility requires that the author provide access to the testbed used. Both these cases, however, are more like product testing than science and are not our main focus here.

Complicating the whole issue of reproducibility is the fact that one key algorithmic measurement, the one we are often most interested in, is inherently irreproducible in the broad sense I have been advocating. This is running time. Broadly reproducible results should not be machine-dependent, but even if one fixes an implementation and an instance, running times are dependent on machine, compiler, operating system, system load, and many other factors. The best one can hope for is to conclude that the running times on the different combinations of machines, operating system, etc. are in some sense consistent with other measurements of the relative speeds of the combinations. We will have more to say about the inexact science of making such comparison in our discussion of the next Principle (Ensure Comparability).

The Principle of Reproducibility is perhaps the most violated one in the literature today. Besides simple failures to report key information and when appropriate provide access to code and/or instances, there are less obvious infractions:

PET PEEVE 7. *Irreproducible standards of comparison.*

Suppose you are experimentally evaluating approximation algorithms and have followed my advice and not restricted attention to instances for which the optimal solution value is known. You are then confronted with the question of how to measure the relative goodness of a solution. Here is a list of the answers to that question that I have encountered, several of which have associated reproducibility drawbacks, some of them fatal (see also [**McG96**].)

- Simply report the solution value.

  This certainly is reproducible in the narrow sense, but not in the broader sense that one can perform experiments on similar instances and determine whether one is getting similar results. It also provides no direct insight into the quality of the algorithm.
- Report the percentage excess over best solution currently known.

  This is narrowly reproducible if you explicitly state the current best and also make the instance available to other researchers. Unfortunately, many authors omit at least one of these two actions. Moreover, even if you provide both instance and value, this approach does not yield reproducible results in the broader sense. Furthermore, "current bests" represent a moving target and one usually can't tell whether all the "current bests" for the overall testbed are equally good. Thus we again may be left without a clear picture of the algorithm's true quality.
- For randomly generated instances, report the percentage excess over an estimate of the expected optimal.

  This approach leads to reproducible results only if one explicitly states the estimate or completely specifies the method for computing it. It leads to *meaningful* results only if (i) the estimate is in fact consistently close to the expected optimal, and (ii) the values of the true optima under the distribution have relatively low variance. In most applications of this approach that I have seen, at least one of these two requirements was not satisfied.
- Report the percentage excess over a well-defined lower bound.

  I have already given an example of this approach in the discussion of Principle 4, when I described the use of the Held-Karp TSP lower bound [**HK70, HK71, JMR96**] for variance reduction. Assuming the lower bound is usually close to the optimal solution, as is the case for the Held-Karp bound, this can be a useful approach. It is only reproducible, however, if the lower bound can be feasibly computed or reliably approximated. When I first started using the Held-Karp lower bound as a standard of comparison for the TSP [**Joh90**], it probably did not completely meet these criteria, as we could only compute estimates whose quality we could not guarantee. Indeed, subsequent validation experiments showed that our estimates were only reliably close to the true value when we were dealing with randomly generated instances. Now however, the bound can be calculated exactly for instances as large as 1,000,000 cities using the publicly available `Concorde` code of [**ABCC98**]. Unfortunately, not all problems have such good and computable bounds.
- Report the percentage excess/improvement over some other heuristic.

  This appears to be the ultimate fallback option. It is reproducible so long as the "other heuristic" is completely specified. Unfortunately, it can be difficult to specify that other heuristic if it is at all complicated, and too often authors have settled for simply naming the heuristic, simply saying

"2-Opt," "Lin-Kernighan," or (my favorite example of gross underspecification) "simulated annealing." For all these algorithms, there are variants having a wide range of behaviors, and the name itself does not provide enough detail to distinguish between them (nor do most references). If one is to apply this approach successfully, it is best to use a very simple algorithm as the standard, one that *can* be specified precisely in a few words, and preferably one that is deterministic. If a more complicated benchmark algorithm is desired, then the only viable option is to provide the source code for an implementation, or use one whose source code is already available on the Web.

PET PEEVE 8. *Using running time as a stopping criterion.*

Many types of approximation algorithm, for example multiple-start local search and truncated branch-and-bound, can provide better and better solutions the longer one lets them run. In a practical situation where limited computation time is available, one may well want to simply "run the code for an hour" and take the best solution found so far. Note, however, that "run the code for an hour" is not a well-defined algorithm and will not yield reproducible results. Should one use a machine with a different processor or operating system, or just a more/less efficient implementation of the algorithm on the same machine, one might get solutions having a distinctly different level of quality. Thus defining an algorithm in this way is not acceptable for a scientific paper.

The temptation to use this stopping criterion is especially strong when one is comparing a variety of different algorithms. Many authors, in hopes of providing a "fair" comparison, have performed experiments in which each algorithm was allowed the same amount of running time, say 60 minutes. However, these comparisons are not reproducible. If one reruns the same test on a machine 10 times faster, the algorithms will presumably all do better but their relative rankings may change substantially.

So what is one to do if one wants to make reproducible "fair" comparisons? One solution is to design your codes so that some readily measurable combinatorial count (number of neighborhoods searched, number of branching steps, etc.) is used as the stopping criterion. You then have a well-defined algorithm, for which running time and quality of solution can be measured as a function of the combinatorial count, and the latter is (or should be) reproducible. Given data on the average values of these two metrics as a function of count, one can then *derive* a table that reports results for a specific running time, but also includes the combinatorial counts associated with the running time for each algorithm. Subsequent researchers can then in principle reproduce the table for the given counts, and observe how the differences caused by their machines and implementations affected the various running times (which may or may not remain roughly equal).

PET PEEVE 9. *Using the optimal solution value as a stopping criterion.*

My complaint here is not about optimization algorithms, which stop when they have found an optimal solution and *proved* that it is optimal. Rather, it is about a practice that I have encountered in more than a few papers in the metaheuristic literature, where the algorithms concerned have no mechanism for verifying optimality but simply look for a very good solution until some stopping criterion is reached. In the papers in question, the algorithms are given the instance and the optimal solution value (if known), and are halted early should a solution with the optimal value be found. (The algorithms typically have a back-up stopping criterion for instances with unknown optima and for runs that fail to find a known optima.) The temptation to truncate searches in this way is I guess natural: if you already know what the optimal solution value is, why let your heuristic waste time after it has reached that goal?

The drawback to this approach is that in practice one would not typically run an approximation algorithm on instances for which an optimal solution is already known. Hence in practice one would not know when the optimal solution value had been reached, and so this stopping criteria cannot be used. Thus the tests for instances with known optima need not reflect performance in practice (where the benefit of early stopping will never be felt), and would not be "reproducible" in the sense that dramatically different running times might be reported for similar (or even the same) instances, depending on whether one knew the optimal value or not.

PET PEEVE 10. *Hand-tuned algorithm parameters.*

Many heuristics have parameters that need to be set before the algorithm can be run. For instance, in a multiple-start local optimization algorithm, one must specify the number of starts. More elaborate metaheuristics such as simulated annealing, tabu search, genetic algorithms, etc. can come with whole ensembles of adjustable parameters. For such an algorithm to be well-defined, one must either fix those parameters or define them in a way that depends on measurable aspects of the instance being handled. In the former case (fixed parameters) there is no problem of reproducibility as long as the paper reports the settings chosen (although the paper might be more informative and useful if some insight is provided on how performance would be affected by changes in the settings). In the latter case, however, many papers use different settings for different instances without explaining how those settings were derived beyond perhaps the words "after experimentation, we found the following settings to work well for this instance/class of instances."

There are at least two drawbacks to this approach. First, it means that the algorithm is ill-specified, since the parameter-setting process is not explained in detail. (Indeed, since it involved human experimentation and judgment, it may not have involved any sort of codified procedure.) Second, since the reported running times typically do not include the time spent in determining the parameters, it leads to a serious underestimate of the computing time needed to apply the algorithm to a new instance/class of instances.

The rule I would apply is the following: If different parameter settings are to be used for different instances, the adjustment process must be well-defined and algorithmic, the adjustment algorithm must be described in the paper, and the time for the adjustment must be included in all reported running times.

PET PEEVE 11. *The one-run study.*

Unless a study covers a wide enough range of instances (and a large enough number of runs in the case of randomized algorithms), the conclusions drawn may well be *wrong*, and hence irreproducible for that reason. The amount of data needed will of course vary with the detail of the conclusions. A first paper on a given algorithm may well settle for trying to indicate general trends in its performance without quantifying them, and this may require fewer test instances and/or fewer runs per test instance than a subsequent paper that wishes to characterize specific aspects of performance more accurately. However, it should be remembered that randomly-generated instances from the same distribution can have widely varying properties, especially when the instances are of small size, and that many randomized algorithms can also yield widely-varying results for the same instance. Thus it can be dangerous to infer too much from a single run on a single instance.

PET PEEVE 12. *Using the best result found as an evaluation criterion.*

With randomized algorithms, one can avoid the dangers of the one-run study by performing multiple runs on each instance. These, however, can lead to other temptations. In providing tables of results of randomized approximation algorithms, many papers include a column for the best result found as well as (or instead of) one for the average result found. The objections to this are twofold. First, the best solution found is a sample from the tail of a distribution, and hence less likely to be reproducible than the average. Second, in such tables, the running times reported are usually for a single run of the algorithm, rather than for the entire ensemble of runs that yielded the reported "best." Thus the time for obtaining this answer is obscured. Indeed if, as is often the case, the number of runs actually performed is not clearly stated, there is no way to determine the running time. And even if the number of runs is stated, note that the simple process of multiplying the running time by the number of runs may *overestimate* the time needed, given that certain actions, such as reading the instance and setting up data structures, may need to be done only once when multiple runs are performed.

If you think that in practice users may want to perform many runs and take the best, a more appropriate experimental approach would be to evaluate the algorithm "Perform k runs and take the best" directly, reporting both running time and solutions for this iterative approach. As we already saw in the discussion of Principle 4, there are efficient techniques for performing such evaluations using bootstrapping.

Principle 7. Ensure Comparability

This Principle is essentially the reverse side of the Principle about tying your paper to the literature. That earlier principle referred to the past literature. This one refers to the future. You should write your papers (and to the extent possible make relevant data, code, and instances publicly available in a long-term manner) so that future researchers (yourself included) can accurately compare their results for new algorithms/instances to your results. Part of this is simply following the above recommendations for ensuring reproducibility, but there are additional steps necessary. In trying to compare my own results to the literature, I have encountered several difficulties due to omissions of various sorts in past papers.

PET PEEVE 13. *The uncalibrated machine.*

Although most papers at least mention the machine on which their experiments were run, they often omit other key factors such as processor speed (not always evident from the machine model name), operating system and language/compiler. And even when they present all this information, it can still be difficult to estimate the relative difference in speeds between the earlier system and your own, a difficulty that only gets worse as time passes and machines get outdated and forgotten. When talking about machines several generations apart, even if one knows the quoted processor speeds for the two machines, e.g. 20 Mhz versus 500 Mhz, the raw speed of the processor in Megahertz is a notoriously unreliable predictor of performance. (Even for processors currently on the market, differences in machine architecture render comparisons based solely on quoted processor speed highly suspect.)

SUGGESTION 6. *Use benchmark codes to calibrate machine speeds.*

The benchmark is distributed as portable source code that preferably involves data structures and algorithmic operations somewhat similar to those used in the algorithms studied. You compile and run the benchmark code on the same machine and with the same compiler that you use for the implementations you are studying reporting its running times for a specified set of publicly available test instances of varying size. Future researchers can then calibrate their own machines in the same way and, based on the benchmark data reported in the original paper, attempt to normalize the old results to their current machines.

In the world of scientific computing, where floating point computation and `Fortran` are the dominant computational paradigms, this approach is widely practiced. The benchmark codes are from the `LINPACK` suite described in [**Don00**], a report that lists, for various combinations of machine, operating system, and compiler, the number of megaflops (millions of floating point operations per second) performed on each of three benchmark computations. These benchmark codes have certain drawbacks for our purposes, however. Being written in `FORTRAN` and dominated by highly structured loops of floating point operations, they may not adequately reflect the codes that many of us study, which are combinatorial in nature and written in `C` or `C++`. Furthermore, because the `LINPACK` benchmarks are limited to just three computations, the derived numbers may not adequately quantify memory hierarchy effects.

Thus in the world of combinatorial algorithms it may be worthwhile to promulgate new and more relevant benchmark codes. This is the approach taken in several DIMACS Implementation Challenges. For example, see the Web site for the DIAMCS TSP Challenge at `http://www.research.att.com/~dsj/chtsp/`). Here the benchmark algorithm is itself a nontrivial TSP heuristic, and the instances cover a large range of sizes, from 1,000 to 10,000,000 cities. Given the benchmark results for two machines, one can plot the relative speeds of the two machines as a function of instance size, and use interpolation to normalize the time of an algorithm for a specific instance on one machine to what it would likely be on the other. There are limits on the accuracy of this approach, of course, and preliminary data from the DIMACS TSP Challenge suggests that one cannot hope that the normalized results will be closer than a factor of two to what one would have gotten had the same system been used for both studies. This, however, is much better than nothing, since many other factors can introduce discrepancies this large.

PET PEEVE 14. *The lost testbed.*

As I mentioned earlier when talking about variance reduction, there is much to be gained when comparing algorithms if one can run them on the same instances. (This is less important for reproducibility, where what really wants to verify are the conclusions of the study, which typically are independent of the precise answers given for various instances.) Thus for the sake of future researchers, you should do your best to perform many of your runs on instances to which subsequent researchers will have access. These days the standard solution is to make sure that the instances (or their generators) are available on the Web. This is of course less crucial if your testbed includes many samples from each distribution studied, as this enables you to average out much of the variability encountered in individual instances. However for individual instances, the future researcher may have no insight into whether that instance was particularly easy or hard or atypical in other ways without having access to the instance itself.

Admittedly, this requirement does open up possibilities for abuse. Future researchers interested in winning horse races might be tempted to optimize their codes for precisely those instances you studied, and thus beat you based on instance-specific code-tuning alone. This, however, is less likely if your testbed is sufficiently large and varied.

Another alternative to resolving the above two pet peeves is simply to make the source code for your algorithm available. What better way of ensuring comparability? (It would however still be worthwhile to also provide machine calibrations and your testbed instances, if only to enable future researchers to verify that the code you provide does indeed correspond to the one whose results you reported.) There can of course be obstacles to making the code available. Depending on the policies of your employer, it may or may not be possible to release your code to the public. Even if it is allowed, you may not want to release it until you are finished performing your own experiments with it (or have corrected all the spelling errors and put in all those comments that good programming style recommends). However, even if you are willing to make the source code available, there is still one more obstacle that may be encountered.

PITFALL 6. *Lost code/data.*

If you lose your code, you lose your best approach to obtaining comparability between it and future algorithms designed by yourself and others. If you lose the data on which the summaries reported in your papers are based, you lose the chance of going back and answering more detailed questions raised by readers or future papers. So why would one allow this to happen? I can mention several ways from bitter personal experience.

- Modifying the code without saving a copy of the original version.
- Unthinking responses to pleas of systems administrators to "clean up."
- Failure to keep back-up copies.
- Poorly organized directories containing multiple variants on code/data without clearly identifying the crucial ones.

(Fortunately, for me the last is the most common, and with effort one can recover from it.)

Principle 8. Report the Full Story

Although it is typically overkill to present all your raw data, if you are overly selective you may fail to reach accurate conclusions or adequately support them. You may also impair your paper's reproducibility and comparability. If you report only averages, you should say how many instances (and how many runs in the case of randomized algorithms) you based the averages on. If the precise values of these averages are important for your conclusions, you should also provide information about the distribution of the results. The latter might simply be standard deviations if the data appears roughly normally distributed, but might need to be more pictorial (histograms, boxplots) if the distribution is more idiosyncratic. And any scaling or normalizing of measurements should be carefully explained so that the raw averages can be regenerated if desired. In particular, although pictorial summaries of data can often be the best way to support your overall conclusions, this should not typically be the only presentation of the data since pictures typically lack precision. Tables of data values/averages may be relegated to an appendix, but should be included.

Of course, one can go overboard.

PET PEEVE 15. *False precision.*

One of the most common statistical abuses is the presentation of averages to far more digits of accuracy than is justified by the data, with the subsequent temptation to draw conclusions about differences that are basically just in the noise. In the case of running times, even reporting individual measurements can be misleading because of the imprecision of the timing mechanisms in most operating systems and the unpredictable effect that other users and system effects may have on reported running times.

Admittedly, one can be lead to including all that extra precision simply for data layout reasons. For example, consider a table that includes average running times for a large range of instance sizes. In this case, one may need to go down to units of 10^{-2} to even get two digits of accuracy on the smallest instances, and once the column has some entries with two digits to the right of the decimal point, the temptation is to keep them even when the entries for large instances may be bigger than 10^6. My own solution (when I'm not violating this Pet Peeve myself) is simply to replace the insignificant digits with 0's and add a comment in the text or caption to explain what I'm doing.

A second major part of telling the "full story" concerns anomalous results. You should not hide them, either by omitting them or by failing to point them out when they are present. For reasons of intellectual honesty one should of course include results that are only "anomalous" in that they are inconsistent with the conclusions you wish to draw (e.g, results for instances where the code that you wish to champion underperforms). However, one should also report any strange (but reproducible) phenomena one encounters in one's experiments. Ideally, one should also provide explanations for such anomalies, but even if you have none, the reader should know of their existence. Currently unexplainable anomalies may eventually prove to be the key to major insights into the algorithms, implementations, or test data.

PET PEEVE 16. *Unremarked anomalies.*

The worst anomaly is the one you don't notice. Unfortunately, many papers contain them, leaving the reader to wonder whether it is a true anomaly or simply a typographical error (or evidence of an implementation bug). Anomalies are important. Look for them.

PET PEEVE 17. *The* ex post facto *stopping criterion.*

This is similar to my earlier pet peeve about using the optimal solution value as a stopping criterion, but concerns telling the full story rather than reproducibility. Many search heuristics do not stop when they find a local optimum, but continue looking for good solutions even if this means examining solutions that are worse than ones you have already seen. Typically one runs such a heuristic for some fixed number of steps and then returns the best solution encountered. Similarly, when performing multiple-runs of randomized algorithms, one typically fixes the number of runs in advance and on completion takes the best result found.

Unfortunately, when studying such algorithms, some authors don't report the total running time, but merely the time until that best solution was first encountered. In effect they are investigating a clairvoyant algorithm that knows in advance the best solution value it will ever see and so stops as soon as a solution with that value is encountered. This is not something we can do in the real world. Thus, although the statistic reported is presumably reproducible, it obscures the full story by underestimating the total time that the algorithm would take.

A better approach taken by many authors is to report, in addition to full running times, the number of steps/iterations taken before the best solution was found. Such information may help in determining general rules for how to set the parameter governing the total number of steps/iterations to be performed.

The above is a special case of the following more general (and perhaps more controversial) complaint:

PET PEEVE 18. *Failure to report overall running times.*

Even if your main subject is not running times, you should report yours. As noted above, running time is an important component of newsworthiness, and so a reader may legitimately want to know this information before committing time to a detailed study of your results. Here are some of the common reasons stated for *not* reporting overall running times. For each stated reason, I give a counter-argument as to why overall running time is still of interest.

(1) The main subject of your study is only one component of the running time (say the local optimization phase). However: readers may legitimately want to know how important the contribution of the component being studied is, and for this they need information on overall running time.
(2) The main subject of your study is a combinatorial count related to the algorithm's operation. However: readers may legitimately expect you to establish the meaningfulness of the count in question, which presumably means studying its correlations with running time. For example, I have seen studies of different pruning strategies for an exhaustive search algorithm that measure only the number of subproblems explored under each. This can be misleading if in fact the "better" pruning scheme uses far more time in processing each node and hence leads to a larger overall running time.
(3) Your paper concerns approximation algorithms and your main concern is simply in measuring the quality of the solutions they produce. However: a key reason for using approximation algorithms is to trade quality of solution for reduced running time, and readers may legitimately want to know how that tradeoff works out for the algorithms in question.
(4) Your paper's goal is to estimate average-case solution quality for a well-studied approximation algorithm whose overall running time has previously been studied. This is actually a pretty good excuse (I've used it myself). However (and this argument applies to all the cases above as well): a reader interested in reproducing your results may well want to

know how much computation will be involved in doing so. The same goes if what you are really doing is simply using algorithms as as tool in experimental mathematics (estimating asymptotic constants, determining properties of distributions, etc.).

Note that although the above may be the stated reasons for not reporting overall running time, the real reason is typically either that it takes a bit more effort to record running times or that the current code is sufficiently slow that reporting its running times may cast doubts on the significance of the results being reported. However: the need for a minor bit of extra work is not an excuse, nor, according to Principle 5, is failure to use efficient implementations.

Principle 9. Draw Well-Justified Conclusions and Look for Explanations

The purpose of doing experiments with algorithms is presumably to learn something about their performance, and so a good experimental paper will have conclusions to state and support. This is worth emphasizing, since, based on conference submissions I have seen, many beginners apparently do not realize it.

PET PEEVE 19. *Data without interpretation.*

It is not enough simply to perform tests, tabulate your results, and leave the reader the job of finding the implications of the data. (If there aren't any implications that you can find or express, then you've done the wrong experiments and shouldn't be writing a paper yet, as you've failed the "newsworthiness" test.) At a minimum, one should be able to summarize patterns in the data. Ideally, one might also be able to pose more general conjectures that the data supports and which subsequent research (experimental or theoretical) may try to confirm or deny.

Note that the conclusion might well have to be "the data is inconclusive," but if you've set up your study in order to answer interesting questions (as I've recommended), you should be able to derive an answer of some sort. You also need to make a convincing case that your data does indeed support the answers you state.

PET PEEVE 20. *Conclusions without support.*

It is surprising how often papers state conclusions that are not well-supported by the data they present, either because of glaring exceptions they don't comment on, trends they don't notice, or some other failure. As an example of the second failing, consider a paper I recently read that claimed two algorithms to be equally good because each was better half the time, but failed to notice that one was better only on the smaller instances in the testbed, and the other was better (by increasing margins) as instance size increased. A particularly common example of poorly-supported conclusion is the following.

PET PEEVE 21. *Myopic approaches to asymptopia.*

Given that theorists are interested in asymptotics (asymptotic running times, asymptotic worst-case ratios, etc.) it is natural for experimentalists from that community to try to address such questions experimentally. However, if there is anything one learns in this field, it is that behavior on small (or even relatively large) instances does not always predict behavior for *very* large instances. Thus studies that try to extrapolate asymptotic running time by studying times for instances of size 1000 or less can often be led astray. My own early bin packing experiments in [**Joh73**], based on experiment with 200-item lists were also woefully misleading. I concluded that for item sizes uniformly distributed between 0 and 1, Best Fit was on average 5.6% worse than optimal. Subsequent experiments with lists of 100,000 items or more [**BJLM83**] implied that Best Fit was in fact asymptotically optimal, as has now been proved [**Sho86**]. Similarly, for many TSP heuristics, the relative quality of the tours found by two heuristics on 100-city instances can be far different from the relative quality found for 10,000-city instances (in either direction) [**JBMR03**]. If one is interested in asymptotics, one should study as large instances as possible. In addition, if one is interested in running time, it pays to study it in as much detail as possible.

SUGGESTION 7. *Use profiling to understand running times.*

An algorithm's running time is typically made up of many components, each with its own growth rate. A $\Theta(n)$ component with a high constant of proportionality may dominate a $\Theta(n^2)$ component when n is small, although the latter will eventually determine the algorithm's behavior. Profiling your code, which can provide you with both the number of calls to the various subroutines as well as the time spent in them, can help you spot those higher-exponent components of running time well before they make a significant contribution to the overall time.

Note that in helping us get a better estimate of the true asymptotic running time, profiling also provides an explanation of how that running time comes about. Such explanations are a key part of an experimental analysis paper. In the real-world, the key performance characteristics of an algorithm are it's resource requirements (running time, memory usage, etc.) and (with approximation algorithms) the quality of the solutions it generates. It is thus natural to concentrate on measurements of these quantities when performing a first experimental analysis. However, if our goal is understanding, we must soon turn to the question of explaining why the observed measurements occur. (Plausible explanations also add to the credibility of the experimental results themselves.)

Explanations are at their most believable if backed up by compelling evidence. When a worst-case $\Theta(N^2)$ algorithm appears to be taking $\Theta(N \log N)$ in practice, what part of the worst-case analysis proved to be overly pessimistic? Why does a seemingly more complicated algorithm take less time in practice than a supposedly simple and efficient one? Often these questions can be answered by profiling or by instrumenting the code to perform additional measurements. (Measurements of this sort have also on more than one occasion led to the "explanation" that an implementation was defective, something one would definitely like to know before publishing results about it.)

Principle 10. Present Your Data in Informative Ways

The best way to support your conclusions (and sometimes also the easiest way to derive them) is to display your data in such a way as to highlight the trends it exhibits, the distinctions it makes, and so forth. There are many good display techniques depending on the types of points one wants to make. Illustrating them all would unfortunately require a much longer paper than this. For now, readers are best advised to take a critical look at the examples of good experimental papers listed in this and other papers, and try to adapt those techniques they themselves find most informative. For additional ideas, one can also consult the general literature about data display (e.g., see [**Cle85, Cle93, Tuf83**]). My approach here, as with the other Principles, will be to organize the discussion around warnings about potential mistakes and suggestions about how to avoid them.

PET PEEVE 22. *Tables without pictures.*

Tables by themselves are usually a very inefficient way of telling your story. Most readers (and talk attendees) *hate* presentations where the punch line is a large, multi-columned table in fine print. If there is any graphical way to summarize the data and reveal its message, it is almost always to be preferred to a table alone.

PET PEEVE 23. *Pictures without tables.*

On the other hand, although pictures can often tell your story more quickly, they are usually a poor way of presenting the details of your results. I don't want to have to get out a ruler to estimate the value of the solution your algorithm found so that I can compare it with the results of my own algorithm. So a good paper should contain *both* pictures and tables, although feel free to stick the tables in an appendix so that readers who just want to see the big picture don't have to deal with them.

PET PEEVE 24. *Pictures yielding too little insight.*

Although pictures can add much to our understanding of the data, not all pictures are equally useful. Care must be taken in figuring what to display and how to display it, and without such care one can get figures that tell us very little. Suppose for example we wish to construct a meaningful display about running time growth. (I choose this example because so many papers do a poor job of it.) Suppose we have tested five algorithms on TSP instances ranging in size from 100 to 1,000,000 cities, going up by factors of roughly $\sqrt{10}$, and the table below gives the average running times we obtained (no doubt stated with more precision than is justified for the larger instances and less than we would like for the smallest ones).

	100	316	1,000	3,162	10,000	31,623	100,000	316,227	1,000,000
Alg A	0.00	0.02	0.08	0.29	1.05	5.46	23.0	89.6	377
Alg B	0.00	0.03	0.11	0.35	1.38	6.50	30.6	173.3	669
Alg C	0.01	0.06	0.21	0.71	2.79	10.98	42.7	329.5	1253
Alg D	0.02	0.09	0.43	1.64	6.98	37.51	192.4	789.7	5465
Alg E	0.03	0.14	0.57	2.14	10.42	55.36	369.4	5775.0	33414

Simply staring at this table is not going to give us much insight other than the fact that the algorithms have been roughly ordered by speed, with the same ranking holding for each instance size. Can a picture tell us more? Figure 1 illustrates four different ways we might display the data, all of which I have seen in experimental papers, and only one of which (I would argue) gives much useful additional insight.

The display in the upper left hand corner of Figure 1 simply charts running time versus number of cities. Note that a large majority of the data points are concentrated in the leftmost tenth of the figure and have y-coordinates that are hard to distinguish from 0. So from this picture all we can conclude (or would be able to conclude if I had labeled the curves) is that for large instances Algorithms

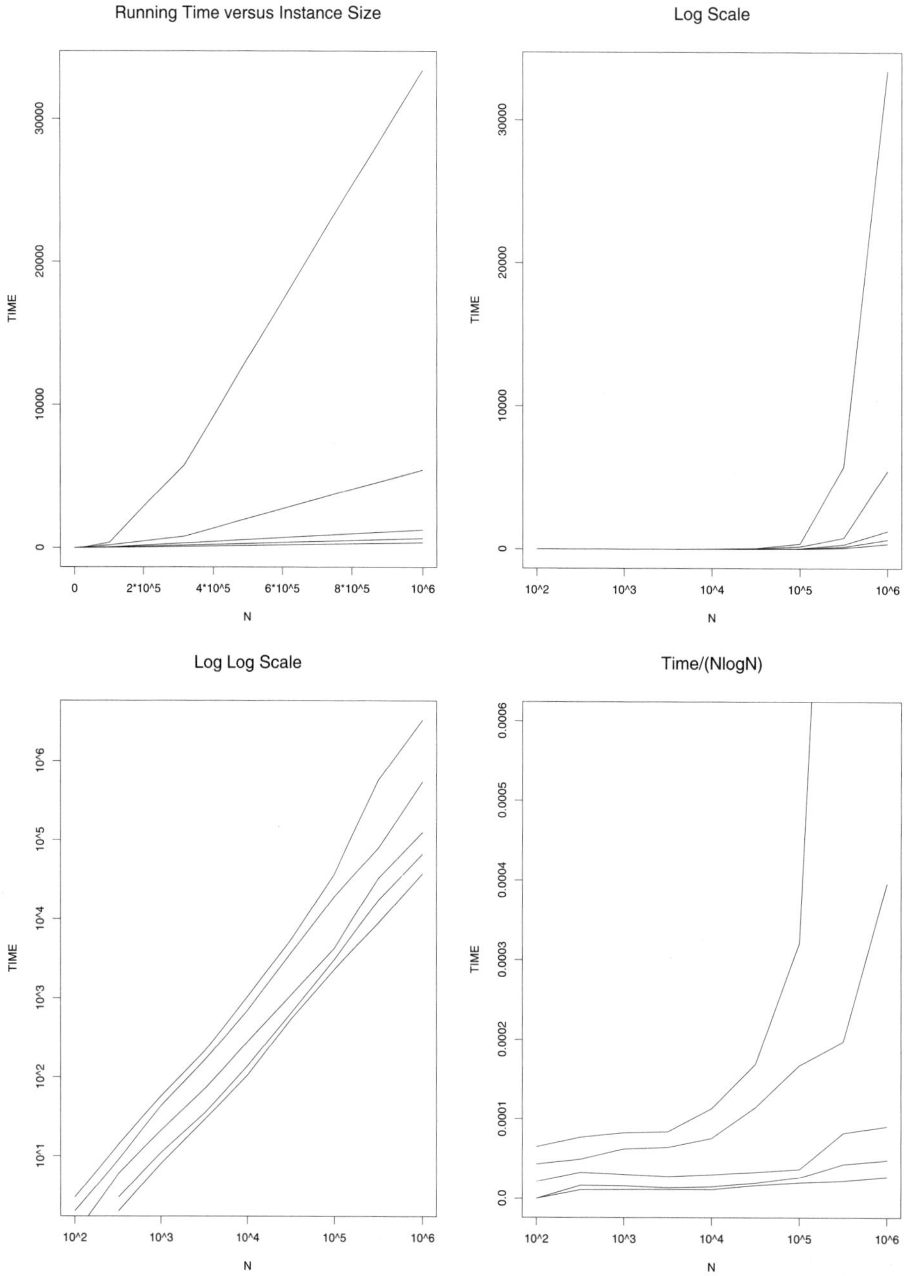

FIGURE 1. Displaying running time as a function of instance size.

D and E are a lot slower than the others, with the gap increasing. We have lost the insight that the relative rankings are consistent for all instance sizes.

The display in the upper right hand corner of Figure 1 uses a logarithmic scale for the x-coordinate, and so now the data points are evenly spread in the x direction, but because the running times for instances with 100,000 or fewer cities are still so small in comparison to those for larger instances, we get no more insight than we did from the previous display.

The display in the bottom left uses logarithmic scales for both axes, and now the consistent ranking of the algorithms for the different instance sizes is visible. Moreover, in theory one could determine something about the running time growth rates by measuring the slopes of the five curves. However, visually the slopes all look more or less the same and it is essentially impossible to estimate their values without resorting to a ruler and scratch paper.

The final display (bottom right hand corner) exploits the following suggestion.

SUGGESTION 8. *Display normalized running times.*

Having determined from our theoretical understanding of the algorithms and detailed analysis of the data that the fastest three algorithms have running times that grow as roughly $n \log n$, we divide all the running times by this quantity, and chart the resulting normalized times using a logarithmic x-axis. The resulting picture then reveals not only that the running time rankings are consistent and that algorithms D and E are much slower than the first three, but also that those first three have close to $\Theta(n \log n)$ running times, and that the latter are asymptotically much worse. We also get a clearer idea of the relative speeds of A, B, and C (or would if one added horizontal grid lines at appropriate intervals.) The one thing we lose is a clear picture of what the actual running times are, but that's what tables are for. We also get an illustration of another of my pet peeves.

PET PEEVE 25. *Inadequately or confusingly labeled pictures.*

Clearly if the data were real the curves in Figure 1 should have been labeled with the algorithms to which they correspond. A common practice is to use different symbols for the data points on the curve, but often the symbols are not sufficiently distinct to distinguish without a magnifying glass. Moreover, they can become almost totally indecipherable when data points are close together or coincide, as can happen in situations like the following.

PET PEEVE 26. *Pictures with too much information.*

Pictures do their job best when they are clear and uncluttered. If the bottom right display of the previous discussion had covered 20 algorithms instead of 5, it might well have lost its impact by making it difficult to distinguish (or even keep track of) the trend lines for the different algorithms. In general, the more algorithms you try to cover in a single figure, the harder it is to make your points clearly. In addition, to the extent that you include algorithms with widely different run times, you may be forced to compress data and obscure distinctions in order to fit everything in. A better solution might be to have multiple figures, each devoted to a subset of the algorithms in a given performance range. You can still provide an overall view that links all the results together if you use overlapping sets.

PET PEEVE 27. *Confusing pictorial metaphors.*

Too much creativity can be a dangerous thing. If you can't explain a figure in a short caption (or perhaps a short caption and an additional short paragraph in the text), then you may not be able to get your message across to your readers.

PET PEEVE 28. *The spurious trend line.*

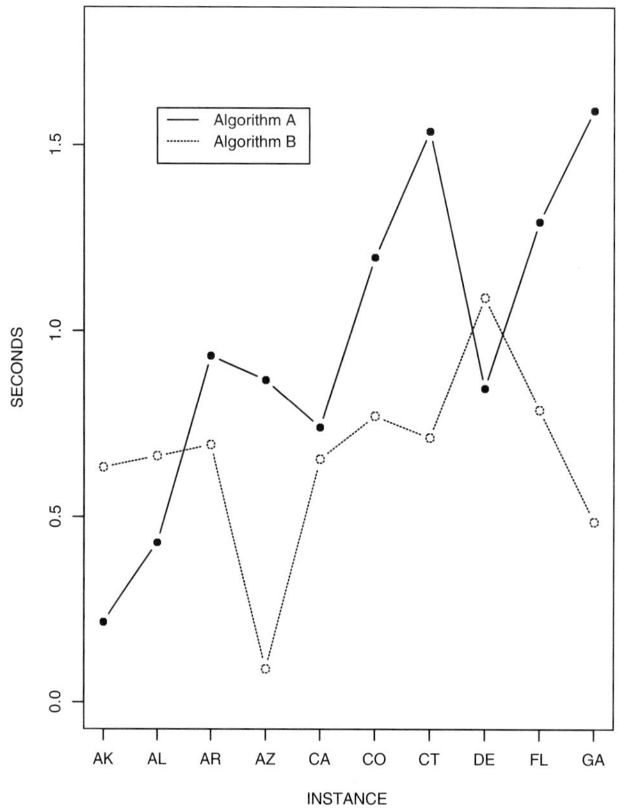

FIGURE 2. Spurious trend lines.

This common but aggravating practice is illustrated in Figure 2. Here we have performed experiments on a collection of 10 instances. They might be 10 samples from the same instance distribution or simply 10 members of some standard testbed. Each instance has a name, and after sorting the names into alphabetical (or some other arbitrary) order, we plot our running times (or other metrics) for the 10 instances, and then for each algorithm *connect the data points by lines*.

The reasons this is done are understandable. Some plotting software packages do it automatically. Or perhaps one is concerned that the data points for the algorithms might be confused and so links them up to clarify which ones go with which algorithm. However, linking data points together in this way normally has certain implications. It suggests that there are underlying trends in behavior as you move from left to right. It also sometimes suggests the conjecture that one can interpolate between the results presented based on the curves shown. Neither of these inferences is typically warranted in this situation however, unless one seriously means to suggest that algorithmic performance is influenced by the alphabetic ranking of an instance's name.

PET PEEVE 29. *Poorly structured tables.*

Even if you are going to relegate your table to an appendix, but especially if you haven't figured out how to make your point graphically, it is important to order the rows and columns so as to highlight important information. For example, even though it is fairly common, it is usually not a good idea simply to sort your columns or rows by instance or algorithm name. The danger is not (as in the previous discussion) that you will suggest false trends, but rather that you will obscure true ones. Ordering instances by size makes a lot more sense than ordering them by name, since one can then more readily spot trends in time or solution quality that correlate with size. Ordering algorithms by solution quality or running time also makes these relationships more visible. Finally, if a single table reports values for several metrics, thought should be given to how best to order the columns/rows for the metrics.

PET PEEVE 30. *Making your readers do the arithmetic.*

This is another common problem with tables, and refers to what might be called the "missing column." As an example, suppose you are evaluating an approximation algorithm on instances for which good lower bounds (or the optimal solution values) are known. In this case, do not simply present a table of the solution values found by the algorithms, thus leaving readers with the task of performing the division that will tell them how close those solutions are to the corresponding lower bounds (which is the information a reader would typically want to know). This derived statistic should have been in the table to begin with.

PET PEEVE 31. *The undefined metric.*

This typically occurs in tables, although the same thing can show up on the axis labels for figures: A cryptic or ambiguous label is given to a column/axis and remains unexplained, either in caption or the text of the paper. The most common example is the running time column where it is not clear if the times reported include instance reading or preprocessing times (the latter of which can for some algorithms be substantial), or whether it refers to the time for a single run or the total time for all the runs performed. Another example is the column marked "number of iterations" when nowhere in the paper is it clearly stated what constitutes an iteration. Another is the column marked "time" with no indication of whether it is measured in seconds, microseconds, or what. It really isn't difficult to spell such things out clearly, and there is no excuse for not doing so.

PET PEEVE 32. *Comparing apples with oranges.*

My prime example of this problem is the table that presents running times for various algorithms on a given set of instances, but for each algorithm the entries have been taken from an earlier paper whose experiments were performed on a different (and often much slower) machine. Even when the caption or text does contain the caveat that different machines were involved, a reader skimming the paper is likely to be seriously misled about the relative running times of the algorithms. Readers who want a more accurate comparison are left with the task of normalizing the running times for themselves, making this another illustration of the problem of making the reader do the arithmetic.

PET PEEVE 33. *Detailed statistics on unimportant questions.*

If one is to get the full picture of an algorithm's performance, one must perform tests on many instances. The precise determination of results for one instance (or one random distribution of instances) may be less important than the overall picture. Doing a thousand runs to get narrow confidence limits on one such data point is usually a mis-allocation of resources, since it may prevent you from examining other data points.

Another example of misguided use of statistics is the use of detailed tests to determine with what confidence we can say that algorithm A is better than algorithm B on a particular instance or class of instances. If the class is narrow, the results are too narrow to be of interest (for example, applying this approach to a set of small instances and ignoring the fact that relative performances may change drastically as instance size increases). If the class is broad, such tests may obscure the much more interesting fact that the identity of the better algorithm may depend on the type of instance. Moreover, if one really needs sophisticated statistical tests to distinguish the performance of two algorithms, a more appropriate conclusion might be that for practical purposes their performance with respect to the given metric is "about the same" and hence the decision on which algorithm to use should be based on other grounds.

Statistics are useful, but should be used to support general conclusions (or particularly interesting specific ones). In particular, they do have a necessary role to play in experimental average-case papers, as for instance in [**JMR96, PM96**].

PET PEEVE 34. *Comparing approximation algorithms as to how often they find optima.*

One situation in which one *should* be interested in details of the distribution of results is the case of randomized approximation algorithms. Here, as has already been mentioned, one has the opportunity to run the algorithm multiple times and thus exploit the variability of the distribution of solutions.

One aspect of such distributions that is definitely of interest in certain situations is the probability that the algorithm will find an optimal solution for a given instance. For example, it is my observation that for most instances of the TSP with 50 cities or less, the Lin-Kernighan algorithm (randomized by its choice of starting solution) typically finds the optimal solution with high probability.

However, using the frequency with which optimal solutions are found as the primary metric in comparing algorithms has serious limitations. First, it restricts attention to test instances for which optimal solutions are known (see Pet Peeve 4). Second, it ignores the question of how near to optimal the algorithm gets when it does not find the optimum. And finally, it is a metric that will fail to make any distinctions at all between algorithms once instances get reasonably large and, as expected, the probability of finding an optimal solution goes to zero for all the competitors.

PET PEEVE 35. *Too much data.*

In doing an experimental study, getting additional data is almost always valuable. However, in writing up your studies once you have fully analyzed your data, presenting too much data can overwhelm your readers and obscure your main points. Raw data should be replaced by averages and other summary statistics when appropriate. If several instance classes yield basically the same results, choose a representative one and present the data for that one only, while pointing out in the text which other classes behave similarly. Algorithms that are dominated and not interesting for other reasons should be dropped from tables and charts. Data thus omitted may be included in appendices, or perhaps better yet be relegated to a Web archive where interested readers can access it. (With the growing popularity of online journals, the distinction between appendix and Web archive of course is beginning to disappear).

Section 2. Extensions and Other Points to Ponder

This paper has attempted to give advice about how best to analyze algorithms experimentally and report your results. Much of the discussion has been about what *not* to do, but I hope that the reader has come away with ideas about good practices as well, and that those who do not agree with all the points I have made have at least been stimulated to think more deeply about the issues involved.

The discussions of the preceding sections were primarily addressed to the experimentalist interested in studying sequential algorithms for the "classic problem" in which one is given a single input and asked to produce a single output (whose quality can be measured by a single-valued objective function). Not all computational tasks fit this paradigm, but many of the issues raised and suggestions made apply more broadly. I leave it as an exercise to the reader to determine which ones apply and which need to be modified in other situations, such as the following:

- Parallel/distributed algorithms for classic problems.
- Algorithms for problems with multi-valued or imprecise objective functions.
- Algorithms for program testing/checking/correcting.
- Dynamic/reactive algorithms that are required to respond to a sequence of requests with a conceptually infinite time horizon.

Given that the operating principle of this paper has been basically to present lists of aphorisms, let me conclude with one additional list, this one addressing the extent to which we should rely on various common resources without constant vigilance.

Whom can you trust?

(1) Never trust a random number generator.
(2) Never trust your code to be correct.
(3) Never trust a previous author to have known all the literature.
(4) Never trust your memory as to where you put that data (and how it was generated).
(5) Never trust your computer to remain unchanged.
(6) Never trust backup media or Web sites to remain readable indefinitely.
(7) Never trust a so-called expert on experimental analysis.

References

[ABCC98] D. Applegate, R. Bixby, V. Chvatal, and W. Cook, *On the solution of traveling salesman problems*, Documenta Mathematica Journal der Deutschen Mathematiker-Vereinigung **ICM III** (1998), 646–656, Additional information and source code for the `Concorde` package is available at `http://www.keck.caam.rice.edu/concorde.html`.

[Ben92] J. L. Bentley, *Fast algorithms for geometric traveling salesman problems*, ORSA Journal on Computing **4** (1992), no. 4, 387–411.

[BGK+95] R. S. Barr, B. L. Golden, J. P. Kelly, M. G. C. Resende, and W. R. Stewart, *Designing and reporting on computational experiments with heuristic methods*, Journal of Heuristics **1** (1995), no. 1, 9—32.

[BJLM83] J. L. Bentley, D. S. Johnson, F. T. Leighton, and C. C. McGeoch, *An experimental study of bin packing*, Proceedings of the 21st Annual Allerton Conference on Communication, Control, and Computing (Urbana), University of Illinois, 1983, pp. 51–60.

[CGR94] B. V. Cherkassky, A. V. Goldberg, and T. Radzik, *Shortest paths algorithms: Theory and experimental evaluation*, Proceedings of the Fifth ACM-SIAM Symposium on Discrete Algorithms, ACM-SIAM, New York, Philadelphia, January 1994, pp. 516–525.

[Cle85] W. S. Cleveland, *Elements of graphing data*, Wadsworth, Monteray, CA, 1985.

[Cle93] ———, *Visualizing data*, Hobart Press, Summit, NJ, 1993.

[CS00] M. Coffin and M. J. Saltzman, *Statistical analysis of computational tests of algorithms and heuristics*, INFORMS J. Computing **12** (2000), no. 1, 24–44.

[Don00] J. J. Dongarra, *Performance of various computers using standard linear equations software*, Tech. report, No. CS-89-85, Computer Science Department, University of Tennesssee, Knoxville, TN, August 24, 2000, The currently most up-to-date version should be available from `http://www.netlib.org/benchmark/performance.ps`.

[FJMO95] M. L. Fredman, D. S. Johnson, L. A. McGeoch, and G. Ostheimer, *Data structures for traveling salesmen*, J. Algorithms **18** (1995), no. 3, 432–479, Preliminary version: *Proceedings of the Fourth ACM-SIAM Symposium on Discrete Algorithms*, pages 145–154, SIAM, Philadelphia, 1993.

[HK70] M. Held and R. M. Karp, *The traveling-salesman problem and minimum spanning trees*, Operations Research **18** (1970), 1138–1162.

[HK71] ———, *The traveling-salesman problem and minimum spanning trees: Part II*, Math. Prog. **1** (1971), 6–25.

[Hoo93] J. Hooker, *Needed: An empirical science of algorithms*, Operations Research **42** (1993), no. 2, 201–212.

[JBMR03] D. S. Johnson, J. L. Bentley, L. A. McGeoch, and E. E. Rothberg, *Near-optimal solutions to very large traveling salesman problems*, Monograph, in preparation, 2003.

[JM97] D. S. Johnson and L. A. McGeoch, *The traveling salesman problem: A case study in local optimization*, Local Search in Combinatorial Optimization (E. Aarts and J. K. Lenstra, eds.), John Wiley & Sons, 1997, Preliminary draft available at `http://www.research.att.com/~dsj/`, pp. 215–310.

[JMR96] D. S. Johnson, L. A. McGeoch, and E. E. Rothberg, *Asymptotic experimental analysis for the held-karp traveling salesman bound*, Proceedings of the Seventh Annual ACM-SIAM Symposium on Discrete Algorithms (Atlanta), January 1996, pp. 341–350.

[Joh73] D. S. Johnson, *Near-optimal bin packing algorithms*, Ph.D. thesis, Project MAC TR-100, MIT, Cambridge, MA, June 1973.

[Joh90] ———, *Local optimization and the traveling salesman problem*, Proc. 17th Colloq. on Automata, Languages, and Programming, Lecture notes in Computer Science 443, Springer-Verlag, Berlin, 1990, pp. 446–461.

[Joh96] ———, *A theoretician's guide to the experimental analysis of algorithms*, 1996, Seven page preliminary draft of this paper.

[McG92] C. C. McGeoch, *Analyzing algorithms by simulation: Variance reduction techniques and simulation speedups*, ACM Computing Surveys **245** (1992), no. 2, 195–212.

[McG96] ———, *Toward an experimental method for algorithm simulation*, INFORMS Journal on Computing **1** (1996), no. 1, 1—15.

[MM99] C. C. McGeoch and B. M. E. Moret, *How to present a paper on experimental work with algorithms*, SIGACT News (1999), no. 113, 85–90, Also available at `www.cs.amherst.edu/~ccm/howto.ps`.

[PM96] A. G. Percus and O. C. Martin, *Finite size and dimensional dependence in the euclidean traveling salesman problem*, Phys. Rev. Lett. **76** (1996), no. 8, 1188–1191.

[Rei81] G. Reinelt, *TSPLIB–a traveling salesman problem library*, ORSA Journal on Computing **3** (1981), 376–384, Website: `http://www.iwr.uni-heidelberg.de/iwr/comopt/software/TSPLIB95/`.

[RU01] R. L. Rardin and R. Uzsoy, *Experimental evaluation of heuristic optimization algorithms: A tutorial*, J. Heuristics **7** (2001), 262–304.

[Sho86] P. W. Shor, *The average case analysis of some on-line algorithms for bin packing*, Combinatorica **6** (1986), 179–200.

[Tuf83] E. R. Tufte, *The visual display of quantitative information*, Graphics Press, 1983.

Appendix

This appendix collects together into separate lists the "Pet Peeves," "Pitfalls," and "Suggestions" we highlighted during the course of the discussions in Section 2.

Pet Peeves

(1) Authors and referees who don't do their homework
(2) Concentration on unstructured random instances.
(3) The millisecond testbed.
(4) The already-solved testbed.
(5) Claiming inadequate programming time/ability as an excuse.
(6) Supplied code that doesn't match a paper's description of it.
(7) Irreproducible standards of comparison.
(8) Using running time as a stopping criterion.
(9) Using the optimal solution value as a stopping criterion.
(10) Hand-tuned algorithm parameters.
(11) The one-run study.
(12) Using the best result found as an evaluation criterion.
(13) The uncalibrated machine.
(14) The lost testbed.
(15) False precision.
(16) Unremarked anomalies.
(17) The *ex post facto* stopping criterion.
(18) Failure to report overall running times.
(19) Data without interpretation.
(20) Conclusions without support.
(21) Myopic approaches to asymptopia.
(22) Tables without pictures.
(23) Pictures without tables.
(24) Pictures yielding too little insight.
(25) Inadequately or confusingly labeled pictures.
(26) Pictures with too much information.
(27) Confusing pictorial metaphors.
(28) The spurious trend line.
(29) Poorly structured tables.
(30) Making your readers do the arithmetic.
(31) The undefined metric.
(32) Comparing apples with oranges.
(33) Detailed statistics on unimportant questions.
(34) Comparing approximation algorithms as to how often they find optima.
(35) Too much data.

Pitfalls

(1) Dealing with dominated algorithms.
(2) Devoting too much computation to the wrong questions.
(3) Getting into an endless loop in your experimentation.
(4) Start by using randomly generated instances to evaluate the behavior of algorithms – End up using algorithms to investigate the properties of randomly-generated instances.
(5) Too much code tuning.
(6) Lost code/data.

Suggestions

(1) Think before you compute.
(2) Use exploratory experimentation to find good questions.
(3) Use variance reduction techniques.
(4) Use bootstrapping to evaluate multiple-run heuristics.
(5) Use self-documenting programs.
(6) Use benchmark algorithms to calibrate machine speeds.
(7) Use profiling to understand running times.
(8) Display normalized running times.

AT&T Labs – Research, Room C239, Florham Park, NJ 07932-0971
E-mail address: dsj@research.att.com

DIMACS Series in Discrete Mathematics
and Theoretical Computer Science
Volume **59**, 2002

A Bibliography of Algorithm Experimentation

Catherine C. McGeoch

This annotated bibliography lists sources that address methodology, tools and techniques, and standards for experimental research on algorithms. I've tried, in the annotation, to summarize both the content and the technical level. No attempt has been made to catalog the huge number of published *examples* of experimental and computational research on algorithms, although some general publication venues are listed.

We begin with a shortlist of resources for the beginning experimentor. These sources, taken together, provide good overall coverage of the main issues of experimental research, at about the graduate student level. The reference list that follows contains works on more specialized, advanced, and technical topics.

A Beginner's Reading List.

- For general advice, tips, and guidelines on algorithmic experimental resaerch, read Barr et al. [**BGK$^+$95**], McGeoch [**McG96b**], [**McG00**], Johnson [**Joh01**], and Moret [**Mor01**].
- Bentley [**Ben91**] shows how to build a Unix environment that supports efficient testing and data collection. Some remarks on this subject may also be found in [**McG01b**].
- Ahuja, Magnanti, and Orlin [**AMO93**] discuss algorithmic performance measures that closely predict running times and that (to some extent) can be extrapolated across machine environments.
- For an introduction to statistical concepts and techniques that are most relevant to experimental research on algorithms, read the book by Cohen [**Coh95**] and/or the article by Coffin and Saltzman [**CS00**]. Both of these sources contain examples and illustrations drawn from algorithmic research problems. For a readible and authoritative discussion of techniques of graphical data analysis, see Chambers et al. [**CCKT83**].
- Crowder, Dembo, Mulvey [**CDM78**], and the follow-up article by Jackson et al. [**JBNP91**] give criteria and standards for presentation of experimental research in published work. The first provides a handy checklist for reviewers. See also Johnson [**Joh01**] for advice on what kind of information to include in your talk or paper. McGeoch and Moret [**MM99**] give guidelines for presenting talks on experimental research on algorithms.

References

[AMO93] R. K. Ahuja, T. L. Magnanti, and J. B. Orlin, *Network flows: Theory, algorithms, and applications*, Prentice Hall, Englewood Cliffs, NJ, 1993, •Chapter 18 contains good advice on selecting appropriate cost measures.

[And01] R. Anderson, *The role of experiment in the theory of algorithms*, this volume, 2001.

[Bar87] R. R. Barton, *Testing strategies for simulation optimization*, Proceedings of the 1987 Winter Simulation Conference (A. Thesen, H. Grant, and W. D. Kelton, eds.), Society for Computer Simulation, 1987, pp. 391–401.

[BB98] R. Battiti and A. Bertossi (eds.), *Alex'98: Workshop on algorithms and experiments*, *rtm.science.unitn.it/alex98/*, 1998, •Submitted and invited papers by workshop participants.

[Ben82] J. L. Bentley, *Writing efficient programs*, Prentice Hall, Englewood Cliffs, NJ, 1982, •Describes a systematic methodology for reducing constant factors in implementations.

[Ben84] J. L. Bentley, *A case study in applied algorithm design*, Computer **17** (1984), no. 2, 75–88, •TSP algorithms applied to a problem in pen-plotter scheduling.

[Ben90] J. L. Bentley, *Experiments on traveling salesman heuristics*, Proceedings of the First ACM-SIAM Symposium on Discrete Algorithms, ACM-SIAM, New York, Philadelphia, 1990, •Discusses both the research problem and the experimental methodology., pp. 91–99.

[Ben91] J. L. Bentley, *Tools for experiments on algorithms*, CMU Computer Science: A 25th Anniversary Commemorative (R. F. Rashid, ed.), ACM Press, New York, 1991, •How to build Unix tools to make an efficient and reliable experimentation environment. Check out the 'Ten Commandments of Experimentation on Algorithms.'.

[Ben99] J. L. Bentley, *Programming pearls, second edition*, Addison Wesley, Reading, MA, 1999, •A must-read for algorithm engineers. Part II considers both asymptotic and constant-factor performance issues.

[BFS83] P. Bratley, B. L. Fox, and L. E. Schrage, *A guide to simulation*, Springer-Verlag, New York, 1983, •A textbook aimed at the first-year graduate level. Covers statistical techniques as well as implementation issues, with attention to practical concerns.

[BGK+95] R. S. Barr, B. L. Golden, J. P. Kelly, M. G. C. Resende, and W. R. Stewart, *Designing and reporting on computational experiments with heuristic methods*, Journal of Heuristics **1** (1995), no. 1, 9—32, •Advice and standards for experimental research on heuristic algorithms.

[BS01] A. Buchsbaum and J. Snoeyink, *ALENEX01: Workshop on Algorithm Engineering and Experiments*, *www.research.att.com/~alb/ALENEX01/*, Washington, D.C., January 2001, •Third in an annual series of workshops. The website has links to previous meetings.

[CCKT83] J. M. Chambers, W. S. Cleveland, B. Kleiner, and P. A. Tukey, *Graphical methods for data analysis*, Duxbury Press, Boston, 1983, •Readible and authoratative reference on graphical analysis techniques.

[CDM78] H. P. Crowder, R. S. Dembo, and J. M. Mulvey, *Reporting computational experiments in Mathematical Programming*, Mathematical Programming **15** (1978), 316–329, •This classic paper stands the test of time. The authors present criteria for reporting experimental results and provide a handy checklist for reviewers.

[Che82] R. C. H. Cheng, *The use of antithetic variates in computer simulation*, Journal of the Operations Research Society **33** (1982), 229—237, •Illustrates the application of a variance reduction technique.

[Cle85] W. S. Cleveland, *Elements of graphing data*, Wadsworth, Monteray, CA, 1985, •A good general reference covering both analysis and presentation.

[Cle93] W. S. Cleveland, *Visualizing data*, Hobart Press, Summit, NJ, 1993, •Graphical and visualization tools for getting better views of data.

[Coh95] P. R. Cohen, *Empirical methods for artificial intelligence*, MIT Press, Cambridge, 1995, •Statistical methods and practical advice for algorithm experimentation. This textbook is relevant to all kinds of algorithmic research, not just heuristics in Artificial Intelligence.

[CS00] M. Coffin and M. J. Saltzman, *Statistical analysis of computational tests of algorithms and heuristics*, INFORMS Journal on Computing **12** (2000), no. 1, 24–44, Introduction and survey of statistical techniques most relevant to algorithmic experimentation.

[Dev86] L. Devroye, *Non-uniform random variate generation*, Springer-Verlag, New York, 1986, •Algorithms, code, theory: a must-have reference.

[DG87] J. J. Dongarra and E. Grosse, *Distribution of mathematical software via electronic mail*, Communications of the ACM **30** (1987), no. 5, 403–407, Available through the mail server `netlib@research.att.com`. •The NETLIB collection of instances for network problems.

[FMS00] R. Fleischer, B. M. E. Moret, and E. M. Schmidt (eds.), *Dagstuhl seminar on experimental algorithmics*, Schloss Dagstuhl Seminar No. 00371, September 2000, Abstracts: *www.dagstuhl.de/DATA/Seminars/00/*. Full papers to appear in *Lecture Notes in Computer Science*, Springer Verlag, 2001.

[FR92] G. S. Fishman and D. S. Rubin, *Bounding the variance in Monte Carlo experiments*, Operations Research Letters **11** (1992), 243–248, •How to use variance estimations to decide how many tests are needed.

[FY97] G. S. Fishman and L. S. Yarberry, *An implementation of the batch means method*, INFORMS Journal on Computing **9** (1997), no. 3, 296–310, •Illustrates a variance reduction technique.

[GAWB86] B. L. Golden, A. A. Assad, E. A. Wasil, and E. Baker, *Experimentation in optimization*, European Journal of Operational Research **27** (1986), 1–16, •General advice and tips on experimentation.

[GM99a] A. V. Goldberg and B. M. E. Moret (eds.), *CATS: Combinatorial Algorithms Test Sets*, *www.jea.acm.org/CATS/*, since 1999, •A repository for input sets for combinatorial algorithms. Contains test sets for several graph problems and NP-Hard problems, with links to related sites.

[GM99b] M. C. Goodrich and C. C. McGeoch (eds.), *Workshop on algorithm engineering and experimentation (alenex99)*, Lecture Notes in Computer Science, no. 1619, Springer Verlag, 1999.

[Gre90] H. Greenberg, *Computational testing: Why, how, and how much*, ORSA Journal on Computing **2** (1990), 94–97, •A short article on larger issues of computational testing.

[GS85] B. L. Golden and W. R. Stewart, *Empirical analysis of heuristics*, The Traveling Salesman Problem: A Guided Tour of Combinatorial Optimization (E. Lawler, J. K. Lenstra, A. Rinnooy Kan, and D. Shmoys, eds.), Wiley Interscience, New York, 1985, •A case study with emphasis on statistical techniques.

[HA80] D. C. Hoaglin and D. F. Andrews, *The reporting of computation-based results in statistics*, The American Statistician **29** (1980), 122—126, •A statistician's view of computational experimentation.

[Hig97] J. L. Higle, *Variance reduction and objective function evaluation in stochastic linear programs*, INFORMS Journal on Computing **10** (1997), no. 2, 236—247, •Tutorial discussion of variance reduction techniques.

[Hoo93] J. Hooker, *Needed: An empirical science of algorithms*, Operations Research **42** (1993), no. 2, 201–212, •Hooker laments the state of algorithmic experimentation in operations research and suggests ways to make practice more rigorous.

[Hoo96] J. N. Hooker, *Testing heuristics: We have it all wrong*, Journal of Heuristics **1** (1996), 33—42, •Proposes new approaches to algorithmic research.

[HP01] M.G. Hall and M. E. Posner, *Generating experimental data for computational testing with machine scheduling applications*, Operations Research **49** (2001), no. 7, 854–865, Survey of good principles of data generation, together with specific critiques and illustratoins from machine scheduling.

[JBNP91] R. H. F. Jackson, P. T. Boggs, S. G. Nash, and S. Powell, *Guidelines for reporting results of computational experiments. report of the ad hoc committee*, Mathematical Programming **49** (1991), 413–425, •A useful update to the classic article [CDM78].

[JM78] R. H. F. Jackson and J. M. Mulvey, *A critical review of comparisons of mathematical programming algorithms and software (1953–1977)*, Journal of Research of the

National Bureau of Standards **83** (1978), no. 6, 563–584, •Critique of the literature circa 1978, still relevant today.

[JM91] D. S. Johnson and C. C. McGeoch (eds.), *Network flows and matching: First dimacs implementation challenge*, DIMACS Series in Discrete Mathematics and Theoretical Computer Science, vol. 12, American Mathematical Society, Philadelphia, 1991, Programs and test instances available from *dimacs.rutgers.edu/Challenges/"*. •A collection of experimental papers and commentary.

[Joh01] D. S. Johnson, *A theoretician's guide to the experimental analysis of algorithms*, this volume, 2001, Also available at *www.research.att.com/~dsj/papers/experguide.ps.* •A survey of pitfalls of experimentation and presentation, with advice on how to avoid them.

[JT96] D. S. Johnson and M. Trick (eds.), *Graph Coloring, Vertex Cover, and Satisfiability: Second DIMACS implementation challenge*, DIMACS Series in Discrete Mathematics and Theoretical Computer Science, vol. 26, American Mathematical Society, Philadelphia, 1996, •A collection of experimental papers and commentary.

[Kel94] W. D. Kelton, *Perspectives on simulation research and practice*, ORSA Journal on Computing **6** (1994), no. 4, 318–328.

[KG92] J. Kleijnen and W. Van Groenendaal, *Simulation: A statistical perspective*, John Wiley & Sons, New York, 1992.

[Knu93] D. E. Knuth, *The stanford graphbase: A platform for combinatorial computing*, ACM Press and Addison-Wesley, New York and Reading, MA, 1993, Available by anonymous ftp at `labrea.stanford.edu`. •Collection of graph algorithms and graphs with real-world structure.

[L'E90] P. L'Ecuyer, *Random numbers for simulation*, Communications of the ACM **33** (1990), 85–97, •A standard reference on random number generators.

[L'E92] P. L'Ecuyer, *Testing random number generators*, Proceedings of the 1992 Winter Simulation Conference (1992), 305–313.

[L'E94] P. L'Ecuyer, *Uniform random number generation*, Annals of Operations Research **53** (1994), 77–120.

[L'E96] P. L'Ecuyer, *Simulation of algorithms and performance analysis*, ORSA Journal on Computing **1** (1996), no. 1, 16–20, •Short commentary on [McG96b] discussing statistial analysis and random number generation.

[LED89] *Leda research*, since 1989, •A large repository of efficient C++ implementations of algorithms and data structures.

[LR80] B. W. Lin and R. L. Rardin, *Controlled experimental design for statistical comparison of integer programming algorithms*, Management Science **25** (1980), no. 12, 1258–1271.

[McG86] C. C. McGeoch, *Experimental analysis of algorithms*, Ph.D. thesis, Technical Report CMU-CS-87-124, Department of Computer Science, Carnegie Mellon University, Pittsburgh, 1986, •Case studies and methodologies for algorithm experimentation.

[McG92] C. C. McGeoch, *Analyzing algorithms by simulation: Variance reduction techniques and simulation speedups*, ACM Computing Surveys **245** (1992), no. 2, 195–212, •A tutorial on variance reduction techniques in the context of algorithm analysis, with examples.

[McG96a] C. C. McGeoch, *Challenges in algorithm simulation*, ORSA Journal on Computing **1** (1996), no. 1, 27–28, •Brief reply to commentaries on [McG96b].

[McG96b] C. C. McGeoch, *Toward an experimental method for algorithm simulation*, INFORMS Journal on Computing **1** (1996), no. 1, 1—15, •A survey of issues in computational experiments on algorithms.

[McG00] C. C. McGeoch, *Experimental analysis of optimization algorithms*, Handbook of Combinatorial Optimization (P. M. Pardalos and M. G. C. Resende, eds.), Oxford University Press, 2000, A chapter surveying issues in experimentation.

[McG01a] C. C. McGeoch, *A bibliography of algorithm experimentation*, this volume, 2001.

[McG01b] C. C. McGeoch, *Experimental analysis of algorithms*, Handbook of Global Optimization, Volume 2: Heuristic Approaches (P. M. Pardalos and E. Romeijn, eds.), Kluwer Academic Publishers, 2001, A chapter on experimental methodology.

[MM99] C. C. McGeoch and B. M. E. Moret, *How to present a paper on experimental work with algorithms*, SIGACT News **30** (1999), no. 4, 85–90, Also available at `www.cs.amherst.edu/~ccm/howto.ps`. •Advice on giving talks on experimental research in algorithms.

[Mor96] Bernard M. Moret (ed.), *Journal of Experimental Algorithmics*, *www.jea.acm.org/index.html*, since 1996, •An on-line journal published by The Association for Computing Machinery.

[Mor97] B. M. E. Moret, *Bridging the gap between theory and practice*, September 1997, Available at *www.press.umich.edu/jep/03-01/JEA.html* •A survey of issues and opportunities in experimental algorithmics.

[Mor01] B. M. E. Moret, *Toward a discipline of experimental algorithmics*, this volume, 2001, •General advice on experimental methodology.

[MS01] B. M. E. Moret and H. D. Shapiro, *Algorithms and experiments: the new (and the old) methodology*, Journal of Universal Computer Science **7** (2001), no. 5, 434–446, •Historical survey of methodology.

[MSF+01] C. C. McGeoch, P. Sanders, R. Fleischer, P. Cohen, and D. Precup, *Searching for Big-Oh in the data: Inferring asymptotic complexity from experiments*, Experimental Algorithmics, the State of The Art:, to appear as a volume of *Lecture Notes in Computer Science*, Springer Verlag, 2001, •Advice and techniques for inferring asymptotic behavior from data.

[NRLMF87] R. E. Nance, Jr. R. L. Moose, and R. V. Foutz, *A statistical technique for comparing heuristics: An example from capacity assignment strategies in computer network design*, Communications of the ACM **30** (1987), no. 5, 430–442.

[Orl96] J. B. Orlin, *On experimental methods for algorithm simulation.*, ORSA Journal on Computing **1** (1996), no. 1, 21–23, •Short commentary on [McG96b] focusing on performance measures.

[Paw90] K. Pawlikowski, *Steady-state simulations of queueing processes: A survey of problems and solutions*, ACM Computing Surveys **22** (1990), no. 2, 123–170.

[PB85] P. W. Purdom, Jr. and C. A. Brown, *The analysis of algorithms*, Holt, Reinhart and Winston, 1985, •Contains a chapter on experimentatal methodology.

[PM88] S. K. Park and K. W. Miller, *Random number generators: Good ones are hard to find*, Communications of the ACM **31** (1988), no. 10, 1192–1201, •A comparison of random number generators, with advice to practioners.

[Raw98] J. O. Rawlings, *Applied regression analysis: A research tool*, Wadsworth and Brooks/Cole, Pacific Grove, CA, 1998, •A very readible advanced textbook.

[Rei81] G. Reinelt, *TSPLIB–a traveling salesman problem library*, ORSA Journal on Computing **3** (1981), 376–384, Available through the mail server `netlib@research.att.com`.

[San90] L. A. Sanchis, *On the complexity of test case generation for NP-Hard problems*, Information Processing Letters **36** (1990), 135–140.

[San93] L. A. Sanchis, *Some complexity issues involved in the construction of test cases for NP-Hard problems*, Complexity in Numerical Optimization (Panos M. Pardalos, ed.), World Scientific, 1993.

[San95] L. A. Sanchis, *Generating hard and diverse test sets for NP-Hard graph problems*, Discrete Applied Mathematics **58** (1995), 35–66.

[Shi96] D. B. Shier, *On algorithm analysis*, ORSA Journal on Computing **1** (1996), no. 1, 24–26, •Short commentary on [McG96b] describing a conceptual framework for algorithm analysis.

[Ski97] S. S. Skiena, *The Stony Brook Algorithm Repository*, *www.cs.sunysb.edu/~algorith/*, since 1997, •A repository of implementations in several programming languages.

[Ski98] S. S. Skiena, *The algorithm design manual*, Springer-Verlag/TELOS (The Electronic Library of Science), 1998, •Much information about algorithms and applications. Great war stories.

[Spa01] A. Marchetti Spaccamela, *Workshop on Algorithm Engineering (WAE 2001)*, *www.brics.dk/wae2001/*, Denmark, August 2001, •Fifth in an annual series of workshops. The website has links to previous meetings.

[Tod94] M. J. Todd, *Theory and practice for interior-point methods*, ORSA Journal on Computing **6** (1994), no. 1, 28–31.

[Tuk77] J. W. Tukey, *Exploratory data analysis*, Addison Wesley, Reading, MA, 1977, •A seminal work on non-parametric data analysis.

Department of Mathematics and Computer Science, Amherst College, Amherst, MA 01002

E-mail address: ccm@cs.amherst.edu

Titles in This Series

TITLES IN THIS SERIES

30 **Sandeep N. Bhatt, Editor,** Parallel Algorithms: Third DIMACS Implementation Challenge

29 **Doron A. Peled, Vaughan R. Pratt, and Gerard J. Holzmann, Editors,** Partial Order Methods in Verification

28 **Larry Finkelstein and William M. Kantor, Editors,** Groups and Computation II

27 **Richard J. Lipton and Eric B. Baum, Editors,** DNA Based Computers

26 **David S. Johnson and Michael A. Trick, Editors,** Cliques, Coloring, and Satisfiability: Second DIMACS Implementation Challenge

25 **Gilbert Baumslag, David Epstein, Robert Gilman, Hamish Short, and Charles Sims, Editors,** Geometric and Computational Perspectives on Infinite Groups

24 **Louis J. Billera, Curtis Greene, Rodica Simion, and Richard P. Stanley, Editors,** Formal Power Series and Algebraic Combinatorics/Séries Formelles et Combinatoire Algébrique, 1994

23 **Panos M. Pardalos, David I. Shalloway, and Guoliang Xue, Editors,** Global Minimization of Nonconvex Energy Functions: Molecular Conformation and Protein Folding

22 **Panos M. Pardalos, Mauricio G. C. Resende, and K. G. Ramakrishnan, Editors,** Parallel Processing of Discrete Optimization Problems

21 **D. Frank Hsu, Arnold L. Rosenberg, and Dominique Sotteau, Editors,** Interconnection Networks and Mapping and Scheduling Parallel Computations

20 **William Cook, László Lovász, and Paul Seymour, Editors,** Combinatorial Optimization

19 **Ingemar J. Cox, Pierre Hansen, and Bela Julesz, Editors,** Partitioning Data Sets

18 **Guy E. Blelloch, K. Mani Chandy, and Suresh Jagannathan, Editors,** Specification of Parallel Algorithms

17 **Eric Sven Ristad, Editor,** Language Computations

16 **Panos M. Pardalos and Henry Wolkowicz, Editors,** Quadratic Assignment and Related Problems

15 **Nathaniel Dean and Gregory E. Shannon, Editors,** Computational Support for Discrete Mathematics

14 **Robert Calderbank, G. David Forney, Jr., and Nader Moayeri, Editors,** Coding and Quantization: DIMACS/IEEE Workshop

13 **Jin-Yi Cai, Editor,** Advances in Computational Complexity Theory

12 **David S. Johnson and Catherine C. McGeoch, Editors,** Network Flows and Matching: First DIMACS Implementation Challenge

11 **Larry Finkelstein and William M. Kantor, Editors,** Groups and Computation

10 **Joel Friedman, Editor,** Expanding Graphs

9 **William T. Trotter, Editor,** Planar Graphs

8 **Simon Gindikin, Editor,** Mathematical Methods of Analysis of Biopolymer Sequences

7 **Lyle A. McGeoch and Daniel D. Sleator, Editors,** On-Line Algorithms

6 **Jacob E. Goodman, Richard Pollack, and William Steiger, Editors,** Discrete and Computational Geometry: Papers from the DIMACS Special Year

5 **Frank Hwang, Fred Roberts, and Clyde Monma, Editors,** Reliability of Computer and Communication Networks

4 **Peter Gritzmann and Bernd Sturmfels, Editors,** Applied Geometry and Discrete Mathematics, The Victor Klee Festschrift

3 **E. M. Clarke and R. P. Kurshan, Editors,** Computer-Aided Verification '90

2 **Joan Feigenbaum and Michael Merritt, Editors,** Distributed Computing and Cryptography

1 **William Cook and Paul D. Seymour, Editors,** Polyhedral Combinatorics